Routledge Revivals

Willam Gager : The Complete Works

Willam Gager : The Complete Works

Edited by
Dana F. Sutton

First published in 1994 by Garland Publishing, Inc.

This edition first published in 2019 by Routledge
2 Park Square, Milton Park, Abingdon, Oxon, OX14 4RN
and by Routledge
52 Vanderbilt Avenue, New York, NY 10017, USA

Routledge is an imprint of the Taylor & Francis Group, an informa business

© 1994 by Dana F. Sutton

All rights reserved. No part of this book may be reprinted or reproduced or utilised in any form or by any electronic, mechanical, or other means, now known or hereafter invented, including photocopying and recording, or in any information storage or retrieval system, without permission in writing from the publishers.

Publisher's Note
The publisher has gone to great lengths to ensure the quality of this reprint but points out that some imperfections in the original copies may be apparent.

Disclaimer
The publisher has made every effort to trace copyright holders and welcomes correspondence from those they have been unable to contact.
A Library of Congress record exists under ISBN:

ISBN 13: 978-0-367-19666-0 (hbk)
ISBN 13: 978-0-367-19669-1 (pbk)
ISBN 13: 978-0-429-20385-5 (ebk)

THE RENAISSANCE IMAGINATION

Important Literary and Theatrical Texts
from the Late Middle Ages through
the Seventeenth Century

edited by
STEPHEN ORGEL
Stanford University

A GARLAND SERIES

WILLIAM GAGER:
THE COMPLETE WORKS

VOLUME I
THE EARLIER PLAYS

Edited with translation and commentary by
DANA F. SUTTON

GARLAND PUBLISHING, INC.
NEW YORK & LONDON / 1994

Copyright © 1994 by Dana F. Sutton
All rights reserved

Library of Congress Cataloging-in-Publication Data

Gager, William, fl. 1580–1619.
   [Works. 1994]
   William Gager : the complete works / edited, with a translation and commentary, Dana F. Sutton.
     p. cm. — (The Renaissance imagination)
   Includes bibliographical references and index.
   Contents: v. 1. The earlier plays — v. 2. The Shrovetide plays — v. 3. Poems — v. 4. Juvenilia, Pyramis, collected prose.
   ISBN 0-8153-1692-5
   1. Latin literature, Medieval and modern—England—Oxford. 2. Renaissance—England—Oxford. 3. Humanists—England—Oxford. I. Sutton, Dana Ferrin. II. Title III. Series: Renaissance imagination (Unnumbered)
PA8520.G127   1994
872'.04—dc20   93-38853
                                                          CIP

Printed on acid-free, 250-year-life paper
Manufactured in the United States of America

Contents

Preface	v
General Introduction	ix
Oedipus	1
Introduction	3
Text and Translation	6
Textual Commentary	23
Meleager	27
Introduction	29
Text and Translation	34
Textual Commentary	163
Rivales	223
Introduction	225
Fragments and Testimonia	228
Textual Commentary	235
Dido	239
Introduction	241
Text and Translation	254
Textual Commentary	347
Appendix: Gager in his Pointing: On Pointing Gager	365

Preface

n the Renaissance the enterprise of English school and University education was conducted in Latin,[1] so educated England was a bilingual society, and there are two distinct, although mutually influential, literatures of the Tudor and Jacobean periods. This second, Anglo-Latin remains imperfectly known.[2] Writers who wrote in Latin because of their situation or out of personal inclination[3] tend to remain comparatively obscure. Surely one of the causes of this situation is the dearth of readily available critical editions, translations, and commentaries.

An excellent case in point is Dr. William Gager of Christ Church, Oxford, at least arguably the best Latin playwright of the Tudor period. He was counted in the same breath with a group of poets including Shakespeare as "our best for comedy" by the judicious Francis Meres;[4] absurdly rated above anybody else, Shakespeare included, by the seventeenth-century antiquarian Anthony à Wood;[5] no less foolishly ranked ahead of Horace by William Vaughan;[6] identified, with Richard Hakluyt, as one of the two literary hopes of the nation by Gabriel Harvey.[7] Another contemporary appraisal is saner but nonetheless flattering. A dedicatory poem prefacing the 1603 *editio princeps* of Matthew Gwinne's play

---

[1] Evidently the idea of conducting higher education in the vernacular was not given serious consideration prior to the foundation of Gresham College, London, when the issue came in for considerable debate. The 1597 College statutes reflect the compromise solution that lectures were to be given in Latin mornings and repeated in English in afternoons: cf. John Ward, *The Lives of the Professors of Gresham College* (London, 1740, repr. New York - London, 1967) v.

[2] The recent survey by J. W. Binns, *Intellectual Culture in Elizabethan and Jacobean England: The Latin Writing of the Age* (Leeds, 1990) goes a long way towards remedying this situation. There exists an excellent survey of drama written in Latin, Frederick S. Boas, *University Drama in the Tudor Age* (Oxford, 1914, repr. New York, 1966), and a more cursory look at non-dramatic poetry in the first chapters of Leicester Bradner, *Musae Anglicanae: A History of Anglo-Latin Poetry 1500 - 1925* (New York, 1940, repr. New York, 1965). For drama, cf. also G. B. Churchill and Wolfgang Keller, "Die lateinischen Universitäts-Dramen Englands in der Zeit der Königin Elisabeth," *Jahrbuch der Deutschen Shakespeare-Gesellshaft* 35 (1898) and Binns, *ib.*, Chapter Eight.

[3] Another possible motivation is suggested by J. W. Binns, *The Latin Poetry of English Poets* (London, 1974) viii: "There was then a simple but compelling reason for a sixteenth- or seventeenth-century English poet to wish to write in Latin: the desire for an international audience and international recognition." At least in Gager's case, this generalization is wholly inapplicable. There is no evidence that he either had or sought an international reputation. He wrote for the consumption of the segment of his own English society in which he moved.

[4] Quoted in the introduction to *Rivales* in the present volume.

[5] *Athenae Oxonienses* II.87 (in the edition of Philip Bliss, London, 1813 - 22, repr. Hildesheim, 1969).

[6] *Poematum Libellus* (1598), sig. C 4ʳ:

> hic ubi multimodis Flacco, Gagere, camoenis,
> o mihi post nullos, Doctor amande, praeis.

But if the assessment of Gager as Horace's superior is silly, the appellation *Doctor amandus* is nevertheless worth keeping in mind.

[7] Cf. C. G. Moore Smith, *Gabriel Harvey's Marginalia* (Stratford-upon-Avon, 1913) 233.

Nero by John Sandsbury of St. John's College, Oxford, is addressed to the great Flemish Humanist Justus Lipsius:

> *Lipsi, Neronem nunc habe; votis tuis*
> *oculisque dignum: quique puerilem putas*
> *Octaviam illam, quam rudis mundus iubet*
> *Senecae imputari, Iuste, praestentem loco*
> *substitue: Seneca sic enim iratus iubet.*
> μετεμψύχωσιν *ille millenam miser*
> *sensit, querelas antequam posset suas*
> *lingua referre propria; tandem tamen*
> *ex ore Gwinni pristinum servat decus.*
> *Gagere, Buchanane, nec Beza invide.*
> *videte; talis Seneca qui Gwinnus fuit.*
> *qui iudicas, fatere; qui nescis, tace.*

["Lipsius, now you have a Nero worthy of your desires and your reading. Since you think that *Octavia* to be puerile stuff which the unlearned world bids us ascribe to Seneca, you can substitute the present work in its place. Thus commands angry Seneca. The poor man has experienced his thousandth soul-migration before being able to give his own tongue to his complaints. But at length let him retrieve his former glory through Gwinne's mouth. Gager, Buchanan, Beza, be not envious. Observe. Gwinne is as Seneca was. You who have judgment, confess it. You who are ignorant, keep still."]

The casual assumption that Gager is on a par with the leading continental Humanist playwrights is more eloquent than any amount of bombastic praise.

In the eyes of modern writers on the Renaissance drama and literature, Gager's reputation has not greatly deteriorated. In the single important survey of English University drama, two out of the thirteen chapters are devoted, wholly or in large part, to describing his plays, and to praising their quality.[1] Another chapter in the same study[2] is chiefly devoted to an account of his celebrated dispute with Dr. John Rainolds about the propriety of acting, required reading for any student of contemporary opposition to the stage. Gager figures no less prominently, and is handled with equal respect, in the standard handbook on Anglo-Latin poetry.[3]

And with good reason. As his contemporaries were not slow to grasp, Gager was an extraordinarily gifted playwright. His plays tended to performed as official entertainment for distinguished University visitors. His printed plays and poetry played an important role in the early history of the nascent Oxford University Press. He was selected to edit the University's anthology of poetry commemorating the death of Sir Philip Sidney, the first Oxford volume of its kind. As intimated above, he came forth as an outspoken champion of the propriety of the theater. In what he has to say about literature both in this work and

---

[1] Boas, *op. cit.*, Chapters VIII and IX.
[2] Chapter X.
[3] Bradner, *op. cit.*, 61 - 6.

elsewhere, in prologues, epilogues, and prefatory material written in prose, and in his oration *Eloquentiae Encomium*, he displays a lively intellect. He also left behind a considerable body of private poetry, much of it remarkably passionate and self-revealing.

Another mark of a writer's stature is his influence on others. This is a subject that cannot be pursued in the present work, but I believe a canvass would show that Gager exerted considerable influence on his contemporaries. Specific imitation by such other writers as Matthew Gwinne and Richard Burton will be noted in the course of this edition. Signs of more general influence abound. To mention one particularly fine example, the cycle of lyric poems written for Elizabeth's 1592 visit by John Sanford of Magdalene College[1] is very consciously cast in the mold of Gager's printed lyrics. Gager did much to elevate the general tone of Oxonian literature.

In the course of his "Life of Milton" Dr. Johnson rather absurdly opined that William Alabaster, author of the sanguine revenge play *Roxane* and a providentially unfinished epic poem about Elizabeth, as the best Latin poet England had produced prior to Milton. Gager is one of a small handful of poets who might better warrant this accolade. He was also a highly adroit and versatile playwright. But, though his name may be frequently encountered, he is little read. Take, for example, the plays. The one that is usually disparaged as hasty hack work because of the peculiar conditions under which it had to be written, *Dido*, has been edited and translated repeatedly, thrice in the past twenty years. The two that are praised as his masterpieces, *Meleager* and *Ulysses Redux*, remain completely untouched. Some of Gager's poetry has been presented in various scholarly journals and organs of learned societies, but the bulk of the available material consists of items printed in his own lifetime. Save for a few individual items, his large body of unpublished work has never seen the light of day.

The late Professor C. F. Tucker Brooke of Yale University had published a fraction of Gager's work, and was working on an edition of the complete works at the time of his death in 1943. Brooke's intended biographical Introduction was given independent publication posthumously.[2] A nearly complete set of texts and translations was left behind, but in too inchoate a state to merit printing. In the interim, some more individual items have been published, chiefly by Professor J. W. Binns of the University of York. But a great deal remains entirely unedited, and of course a prolific writer's life work looks considerably different (and considerably more intelligible) when collected in one place. For all these reasons, a complete critical edition of Gager's works, translated and annotated, seems a worthwhile project.

Gager was prolific, and so the result has proved alarmingly large, considerably more so than I had at first anticipated. Together with introductory material, facing English translations, and appended textual Commentaries, four volumes are required: two of plays, one of

---

[1] Printed in the same year by Joseph Barnes under the title *Apollonis et Musarum Εὐκτικά Εἰδύλλια*, reproduced by Charles Plummer (ed.), *Elizabethan Oxford* (Oxford, 1887) 277 - 99.

[2] Brooke's manuscript does not contain *Pyramis*. Doubtless this is because he felt the edition of this long poem he had already published was sufficient; certainly both his biographical essay and the quality of his edition of *Pyramis* give an intimation of the high quality his proposed edition would have attained.

At *The War Against Poetry* (Princeton, 1970) 60 n. 29, Russell Fraser wrote of a forthcoming edition of Gager's complete works by J. W. Binns. This would appear to be the only published mention of such a project, and if Binns did contemplate a complete edition, the appearance of his editions of *Dido* and of some of Gager's poetry in the 1970's seems to indicate that he abandoned the idea.

occasional poetry, and one serving as a repository for miscellaneous stuff (juvenilia, an epyllion on the Gunpowder Plot, various prose works in English and in Latin). But in view of Gager's stature, I do not think any serious apologies are in order.

In doing this work, I have managed to run up a number of important debts, and it would be well to acknowledge them at the outset. First and foremost, I am under great obligation to previous students of Gager: Professors Frederick S. Boas of the Queen's University, Belfast, and Karl Smith of the University of Wisconsin, as well as Brooke and Binns. Although I occasionally diverge from these men on points of detail or of interpretation, any reader familiar with their publications will agree, I am sure, that the present edition would have been difficult, or more likely impossible, in the absence of their groundbreaking work. Unfortunately only the last of these is still alive to receive my thanks, and so I take this opportunity to thank Professor Binns personally for his advice and friendly encouragement.

I am also indebted to various individuals and institutions for supplying materials, information, and advice: the Library of the American Philosophical Society, Philadelphia; the British Library, London; Peter Cane, Fellow Librarian of Corpus Christi College, Oxford; Mark Curthoys, Archivist of Christ Church, Oxford; Melissa Dalziel, Senior Library Assistant, the Bodleian Library, Oxford; J. M. Farrar, County Archivist, Cambridgeshire; Mrs. C. M. Heald, Chapter Clerk of Ely Cathedral; the Huntington Library, San Marino, California; the National Library of the Victoria and Albert Museum, London; Dr. Mark Nicholls, Department of Manuscripts and University Archives, the Cambridge University Library; D. A. Rees, Archivist of Jesus College, Oxford; Christine N. Ritchie, Librarian of University College, Oxford; Mr. George Rombach (a descendant of Edwin and Cicely Sandys); the Reverend C. J. Sansbury, Vicar of Holy Trinity Church, Long Melford, Suffolk; and the Suffolk County Records Office, Bury St. Edmunds.

Finally, and most important of all, I am once again indebted to my wife, Dr. Kathryn A. Sinkovich, who has had to tolerate me as I have worked on this project and, I suspect, who has been obliged to hear a good deal more about William Gager than she really wanted to.

CORONA, CALIFORNIA
AUGUST 5, 1993

General Introduction

The performance of classical plays and also of original works, mostly in Latin, was favored by Humanistic educators, and plays could be employed as vehicles for salubrious moral lessons.[1] But something else was equally, although perhaps less officially, at stake. The Tudor educational curriculum was undeniably dreary and still somewhat medieval in contents and method. Especially as both students and faculty tended to be appreciably younger than their modern equivalents, schools and Universities were largely populated by young men who had few legitimate outlets for high spirits, and few opportunities for wholesome recreation or entertainment. The production of plays was one sanctioned such opportunity,[2] and had the added advantage that plays could suit institutional purposes, for example by serving as entertainment on important occasions.

Hence as early as ca. 1540[3] a flourishing theatrical tradition grew up, not only at Oxford and Cambridge, but at the leading public schools, and also the Inns of Court. There was a good reason for this quickening of academic theatrical life long before the rise of popular and vernacular drama. Academic drama was imitative of classical models. Therefore there was ready at hand a prefabricated set of understandings about how high drama was supposed to work, and also a preexisting poetics to employ in writing plays. Academic playwrights, performers, and audiences were not obliged to confront problems involved in building a sophisticated theatrical tradition from scratch. Hence, although in the early 1580's, when Gager began to write, Sidney could bleakly survey the vernacular theater of the nation, and not much later Marlowe could mordantly disdain the *jigging veins of rhyming mother wits / and such conceits as clownage keeps in pay*, a lively tradition of academic drama had been thriving for more than a generation. And so it is no accident that those milestones in the development of the English national theater, *Gammer Gurtons Nedle*, *Ralph Roister Doister*, and *Gorboduc*, were created in school or University environments. Nor is it an accident that the schools and Universities served as incubators from which many a future London playwright was hatched.

One unfamiliar with Tudor University drama might easily entertain some misapprehensions.[4] The generic title "University drama" might strike the reader as a monstrous and repelling oxymoron: he might anticipate that academic plays were exercises in frigid neoclassicism, and that the academics who wrote and performed them were not practical men of the theater; he might also assume that this title implies these plays were produced in such

---

[1] See the first chapter of Bruce R. Smith, *Ancient Scripts & Modern Experience on the English Stage 1500 - 1700* (Princeton, 1988).
[2] And, like all such opportunities, it was occasionally abused. We hear of occasions of intermural rioting, window-smashing, etc. in connection with University performances.
[3] At least if Thomas Watson's *Absalom*, written about this time, was actually performed at Cambridge.
[4] Misapprehensions that would be impossible to sustain after a reading of Boas' highly intelligent and sympathetic *University Drama in the Tudor Age*. Although this general survey can be supplemented or corrected in details, it remains the magisterial treatment of the subject, and one only wishes that he had included Jacobean academic drama within his scope.

a rarified intellectual atmosphere that there existed some kind of impermeable barrier between University drama and the popular theatrical life of the nation.

An excellent corrective to any such possible misunderstandings is a reading of the plays of William Gager of Christ Church, Oxford (1555 - 1622). Since academic playwrights wrote as an avocation, none of them was especially prolific, but Gager wrote more than any other, and he was evidently unique in working in the three different dramatic genres of tragedy, comedy, and tragicomedy. With the arguable exception of his Cambridge contemporary Thomas Legge (1535 - 1607), the inventor of the Chronicle play, Gager was the outstanding playwright of the University theater.

Gager and Legge wrote with very different aims, but some of the qualities that elevate them above the common run of academic dramatists are the same. Although both indeed are capable at times of frigid rhetoric, and also, perhaps, of excessive imitation of classical models, the undeniable faults associated with this dramatic tradition, these tendencies are more than slightly counterbalanced by others: intense verve and energy, considerable gifts for characterization, a genuine sense of theater and of what can and should be done on the stage (the number and detail of Legge's stage directions are astonishing), and a willingness to cater to popular taste by importing elements from the vernacular theater, by providing plenty of visual spectacle, and by appealing to patriotic sentiment. Gager was also equipped with something evidently denied to Legge, a lively sense of humor. In the address *ad Criticum* prefacing the printed version of *Ulysses Redux*, he declares his aim in writing that play:

> *nam ut vivendi, sic etiam scribendi ratio mihi imprimis probatur ea, quae est paulo liberior ac pene dissolutior, quaeque non tam doctissimis, quam imperitis placeat...equidem ego hanc sive tragaediam, sive fabulam, sive narrationem historicam, sive quicquid eam dici ius fasque est, non ad exquisitam Artis Poeticae tanquam aurificis stateram, sed ad popularis iudicii trutinam exigendam proposui, et effudi potius quam scripsi.*

> ["For, just as in living, so in writing my method is somewhat free and relaxed, of a sort which pleases the learned less than the unskilled...For my part, I have produced this tragedy, or play, or historical narrative, or whatever it is right and proper to call it, not according to the exacting standards of the *Art of Poetry* employed as some sort of goldsmith's balance, but rather measured according to the exacting standards of popular taste, and I have poured it forth rather than composed it."]

Although here he is defending his decision to write a tragicomedy, in disregard of Horace's canons of strict literary propriety, in a larger sense these words may be taken as a declaration of the artistic intent that permeates all his plays. Gager was well aware of the popular theater and its attractions (at one point in a preface, he begs his audience to pay as much attention to his play as they would to a vernacular one),[1] and cut his cloth accordingly. Another sign of disinterest in neoclassical strictness is that in each of his plays the canonical Unities are somehow violated: Gager even managed to introduce a violation of

---

[1] *Panniculus* 32f. Robert Burton was so impressed with these lines that he appropriated them for his own Latin play, *Philosophaster* (cf. the Commentary note *ad loc.*).

x

the Unity of Place into his expanded version of Seneca's *Hippolytus*. There is also abundant reason for thinking that he employed his plays as a means of working out a deep-seated psychological conflict,[1] and his use of plays to grapple with a gnawing personal issue infuses them with extra energy and intensity that helps elevate them beyond the ordinary. Gager, in sum, deserves to be recognized and appreciated as a significant figure in the history of the English national theater.

※ ※ ※

William Gager was born on July 24, 1555, at Long Melford, Suffolk, the son of Gilbert Gager and Thomasina Cordell Gager.[2] Thomasina was the sister of Long Melford's leading citizen, Sir William Cordell of Melford Hall. Cordell was one of those Tudor thrusters, a yeoman's son who did well under Henry VIII, and there is rich symbolism in the fact that Melford Hall was erected on the foundations of a hunting lodge of the Abbots of Bury St. Edmunds, confiscated and ceded to him by royal grant.[3] Gager's maternal grandfather, John Cordell, had been a servant of Long Melford's squire, Sir William Clopton. A sign of Sir William Cordell's upward mobility was that he married Clopton's granddaughter, Mary. In his life he held an impressive number of titles: Member of Parliament, Solicitor-General, Speaker of the House of Commons, member of the Privy Council (under Mary), and Master of the Rolls[4] under both Mary and Elizabeth. Although at least reputedly Cambridge-educated, Cordell, like his nephew, had Oxford connections. He is supposed to have drafted the statutes of St. John's College, and was Visitor of that College. A mark of his standing is that in August of 1578 he played host to the Queen at Melford Hall, after she had been entertained by academic disputations and a play by Cambridge men at Audley End.[5] Cordell's siblings rode the social escalator in his wake: sister Jane married well and brother Edward also made his fortune, of which we shall hear more below.

There are strong indications that Thomasina and her sons were regarded as poor relations by the Cordells, perhaps because Gilbert was something of a wastrel.[6] We have records of

---

[1] In the same way, he employed some of his unpublished occasional poetry to vent personal feelings about his family life and other issues. A previously unedited example is quoted below.
[2] Like all subsequent writers on Gager, I heavily depend for my biographical sketch on C. F. Tucker Brooke, "The Life and Times of William Gager (1555 - 1622)," *Proceedings of the American Philosophical Society* 95 (1951) 401 - 31. There is also a biography in the *D. N. B.* What I have managed to ascertain about Gager's family connections is set forth in the Introduction to Volume III.
[3] Currently the seat of Sir Richard Hyde Parker, 12th Baronet Melford, Melford Hall has been transferred to the National Trust and is open for inspection by the public; most visitors will be more conscious of other literary associations: in a later century it was the family home of Beatrix Potter. The Hall is the subject of a handsome and informative brochure, "Melford Hall," available from the National Trust (emended edition 1990).
[4] Responsible for custody of legal records, second only to the Chief Justice in the judicial hierarchy.
[5] (August 4 - 5); for particulars of the visit cf. John Nichols, *The Progresses and Public Processions of Queen Elizabeth* (London, 1823, repr. New York, n.d.) II.116f., and for poetry by Gager celebrating the occasion cf. poems LXIX, LXXVI, and LXXVII in Volume III.
[6] So Brooke speculates (p. 403). Or is it possible that Thomasina annoyed her brother by marrying for love rather than advancement? Roger's father John had been a man of some standing in the community, serving for many years as collector of quitrents and the King's taxes, and as parish clerk. Although the Cordells

Cordell doling out money for Gager's education but, as Brooke wrote after examining various family wills,[1] "nothing, indeed, is more remarkable in the testamentary acts of the Cordells than their unanimity in passing over the Gagers." In volumes concerned with Gager's plays there is no need to investigate his family life, with one conspicuous exception to which we shall presently come.

Gager received his first education, including the rudiments of Latin, at the local Melford school. Thence he passed on to the Winchester College. There is no record of his entry there, but Brooke assumes that, if he was twelve at the time, this would have been in about 1567.[2] From Winchester, he went up to Oxford in 1574 as a Queen's Scholar, where he matriculated from Christ Church. He then ascended the academic ladder at the fastest pace statutably possible: admitted to the B. A. in 1577, incepted M. A. in 1580, created Doctor of Civil Law in 1589. Gager attained the status of *theologus* (which did not imply any especial interest in divinity) as a student of Christ Church, and remained in residence until 1593. After that, Christ Church records indicate he was present only rarely. How he passed the next few years is obscure. In 1601 he became surrogate to the Chancellor of the diocese of Ely.[3] Upon the death of the incumbent, Gager was appointed to the Chancellorship *pro termino vitae*. He owned a house in Chesterton, a suburb of Cambridge, which he shared with his wife, the former Mistress Mary Tovey, a widow with two sons by a prior marriage whom he married at some unknown date, where they lived until his death in August, 1622.[4] He is buried in All Saints' Church, Cambridge.

During his Winchester years Gager must have been exposed to two influences which were determinative for his literary future. Leicester Bradner wrote:[5]

> The great public schools generally took their pupils through Vergil, Ovid, Horace, parts of Catullus and Martial, and a few modern poets such as Baptista Mantuan. The study of these authors included detailed attention to their striking phrases and poetical ornaments, which the students were required to note carefully. The more ambitious boys kept commonplace books in which these things were put down for future borrowing or imitation.

Closely linked to this program of reading was a rather ferocious regimen of Latin verse composition, beginning in the fourth form. To be sure, a certain amount of this versification consisted of pasting together tags taken from classical authors according to the

---

were *arrivistes*, we shall see in the Introduction to Volume III that they maintained at least the pretense of an ancient pedigree, a theory to which Gager enthusiastically subscribed.

[1] *Loc. cit.*
[2] *Ib.* 404.
[3] It has been wrongly stated (by David H. Horne, *The Life and Minor Works of George Peele*, New Haven, 1952, 42) that, like his contemporaries Richard Edes and Leonard Hutton, Gager became a clergyman. This was a layman's post, at least usually filled by a lawyer; Thomas Legge, likewise a D. C. L., had previously held this position.
[4] Boas, *op. cit.* 167, wrongly gives the year of his death as 1621.
[5] *Op. cit.* 3f. For an astonishingly rich and detailed account of Elizabethan secondary education, cf. W. T. Baldwin, *William Shakspere's Small Latine & Lesse Greeke* (Urbana, 1944). Two chapters in this study are particularly relevant: Vol. I , Chapter XIV (on Winchester) and Vol. II, Chapter XLI (on the teaching of verse composition).

principle described by Bradner, or lifted out of dictionaries of synonyms and epithets.[1] At its worst, this system of verse composition must have led to little more than the manufacture of centos. But a talented boy could develop a genuine facility as the result of such training.

Winchester also had its own lively theatrical life. Like the Eton College, it contained in its statutes a requirement for annual Latin dramatic productions.[2] Brooke furnishes an impressive list of performances given during the 1560's and early 1570's, mostly but not exclusively of plays by Plautus and Terence.[3] But there was a special feature that distinguished Winchester's dramatic life. The same statute also required that English plays be performed by the boys of the choir, who had their own school presided over by a separate Master:[4]

> This vulgarer band of youths had in Gager's period a very interesting histrionic career. Under their director, John Taylor, they took part in various London city pageants and even appeared at times at Court: once (1572) in a play based on the mediaeval romance of *Paris and Vienne*, and again (Christmas, 1574, during Gager's last year at Westminster) in a kind of moral masque, "Truth, Faithfulness, and Mercy."

Thus, while himself studying and assisting in the drama of ancient Rome, Gager was being constantly exposed (as a rather supercilious spectator, it may be feared) to the influence of pretty much all that the vernacular London drama of his boyhood was accomplishing. The results are important in the judgment of his own plays. On the one hand, he never gave up the opinion, often repeated in later years, that drama in English was unworthy of scholars and gentlemen;[5] he shows no least tendency to write, as [Nicholas] Udall[6] had done, a *Roister Doister*, or as Mr. S. of Christ's College, Cambridge, had done, a *Gammer Gurton's Needle*. And yet he could not write a Latin play without admitting into its emotion and structure traces at least of the larger freedom of the vulgar stage. A good deal of Gager's importance as an Elizabethan dramatist lies in this.

Gager maintained a personal notebook in which he preserved his unpublished work written at Oxford, British Library Additional Ms. 22583. (Because of the frequency with which this manuscript must be cited throughout the volumes of this series, it is henceforth designated A).[7] The first and presumably earliest item in this is a Latin translation of the pseudo-Homeric *Batrachomyomachia* with an appended note *haec lusi Scholaris*, showing

---

[1] Besides the evidence for these cited by Baldwin, Ch. XLI, cf. Appendix C of D. C. Allen, *Francis Meres' Treatise "Poetrie"* (Urbana, 1933). That this approach to versifying remained the mature Gager's working method can readily seen by the large number of tags and more important imitations recorded in the Commentary notes to his plays. I shall return to the character of his poetic technique below.

[2] In the case of Eton, in the original charter; in that of Winchester, in the revised statutes of 1561. The passage is quoted by Brooke, *op. cit.* 405.

[3] *Loc. cit.*

[4] Brooke, *loc. cit.*

[5] [One of Tucker Brook's rare errors: Gager never expressed any such opinion, and one poem, LXXIX, is expressly to the contrary.]

[6] [A former Master of Winchester.]

[7] Cf. the Introduction to Volume III for a detailed description of the manuscript in question.

that this was done during his undergraduate years. Other early work includes a hexameter version of the Biblical story of Susanna, and one of Isocrates' precepts to Demonicus in elegaics. It was probably soon after coming to Oxford that Gager's enthusiasm for Latin versification tried the patience of his masters and earned him a whipping, doubtless for neglecting other responsibilities. A poem about this incident (LIX) is a fine example of Gager's habit of worrying over personal grudges and frustrations in his writings.

When he came up to Oxford, Gager found himself in what was increasingly becoming a hotbed of literary activity, some of national significance. Present in his Christ Church were other talented poets, such the future London playwright George Peele, and the Anglo-Latin poets Richard Eedes and Martin Heton. Then there was Richard Haklyut, whose *Voyages* was a milestone in the development of English prose. College authorities looked favorably on literary efforts. Christ Church took the lead in University dramatic performances. The Dean, Tobie Mathew, and Harbert Westfaling, one of the Canons, were two of the most celebrated preachers of the day in an age when preaching was regarded as a form of epideictic rhetoric.

So Gager had found an ideal environment for exercising his abilities as a poet, and for discovering his talents as a dramatist. In this fostering atmosphere he made rapid progress. The major product of his Bachelor years was a translation of Musaeus' *Hero and Leander*. Of more immediate concern to us here, the notebook also contains sketches for five scenes of a tragedy about Oedipus, the first item in the present volume.[1] As the reader will see, there is much in these scenes that is unpromising. But one scene presents a striking contrast. In a few deft strokes we are given a portrait of Eteocles conceived along the lines of a Renaissance tyrant, a piece of characterization that is remarkably able for a tyro, in which any playwright could take justifiable pride. In these very few lines we can discern evidence for a dramatist of formidable potential.

This potential was swiftly realized, for only a few years later Gager produced his *Meleager* of 1582.[2] The rapidity of Gager's growth is astonishing. *Meleager*'s plotting, characterizations, and overall conception are executed with mature assurance, and in all ways the author is firmly in control of his material. It would be hard to point to any features that are palpably the marks of a maiden performance. Indeed, in this play Gager attained a level of originality and excellence arguably unequaled in his later works. *Meleager* is no mechanical replica of Seneca. Although the play's poetics are predictably Senecan, as is the conception of some of its characters and scenes, Gager made a concerted effort to bypass Seneca and go back to the austerer and more elevated moral grandeur of Attic tragedy, presenting the authentic Greek narrative pattern of a hubristic tragic hero rebelling against the gods and suffering a consequent downfall. Tragedy of this type demands a suitably grand, and suitably wrongheaded, hero at its center, and Gager managed to create such a hero in Oeneus. This god-hating, heaven-storming ranter is one of the genuinely memorable characters of the Elizabethan stage, and several writers have justly compared him with the kind of tragic hero Marlowe was presently to develop. There is room for plenty of debate whether Seneca's plays (and, in consequence, much Renaissance Seneca-based drama)

---

[1] In Volume III, I shall argue that poems CII - CVII, all written in iambic senarii, are also a budding playwright's technical exercises.
[2] Technically 1581/2, since it was produced before March 25 of the year in question. Henceforth all dates will be cited according to the modern calendar.

constitute genuine tragedies. Gager leaves no room for any doubt that *Meleager* is a real tragedy by any standards you care to apply.

Meleager is his most uncompromisingly tragic work. His next play, *Dido*, is a tragedy too, but its tone is lightened by a greater admixture of non-tragic elements designed to provide entertainment. But it is a feature of Gager's overall art that even *Meleager* contains popularizing features redolent of the popular stage. The tone of Actus I is light and witty, and, some characterizations look a little less than entirely serious. And the play contains elements of masquing and song that would be quite out of place in a strictly neoclassical tragedy. Indeed, in each of his surviving plays the gravity and potential tedium of neoclassicism are lightened by features that are winsome, graceful, and witty.

Meleager was put on again three years later as entertainment for a visitation by the Earl of Leicester, Chancellor of the University of Oxford, accompanied by his nephew Sir Philip Sidney.[1] More immediately, in 1583 the University was apprised at very short notice of the impending visit of a foreign dignitary, to be escorted by Leicester, and there was something of a scramble to devise suitable entertainment. The University turned to Gager to write two plays, and supported him with generous resources. One of the works written for this occasion, the comedy *Rivales*, has not been preserved, but must have been quite successful since it provoked Francis Meres' enthusiastic view of Gager's stature as a comic playwright. It was revived in 1592 in connection with the great Shrovetide dramatic exercises, and again in September of the same year for the first royal visitation since 1566.

The other play written for this occasion, *Dido*, is commonly disdained by modern critics who say that it was hastily cobbled together and amounts to little more than a mechanical adaptation of Vergil's story of Dido and Aeneas. It could also be claimed that *Dido*'s considerable elements of entertainment and pageantry do not sit very well with the essentially tragic story. And, as will be shown in the special Introduction to that play, internal evidence tends to establish that Gager farmed out some scenes to a less talented collaborator. But in view of the circumstances under which it was written, *Dido* is a remarkably well-crafted play, and there is much that can be said in its defense. This is not a play that should not greatly detract from its author's reputation.

※ ※ ※

This is far as the story of Gager's career as a dramatist need be carried for the first volume of his plays; this biographical narrative will be resumed in the General Introduction to Volume II. The suggestion has already been made that Gager's plays gain extra intensity and energy because he employed them as a forum for working out a psychological conflict, or perhaps for conducting an interior debate. For the common denominator linking all of his plays is a virtual obsession with the subject of chastity. From first to last, he ceaselessly worries at this topic. Sometimes, chastity is presented in a wholly favorable light. Penelope is shown to be a paragon of virtue in *Ulysses Redux*, and we are given three negative examples of unchastity, and of the disaster to which it leads, in the protagonist of the *Dido*, in

---

[1] The official nature of the visit is indicated by the fact that from London John Lyly arranged to have the Revels Office lend costumes for the plays: cf. the document reproduced by Boas, *op. cit.* 194f.

Phaedra of *Panniculus*, and in Melantho in *Ulysses Redux*. We are likewise treated to the impassioned defenses of celibacy by Atalanta in *Meleager* and by Hippolytus in *Panniculus*.

On the basis of these elements, one might be tempted to construct a picture of Gager as a misogynist or somebody deeply frightened of female sexuality. Until well into the present century, after all, the Universities were intensely masculine societies and for this reason doubtless tended to attract men of both types.

If you wanted to make this case, you could point to certain biographical facts. Following the suggestion of the anonymous "I. C.," probably Dr. John Case of St. John's College, who contributed an epigram prefacing *Meleager*, you could argue that the trouble caused by an allegedly predatory female relative within his own family, who did Gager out of an expected inheritance, left a deep emotional scar, and jaundiced his attitude towards women. Gager's uncle Edward Cordell remarried in late life and then expired in 1590. As often happens in such cases, Gager was bitterly resentful of the loss of an expected inheritance, and he may have blamed his uncle's young bride for poisoning his mind. In his notebook there is a poem on the subject[1] beginning:

> *o fortuna meis semper contraria votis!*
> *o mors! o peius faemina morte malum.*
>
> ["O Fortune, always contrary to my desires! O death! Oh woman,
> more evil than death!"]

This poem is prefaced with the following outburst: *In obitu Avunculi mei Eduardi Cordelli quo sua domina Digbye biennio ante ducta, et sola haerede instituta, tot promissis suis, iureque Civili et Naturali violatis, testamento praeteritus sum Decembris 1590* ["On the death of my uncle Edward Cordell, by whom I was passed over in his will in violation of all his promises and of law both civil and natural, after he had married Mistress Digby two years previously and made her is only heir"]. "I. C." appears to have thought that *Meleager*'s murderous Althaea was modeled on the hateful Mistress Abigail Digby.

It could also be pointed out that some of his nondramatic poems dwell on the theme of the chastity and its loss.[2] Most notably, the youthful *Susanna* (printed here in Volume IV) anticipates the *Ulysses Redux* in telling a story of chastity besieged by unworthy and rapacious suitors. Likewise, since selection of metaphor can be psychologically revealing, one might remark that in his letter to Dr. John Rainolds[3] Gager defined his task:

> Wherin I ame affected as if I weare advocate to a fayre mayden suspected and accused of incontinencye...evne so I fare in this cause, whearin not one, but two fayre maydens, *Tragoedia* and *Comoedia* are not only greevusly suspected, but vehemently and eloquently accused...

Although this is a topic more properly addressed in the Introduction to Volume III, our understanding of Gager's psychological makeup is complicated by the fact that some of his

---

[1] CLXXI.
[2] Such as LXXI - LXXIII.
[3] Cf. Volume IV, p. 260.

notebook poetry attests Platonic homosexual attachments. One might allege this as further evidence for a misogynistic streak in the man. To round out the picture, it could be pointed out that in a 1608 Comitia debate he seems to have upheld the thesis that wife-beating was legally sanctioned.

The trouble with this picture, however, is that as soon as you examine it more closely, it tends to dissolve. Unless "I. C." was writing with tongue and cheek (which his tone scarcely suggests), his interpretation of Althaea's characterization is merely silly, for *Meleager* was written many years prior to Uncle Edward's death (a passage at *Panniculus* 245ff. may or may not reflect such feelings). In the notebook poem Mistress Digby comes in for some harsh words, but Uncle Edward quite properly bears the brunt of the poet's frustration,[1] and in any event the poem and some following ones serve to show that the episode did not produce embitterment, but rather provoked a Christian conversion experience.

Two of his plays, *Meleager* and *Panniculus*, contain debates about chastity's value, and in both debates those arguing the antichastity position give as well as they get. In these debates the representatives of that side unquestionably emerge as the more attractive characters and as the more convincing debaters. In *Meleager* the chaste Atalanta strikes one as more than a little uncouth. Meleager himself may be headstrong and, in his infatuation, a mooncalf. But his friend Philemon is portrayed as a polished and intelligent courtier. In the *Panniculus* debate, Hippolytus is characterized as boorish and more than slightly hysterical, while the Naiad who woos him strikes the reader as wholesome, sensible, and thoroughly attractive.[2] When she suggests that his life-philosophy is based on nothing more than fear and avoidance, adding more than a hint that there is something pathological involved (273 - 97), the spectator cannot help but agree. Seneca's Hippolytus is already characterized as misguided, hysterical, and downright pathological; Gager's additions do nothing to undercut this representation, and much to support it. And he undermines the black-and-white moral scheme that has prevailed throughout *Ulysses Redux* in a final chorus which concludes with the cynically worldly sentiment that, when all is said and done, bad women are to be counted among life's amenities.[3]

Furthermore, the notebook poem entitled *Licet Sapienti Uxorem Ducere* (LXXXI) appears among a series of poems arguing one side of disputational questions, and it is perhaps significant that in the context of a private notebook in which he often opened his heart Gager chose to argue in the affirmative.[4] Certainly it begins with striking vehemence:

---

[1] It is probably for this reason that Gager ripped a page out of his notebook, which began with a vernacular poem addressed to him (CLXIII).
[2] Even Gager's great antagonist Dr. John Rainolds was not immune to her charm: he wrote of "a new Nymph...bringing fewell enough to heate and melt a heart of yse or snow" (in his *Th'Overthrow of Stage-Players* p. 20, with *heale* a misprint for *heate* in the printed text). The Gager - Rainolds controversy will be described in the General Introduction to Volume II.
[3] I do not think that this observation is entirely undermined by the consideration that this chorus translates an anonymous poem in *Tottel's Miscellany*, for the choice of the item in the question is still Gager's. Nevertheless the pert cynicism of this piece represents a voice that is not characteristically his own.
[4] This is especially significant because participants in Oxford academic disputations respondants were free to answer in the affirmative or negative, as they chose, until 1592: cf. A. Clark, *Register of the University of Oxford* (Oxford, 1887) II.i 172.

> *qui dura taedas sapienti lege iugales*
> *deneget, aut puer est, aut sine mente senex.*

["Whoever denies a wise man the wedding torches by a harsh law is either a child or an old fool."]

In 1609 Joseph Barnes printed a tract entitled *An Apologie for Women, or An Opposition to Mr. Dr. G. his Assertion, Who held in the Act at Oxforde, Anno 1608, That it was lawfull for husbands to beat their wives* by "W. H. of Ex. in Ox." The author is identified by Anthony à Wood as William Heale of Exeter College,[1] who adds that the "Dr. G." is Gager; this finds support in the fact that Gager's name is also written in ink in the Bodleian copy of Heale's tract. To be sure, Tucker Brooke[2] pointed out that Convocation granted a dispensation for Thomas Gwin of All Souls to act as respondent at the 1608 Comitia because no Doctor could be found for the purpose, but the chances that Gager did participate in this debate are increased by a some lines of his *Pyramis*, written in the same year (1198ff.):

> *uxori pulsare virum natove parentem*
> *nulla lege licet. contra, natumque parenti*
> *uxoremque viro fas est quandoque. vir est rex,*
> *et pater est populi; populo inviolabilis ergo.*

["No law allows a wife to strike her husband, or a son his father. But on the contrary, from time to time a parent may beat his son, a husband his wife. A king is the husband, and the father of his subjects, and so inviolable to his people."]

But arguing that wife-beating is legal is not the same thing as asserting that it is advisable. Heale's treatise is no careful point-by-point refutation of "Dr. G."'s case, and does not permit the reconstruction of the argument, but in one place (p. 7) he says that this proponent of wife-beating adduced as evidence the case of Publius Sempronius, who divorced his wife for having seen a play.[3] If Gager was the debater, this allusion suggests a bit of clowning, which would scarcely be out of keeping with the spirit of an occasion that encouraged plenty of comedy.[4] Heale may have taken Gager a bit more seriously than the situation warranted. All in all, it would be highly dangerous to see in this episode any evidence for misogyny.

And the argument that Gager's homosexuality necessarily implies some kind of aversion towards women may well be a naive psychological *non sequitur*. The final and definitive refutation of any possible charge that he was a simple misogynist is of course the fact that after leaving Oxford he married (at some unknown date). One might argue that many of the facts considered here support the opposite interpretation just as well if not better. It could be claimed that Gager's obsessive harping on the subjects of chastity and courtship, and also

---

[1] *Athenae Oxonienses* II.89.
[2] "Life and Times" 429 n. 154.
[3] The story comes from Aulus Gellius, *Attic Nights* X.2.
[4] Clark, *op. cit.* II.i 84. The nature and purpose of Comitia debates will be described in the Introduction to Volume III.

his homosexual pashes, reveal a man chafing under the burden of academic celibacy. In his debates about chastity he allows his debaters to score important points both by discoursing on celibacy's sterility (*Meleager* 365ff.), and demonstrating that chastity can exist within marriage (*Panniculus* 287ff.), and in both of these passages the speaker points out the joys of child-bearing. There is little doubt that this he found this attitude attractive, since in the same notebook poem on marriage he writes:

> *nam miseram ducit quisquis sine coniuge vitam*
> *ducit, nec Veneris pignora chara videt.*
> *adde quod indigne telluris inutile pondus*
> *nascitur, ex quo non ortus et alter erit.*

["For he who lacks a wife leads a miserable life, nor knows Venus' dear pledges. Then too, he is born an unworthy burden on the earth, from whom no other is born."]

But even this reading of his character courts oversimplification. Because of the way Gager recurrently plays off the images of good hardness (representing chastity, and virtue) versus bad softness (standing for unchastity, degeneracy, and vice) in a number of his plays, one is obliged to confess that his attitude does not seem unequivocally antichastity and pro-marriage. All and all, it seems fairer to conclude that Gager's plays, and to a lesser extent his other writings, reveal deeply divided feelings. It is likely that the debates he writes on the subject reflect a genuine personal conflict. Just as he used his private poetry to express his frustrations and resentments on a wide range of matters, so he employed his plays to create personified projections of his own conflict. His inner situation is perhaps best summarized by a lapidary two-line notebook poem starkly contrasting the claims of two opposing goddesses (CXXII):

> *non bene conveniunt nec eodem more coluntur*
> *Iuno culta toris, culta Diana choris.*

["These goddesses do not agree with each other, nor are they worshipped in the same way: Juno is worshipped in marriage beds, Diana in choirs."]

* * *

In order to argue for Gager's high stature as a playwright and poet, it is necessary to face squarely the problem of his frequently imitative method of composition. In two of his three complete plays, *Dido* and *Ulysses Redux*, he follows a single literary source more or less closely. When his sources contain speeches that could be adapted to the stage, or descriptive passages that could be converted into speeches or even choral passages, he borrowed without hesitation. Even in those passages of *Meleager* where he could adapt a speech or descriptive passage out of Ovid's *Metamorphoses*, he did so. In passages where he could not follow a model, he would whenever possible pattern a scene after some Senecan prototype. Thus, for example, both Althaea's burning of the brand in *Meleager* and Dido's pretended sacrifice are patterned after Medea's magical rite in Seneca's *Medea*. In the former case, more precisely and more notably, on one side of the stage Althaea momentarily "becomes" Medea, while on the other side Meleager simultaneously "becomes" the tormented protagonist of the *Hercules Oetaeus*. Senecan type-scenes, such as apparitions of furies and ghosts, *domina-nutrix* and *dominus-satelles* dialogues, sacrifices, triumphal processions, ritual lamentations, messenger speeches, and the plotting of crimes, are common.

These generalizations may raise some questions in the reader's mind about originality and quality. A full discussion would take us too far afield, but the main lines of such a possible defense may be sketched. The description of Gager's working method given above simultaneously describes that of most other University dramatists. Many another Tudor academic play also depends more or less closely on literary models (certainly, this generalization is true for Gager's most distinguished academic contemporary, Legge), and this might better be accounted a recognized method for University playwrights than a sign of defective invention or plagiarism. Plays (and, nowadays, films) based on literary models constitute a special dramatic genre, where part of the spectator's pleasure lies in the recognition of the original work being enacted. In this special genre, the important thing is the fidelity and adroitness of the author's adaptation, and judiciousness in selection and arrangement counts for more than originality. The use of generic type-scenes and, to an extent, stereotyped characters, is endemic to University tragedy, and indeed even to Attic tragedy itself. We therefore have no business coming down on Gager for employing well-established dramaturgic practices. Rather, we ought to admire him for exercising the level of independence that he did, while operating within the framework of this tradition.

In his otherwise highly favorable appraisal of *Meleager*, Boas[1] wrote that "Where the play is weakest is in its poetic quality. The rhythm of the verse is lacking in melody, and even the lyrical passages are not fired by the glowing imagination which lends Grimald's *Archipropheta* its peculiar romantic charm." Presumably, if pressed, he would have extended this verdict to all of Gager's dramatic poetry, which is stylistically of a piece. The nature of Gager's poetry, like that of most other University dramatists, is explicable by the fact that he always adhered to the method of composition he had been taught at school, described above. Thus all his plays are liberally interlarded with classical borrowings and imitations. This imitative approach inculcated by the educational system undoubtedly tended to produce poetry that was more serviceable than original or memorable, although Gager's ability to put borrowed or closely imitated material to new and unexpected uses occasionally has the power to astonish.

Imitatio on the level of dramaturgy only served to reinforce this inculcated proclivity to use *imitatio* on the level of poetics. Principally, as one would only expect, in the context of serious drama *imitatio* means imitation of words, phrases, and even larger poetic units taken from the Senecan corpus.[2] But Seneca is not the only classical author laid under

---

[1] *Op. cit.* 175.
[2] I.e, from the spurious *Hercules Oetaeus* and *Octavia* no less than the genuinely Senecan plays; it is doubtful that Gager would have entertained any doubts about the former of these, at least. Many of the authors listed here would have been read at Winchester. But it is noteworthy that Baldwin (*op. cit.* supra) concludes that Seneca was not normally part of the secondary school curriculum before 1600. As a general rule, Gager and the other academic dramatists would have had to read him on their own.

contribution: Gager goes to such other poets as Ovid, Horace, Catullus, Terence, Lucan, Persius, Juvenal, and Statius. Since *Meleager* is the play least dependent on a single classical model, and so displays the greatest originality of conception, one might expect to find that in writing it Gager employed the greatest amount of *imitatio*-free composition. But a look at the borrowings indicated in the Commentary notes to Actus I shows otherwise. While not exactly a cento, to a considerable extent the poetry of *Meleager* is something like a mosaic partially assembled out of bits and pieces of Seneca and other classical authors.

Or perhaps, a modern reader might prefer to think, like a nest made by some thieving magpie out of filched twigs and string. For this method of composition might strike one as seriously at odds with how we tend to understand the operations of the creative process. This problem will become all the more urgent in the case of nondramatic poetry, in which Gager very frequently writes of his Muse and of the poetic inspirations he receives, not always willingly.

Of course, he could have said the same thing in his defense that a Christ Church student of the next generation wrote about a similar method of constructing prose:[1]

> For my part I am one of the number, *nos numerus sumus*: I do not deny it, I have only this of Macrobius to say for myself, *Omne meum, nihil meum*, 'tis all mine, and none mine. As a good housewife out of divers fleeces weaves one piece of cloth, a bee gathers wax and honey out of many flowers, and makes a new bundle of all, *Floriferis ut apes in saltibus omnia libant*, I have laboriously collected this cento out of divers writers, and that *sine injuria*...which nature doth with the aliment of our bodies incorporate, digest, assimilate, I do *concoquere quod hausi*, dispose of what I take. I make them pay tribute to set out this *Macaronicon*, the method only is mine own; I must usurp that of Wecker *e Ter.*, *nihil dictum quod non dictum prius, methodus sola artificem ostendit*, we can say nothing but what hath been said, the composition and method is ours only, and shows a scholar.

But something more needs to be said. In the case of a poet of Gager's obvious standing, the first possibility to come to mind may be dismissed out of hand. He did not write this way because he was incapable of doing otherwise. The considerable swatches of his poetry where *imitatio* is not visible demonstrate this abundantly. And, in his nondramatic poetry, it is in his most formal, polished, and carefully written pieces that we encounter the greatest frequency of borrowing. It is much more likely that his heavy reliance on *imitatio* is to be attributed to the manner of his training and to the poetic tradition in which he was working, and consequently to the expectations of his audience and readers.

And this, ultimately, is the important point to be made. *Imitatio*, both on the levels of dramaturgy and of poetry, comprises the standard working procedure for Gager's time and place, and reliance on this technique does not imply any necessary unoriginality or lack of skill. The artistic challenge confronting the poet was to display originality while working within this system, so that his educated audience could appreciate both his borrowings and the appositeness and originality with which they are employed. This style of writing represents a discourse strategy that is, in its way, no less stylized and specialized than that of a

---

[1] Robert Burton in "Democritus to the Reader" from *The Anatomy of Melancholy* (pp. I.24f. of the Everyman edition).

Homeric bard. For the questions about poetic originality for someone working in this imitative manner are not entirely dissimilar to those that are raised about the individual bard working within the framework of the Greek tradition of epic composition, obliged to construct his verses out of a fund of traditional formulae.[1] In the latter case, too, this understanding of the nature of Homeric composition has profoundly disturbed many modern Hellenists, because he seems to describe an overwhelmingly mechanical poetic *techne* that leaves no room for originality, individual excellence, or, if you want to romanticize the thing a bit, inspirational genius.[2] Could one not arrange for a computer to churn out pseudo-Homeric hexameters or bogus Senecan senarii? Does this system allow a poet to say precisely what he wants, rather than co-opting his voice and his thoughts? Does it permit one poet to be better (or worse)[3] than another? This is not the place to pursue the subject, although Gager's poetry would provide an excellent laboratory for the study of this method of composition and the questions it raises, precisely because his obvious high quality excludes any suspicion that he writes in this way because he could do no better.

To illustrate in detail how a first-rate Humanistic poet trained in this system of composition went about his job, I have tried to identify all his borrowings from the principal classical poets in Actus I of *Meleager*.[4] A similar analysis could have been performed on all of Gager's plays and poetry, but is eschewed here because it would have added a large number of pages to Commentary material that most readers would doubtless regard as tedious. Save for Actus I of *Meleager*, Gager's classical borrowings are only noted selectively, when some point of special literary interest is at stake. Detailed observations of *imitatio* go a long way towards delineating the nature of Gager's craft, and may pave the way for an eventual understanding of his artistry. Certainly, one might observe that this method of composition permits both more or less playful allusiveness and the display of cleverness, qualities scarcely foreign to classical Latin poetry.

Gager's plays and poetry are also characterized by a quite different kind of borrowing. As can be seen from the running textual notes of the Commentaries on his plays, and even more so from the similar notes on his nondramatic poets, he was an inveterate autoplagiarist. Self-borrowing is a feature of his working method second only to *imitatio* of classical poets, and it adheres to a very distinctive pattern. Besides his plays and printed

---

[1] For the system of Homeric composition cf. Adam Parry (ed.), *The Making of Homeric Verse* (Oxford, 1987). This comparison with Homeric formulae is especially cogent because many of the classical tags Gager borrows consist of noun-adjective combinations, and he often employs such tags at the same position in the poetic line of any given meter, as the point where he finds them in his classical sources.

[2] For a recent sustained attempt to defend this formalistic understanding of Homeric *techne* against such accusations, cf. Richard P. Martin, *The Language of Homer: Speech and Performance in the Iliad* (Ithaca, 1989).

[3] For badness is a quality in literature no less distinctive than excellence, and it, like excellence, far transcends the simple issue of technical competence or its absence (as pithily argued by D. B. Wyndham Lewis' Introduction to *The Stuffed Owl: An Anthology of Bad Verse*, London, 1930); a system of poetry that excludes badness is just as dissatisfactory as one that allows no excellence.

[4] I wish to thank the students who participated in a recent seminar on the use of computers for research in the Classics who studied Gager's borrowings in these lines: Theresa Allen, Mark Brighton, Dean Cassella, and Margaret Smith.

To facilitate further study of his poetic technique, I have included more detailed observations of his borrowings in the Commentary notes to his *Batrachomyomachia*, *Susanna*, and *Hero and Leander* and *Pyramis* in Volume IV, where space is not at so great a premium. These commentaries show that Gager's technique did not substantially change over time.

poetry, Gager maintained a private notebook into which he copied a rather large mass of nondramatic poetry. In the Introduction to Volume III I shall argue that he kept this notebook so as to have a repository of unprinted material he could reemploy in the future. For his experience with *Dido* and *Rivales*, when he was obliged to produce two plays on extremely short notice, had taught him an important lesson. As something like the uncrowned laureate of Christ Church, if not of the University as a whole, he might be placed in a similar position again, and it was important to have a repository of material that could be reworked as necessary.

Therefore Gager felt free to appropriate notebook poetry for plays or printed poems. He felt equally free to employ the same passage, or a reworked version of the same poem, in another unpublished poem. But once the material in question had been appropriated for a play or been printed, it was henceforth out of bounds for further use. Gager's self-borrowing rarely involves material that had been made public in any form.

The notebook, in other words, deserves to be regarded as one of Gager's tools. Apparently we have no idea of its history prior to the nineteenth century, and may assume it was preserved by accident. Probably many other poets have employed similar devices, if not always in such a systematic way, but have been more successful in destroying the evidence. So Gager's visible self-borrowings ought in no way to lessen our estimation of him as a poet. Demonstration of his reuse of previous material in Commentary notes is in no way meant to diminish his standing. Rather, we should feel privileged to have this unusual glance into a writer's workshop.

One of the most striking features of Gager's poetry, dramatic and otherwise, is his ability as a metrician. In the lyric portions of his plays, which encompass not only act-ending choruses[1] but also interspersed songs, the distinctive feature is a metrical adventurousness which also marks his nondramatic poetry. He imitates the lyric meters of Senecan tragedy, as follows:[2]

> Anapestic dimeters, consisting of four anapests or equivalents: *Meleager*, Actus III chorus; *Dido*, Actus II chorus; *Ulysses Redux*, Actus I chorus, Actus II chorus, Actus III chorus, Actus IV chorus.

> Anapestic dimeters occasionally rounded off, or at least rounded off at the end of the passage, by one anapestic foot resolved as an Adonic [- ˘ ˘ - ˯]: *Meleager*, Actus I chorus, lyric passage at V.1792ff; *Dido*, song at III.ii, Actus III chorus, Actus IV chorus.

> Sapphic hendecasyllables [- ˘ - - - | ˘ ˘ - ˘ - ˯]: *Meleager*, Actus IV chorus.

> So-called "greater Alcaics": hendecasyllables such as are found as the first two lines of an Alcaic stanza, employed independently [˯ - ˘ - - | - ˘ ˘ - ˘ ˯]: *Ulysses Redux*, song at III.784ff.

---

[1] Unlike Seneca, Gager writes full-length choruses at the conclusion of his plays.
[2] Sapphic and Alcaic stanzas are also employed in his non-dramatic poetry.

Sapphic stanzas consisting of three hendecasyllables followed by an Adonic: song at *Dido* II.321ff; song at *Ulysses Redux* II.610ff.

Stanzas consisting of various other numbers of hendecasyllables followed by an Adonic: *Meleager*, song at III.882ff.; *Dido*, Actus I chorus.

A stanza consisting of two hendecasyllables followed by two iambic pentameters catalectic [˘ ̠ ˘ ̠ | ˘ ̠ ˘ ̠ ̠]: song at *Ulysses Redux* V.1789ff.

Iambic tetrameters: *Meleager*, Actus V chorus.

Lesser Asclepiadics [̠ ̠ | ̠ ˘ ˘ ̠ | ̠ ˘ ˘ ̠ | ˘ ̠]: *Meleager*, Actus II chorus; *Dido*, Actus V chorus; *Ulysses Redux*, Actus V chorus.

An equally prominent feature of Gager's Latin style is found in his occasional poetry more than in his plays, but is worth mentioning here since we are attempting to take his overall measure as a poet. His generally neoclassical style is tempered by a habit that stamps him as a product of his own age: delight in punning and similar word play. Verbal play and pyrotechnics abound. To choose an example nearly at random, consider a New Year's poem addressed to two Christ Church friends (CLIV):

> *anni Iane parens, unum mihi perfice votum*
>   *quod mea cum dederis, strena duobus erit.*
> *quam bene Pollucem memoratur Castor amasse,*
>   *quam bene magnanimum Thesea Perithous,*
> *quam Patroclus erat Pelidi charus, Orestes*
>   *quam Piladi, Niso quam fuit Eurialus:*
> *tam Gualterus amet Thomam, Thomasque vicissim*
>   *Gualterum, et casta flagret uterque face.*
> *cumque nec ortu illis nec sint in amando minores,*
>   *non minus istorum nobilitetur amor.*
> *nobile par iuvenum, annuerit si Ianus, ab ullo*
>   *haud maior vobis strena venire potest.*

The jingle *anni Iane parens* at the beginning sets up the subsequent pun *annuerit si Ianus*. Verbal tomfoolery is more luxuriant in the persistent punning on *par* in the first lines of a later New Year's poem, CLXXXIV, written to accompany the gift of a pair of gloves:[1]

> *par cherothecarum, donum impar, accipe, praesul,*
>   *nec meritove tuo par animove meo,*
> *nec manibus fortasse tuis par, omnia dispar,*
>   *nec tu quale decet, parque erat accipere;*
> *quale tamen fortuna potest tibi mittere nostra.*

---

[1] A more significant form of pun may be operative in this poem, if Gager thought that his surname meant "glove-maker."

> *sola facultati par mea strena meae est.*
> *nam meritis quae digna tuis, quae gratia par sit,*
> *quaeve voluntanti strena sit apta meae?*

A very similar series of puns in an unsigned printed poem (*VI) eliminates any doubt that these lines are Gager's; as often happens, our poet takes pleasure in manufacturing Latin puns and word plays based on English proper names:

> *Parry, parem ingenio cum non agnosceret unum;*
> *non unum voluit crimine ferre parem.*
> *Parry, parem meritis cum vix agnosceret orbem;*
> *orbi reginam nollet in orbe parem.*
> *Parry, parem sceleri cum non offenderet horam;*
> *horam habuit sceleri discutiendo parem.*
> *Parry, parem legi cum nollet ducere vitam;*
> *accepit mortem legibus ille parem,*
> *ante pares sine Parry pari cum pendeat omnes;*
> *succedant omnes quos habet ille pares.*

It would be easy to multiply these examples indefinitely, but better to let the reader have the fun of discovering them for himself. Suffice it to say that in amusing himself, and providing entertainment for the recipients of his poems, Gager shows himself to be a very Elizabethan writer indeed.

✳ ✳ ✳

The sources for the texts of the plays included in this volume are specified in the Introductions to individual works, where discussions of special textual problems may also be found. But I may take the present occasion to explain the general editorial policies adopted for all the volumes in this series.[1]

I have silently expanded abbreviations, modernized the long *s*, adopted the modern usage of *u* and *v*, printed *j* as *i*, separated ligatures not employed in modern typography, and removed diacritical markings. Just as in contemporary vernacular documents, there is no firm convention that only proper nouns are to be capitalized, and in the original texts each line is capitalized at the beginning. Modern usage has been imposed, almost always silently (although instances where a copyist or printer has evidently misinterpreted a proper noun as a common one are noted). In his occasional poetry Gager often introduces abbreviations into his titles, and I have silently expanded these. In his English poetry and prose I have also silently expanded such abbreviations as & and y^e.

Contemporary orthography is rarely problematic (at least if you remember that Gager wrote *x* where Classical Latin would have *xs*, and spelled the perfect forms of *capio* as *caepi* etc. and wrote *caetus* instead of *coetus*), and retention of original spellings help con-

---

[1] More precisely, these policies are followed for the editing of Latin texts. English documents are reproduced as found, save where clearly erroneous.

vey the special flavor of Anglo-Latin no less than does similar retention of contemporary English orthography.

Printers were far from careful about maintaining even spacing between words. Sometimes it is difficult to tell whether one should discern single words such as *iamiam* and *nondum* or double ones like *iam iam* and *non dum*. But Gager's notebook displays a pronounced tendency to write double words. Likewise, in his handwriting Gager employed the same digraph for æ and œ, which are therefore equally conflated in printed texts based on his manuscripts. Whether in his mind and ear he actually collapsed these two diphthongs into one or whether this habit was merely orthographic, his practice is maintained here. On the other hand, although the frequency with which *ceu* and *seu* are confused indicates that Gager pronounced these words the same way, they are distinguished here to reader confusion.

Punctuation is a quite different matter. This edition departs from standard editorial practice for the handling of Renaissance Latin verse by (usually silently) imposing modern punctuation. The justification for this decision, which may strike some readers as controversial, is given in an Appendix to this volume.

In an edition of this kind, where they will doubtless be employed as a "trot" by those whose Latin is imperfect or rusty, accurate but inevitably prosaic translations are preferable to more adventuresome versions. For the plays, extra stage directions (printed within square brackets) are added to indicate such things as entrances and exits, while more substantial questions of stagecraft are discussed in the Commentary notes.

The intention of the Commentaries appended to these plays is merely to explain allusions, and handle problems of textual reading and dramaturgy, identify classical borrowings and self-borrowings, and to show how Gager used his sources. No attempt is made at any sort of running literary exegesis.

OEDIPUS

Introduction

ager's personal literary notebook (A) includes portions of *Dido* preceded by the five passages that comprise the present item.[1] Untitled in the manuscript, these passages are generally referred to as the *Oedipus*. They have been edited and annotated, but not translated, by R. H. Bowers.[2] Bowers objected to Boas' identification of this group as a fragment on the grounds that "it is not a fragment in the sense that parts are lacking, as in the case with the *Niobe* of Aeschylus, which consists of a fragmentary speech of 21 lines."[3] This may be technically true if you narrowly define a fragment as a passage of a lost play quoted out of context or preserved on a scrap of papyrus, but nothing could be more erroneous than Bowers' assertion that "actually it is a complete play, albeit short." At most, we have fragments in the sense that Seneca's so-called *Phoenissae* can be thought of as such: disjointed sketches for a play that was never finished. They ought not even to be called scenes, which would misleadingly convey the impression that they are necessarily fully completed dramatic episodes.[4]

It is very hard to imagine what Gager had in mind. The five passages are identified here as I - V. I is the prologue, in which a citizen of Thebes describes the effect of the horrible pestilence on his household. In II Oedipus learns that he has been accused of killing his father, Laius, and marrying his own mother, Jocasta. In III Eteocles and Polynices squabble in front of their mother. By the end of the passage, they have agreed that the only solution to their quarrel is a fight to the death. IV is a monologue in which Jocasta laments the long string of misfortunes that have spoiled her life, of which the war between her two sons is the most recent. In V a maidservant describes to Creon her suicide by hanging.

And so it looks as if Gager intended a play that would cover both Oedipus' downfall and the fraternal strife that ensued: one play that would go over all the ground dramatized by Seneca in two, *Oedipus* and *Phoenissae*.[5] This seems a remarkably ambitious scheme for a single play.

In some ways, Gager is obviously dependent on Seneca. In that poet's *Oedipus* Creon tells Oedipus that he has learned of Oedipus' guilt from the ghost of Laius (619 - 58). In a variant of this narrative device, it would seem, an invented character named Palaemon informs Oedipus of the ghost's revelation to Creon. But in one crucial respect trying to redramatize these plays involves a tremendous problem. In Seneca's *Oedipus*, as in Soph-

---

[1] The *Oedipus* occupies pp. 57 - 63. These pages are photographically reproduced in *William Gager, Oedipus (Acted 1577 - 1592), Dido (Acted 1583), Prepared with an Introduction by J. W. Binns* (Renaissance Latin Drama in England, First Series, vol. 1, Hildesheim - New York, 1981).
[2] R. H. Bowers, "William Gager's *Oedipus*," *Studies in Philology* 46 [1949] 141-53.
[3] *Ib.* 141 n. 2, reacting to Boas, *op. cit.* 183 n. 2.
[4] Likewise Binns, *op. cit.* 8 says that these passages "may be either surviving scenes from a larger play, or the first attempt at what was supposed to be a longer play, or a playlet complete in itself." The third possibility may be excluded unless someone can adduce a similarly disjointed "playlet." The word "acted" in Binns' title is quite indefensible.
[5] Bowers, *ib.* 145 n. 15 is not unjustified when he expresses doubt over whether this work ought to be entitled *Oedipus, Jocasta,* or even *Thebais*.

ocles, Jocasta kills herself soon after Oedipus' self-mutilation. But in *Phoenissae* Seneca followed a different version of the myth, according to which she did not kill herself but lived on and tried unsuccessfully (as in Euripides' like-named play) to reconcile her two sons. It is not fully clear how Gager proposed to resolve this difficulty, or to motivate her delayed suicide.

It is one thing to write a neoclassical tragedy but quite another to write one on the same subject already handled by a classical poet. In the latter case, one invites direct comparison with his model, and is therefore confronted with the problem of ensuring sufficient originality. As discussed in the introductory Commentary notes to the relevant fragments, we can partially observe how Gager proposed to tackle this challenge, but, again, his masterscheme eludes us.

But he was probably quite unconcerned about such issues. For it is likely that he never meant to write a complete play, and these are merely paper exercises undertaken to get the knack of dramatic composition. They display five typical tragic scenes: a prologue of the narrative type, a stichomythic interrogation designed to elicit information, an *agon* or confrontation scene, again featuring plenty of stichomythia, a monologue, and a messenger speech.

Gager's notebook, as originally conceived, seemingly follows a tripartite structure whereby the first part consisted of works of some length, of which *Dido* is the last, the second of short occasional poems arranged chronologically, and the third of miscellaneous prose items.[1] Chronological order is followed within each section, with consequent overlapping between the sections. Thus the earliest datable poems of the second section are assignable to 1578, considerably earlier than *Dido*.[2]

In the second section of the notebook is a sequence of short iambic poems (CIII - CVII) that look like sketches for possible dramatic speeches. From their position in the notebook, they would appear to emanate from the early 1580's. Indeed, the last of these reappears, in slightly modified form, in *Meleager*, and another found its way into the later *Panniculus*. Heretofore Gager had mainly displayed an ability for writing dactylic hexameters and elegiac distichs. Save for a few efforts in hendecasyllables, he did not yet exhibit the facility for writing in various meters that would later distinguish his work. Thus this series of poems look like exercises designed to develop skills for the writing of iambic senarii, and it is likely that the composition of the *Oedipus* fragments were part of the same effort.

Certainly the length at which Oedipus interrogates Palaemon with a sing-song catechism in II looks like a beginner's clumsy miscalculation. A passage which is supposed to dramatize Oedipus' incredulity has the unintended effect of making him seem rather stupid. On the other hand, one must hasten to add that the thumbnail sketch of Eteocles in III is first-rate work. The striking improvement made over the course of these fragments well accords with the appraisal suggested here.

---

[1] Cf. the more detailed discussion of this manuscript's organization in the Introduction to Volume III.
[2] Therefore the notebook was not begun until after the time of *Dido*'s writing.

I.

CIVIS THEBANVS SECVM DEPLORAT ET VRBIS ET SVAM IN PESTE THEBANA MISERIAM
A p. 57

  quam saeva miseros fata Labdacidas premunt!
quaenam ista regio est dira! quae Thebas nova
semper sequuntur monstra! quot fiunt prius
quam conderentur! conditor Cadmus diu
exul vagatur, hic fugam vacca duce   5
inauspicata sistit. en socii statim
serpente caesi, milites terra editi
anguigena proles. iam stat urbs, mox conditor
fit ipse serpens. postea quanti stetit
regnasse Thebis? factus est Cadmi nepos   10
nova praeda canibus ora dum cervi induit.
par conditori dextera Amphion sua
cum stirpe tota cecidit, at mater furens
Penthea superbum lacerat. istis Laium
adiice nefando nuper extinctum dolo.   15
quid Sphynga dicam? credat an quisquam malis
his maius aliquid posse moliri deos?
tamen ecce maius. iam diu Thebas premit
horrenda pestis. publicam taceo luem,
haud ipse propria flere sufficio mala.   20
 namque ecce totam pestis exhausit domum.
iam quinque natos, coniugem, tres filias
totidemque servos extuli. totum pecus
interiit, unus ecce restabat pater
unusque natus. hos item flammis paro   25
adiicere, sed iam flamma pietati deest,

p. 58   iam nulla maestos sufficit sylva in rogos
(en alia clades), ligna iam desunt mihi
ad utrumque funus, unico vix est satis.
 heu gemina mentem distrahit pietas meam.   30
uter est cremandus? natus hinc, hinc est pater.
uterque charus. tu, pater, careas rogo?
tu, nate, careas? surgit hinc illinc nefas.
posito pudore (quid iuvat miserum pudor?)
certabo ad ignes, filium aliena strue   35
cremabo, meque funus extremum dabo.

---

2. *dira?* A 3. *monstra?* A 4. *conderentur?* A

I.

A THEBAN CITIZEN LAMENTS THE CITY'S MISERY AND HIS OWN DURING THE THEBAN PLAGUE

How the savage Fates are oppressing the poor House of Labdacus! How occursed this land! What strange monstrosities are always harrying Thebes! How many there were even before its settlement! Cadmus, its founder, long wandered as an outcast, but made an end to his flight because of the ill-omened cow. Behold, his comrades were swiftly killed by the snake, and the dragon-born generation of soldiers was born from the earth. Then the city was established, its founder soon became a snake himself. In after times, what was it worth to have been king at Thebes? Cadmus' grandson was made novel prey for his hounds when he took on the appearance of a stag. Amphion, equal in rank to the founder, died by his own hand, along with his entire family. But his raging mother tore apart proud Pentheus. To these you may add Laius, recently killed by criminal deceit. What should I say of the Sphinx? Can anyone imagine the gods could devise anything greater than these evils? But behold a worse: for a long time a horrible plague has been oppressing Thebes. I shall not mention the public misfortune, as I can scarcely bewail my own suffering.

For behold, this pestilence has emptied my home. I have buried five sons, my wife, three daughters, the like number of servants. My whole herd is dead, and behold, my father and one son were left. I am preparing to add them to the pyre, but now fire is lacking for my piety. Now no forest is adequate for our pyres — another form of slaughter — and I have no wood for both their funerals, scarcely enough for a single pyre.

Alas, a twofold piety tears my mind apart. Which is to be burned? On the one hand there is my son, on the other my father. Both are dear. Will you lack a pyre, father? Or you, my son? The prospect of wrongdoing arises in either case. But I shall set aside my shame — what good is shame for a wretch? — and hasten to the fires. I shall cremate my son on someone else's fire, and than I shall finally offer myself for the last funeral of all.

II.

OEDIPVS, PALAEMON

OED. dic age, per omnes oro te magnos deos,
per iura regum perque periturae gravem
patriae ruinam, per tuam semper fidem
nobis probatam: vera memoravit Creon, 40
an illa finxit, regna sibi nostra ambiens?
simulata remove verba, num facile Oedipum
decipere credis? Sphyngis evici dolos.
crimen remitto. sit licet magnum hactenus
simulasse, tenta quid potest regis favor. 45

PAL. magnanime princeps, quid iuvat causae moram
afferre verbis? vera memoravit Creon.

OED. me nominavit Laius?

PAL. te Laius.

OED. Oedipoda?

PAL. prorsus.

OED. qui graves Thebas regit?

PAL. Thebas regentem.

OED. spolia qui Sphyngis tulit? 50

PAL. qui Sphynga fudit.

OED. filium me Laii?

PAL. te filium.

OED. patremque se?

PAL. seque etiam patrem.

OED. coniuge creatum?

---

40. *nobis* corr. in *semper* A

II.

OEDIPUS, PALAEMON

OED. Come, tell me, I pray by all the great gods, by the laws of kings, by the great catastrophe of our nation, going to ruin, by the loyalty you always display towards me, has Creon told me the truth, or did he invent this, aiming at my throne? Dispense with falsehood — do you think you can easily deceive Oedipus? I dispelled the Sphinx' deceits. I absolve you of your guilt. Even if until now you have made a big thing of lying, find out what royal favor can accomplish.

PAL. Great-hearted prince, what point is there in delaying my words? Creon told the truth.

OED. Laius named me?

PAL. He named you

OED. Oedipus?

PAL. Just so.

OED. Who rules mighty Thebes?

PAL. The ruler of Thebes.

OED. Who despoiled the Sphinx?

PAL. The man who routed the Sphinx.

OED. He said I am the son of Laius?

PAL. Yes, his son.

OED. And that he was my father?

PAL. Indeed, your father.

OED. Born of his wife?

PAL. coniuge creatum sua
 tuaque.

OED. nempe est mater et coniux mea
 Iocasta?

PAL. sic est.

OED. reus ego caedis?

PAL. reus. 55

OED. stuprique?

PAL. stupri.

OED. pestis?

PAL. et pestis reus.

OED. dic ista rursus, ipse nunc ista repetam.
 me nominavit Laius? meque Oedipum?
 regemque Thebis? inclytum Spyngis nece?
 quid? filium me? se patrem dixit meum? 60
 uxore genitum? matre Iocasta editum?
 causamque pestis? caedis et stupri reum?

PAL. te nominavit Laius, teque Oedipum
 regemque Thebis, inclytum Spingis nece,
 et filium te se patrem dixit tuum, 65
 uxore genitum, matre Iocasta editum,
 causamque pestis, caedis, et stupri reum.

PAL. Born of his wife and your own.

OED. Then Jocasta is my mother and my wife?

PAL. So she is.

OED. And I am guilty of his murder?

PAL. You are guilty.

OED. And of her debauchery?

PAL. And of her debauchery.

OED. And responsible for the plague?

PAL. And responsible for the plague.

OED. Say these things again, I shall repeat them. Laius named me? Me, Oedipus? The king of Thebes? Me, Oedipus? The man famous for killing the Sphinx? What? He said I am his son? He my father? Born of his wife? Born of Jocasta my mother? Responsible for the plague? For his murder? And guilty of debauchery?

PAL. Laius named you, Oedipus, the king of Thebes, famous for killing the Sphinx, and said you are his son and himself your father. You are born of his wife, born of Jocasta your mother, responsible for the plague and his murder, guilty of debauchery.

III.

POLYNICES, ETEOCLES, IOCASTA

POL. imperia pretio quolibet constant bene.

ET. et regna quovis iure retinentur bene.

POL. aliena?

ET.   sed possessa.

POL.   sed quae possides   70
vi rapta.

ET.   placide, vis tibi iam displicet
qui Graia muris patriis signa admoves?

POL. periure, sceleri patriam obtendis tuo?

ET. tu quid tuo?

POL.   me scelere testes liberant
superi, fidesque pacta.

ET.   sic natus deos   75
fidemque curet?

POL.   ecquid ut fidei datae
sic fratris etiam oblitus, et generis tui es?

p. 60   ET. incaeste, memini matris et patris quoque.
Iocasta nempe est mater et pater Oedipus,
fraterque Polynices. sceleris hoc quod fuit   80
generi imputandum est. colere pietatem solet
tam sancta soboles? ecquis expectat pios
sic procreatos? quaeso, Polynices, palam
uterque fateamur vitia, et ut re sumus
videamur esse. novi ego ingenium tuum.   85
ex aequo uterque incaestus, ex aequo impius
avidusque regni. vel tibi vel iam mihi
fuit exulandum. fuerat in medio scelus
positum occupanti. scelere praerepto doles.
scio quid quaeris, non quod ex regno expuli,   90

III.

POLYNICES, ETEOCLES, JOCASTA

POL. Power is well purchased at any price.

ET. And rule is well retained by any kind of law.

POL. Even somebody else's rule?

ET. But one in my possession.

POL. But what you possess is snatched by force.

ET. You man of peace, does force now displease you, who signalled the Greeks from our ancestral walls?

POL. You false man, do you obtain the nation for your wickedness?

ET. And what are you doing for yours?

POL. The gods, my witnesses, and our sworn pact absolve me from guilt.

ET. Should a man with your pedigree care about gods and agreements?

POL. Are you forgetful of your brother's sworn oath, and of your family?

ET. Unclean man, remember your mother and father. For Jocasta is our mother, Oedipus our father, and Polynices your brother. Whatever crime has occurred is to be imputed to our lineage. Should such a sanctified offspring cultivate piety? Should one expect such children to be pious? I ask you, Polynices, let us openly confess our vices and seem to be what we really are. I know your nature. We are equally unclean, equally impious and hungry for power. You grieve because I stole a march on you in evildoing. Either you or I had to go into exile, the crime lay available for whichever acted first. I know what you were complaining about — not that I exiled you from the kingdom, but that you

              quod ipse non expuleris. hic animus tibi,
              eadem voluntas fuerat. hoc unum obstitit:
              prior occupavi, sors mihi melior fuit.

POL. o impudens, sceleste, labes, perfide,
        coinquinator generis ac stirpis tuae.   95

ET.   hos exul animos?

POL.   qui tuo scelere exulat.

ET.   et exulabit.

POL.   vota si valeant tua.

ET.   scilicet Adrastus spiritus altos facit.

POL. tibi mater animum. quam timide metuens tibi
        duxisti in aciem, sola quae opposito suo   100
        pugnam impediret!

ET.   metuam ego vires tuas?
        ut mater aliquid impetret, patria innocens
        tot liberatur cladibus belli mali,
        ad singulare praelium te provoco.
        in nostra moles capita belli concidat.   105

POL. iam me beas, accipio. sed mihi qua fide
        promissa firmas?

ET.   ipsa res faciet fidem.

POL. quam perdidisti?

POL.   cum tuo magno malo
        primam secunda sanciet.

IOC.   misera hactenus
        tacui, ut furorem verba lenirent gravem   110
        utrinque iacta. saepe post ventos mare
        sequitur quietum. sic ubi animi maximi
        onerantur odiis post graves cessant minas.
        exicite tandem tam feros animos precor.

p. 61

---

96. *nempe* corr. in *qui tuo* A

failed to exile me. This was your intent, you had the same will. This one thing stood in your way: I acted first, I was more fortunate.

POL. Oh impudent man, infamous creature, traitor, who befouls your family and race!

ET. This is the animus of an exile?

POL. Who was thrust into exile by your evildoing.

ET. And who will go into exile again.

POL. If you have your wish.

ET. Presumably Adrastus gives you your high spirits.

POL. And our mother gives you yours. How timidly, fearing for yourself, you dragged her to the battle, the one person who could put off the fight by her interposition!

ET. I should fear your power? So that our mother can achieve something, and our nation be freed from the carnage of an evil war, I challenge you to single combat. Let the weight of this war fall on our heads.

POL. Now you make me happy. I accept. But what guarantee of good faith do you pledge?

ET. The matter itself guarantees faith.

POL. The faith you have broken?

ET. My second show of faith will sanction my first — to your great loss.

JOC. In my misery, so far I have kept silent in the hope that the words hurled on either side would mollify your great madness. Often the sea grows calm after a great storm. Thus when great spirits become laden with hatreds, their grave threats afterwards cease. I pray you, at length dispel this fierce loathing.

ET. absiste, mater. vel hodie me principem   115
     certum videbis vel neci certae datum.

POL. nullumque me lux ista vel regem dabit.

IV.

IOCASTA DEPLORANS MISERIAS SVAS

o nostra nullis asperae sortis mala
aequanda lachrymis. quis meas digne potest
deflere clades? misera quid memorem tuas,   120
furiis Agave instincta, vel, Niobe, tuas?
in me miseriae voluit ostendi gravis
documenta sors maiora. me metam suam
fortuna fecit, quam suis crebro improba
telis feriret, perque tot varias vices,   125
infesta ad istum exercuit semper diem.
  minimum est malorum filium gremio unicum
matris revelli, et parvulum exponi feris.
tamen ecce clades ista tot clades dedit.
occulta sequitur Laii caedes mei.   130
sed adhuc leve hoc est, nisi etiam sit dextera
nati interemptus. hoc quoque etiamnum leve est.
quid? monstra cessant? ecce, quam stragem edidit
Spynx caeca nectens verba et implicitos dolos!
sed hoc repressum est. sicilet eo venerat   135
ut diriori sterneret monstro viam.
idem ille sceptrum patris occisi tulit
matrisque thalamos et sibi fratres dedit
natos parenti. quod simile monstrum extitit?
deinde Thebas dira populatur lues,   140
sibi miser oculis Oedipus sponte erutis
exul vagatur. nata comitatur patrem,
civile fratres invicem bellum gerunt,
mihi sola linquor. quid potest addi malis?

p. 62 *(marginal, at line 132)*

---

120. *deflere fere clades* A, inepte 124. *finxit* corr. in *fecit* A

ET. Leave off, mother. Today you will either see me the certain ruler or see me given over to certain death.

ET. This day will make me king — or nothing.

IV.

JOCASTA, DEPLORING HER WOES

Oh, the evils of our harsh fortune, which no tears can match! Who can suitably bemoan all my losses? In my misery why should I recall yours, fury-driven Agave, or yours, Niobe? A more baleful fortune wanted to make me an example of great misery. Fortune made me her butt, against whom she wantonly shot her frequent darts, and through various misfortunes in her hatred she has hounded me until this very day.

The least of my misfortunes was to have my only son torn from his mother's bosom, and to have the little boy exposed to wild beasts. But behold, that killing engendered so much slaughter. There followed the secret murder of my Laius. But so far this was a light matter, if he were to not killed by the hand of our son. But even that was a trifle. What? Did these monstrosities cease? See what butchery was committed by the Sphinx, contriving her obscure riddles, weaving her snares! But this monster was put down. Evidently it came in order to pave the way for a worse. For this man[1] took his murdered father's scepter and also his mother's bed, and as children for himself, the father, sired brothers. What similar monstrosity ever existed? Then a dire plague ravaged Thebes, and poor Oedipus, voluntarily putting out his eyes, wanders as an exile. His daughter[2] accompanies her father, and her brothers are waging civil war against each other. I am left alone to myself. What can be added to these miseries?

---

[1] Oedipus.
[2] Antigone.

V.

ANCILLA NVNTIANS MORTEM IOCASTAE, CREON

ANC. cum iam furentes senserat caedem invicem 145
spectare fratres, nec regi posse impios,
furibunda thalamos intrat, et magno ciet
clamore questus. unguibus lacerat comas
foedatque vultus. mox ait, "famulae, ocius
exite thalamis." instat impatiens morae. 150
paremus aegre, nec satis tantum mali
miserae timentes, nec tamen vacuae metus.
fores sibi ipsa claudit. at nos sedulum
simulamus abitum, mox tamen tacito gradu
pavidae redimus, qua fatiscentes patent 155
rimae admovetur auris attenta undique.
ast illa tristes Laii manes vocat
vocesque miseras fundit, et saepe Oedipum
natosque saepe memorat, et multa insuper
confusa quae gemitus ad aures detulit. 160
repente planctus inter et lachrymas silet.
iamque omne cessat murmur et minimus sonus,
ut cum furentes ventus abiecit minas
placidumque nullo labitur fluctu mare.
miramur, aures arrigimus, et iam magis 165
magisque dubius occupat mentes pavor.
vocamus "hera Iocasta, regina," at nihil
respondet illa. reddit audaces timor.
pulsamus, ecce rediitur contra nihil.
tum nostra vero maior invasit metus 170
pectora, subitque cuncta metuentes stupor.
posito timore, nitimur iuncto impetu
excutere seram postibus. fractae patent
fores et una panditur dirum nefas.
Iocasta ab alta fregerat collum trabe. 175

CRE. o dura semper numina, et sortem asperam.
quaenam ista regio est horrida, infelix, bove
inauspicata condita? o Thebae graves
laresque Cadmi. proh misera Cadmi domus.
fratremne sic deserere potuisti, soror? 180
o simile nostrae cladibus stirpis malum
tuisque fatis simile! sortita es necem
vitae parem, germana, et aerumnis tuis.
sed heu querelis tota nequicquam dies

V.

A MAIDSERVANT, ANNOUNCING THE DEATH OF JOCASTA, CREON

MAID Now, when she had perceived the brothers were contemplating mutual slaughter, and that these impious men could not be controlled, she furiously entered her chamber, uttering her complaint in a loud voice. With her nails she tore her hair and gashed her face. Soon she said "my slaves, leave this chamber quickly." She insisted, impatient of any delay. Grudgingly, we obeyed, in our unhappiness not fearing enough, nor yet completely free of anxiety. She closed the doors herself. But we pretended an obedient departure; however, in our fear we soon crept back, and attentively clapped our ears to the chinks. Then she called on the shades of Laius, saying piteous things, often recalling Oedipus and her children, saying many indistinct things which her groans brought to our ears. Suddenly the plaints and weeping ceased within. Now the muttering stopped, even the least sound, as when the wind abates its raging threats and the sea flows waveless. We were amazed, pricking up our ears, and now a doubtful terror increasingly invaded our minds. We called out "mistress Jocasta, queen!" but she made no reply. Fear for her lent us courage. We beat on the door, but behold, there was no response. Then, in truth, a greater dread came over our hearts, and numbness overwhelmed us in our terror. We set aside our timidity and strove to break down the bars of the door. The shattered portals opened and all at once the dire crime stood revealed. Jocasta had hanged herself from a rafter.

CRE. O gods, always hard, oh harsh fortune! This land is horrible, unlucky, founded by that ill-omened heifer. Oh great Thebes, household gods of Cadmus! Oh Cadmus' unlucky house! Could you desert your brother, sister? Oh evil, similar to our family's other catastrophes and your own misfortunes! Sister, you have been allotted a death equal to your life and your woes.

teritur, meisque consulere rebus monet 185
confusa regni forma, et incertus status.

But alas, the entire day is being vainly squandered on lamentations. The confused condition of the kingdom and its uncertain state warns me to think of public affairs.

Textual Commentary

I A Theban citizen stands by the corpses of his father and son. It looks as if this passage is meant to serve as a narrative prologue of the standard Euripidean - Senecan kind, which (like those of Sophocles' *Oedipus Tyrannus* and Seneca's *Oedipus*) informs the audience about the plague currently devastating the city.

The idea for this prologue is suggested by Seneca, *Oed.* 52 - 68,[1] which describes the citizenry burning their relatives and, because of the deficiency of wood, shamelessly poaching other people's pyres:

> *nec ulla pars immunis exitio vacat,*
> *sed omnis aetas pariter et sexus ruit,*
> *iuvenesque senibus iungit et gnatis patres*
> *funesta pestis, una fax thalamos cremat,*
> *fletuque acerbo funera et questu carent.*
> *quin ipsa tanti pervicax clades mali*
> *siccavit oculos, quodque in extremis solet,*
> *periere lacrimae. portat hunc aeger parens*
> *supremum ad ignem, mater hunc amens gerit*
> *properatque ut alium repetat in eundem rogum.*
> *quin luctu in ipso luctus exoritur novus,*
> *suaeque circa funus exequiae cadunt.*
> *tum propria flammis corpora alienis cremant;*
> *diripitur ignis: nullus est miseris pudor.*
> *non ossa tumuli lecta discreti tegunt:*
> *arsisse satis est, pars quota in cineres abit?*
> *deest terra tumulis, iam rogos silvae negant.*

Seneca in turn was borrowing such picturesque details from Thucydides' description of the plague at Athens (II.52).

I.4ff. Apollo's oracle had told Cadmus to follow a cow and found a city where she sank down to rest. A notebook poem about the sad condition of Christ Church (CXXII) concludes that the College is:

> *abominanda posteris,*
> *ut inauspicata conditas Thebas bove*
> *fugisse Cadmus dicitur.*

---

[1] The plays of the Senecan corpus will be abbreviated as follows: *Ag.* — *Agamemnon, H. F.* — *Hercules Furens, Hipp.* — *Hippolytus, Me.* — *Medea, Oed.* — *Oedipus, Phoen.* — *Phoenissae, Tr.* — *Troades, Thy.* — *Thyestes, H. Oet.* — *Hercules Oetaeus, Oct.* — *Octavia.* I call the play in question *Hippolytus* rather than *Phaedra* in imitation of Gager's practice. To avoid possible confusion, the title of Gager's *Oedipus* will never be abbreviated.

Notes to pp. 6 - 12.

I.6ff. As Cadmus was founding the city, a snake killed most of his men. After he killed it, Athena ordered him to sow its teeth. When he had done so, a crop of warriors grew up to replace them.

I.1 Bowers noted the appearance of *anguigena* at Ovid, *Metamorphoses* III.531.

I.10 Bowers noted the echo of *Met.s* III.174, *Cadmi nepos*. (Cf. Seneca, *Oed.* 751 - 63).

I.13f. Agave and the bacchantes ripped apart Pentheus after he had set himself in opposition to Dionysus. For *Penthea superbum* Bowers compared *Met.* III.514.

I.34f. Bowers compared *Oed.* 64f.:

> *tum propria flammis corpora alienis cremant;*
> *diripitur ignis; nulla est miseris pudor.*

II. In Seneca, Creon and Tiresias conjure up the ghost of Laius, who identifies Oedipus as the sought-for murderer. Creon then reports this to Oedipus (619 - 58), who refuses to believe his news and thinks that he and Tiresias are trying to eject him as king. Gager manufactures a variant of this situation. One can infer that Oedipus has already been informed of Creon's vision, and remains incredulous. Then, instead of dismissing this report as evidence of a conspiracy, he takes the more rational step of verifying it by interrogating an independent witness, an invented character named Palaemon. The identity of this individual is unknown; from the allusion of his loyalty at lines 39f. we can only ascertain that Oedipus considers him a subordinate or ally.

II.61 *Uxore* is of course deliberately ambiguous: "his wife," and "your wife."

III Oedipus is now blinded and in exile. He has left behind two sons, Eteocles and Polynices, and a daughter, Antigone. The kingship was supposed to be divided in such a way that one son would go into exile annually while the other governed the city. But Eteocles, gaining the kingship, refused to admit Polynices. Polynices has gathered an army, the so-called Seven Against Thebes, and is attempting to assert his rights. The two brothers confront each other in the presence of their mother Jocasta.

The literary model for this passage is the final scene of Seneca's fragmentary *Phoenissae*, which breaks off in mid-course. In that work, Eteocles is already portrayed as a typical Senecan tyrant, utterly frank and brutal about power's acquisition and use. But Gager improves on Seneca's incomplete portrait. Bowers (148 n. 32) wrote "This scene, wherein the dangers of civil war are adumbrated, touches on a political topic which haunted the earlier decades of Elizabeth's reign and which obtained full treatment in such plays as *Gorboduc* and *The Misfortunes of Arthur*." This may be so, but Gager is primarily interested in another Renaissance obsession, the Machiavellian Man, and Eteocles' characterization gravitates into this orbit. In his cheerful cynicism he is the equal of anybody in Seneca's portrait gallery of monsters. Especially if the *Oedipus* is a beginner's work, this is a highly effective piece of characterization.

III.68 Bowers pointed out that this line = *Phoen.* 664. In Seneca the line is spoken by Eteocles, and one must admit that this line would better be put in the mouth of the oppressor Eteocles than in that of his victim-brother.

III.72 He is accusing Polynices of seeking to betray the city to his Greek allies outside the walls.

III.85 Bowers observed the echo of *Thy.* 199, *novi ego ingenium viri* (also spoken in the context of a power struggle between two brothers).

III.88f. Bowers observed the echo of *Thy.* 203f.:

> *aut perdet aut peribit; in medio est scelus*
> *positum occupanti.*

III.98 Adrastus was the leader of the Seven Against Thebes.

III.108f. Bowers' translation.

III.115 Cf. poem CLVI.29 - 32 (based on an anecdote told by Plutarch, *Life of Caesar* vii):

> *vox illa matrem Caesaris ad suam*
> *prudentiae expers, haud placuit tibi:*
> *"summumve, mater, me videbis*
> *pontificem aut hodie exulantem."*

IV.120f. Cf. the Commentary notes on I.12f. and I.13f.

IV.143 Bowers noted the echo of Seneca, *Oed.* 92f.:

> *nec Sphinga caecis verba nectentem modis*
> *fugi.*

V In classical tragedy messengers who deliver eyewitness narratives are usually male, but Gager also uses a woman to describe the distraught heroine in *Dido* Actus V.i.

V.177f. See the Commentary note on I.5. Bowers noted the echo of Seneca, *Oed.* 723f.:

> *deseruit fugas nomenque genti*
> *inauspicata de bove tradidit.*

V.170 See the Commentary note on *Dido* V.1182ff.

V.184ff. This coldly abrupt change of gears is in good accordance with Creon's usual

Notes to p. 18.

characterization, as in Sophocles' *Antigone*. Bowers may or may not have been right to see an allusion to the forthcoming dynastic duel between Creon and Antigone in the final line. Note the imitation of *Tr.* 758f.:

> *non vacat vanis diem conterere verbis.*

MELEAGER

Introduction

oth from Gager's dedicatory epistle to the Earl of Essex and from Christ Church account books, we know that *Meleager* was first performed in February 1582, and was revived three years later, in January, in the presence of the Earls of Leicester and Pembroke, and of Sir Philip Sidney. Especially for a first play, *Meleager* is a highly competent neoclassical tragedy, that well reproduces tragedy's inner spirit as well as its outward form. It has been justly admired by critics. J. W. Binns observed that:[1]

> The taut structure of *Meleager* increases the intense and torrid atmosphere of the play, which is permeated by Fate and a sense of inevitable doom. Gager uses supernatural elements, visions, and dreams to add a somber color to the play, and to suggest that dark and ominous forces are at work beyond the powers of men.

Frederick S. Boas wrote:[2]

> [*Meleager*] deserved its highly favourable reception. Though it was Gager's maiden effort as a dramatist, he had shown remarkable skill in adapting the Ovidian story for the stage. He uses, as a matter of course, the Senecan machinery and technique, and he observes the unities strictly. But it is only a superficial view that would dismiss the play as merely imitative and unoriginal. Gager...shows genuine inventiveness and dexterity in his management of the plot, fusing into an attractive whole episodes of his own devising with those of which Ovid was the direct source. The chief personages are individualized by numerous touches which lift them out of the category of types, and the figure of Oeneus is specially noteworthy as due almost entirely to the playwright, and as tempering the tragic atmosphere with an element of acid humour. The dialogue springs, in the main, naturally from the circumstances of the action, and sententious moralizing is for the most part restricted to the Choruses.
> It is assuredly the most convincing test of the merits of *Meleager* that...it will not stand entirely disadvantageous comparison with the consummate tragedy on the same theme which a later age owes to the genius and the scholarship of Swinburne.

Meleager is Gager's most original creation. In his prose preface he displays awareness of various ancient literary treatments of the subject, only two of which are extant. The version of the story in Book IX of the *Iliad* is radically different and so is essentially irrelevant: no Calydonian boar, no Atalanta, no burning brand, no death of Meleager. This leaves only Ovid, *Metamorphoses* VIII.270 - 546. So, just as Gager's other two plays, *Meleager* is based on a single classical model. Because of the haste with which it had to be written,

---

[1] "William Gager's *Meleager* and *Ulysses Redux*," in *The Drama of the Renaissance: Essays for Leicester Bradner* (ed. Elmer M. Blistein, Providence, 1970), 27 - 41 (the quotation is from pp. 31f.).
[2] *Op. cit.* 175 (Boas discusses the play on pp. 168 - 76).

Dido follows its Vergilian model closely. *Ulysses Redux* displays more independence, at least in its second half. But *Meleager* contains important elements that are either developed from hints in Ovid or are entirely invented. The detailed ways in which he did or did not adhere to Ovid may better be discussed in individual Commentary notes. But Gager's most important innovations can be mentioned here

Meleager's love for Atalanta is a necessary plot element, since it motivates his fatal decision to award her the spoils. Although Ovid gets through this briefly, taking no more than four lines (324 - 8), Gager devotes all but the first speech of Act I to this subject. His characterization of Atalanta as concerned with maintaining her virginity, and the lengthy debate about the value of chastity, have no Ovidian equivalents at all.

Since *Meleager* does not follow a literary model so closely, Gager enjoyed especial scope for what was perhaps his most distinctive gift as a dramatist, the delineation of character. We have already seen an example of his ability to create deft characterization in *Oedipus'* Eteocles. In *Meleager* this talent is displayed far more lavishly. Actus I, for example, contains much that strikes one as less than wholly serious. Atalanta, entirely devoted to the killing of animals, frightening the beasts more than they frighten her, is surely one of the least lovely romantic interests in literature; devotees of the late P. G. Wodehouse will be reminded of Honoria Glossop.[1] Meleager, doting on this creature, occasionally borders on the goonish. The exchanges between Meleager and Philemon may be inspired by Senecan scenes between a leading character and a confidant, but Philemon is no mere stock character who serves to elicit his interlocutor's philosophy by asking questions and raising obvious objections: he is a polished courtier with views of his own and is, we are given to feel, considerably brighter than either Meleager or Atlanta.

Gager can get away with this slightly tongue-in-cheek presentation of Meleager and Atalanta because they are, by some important standards, secondary characters. Oeneus is perhaps not the play's unqualified protagonist in terms of the amount of time he is on the stage or the number of lines he is given to speak, but he dominates in the fascination of his portrayal. Also, the play ends with a carefully controlled series of escalating catastrophes, and his downfall, being reserved for last, is made the most important. As Boas suggested, in Oeneus' magnificently single-minded wrongheadedness, and in his terrific rant, there is something almost Marlovian about this quite literally heaven-storming figure. A character is truly worthy of Marlowe who can exclaim (572ff.):

> *si rueret omne quod vides caelum undique,*
> *et ipse ruerem, fateor, et ruerem libens.*
> *haud ille miser est quisquis ex alto cadit,*
> *cadente mundo pariter.*

---

[1] There are, to be sure, elements of her character derived from Seneca's Hippolytus: her fondness for the hunt, her predilection for the rural life, her disdain of the city (for which cf. Hippolytus' speech at Seneca, *Hipp.* 482ff.). It will be observed that, in presenting Meleager as a lover in Actus I, Gager makes a game out of inverting the situation in Seneca's *Hippolytus*: Atalanta, with her enthusiasm for hunting and devotion to chastity, is already very Hippolytus-like. Gager completes the equation by describing the symptoms of Meleager's love in language borrowed from the *Hippolytus'* description of Phaedra's passion, and further underscores the similarity by adapting a number of other phrases from that play, as noted in the Commentary.

["If this heaven you see everywhere were to fall, and I along with it, I confess I should fall gladly. He is scarcely wretched who falls from a high position, if the universe collapses with him."]

Despite the play's title, surely he is the figure who lasts in the reader's imagination.

The fact that he is not closely following a literary model has the effect of allowing Gager to gravitate further into the orbit of Senecan tragedy. Although there are plenty of ways in which *Meleager* does not strictly imitate Seneca's tragic outlook or his dramatic technique (I shall return to this subject below), there is a good deal in this play that is very much in the Senecan vein. The play's crucial scene, in which Althaea burns the log and destroys her son, imitates the sacrifice scene in Seneca's *Medea*. The scenes between Althaea and the Nurse remind us of *domina-nutrix* scenes in such plays as the *Hippolytus* and the *Medea*, and scenes between Oeneus and the unnamed Old Man remind us of dialogues between Senecan kings and their more prudent and level-headed advisers. Indeed, Gager embroiders on this Senecan scene-type by multiplication: there is a balanced symmetry between the pairings of Meleager and Philemon, Althaea and her Nurse, and Oeneus and his Old Man.

Gager is being equally Senecan when he adds heavy elements of the supernatural: a prologue-speaking Fury who, we are given to believe, manipulates the action from behind the scenes, reported ghost-apparitions, dire portents and prophecies. All of this machinery, especially the Fury, is quite unnecessary, since the anger of Diana by itself supplies a sufficient element of divine intervention. Gager adds these superfluous supernatural elements both because they are traditionally Senecan and because they are colorful and exciting, and cater to contemporary tastes for the macabre.

But he is capable of declaring his independence of Senecan models. Even the tragic *Meleager* contains elements of song and masquing, destined to play a greater role in his subsequent works. More significantly, although in the proper Senecan manner *Meleager* is heavily interlarded with references to the power of Fortune and the Fates, at one point (V.1529ff.) Gager rebels against this philosophy and places in the mouth of his Old Man a denial that Fortune exerts any influence over human affairs whatsoever.

In fact, if one can look past the very obvious evidence for Senecan influence on levels ranging from poetry to dramaturgic technique to philosophical outlook, there is good reason for thinking that the most important influence on this play is not Seneca, but rather Sophocles.[1] In one of the most important studies of Sophocles written in this century,[2] Bernard M. W. Knox has shown that each Sophoclean tragedy but one focuses on a strong and single-minded individual on the day of greatest crisis in his or her life. This character's monomania is carried to the point of self-destructive obsession. The exception is *Antigone*, in which two such characters are placed on an inevitable collision course against each other.

This type of tragic hero is, as said above, peculiarly Sophoclean, and it certainly is not Senecan. It is also very much in accord with the kind of Elizabethan tragic hero that Marlowe was about to invent. But rather than giving us one or at most two such characters, Gager populates the play with no less than four: Meleager, blindly in love with Atalanta; Atalanta, rendered equally blind by the all-dominating idea of maintaining her chastity;

---

[1] Equally redolent of Sophocles is Gager's frequent use of proleptic irony: for example, Meleager's passion for Atalanta is frequently described in terms of fire imagery.
[2] *The Heroic Temper* (Berkeley - Los Angeles, 1964).

Oeneus, with his hubristic self-confidence and thunderous disdain of the god; and Althaea, engaged in a quest for settling a score that would do justice to an Electra. With the possible exception of Atalanta (who dooms herself to a life that, the reader may care to think, is correctly diagnosed as sterile by Philemon), each of these characters is ruined by his or her particular obsession, and by the kind of destructive tunnel vision and spiritual isolation it implies.

Of these characters, Oeneus is by far the most interesting. On the Sophoclean stage, there is a religious dimension to the hero's wrongheadedness which, at the risk of annoying classical scholars who debate precisely what this word and concept are all about, may provisionally be called hubris. Thus, for example, part of Oedipus' problem is his idea that he can control his destiny, and part of Creon's is that he is so dead sure that what he wants and what the gods want are one and the same thing. Oeneus' confidence in the prosperity of himself and his kingdom and his contempt for the gods, which eventuates in his final demented attempt to assault them physically (thus replicating the efforts of the heaven-storming Giants of classical mythology), are as starkly hubristic as anything one could hope to find in the classical repertoire. The play's mounting catastrophes achieve a climax in Oeneus' madness and death, which involves (as a good tragic ending should) a reassertion of divine power and of a morally orderly universe.

To further emphasize the nature of his heroes and heroines, Sophocles had a trick of playing them off against characters who are more realistic and accommodating, but also made of weaker spiritual stuff. Thus Electra is matched against Chrysothemis, and Antigone against Ismene. The figures of the advisor and the nurse may be stock characters of the Senecan repertoire, but Gager uses Philemon, the Old Man, and the Nurse for a very similar purpose.

Senecan tragedy is not classical tragedy. Standing at several centuries' remove from the great days of the Athenian theater, his plays are better regarded as a kind of Roman exercise in neoclassicism. He had a completely different theology, based on an admixture of his peculiar brand of Stoicism[1] and blind fatalism, and completely different fish to fry, such as the investigation of tyranny. In *Meleager*, Gager makes a strenuous and remarkably successful effort to get behind Seneca and replicate the spirit and contents of Attic tragedy.

I shall close by quoting, without evaluation, a paragraph from Tucker Brooke's biographical article:[2]

> Another plays on this occasion [of *Meleager*'s first performance] was probably the *Caesar Interfectus* of Gager's friend [Richard] Edes, of which only the epilogue remains on a fragment of paper in the Bodleian dated 1582. This epilogue, unlike those that Gager wrote for his plays, is in prose, and so the entire piece may have been, for though Edes could write tolerable hexameters, there is no evidence that he attempted the tragic metres. However this be, if there is anything in the strangely persuasive arguments of Professor Smart that Shakespeare must have seen Edes'

---

[1] If one can think that his tragedies are Stoic at all. To be sure, they reproduce one major theme of contemporary Stoicism, the glamorization of suicide. But in his plays Fortune and the Fates almost completely supplant Providence as governors of the universe, and a world view that excludes Providence can scarcely be said to be genuinely Stoic.

[2] "Life and Times," 415.

Caesar,[1] it would be difficult not to believe that he was remembering *Meleager* as well as Ovid when he wrote the lines in *2 Henry VI* 233 - 6,

> *Methinks the realms of England, France, and Ireland*
> *Bear that proportion to my flesh and blood*
> *As did the fatal brand Althaea burnt*
> *Unto the prince's heart of Calydon.*

For they describe the great climax of Gager's play.

※ ※ ※

The text of *Meleager* is preserved by the edition of Joseph Barnes, printer to the University, issued in 1593.[2] This is a 16º in eights consisting of 96 pages (sigs. A - F 8), with poetry set in handsome pica Italic and prose in pica Roman. The printed text contains some typographical errors, or perhaps in some cases printer's misreadings of the manuscript. Two extant copies contain a few hand corrections, and some necessary corrections are noted in an appendix to Tucker Brooke's unpublished manuscript.

---

[1] John Semple Smart, *Shakespeare Truth and Tradition* (London, 1928) 179 - 82. [Brooke's note].
[2] Together with prefatory material, the play occupies sigs. A 2ʳ - E 7ᵛ. Five copies survive, owned by the British Library, the Dyce Collection of the National Library of the Victoria and Albert Museum, the Bodleian Library, the Library of Corpus Christi College, Oxford, and the Yale University Library. A photographic reprint has been issued in *William Gager, Meleager, Ulysses Redux, Panniculus Hippolyto Senecae Tragoediae Assutus Prepared with an Introduction by J. W. Binns* (vol. I.2 in the Renaissance Latin Drama in England series, Hildesheim, 1982), pages unnumbered. In the General Introduction to Volume II, I shall say something about the circumstances under which the printed text was issued.
  It is possibly worth stressing again that this edition was issued sometime after January 1, 1593 (modern style), since Falconer Madan, *Oxford Books, A Bibliography of Printed Works Relating to the University and City of Oxford or Printed or Published There* (Oxford, 1895) I.33, registers it under the year 1592. To be sure, the date of the dedicatory letter, 1592, is written in quotation marks, presumably to indicate that it is old style; nevertheless, the fact that this book is listed before *Ulysses Redux* creates a wrong impression of the order in which these volumes were issued.

Meleager
tragoedia nova

bis publice acta in
Aede Christi
Oxoniae

Meleager
a new tragedy

twice publicly acted at
Christ Church,
Oxford

ILLVSTRISSIMO AC NOBILISSIMO HEROI, ROBERTO ESSEXIAE COMITI, AVREAE PERISCELIDIS SODALI, EQVORVMQVE REGIORVM MAGISTRO, FOELIX FAVSTVMQUE NOVI ANNI AVSPICIVM PRECATVR

sig. A 2ʳ

annus iam pene undecimus agitur, nobilissime comes, ex quo Meleager primum, octavus ex quo iterum in scenam venit ac primum quidem volens, ac sponte sua. triennio post, invitatus, publiceque evocatus, secundum prodiit, assidentibus ac spectantibus clarissimis comitibus, Penbrochiensi ac Lecestrensi, cancellario tum nostro, una cum nobilissimo Philippo Sidnaeo, nonnullisque illustribus aulicis. qua tum approbatione acceptus sit, nec iam memini, nec magni unquam feci. satis ad laudem Meleagro fuit, si qua tamen ea laus sit, quod politissimarum aurium discrimen bis subierit, nullo sane insignis fastidii dehonestamento. ecce iam tertium exit, non quidem in scenam, sed in lucem; id est conspectum tuum. tanto iam maius periculum aditurus, quanto lucis, quam scaenae, solis, quam taedarum, oculorum, quam aurium, longe gravius est iudicium. atque [sig. A 2ᵛ] ille quidem diu spretus, ac pene pro exposititio habitus, vix nomen, nedum charitatem filii, apud me obtinebat. erga quem, nescio quo pacto, iniquiore semper animo fui, atque alieniore. sed cum primogenitus meus esset Meleager, multique saepe suaderent, enutriendum potius puerum, quam tineis blattisque escam relinquendum, atque ipsi etiam clam me, sed mendose ac perperam educarent, puerique indolem apud me laudare non desisterent, misertus sum, fateor, tandem prolis meae, caepique paulatim eius non pudere, quemadmodum adolescens genui. vereor ne vel a puero susceptus, vel puerili potius more panniculis efformatus,[1] quam verus faetus videatur. cum itaque hoc quicquid quod genueram, decrevissem tollere, ac pro meo palam habere, caepi mecum cogitare, cuius mihi inprimis gratiam e potentioribus conciliarem, quem sectaretur, cuiusque praesidio nixus Meleager, non solum innotesceret, sed etiam viveret. ex omnibus, sola mihi amplitudo tua satisfecit, clarissime Roberte, cum pro illa excellenti fama, quae de illustri tua familia, humanitate, magnificentia, ingenio, literis, magnitudine animi, scientia militari, omnique virtute heroica domi forisque excitata est. tum pro illa dulcissima consuetudine, quae mihi cum generosissimo fratre tuo Gualtero, Oxoniae agente, intercessit, qua ille me complecti dignatus est, ego illum quoad vixit colui, defunctumque memoria colam [sig. A 3ʳ] sempiterna. cuius immaturo, supraque Sidnaei fatum miserando interitu, et respublica fortissimo iuvene, et tu florentissimo ac suavissimo fratre, et ego nobilissimo amico ac praesidio orbatus sum. sed parcam oculis tuis, non solum dolori meo. quocirca, illustrissime domine, pusionem tibi hunc meum duodecim annos natum, et animi in te mei testem, et novi anni munusculum trado, consecroque, tuique eum iuris ac potestatis totum facio. quem, humillime[2] peto, ut in tanta hodie strenarum magnificentia, non solum aspicere velis, sed etiam in tuorum numerum recipere digneris. qui, ut nulla alia re, certe fide, atque observantia commendatus ad te veniet. tuo enim famulatu Meleagrum victurum, moriturumque promitto, ac spondeo. vale, ex Aede Christi Oxoniae, Calendis Ianuarii, MDXCII.

honoris tui studiosissimus,
GVILIEMVS GAGERVS

---

[1] *deformatus* potius legendum?   [2] *humilime* liber

THE PROSPECT FOR A HAPPY AND PROSPEROUS NEW YEAR IS WISHED FOR THE MOST ILLUSTRIOUS ROBERT, EARL OF ESSEX, MEMBER OF THE ORDER OF THE GOLDEN GARTER, AND MASTER OF THE QUEEN'S HORSE

Now it is almost the eleventh year, most noble Earl, since Meleager came upon the stage, the eighth since he came again; at first he came freely of his own volition, and three years later, invited and summoned by the public, he came forward a second time. Present in the audience were the very distinguished Earls of Pembroke and Leicester (who was our Chancellor at the time), together with the most noble Philip Sidney and a number of illustrious gentlemen of the Court. I do not recall the approbation with which he was received, nor was I greatly concerned. It was sufficient praise for Meleager (if there is to be any praise) that he twice submitted to the judgment of our most discriminating hearers without incurring any mark of disgrace. And behold, he now makes his entry for a third time, not onto the stage, but into the light, that is, into your sight. He is going to undergo a greater risk, to the extent that the judgement of the day, of sunlight, and of the eye, is severer than that of the stage, of torchlight, and of the ear. He was long spurned by me, all but sentenced to exposure: I scarcely acknowledged him, let alone gave him the affection due a son. For some reason I do not understand, I always maintained a somewhat cold and unfriendly attitude toward him. But since Meleager was my firstborn, and many people urged that this child ought to be nurtured and not be abandoned as food for the bookworms and the moths, and they themselves, unbeknownst to me, falsely and wrongly brought him up, and did not cease praising his character to me, I confess that at length I took pity on my child, and little by little I ceased to be ashamed for him, since I had sired him in my youth. I fear lest he appear to be adopted in boyhood or to be disfigured by wearing rags, as urchins are wont to do, rather than to be my true offspring. Therefore, when I had decided to pick up this thing I had engendered, and acknowledge it as my own, I began to ponder to whom among the grandees I should ingratiate myself, on whom I should attend, on whose protection Meleager might rely, not only to become known, but also to thrive. Among them all, only your greatness satisfied me, dearest Robert, in view of your most excellent reputation, your illustrious pedigree, humanity, magnificence, wit, learning, magnanimity, military science, and every form of heroic virtue both private and public; and then in consideration of that most pleasant association in which your brother Walter was kind enough to include me while he was at Oxford; I cherished him as long as he lived, and now that he is dead I shall cherish his memory always. By his untimely passing, even more lamentable than that of Sidney, the nation has been deprived of a most valiant young man, you of a most flourishing and pleasant brother, and I of a very noble friend and patron. But I shall spare your eyes, let alone my own sorrow. Wherefore, most noble Lord, I give you my little boy, twelve years of age, a proof of my devotion to you and a small New Year's gift, and dedicate him to you. I give you power and authority over him. I very humbly request that among all today's magnificence of New Year's presents, you not only condescend to notice him, but also to admit him into your company. He will come to you recommended, if by nothing else, by his loyalty and dutifulness towards you. For I convey and bequeath Meleager to live and die in your service. Farewell. Written at Christ Church, Oxford, January 1, 1593.

Most devoted to your honor, WILLIAM GAGER

RICHARDVS EDES THEOLOGVS DOMINVS AEDISQUE CHRISTI PREBENDARIVS IN MELEAGRVM GVILIEMI GAGERI

sig. A 3ᵛ

    qui Meleager erat multorum cura dierum,
        in multos annos non sine laude tibi.
    fallor, an et Musae fortunam fecit eandem,
        quam misere fertur sustinuisse, tuae?
    scilicet unius pene expiravit ad horae
        lumen, ad ardentem sicut et ille facem.   5
    nunc Musae, et pariter Meleagro consulis, illis
        dum lux extinctis non peritura redit.

DEL S. ALBERICO GENTILE.

    te, che materno sdegno, infesto nume,
    nobil campione, ancise, e quelle mani,
    che te rapiro a fiamme horrende, immani:
    onde qui aggiungi a rivedere il lume?
    Accio e quivi? od' è ver, ch' il tristo fiume   5
    varcasti anchora, e là tanto rimani
    infra d' ombre volanti, e corpi vani,
    ch' il mio Guigliemo te ravvivi, e allumi.
    nascesti per morire a un punto, e poi
    moristi di crudele, e empia morte: 10
    e rinasci, e dinuovo mori. ahi fato.
    ma godi. si questi hor eo versi suoi
    t' assicura un vigor vivaci, e forte,
    che non hai da temere il mondo irato.

I. C. SALVTEM DICIT AMICISSIMO SVO GVILIEMO GAGERO

sig. A 4ʳ

    non tibi necquiquam, Gagere, tragoedia cordi est
        cui cor Fortunae tot pupigere mala.
    res sit digna viro licet ipsa tragoedia docto,
        illa tamen cura te propriore tenet.
    scilicet ut verum planxit Polus histrio natum,   5
        Electram Sophoclis cum simulatam ageret,
    sic tua deploras alieno fata cothurno,
        veraque mentito nomine damna gemis.
    sic proprium absumis sub ficto imitamine luctum,
        dumque videtur agi fabula, res agitur.   10

DOMINUS RICHARD EDES, THEOLOGUS AND CANON OF CHRIST CHURCH, ON WILLIAM GAGER'S *MELEAGER*

For many days Meleager was your care, and will bring you praise for many years. Am I wrong, or has he created the same fortune for your Muse which he is said to have miserably undergone? For the play expired in about the space of a single hour, just as he expired along with the burning brand. Now you are taking thought for your Muse, and also for Meleager. For although the both of them are extinguished, their light returns, which will not perish.

BY SIGNOR ALBERICO GENTILI

You, noble champion, whom a mother's spite and hostile fate destroyed, and those cruel hands that dragged you to dreadful flames: whence do you come hither to view the light again?

Is Accius there? Or is it true that you have not crossed over the river of mourning, and remain there among the flitting shadows and unsubstantial bodies, 'til my William reanimates and enlightens you?

You were born to die at a fated time, and then you died by a cruel and unhallowed death; and you are born again and die anew: alas, the fate! But be glad that this poet now with his verses assures you a living and powerful vigor, so that you have not to fear the angry world.

I. C. GREETS HIS DEAR FRIEND WILLIAM GAGER

Not without reason, Gager, is tragedy dear to your heart, whose heart has been most grieved by Fortune's ills. Albeit tragedy herself is suitable for a learned man, she grips you with a more particular concern. For just as Polus the actor mourned his own son while playing the role of Sophocles' Electra, so do you bewail your fate while wearing another man's buskin, lamenting real injuries under an artificial name. Thus you make a personal plaint under a fictitious guise, and while a play seems to be performed reality is being

iam quoque quod promis, carmen fatale putarim,
   mire argumento conveniente tibi.
nomine quam prope te Meleager, et omine tangit!
   quam prope nomen habes, tam prope et omen habes.
prava suorum illi, nocuit tibi prava tuorum   15
   invidia, et spreti sanguinis improbitas.
tu magis, immerito, et iuvenes periistis uterque;
   utrique exitium faemina dira tulit.
expulit illi animam mater, tibi quam prope mater,
   vivendi causas abstulit, atque animam!   20
occultis perit ille odiis, tu clam periisti.
   ille veneficiis, carminibusque iacet,
tuque veneficio muliebri, fraude, doloque,
   artibus, insidiis, malitiaque iaces.
vita etenim non est sine rebus vivere vitae,   25
   illa vita perit, cui perimuntur opes.
salva tamen res est, forsan vivetis uterque,
   carmine non magico, carmine sed tragico.

AD LECTOREM ACADEMICVM

sig. A 4ᵛ

quem nocturna olim spectasti ad lumina, lector,
   quique bis applausum, te tribuente, tulit,
luce tibi clara Meleagrum sisto legendum,
   et nudum media conspicuumque die.
quam differre procul spectatis lecta putabis?   5
   et fucum fecit larva lucerna mihi,
vixque idem est, dices, Meleager, qui fuit ante,
   et te damnabis, iudiciumque vetus.
et tamen est idem: forsan mutatus ab annis.
   spectasti infantem, iam puer esse potest.   10

"I.C." 13. *tangit?* liber: sic interpunxit Boas, p. 178   19 sq. *mater?...animam.* interpunxit lib., *mater* (sine interpuncto)...*animam?* Boas, sed *animam!* malo

enacted. Now I should imagine that this lethal song you sing agrees wonderfully with your own story. How nearly Meleager touches you, in name and in significance! You almost have his name, and nearly share his fate. He was injured by the criminal invidiousness of his family, and you by yours, and by the wickedness of family ties scorned. For your youths were both ruined unjustly, and a horrible woman visited destruction on the both of you. His mother took away his life — how a woman who was almost your mother took away your reason for living! He died because of hidden hatreds, you were secretly ruined. He was laid low by poisons and incantations, you by a poisonous woman, her fraud and deceit, her arts, wiles, and malice. For life does not exist without the means of living, and she took your life when your fortune was destroyed. But the situation is not lost, and perhaps the both of you will live, not by a magical incantation, but by the song of tragedy.

TO THE ACADEMIC READER

Meleager, whom you once witnessed by nocturnal illumination, and who twice received applause as you granted it, I now provide to be read by you in the bright light, here to be seen in the middle of the day. How much will you think that you read differs from what you saw? You will say that my larva has produced a drone, that Meleager is scarcely what he used to be, you will condemn yourself and your previous opinion. But he is the same, though possibly the years have changed him. You saw him as an infant, now he can be regarded as a boy.

antiquissima est haec fabula, et ad ea tempora refertur, quae expeditionem Argonauticam (in qua noster etiam Meleager socius enumeratur) proxime sequebantur. bellum vero Troianum, toto pene seculo, praecedebat.[1] nam et illa ab iisdem fere ipsis heroibus, qui sunt hic venatores, suscepta, et hoc ab eorum filiis gestum est. istius autem negotii venatorii facile princeps extitit Meleager. quem antiquus poeta, quisquis ille fuit, τὸν Ἑλλάδος κλεινὸν γόνον[2] non dubitavit appellare, quemque Homerus ἀρηίφιλον vocat. Antipho vero tantopere extollit, ut reliquam procerum cohortem convenisse dicat,[3]

οὐχ ἵνα κτάνωσι θῆρ, ὅπως δὲ μάρτυρες
ἀρετῆς γένωνται Μελεάγρῳ πρὸς Ἑλλάδα.

atqui duo potissimum sunt in hac tragoedia, quae fabuloso integumento obvoluta, veram historiae lucem desiderant: aper et stipes [sig. A5ʳ] fatalis. atque aprum quidem Calydonium, insignem fuisse latronem narrant, ferae cuiusdam mulieris Corinthiae filium, quam poetae suem Chromyoniam appellant, a Theseo occisam, ex qua aprum Calydonium procreatum esse refert Strabo.[4] quod si cuiquam mirum videatur, tot principes Graeciae ad latronem opprimendum confluxisse, is si Viriatum Lusitanum, Spartacum gladiatorem, Othomanum primum, Tamburlanem Scytham, aliosque famosos praedatores cogitaverit, mirari statim desinet. stipitem vero fatalem, aut veneficium aut magicas artes fuisse credibile est, quibus Althaea Meleagro interitum machinata est. quod et Homerus[5] videtur innuere. a quo longe aliter, quam ab Ovidio,[6] ab isto, quam ab aliis, tota haec fabula tradita est, pro suo cuiusque arbitratu. neque enim dubito, quin aliter ab Antiphonte, aliter ab Euripide[7] etiam, ac fortasse ab Accio,[8] distributa, ac pertractata sit. quo magis et mihi fas esse existimabam, Atalantam, quaecunque ea fuerit, a coniugio abhorrentem, Oeneum superbum ac deum contemptorem, vitamque sibi praecipitio finientem introducere, ut tragoediae argumentum, maiore cum varietate, tum atrocitate pertexeretur. nam et sorores Meleagri in aves Meleagridas conversae idcirco excludebantur, ne omnis haec fabula in catastrophen potius prodigiosam, quam in exitum, effectumque vere tragicum quasi in piscem certe

turpiter atram
desinat in volucrem, mulier formosa superne.

---

[1] *praecedebant* lib. [2] *Arist. Rhe. l. 2, c. 23.* script. marg. [3] *ibidem.* script. marg. [4] *Geogra. l. 8.* script. marg. [5] *Ilias.* script. marg. [6] *Meta. 8* script. marg. [7] *Aristoph. in Ranis Act. 3, sc. 2.* script. marg. [8] *Nonius Marcellus.* script. marg.

This story is very ancient and pertains to that epoch which immediately follows upon the expedition of the Argonauts (in which our Meleager was included); indeed, it antedated the Trojan War by almost a full generation. For the expedition was undertaken by just about the same heroes who are the hunters here, and the War by their sons. However, in this business of the hunt, Meleager easily stood out as the leader, he whom an ancient poet (whoever he was) did not hesitate to call "the famous son of Greece," and Homer called him "beloved of Ares." Antiphon, indeed, praised him to the extent that he said that the remaining band of princes had gathered "not so that they might kill the beast, but so that they could attest to Meleager's virtue in the eyes of Greece."

Now, there are two elements in this tragedy which, wrapped in the guise of myth, lack the true illumination of history: the boar and the fatal brand. For some say that the Calydonian boar was a notable robber, the son of some feral Corinthian woman named by the poets the Chrommyonian Sow, killed by Theseus, from whom the "Calydonian Boar" was born according to Strabo. And if somebody should think it strange that so many Greek princes came together to suppress a robber, if he were to reflect on Viriatus of Lusitania, the gladiator Spartacus, the first Ottoman, Tamburlane the Scythian, and other notorious bandits, he would immediately cease to be amazed. It is plausible that the fatal brand was a poison, or magical arts by which Althaea encompassed Meleager's death, with which Homer appears to agree. For by him the whole story is told very differently than by Ovid, and by Ovid very differently than by others, according to each writer's judgment. Nor do I doubt that it was told still otherwise by Antiphon, and that it was yet differently arranged and handled by Euripides, and perhaps by Accius. Wherefore I determined all the more to introduce Atalanta (whatever she may have been) averse to marriage, and Oeneus arrogant and scornful of the gods and rashly ending his life, so that the tragedy's plot might be embroidered with greater variety and horror. And for the same reason I excluded the transformation of Meleager's sisters into birds, the Meleagrides, lest this play end with a miraculous turn of events rather than a conclusion having a genuinely tragic feeling, like a fish which "trails off into a loathsome bird, being a beautiful woman above."

PERSONAE

sig. A 5ᵛ

PROLOGVS 2	ARVSPEX
MEGAERA	THESEVS
PHILEMON	PLEXIPPVS
MELEAGER	TOXEVS
ATALANTA	NVNCIVS
CHORVS CIVIVM	VENATORES
OENEVS	NVTRIX
SENEX	MATRES CALYDONIDES
ALTHAEA	EPILOGVS 2

DRAMATIS PERSONAE

TWO PROLOGUES SOOTHSAYER
MEGAERA   THESEUS
PHILEMON   PLEXIPPUS
MELEAGER   TOXEUS
ATALANTA   MESSENGER
CHORUS OF CITIZENS HUNTERS
OENEUS   NURSE
OLD MAN   CALYDONIAN MATRONS
ALTHAEA   TWO EPILOGUES

PROLOGVS AD ACADEMICOS

sig. A 6ʳ

cygno poeta similis est, academici:
candidus uterque, uterque cantando valet,
uterque fluviis gaudet et amoenis locis,
uterque Phaebo gratus. at cygnum ferunt
afflante Zephyro canere. quin ergo canat 5
noster poeta (nominis detur sacri
usura nobis, quaeso) cum vestrae undique
attentionis tantus aspiret favor,
et aura facilis, lenior Zephyro levi?
lugubre carmen ille moriturus canit, 10
lugubre carmen noster et vates, quasi
ipse moriturus. nempe morituri canit,
funebre, tragicum, forsan etiam ipsi ultimum.
veniam poetae quaeso nascenti date.
hic tranat auras primum et immensum aethera, 15
pennisque fidit, nigrior quibus vix color
discessit. alas nidulo hic primum exerit,
vocemque tollit, proximi quae nec freti,
nec cuncta proprii fluminis penetret loca.
vicina satis est ripa si referat sonum. 20
nunc cantionis accipite summam novae.

ARGVMEMTVM TRAGOEDIAE

en alta Calydon, gentis Aetolae caput,
en aula regum. clarus hic rerum senex
potitur Oeneus. ille primitiis novi
dum laetus anni sacra caelicolis facit, 25

sig. A 6ᵛ

solam Dianae thuris expertem ferunt
aram stetisse. seu fuerit illud scelus,
sive error, iram movit horrendam deae.
  namque ecce, spreti vindicem cultus, aprum
immittit agris. ille dat clades ferox, 30
nec tota vasto sufficit Calydon malo.
stomachatur Oeneus, nec deam curat prece
placare demens. Graeciae implorat duces.
adsunt, et una Schaenei proles adest
Atalanta regis Arcadum. hanc iuvenis statim 35
Meleager ardet, filius is est Oenei.
  subinde venatum itur. at pacti prius,
ut victor hirti ferret exuvias apri.
venatur. ecce prima dat calamo eminus
Atalanta plagam. comminus mactat feram 40

PROLOGUE FOR ACADEMICS

A poet is like a swan, good schoolmen: both are pale, both are good at singing, both rejoice in streams and pleasant places, both are dear to Phoebus. But they say that the swan sings when the West wind blows. Why shouldn't our poet (and I beg that you lend me the use of this word) sing when the favor of your attention wafts on him from all sides, a gentle breath of favor, gentler than the mild Zephyr? About to die, the swan sings a doleful song, and our poet, as if moribund himself, sings a dying swan-song: funereal, tragic, as if it were his last. Pray pardon a novice poet. For the first time he glides through the air, the vast sky, trusting in his wings, from which the black color has scarcely departed. For the first time he has taken wing from his little nest and raised his voice, of a kind that does not reach the nearby sea or all the parts of his own river. It is enough if the neighboring bank echoes his noise. Now hear the gist of his novel song.

THE TRAGEDY'S ARGUMENT

See lofty Calydon, capital of the Aetolian race, and the royal palace. Here distinguished king Oeneus holds sway. While he was joyously sacrificing the year's firstfruits to the heavenly gods, they say that only Diana's altar stood bereft of incense. Whether this was a crime or a mistake, it aroused the goddess' terrible wrath. And now, behold, she sends a boar against the fields, an avenger of her scorned cult. Fiercely he metes out slaughter, nor does all Calydon suffice for his great bane. Oeneus is peevish, and in his folly he does not trouble himself to propitiate the goddess by prayers. He begs Greece's champions. They appear, together with Atalanta, daughter of Schoeneus, king of the Arcadians. Young Meleager (he is Oeneus' son) immediately burns for her. Next they go off on the hunt, having first agreed that the victor willcarry off the spoils of the bristling boar. The hunt takes place. Behold, Atalanta is the first to strike it from afar with her dart, and

sig. A 7ʳ

    Meleager. ille gloriam victor suam
cedit Atalantae. avunculi facto invident
Plexippus et Toxeus. statim rixa invicim
exoritur ingens. virgini spolia auferunt.
  accensus ira, uterque Meleager latus   45
mucrone figit. rescit admissum nefas
Althaea mater. aestuat, queritur, furit,
ultura fratres, filio lethum parat.
instruitur ara, stipes iniicitur rogo
fatalis, illo vita Meleagri latet.   50
Meleager, illo stipite absumpto, occubat.
  regina crimen fassa sibi pectus fodit,
dirus superbum corripit regem furor,
et arce ab alta praecipite lapsu cadit.
squalore Calydon tota miserando iacet,   55
planguntque matres, fastus hunc habet exitum.

PROLOGVS AD ILLVSTRISSIMOS PENBROCHIAE AC LECESTRIAE COMITES

  solent poetae carmen orsuri prius
sacrum invocare numen, aut Phaebum patrem,
doctam aut Minervam, deve Musarum choro
aliquam sororem, cuius ausipiciis opus   60
rite inchoatum, quem petunt, ferat exitum.
  praeclare vir, Penbrochiae lumen tuae,
et tu comes, Lecestriae sydus tuae,
idemque nostrae columen, ac splendor scholae,
vos numen unum noster implorat chorus.   65
vos Musa, vos Minerva, vos Phaebus pater.
tua trepidantem dirigat gressum manus,
tuus malevolos arceat baculus procul.
tuus poetam protegat nostrum draco,
tua cynosura fabulae cursum regat,   70
coniuncta caelo signa, sed terra magis.
Sidnaeus etiam benevolum aspectum velit
praestare, nostri lucidum sydus poli.
  at vos, quod annos ante tres factum est semel,
iterum benignas quaeso nunc aures date.   75

45. *utrique* lib.

Meleager draws near and kills the beast. He, the victor, yields his glory to Atalanta. His uncles Plexippus and Toxeus begrudge this gesture. Immediately a quarrel arises, they snatch the spoils from the maiden, and Meleager, incensed with anger, stabs both in the side with his dagger. His mother Althaea discovers this crime when he admits to it. She burns, complains, rages, and prepares death for her son to avenge her brothers. An altar is built, a log is laid on the pyre, in which the life of Meleager himself lies concealed. When the log is consumed, Meleager dies. Having confessed her crime, the queen stabs herself in the breast. A dire madness overcomes the haughty king, and he throws himself headlong from the high citadel. All Calydon is laid low in miserable squalor and mothers' lamentations, and pride has this outcome.

PROLOGUE FOR THE ILLUSTRIOUS EARLS OF PEMBROKE AND LEICESTER

Poets beginning their works are accustomed beforehand to invoke some divinity, either father Phoebus, learned Minerva, or some sister from the Muses' choir, by whose auspices the work, properly begun, may have the desired outcome. Distinguished sir, light of your Pembroke, and you, his companion, star of your Leicester, at once the mainstay and the glory of our University, our chorus implores only your divinity. Your are our Muse, our Minerva, our father Phoebus. Let your hand direct my hesitant step, and your staff make ill-wishers keep their distance. Let your dragon protect our poet, and your cygnet direct the course of our play, two signs conjoined in heaven but even more so on earth. And let Sidney, that shining star of our firmament, choose to present a friendly countenance.

But you gentlemen, since this has been acted once three years ago, I ask that now you give it a second kindly hearing.

sig. A 7ᵛ

Actus Primus

MEGAERA

    vastam relinquens noctis aeternae plagam,
    silentis Erebi, et manium tristes domos,
    Megaera superas extuli ad sedes gradum.
    en fervet odio pectus, exundat furor,
    maiorque rabies crescit aspectu loci.   80
    hic tumidus Oeneus opibus, ac sceptro potens,
    gentem superba fraenat Aetolam manu.
    Althaea thalami socia, Meleager patris
    indigna proles, sed tamen proles patris.
    in hos opaci claustra laxavi Iovis,   85
    iustis Dianae precibus, atque irae favens.
    casura iam iam est vulnere alterno domus,
    malos avunculos dabit letho nepos,
    soror nepotem, filium mater suum,
    melior parente, sed tamen nequam soror.   90
    iam scelera prope sunt, iam minae, caedes, furor.
    paratur ignis. funeris causae tui,
    Meleager, instant, stipes effertur, novo
    urendus interim matris iratae rogo.
    video cremantem, teque torrentem simul.   95
    venit dies tempusque, quo ferro latus,
    Althaea, solves, quo graves, Oeneu, dabis
    paenas Dianae, et pessimo letho cades
    ab arce praeceps. percitos furiis agam,
    miscebo cuncta. cur adhuc tanto vacat   100
    Althaea scelere? quam diu est domus innocens?

sig. A 8ʳ

    cur tota non dum planctibus Calydon sonat?
    iam personabit. ibo, et evertam omnia.

PHILEMON, MELEAGER

\<PHIL.\> magnanime Meleager, genus clarum Iovis,
    et post paternum proximum nobis decus,   105
    quid est quod istos pene iam septem dies,
    cum tota Calydon laeta feriatur novis
    hospitibus, aula nobili exultat grege,
    et nisi choreis, luxui, ac dapibus vacat,
    in publico tu gaudio tacitus gemas,   110
    palam serenes, clam gravem frontem geras,
    vix dignitatis aut tuae, aut patriae memor.
    sed maestus et confusus et pessundatus,

- Act I -

MEGAERA

Leaving the vast expanse of everlasting night, the home of Erebus and the sad shades, I, Megaera, have come to the upper regions. Lo, my heart seethes with hatred, madness floods it, and my insanity grows greater at the sight of this place. Here dwells Oeneus who, swollen with prosperity and mighty with his scepter, governs the Aetolian race with his arrogant hand. His consort is Althaea, and Meleager the unworthy offspring of his father, but nevertheless his offspring. Against these people I have loosened the restraints of Jupiter of the Dark, favoring Diana's legitimate requests, her wrath. This house is presently to fall by mutual woundings: a nephew will kill his wicked uncles, a sister will kill a nephew, a mother her son, a better sister than mother, but still an evil sister. Now these crimes are at hand, now at hand are menaces, murder, madness. The fire is being made ready. The causes of your death impend, Meleager. The log is being brought forth, to be burned again on your enraged mother's pyre. I see it burning, and you ablaze also. The day and hour have come, on which, Althaea, you will open your side with steel, on which, Oeneus, you will pay your penalty to Diana, plunging headlong off the citadel in foulest death. I shall drive you, goaded by Furies. I shall throw everything into confusion. Why is Althaea still free of crime? How long is this household to remain innocent? Why does all Calydon not yet ring with lamentations? Now it will resound. I shall go, overturning everything. [*Exit. Enter Philemon and Meleager.*]

PHILEMON, MELEAGER

PHIL. Noble-minded Meleager, born of Jove's distinguished stock, our greatest glory after your father, why is it that for about this past week, while all happy Calydon has been holding holiday with its new victims, the court has been rejoicing in its noble assembly, having no time for anything but dancing, merrymaking, and feasting, you are gloomy amidst the public joy? Why do you openly appear serene, but frown in private, scarcely

	tecum seorsim cogites, tecum ambules,	
	oculisque somnum, corpori pastum neges?	115
	licet ipse nolis, sponte se prodit dolor.	
	quin me laboris, quicquid est, socium facis?	
	effare, quae te causa sollicitum tenet?	

MEL. ut sum, Philemon, oro te, sine sim miser.

PHIL. miser? quid hoc est? unde tam tristis tibi 120
vox ista venit? sospes est certe parens
uterque, tota sorte faelici domus
beata floret. nulla te miserum facit
fortuna. merito est, sponte quicunque est miser.

MEL. ut vera fatear, multa quae memoras bona, 125
mihi tamen animum maior excruciat metus
furente ab apro, qui magis solito furit,
solitoque propius saeva praedatur lues.
ancepsque metuo, quo dabit sese malum.

PHIL. haec causa gemitus? pelle degeneres metus, 130
animosque veteres advoca, et totum tibi
redde Meleagrum. frontis hanc nubem excute,
solitamque vultus recipe laetitiam tui,
bene te decentem. patriae vulnus novum
resarcietur. pestifer nostris aper 135
pelletur agris, et tibi forsan dabit
novos honores. ecce, te spero manet
spolium superbum capitis, ac tergi decus.

MEL. utinam, Philemon. interim victor novos
ducit triumphos, et spolia nostri abstulit. 140

PHIL. Meleager, unde tantus incessit pavor
animo virili? quo tibi casu excidit
virtus, et ardens pectoris robur tui?
aliam subesse tam gravi causam reor
dolore dignam, tantulae certe pudet. 145
sed ut sit illa quam refers (miror tamen),
quam lecta iuvenum turma convenit, vides.
adsunt creati Tindaro fratres, equi
Castor peritus, caestibus Pollux valens,
fidoque Theseus comite stipatus suo. 150

sig. A 8ᵛ (at line 129)

127. *quo* lib.

mindful of the nation's dignity or your own, sad, confused, and downcast? Why do you brood alone, take walks by yourself, denying your eyes sleep and your body sustenance? Even against your will, your sadness betrays itself. Why not share your trouble with me, whatever it is? Tell me, what matter disturbs you?

MEL. I beg you, Philemon, let me remain unhappy, as I am.

PHIL. Unhappy? What's this? Whence this doleful statement? Surely both your parents are safe, your entire household flourishes. No misfortune is making you miserable. Whoever is unhappy of his own free will suffers deservedly.

MEL. To tell the truth, much of what you say is valid, but a greater anxiety is troubling me, because of the raging boar who rampages strangely, a savage plague which does his plundering unusually close to home. I am fearful in my perplexity about what this evil will portend.

PHIL. This is the cause of your groaning? Dismiss your ignoble fears, summon your old courage, give yourself back the entire Meleager. Dispel this cloud from your brow, assume that usual happy look which so becomes you. Our nation's new wound will be healed. This boar will be driven from your fields, and will perhaps give you new glory. Look, I hope there awaits you the proud trophy of his head, the glory of his hide.

MEL. Would that it were so, Philemon! Meanwhile, this victorious boar celebrates new triumphs, despoiling us.

PHIL. Meleager, whence has such great fears invaded your stalwart mind? By what mishap has your courage departed, the ardent strength of your heart? I suspect that some further cause for such great sorrow lies hidden, for surely this small one is shameful. But suppose this is the case (although I doubt it), you see what a chosen band of youths has gathered. Present are those brothers born of Tyndarus, Castor, skilled at horsemanship, and Pollux, valiant at boxing, and Theseus, accompanied by his loyal friend. Present too is

		adest Licaei nemoris Atalante decus,	
		omnisque Graii splendor ac robur soli.	
		si Thesea reliquosque cognovi duces,	
		praedator ille, tergore superbus licet,	
		supplicia iam iam digna tibi, Calydon, dabit.	155
	MEL.	erras, Philemon. quem putas esse unicum,	
		is geminus est. unum quidem arcitenens dea	
		immisit Oetae montis infesti iugo.	
sig. B 1ʳ		non levior illa, nec trucem minus, alterum	
		pharetratus etiam misit Arcadia deus.	160
		ille per agros et laeta grassatur sata,	
		hic propius urget. intus est, intus furit	
		indomitus, ardens. quodque mireris magis,	
		cui nulla procerum sufficiat unquam manus.	
	PHIL.	quis alter iste, quem mihi memoras, aper?	165
		perplexa remove verba. quodcunque est, tegam.	
	MEL.	ignosce quaeso. quisquis impatiens sui est,	
		magis est suorum.	
	PHIL.	quod novum merui nefas?	
		quae nota fraus, quae suspitio fraudis, meam	
		fidem allevavit? tale quod tecum scelus	170
		gessit Philemon, ut tuum quicquid premit	
		animum doloris, id animum velles meum	
		celare? tutum pectus hoc quondam fuit,	
		iocisque seriisque spectatum suis,	
		idem iam nunc, quod fuit semper, manet.	175
	MEL.	absiste tandem, nosse quid causam iuvat?	
		tibi sat superque est scire, quod peream miser,	
		nec sponte luctus, quos fero, tantos sequi.	
	PHIL.	silere pergis? precibus ac iussu patris	
		cogam fateri, quicquid hic fari abnuis.	180
		ipse ad penates regios gressus feram,	
		patremque ducam, cuius imperium extrahat	
		abstrusa mentis. tene ego ut tacitis sinam	
		perire curis?	
	MEL.	ipse iam prodam, mane.	
	PHIL.	dic tandem aperte.	

Lycaeus' daughter Atalanta, glory of the forest, and the splendor of all Greece, the strength of our land. If I know Theseus and the other champions, that ravager, though he be arrogant with his crest, will soon pay a fitting penalty to you, Calydon.

MEL. You are mistaken, Philemon. The boar whom you think to be single is double. Indeed, the bow-wielding goddess[1] sent one from the perilous ridge of Mt. Oetea. No kinder than she, the quiver-bearing god[2] sent another, no less savage, from Arcadia. That one rages through the fields and gladsome crops, he presses close. This one is inside, inside he rages unconquered, ardent. And, more marvellous, he is of a sort that no prince's hand will ever suffice to quell.

PHIL. Who is this other boar of whom you speak? Dispense with your riddles. Whatever it is, I shall keep the secret.

MEL. Forgive me, I beg you. Who is impatient with himself is even more so with others.

PHIL. What new insult have I deserved? What deceit has come to light, what suspicion of deceit, to diminish my trustworthiness? What sort of crime has Philemon committed in your presence, that some pain vexes your mind, and you want to conceal this thing from my notice? This heart of mine was once safe enough, well tested both in its play and its seriousness, and now it remains the same as it has always been.

MEL. At length, leave off — what's the help in knowing the reason? It is more than enough for you to know that I am perishing miserably. Don't wish to pursue the great sorrows I endure.

PHIL. You persist in silence? By my entreaties and your father's command I shall force you to admit what you refuse to say here. I myself shall go to the palace and bring your father, whose authority will drag out your mind's secrets. Shall I permit you to perish by silent cares?

MEL. Wait, I shall explain now.

PHIL. At last, speak out.

---
[1] Diana.
[2] Cupid.

| | MEL. | pectus insolitum vapor | 185 |

amorque torret, et velut saevus vorat
aper medullas. iste per venas ruens
visceribus imis instat, et totos ferox
sig. B 1ᵛ populatur artus, et fibras subtus rapit.
pudet fateri, ferre quod nequeo iugum, 190
iuvenumque primus est verecundus calor.
nunc, si quid unquam gratia nostra velis,
intende nervos, res tua digna est fide.
Atalanta, virgo est, illa me cruciat fera.

PHIL. hiccine aper ille? tantus huc rediit timor? 195
mirabar ubi se frangeret tantus dolor.
sed illa, fateor, Arcadica vere fera est,
feritate vix Oetea quam superet truci.
quis huius unquam pectus indomitum domet?
exosa prorsus nomen exhorret viri, 200
vitat himenaeos, caelibem vovit torum.
proin, negatum sperne, iuvenilem impetum
ratione fraena. quam cupis, frustra cupis.
quod vis ubi vetant fata, quod possis velis.

MEL. haec est dolorum causa, medicinam expete. 205
hinc iste pallor, tantus hinc torsit furor,
quod dura, quod animosa, quod sylvas colens,
amare nescit. et tamen talem meis
sociare thalamis quolibet statui modo.

PHIL. quis flectat illam?

MEL.   dura sit, victoria 210
praeclarior erit. eruere quercum libet,
namque aura cannam quaelibet moveat levem.
ut cera formam sumit, ac ponit statim,
vix patitur ullam marmor artificis notam,
sed vix remittit. stipula mox accenditur 215
restinguiturque. non facile ferrum uritur,
nec facile friget. illa sic quo durior,
hoc acriore forsan ardebit face.
sig. B 2ʳ non aequet illam velleris spolium aurei,
aprive caesi, nullus Herculeus labor. 220
una haec triumphi materia digna est mei.

---

191. *color* potius legendum? vid. Hor., *Epod.* xvii.21   210. *victoriae* lib.

MEL. An unwonted warmth and love burn my breast, and like a savage boar scorch my marrow. Rushing through my veins it harries my vitals, devastating all my limbs and ravishing my entrails below. I am ashamed to admit that I cannot endure this yoke, this is is a young man's first bashful blush. Now, if ever you wish to do something to gain my favor, exert your strength. The matter is worthy of your loyalty. Atalanta is the girl, she tortures me savagely.

PHIL. So this is the boar? Has your great fear come down to this? I was wondering where such pain would dash itself. But I must confess that this Arcadian girl is in truth savage, whom a woman of Mount Oete would scarcely surpass in uncouth wildness. Who should ever win her unconquered heart? Hating even the word "husband," she shudders, shuns marriage, vows a chaste bed. So spurn this marriage denied to you, and govern your youthful impulse by reason. When the Fates refuse what you want, you must desire that which you can achieve.

MEL. This is the cause of my sorrows, find me a medicine. Hence my pallor, hence this great frenzy has been torturing me, because this hard, spirited, forest-dwelling girl does not know how to love. But I have decided to join her to my marriage-chamber by any means at all.

PHIL. Who might sway her?

MEL. Let her be hard. Whoever wins her will be all the more distinguished for his victory. One wants to fell an oak, for any light breeze can move a frail reed. As wax assumes any shape but quickly loses it, while marble grudgingly accepts any sculptor's mark, as a straw swiftly catches fire and is extinguished, but iron is not readily melted nor easily cooled, so too since she is more resolute, perhaps for this reason she will burn with a hotter fire. Her conquest would not be equalled by the taking of the Golden Fleece, by the killing of our boar, or by any labor of Hercules. This one matter for victory is worthy of me.

PHIL.	tibi mutet animum, quae viros omnes pari prosequitur odio?
MEL.	precibus haud flecti potest?
PHIL.	fera est.
MEL.	amor, tempusque vicerunt feras.
PHIL.	genus omne profugit.
MEL.	careo rivalis metu. 225
PHIL.	nullamne tota virginem Calydon habet, quae placeat?
MEL.	animum non capit Calydon meum.
PHIL.	quid patria tellus?
MEL.	fortibus multo viris, quam procreandis faeminis apta est magis.
PHIL.	rudis est.
MEL.	at ista virginem ruditas decet, 230 qualis Dianae convenit. vestem extimam sic pulchra morsu fibula innectit levi, sic illa nodo simplices crines ligat, sic pendet humero phraretra, sic arcum manu gestat sinistra. quamque virgineam putes 235 habere faciem, quamque puerilem putes! proinde monitis abstine. hac citius queam caeli carere luce. vel coniux erit, vel mors repulsam nostra cumulabit gravem.
PHIL.	si tam obstinatus pectori furor incubat, 240 tentemus animam virginis saevae trucem. atque ecce, credo sola venatu redit. progreditur, ipsa est. initium casus dedit, facilem deinceps exitum praestet Venus.

ATALANTA, MELEAGER, PHILEMON

<AT.>	Meleager, ecce te mihi ex voto locus 245 tempusque praebent.

PHIL. Will she, who loathes all men alike, change her mind for your sake?

MEL. Can't she be swayed by entreaties?

PHIL. She is wild.

MEL. Affection and time have tamed wild beasts.

PHIL. She shuns the whole race of men.

MEL. Because of the fear she inspires, I lack rivals.

PHIL. Has all Calydon no girl who might please you?

MEL. Calydon is not to my taste.

PHIL. What about your native land?

MEL. She is far more fit for bearing brave men than girls.

PHIL. She's uncouth.

MEL. But this uncouthness befits the girl, as it does Diana. Thus a handsome brooch-pin clasps her outer garment, thus she binds her simple locks in a knot, thus a quiver hangs from her shoulder, thus she wields a bow in her left hand. What a girlish face you'd think she has, how child-like you'd think her! So cease giving me advice. I could sooner do without this light of day. Either she'll be my wife, or my death will put the capstone on my sad rebuff.

PHIL. If such obdurate madness falls forcibly on your heart, let us put the savage girl's harsh soul to the test. And see, I believe she's returning alone from the hunt. Here she comes, it's she. Chance has given us a beginning, and let Venus then provide a happy end. [*Enter Atalanta.*]

AT. Meleager, see how this time and place offer my desired opportunity.

sig. B 2ᵛ

MEL.   et quidem multo advenis,
Atalanta, nobis gratior. sed quid rei?
quae causa voti est?

AT.   ut tibi accusem moras
tam segnis aulae. dapibus ac ludis datum
satis superque est. ipsa quam nimio fui   250
accepta cultu! restat idcirco, mea
aliquam rependi gratiam dextra. pudet
pigetque luxus, interim Aetolos aper
dum vastat agros, in sata ac pecudes furens.

MEL. magnanima virgo, regia stirpe edita   255
Atalanta, meritis gratiam nostris parem,
et superiorem, merita retulerunt tua,
quod prima nobis ipsa contuleris opem,
tantaeque nostra sint tibi curae mala.
sed eam remitte, lux sequens tollet moras.   260
at tu quid isto sola, tam pleno metus,
pleno ferarum nemore? terribiles lupos
habet et leones sylva, et immanes apros
ursosque, vel si gravius his aliquid furit.

AT. assueta sylvis, incolas sylvae minus   265
formido, maior ipsa quibus fio metus.
et abstulisse iam mihi videor diu.
proinde prima luce, pertaesa otii,
pertaesa somni, placuit in vestris feris
arcum experiri, et studia venandi nimis   270
remissa colere, nec labor vanus fuit.
fulvum sub alto montis errantem iugo
stravi leonem, nec mihi Aetolus tamen
tantus videtur, quantus Arcadicus leo.

MEL. hui! leonis virgo mactatrix feri?   275
si te libido tanta venandi capit,

sig. B 3ʳ   insequere lepores potius, aut damas leves
agilesve cervos, aut gravem certe lupum,
cum maius aliquod facinus audere expetit
generosus ardor. improbas prudens fuge   280
natura quas armavit in caedem feras.
non tangit illas ista quae nimium potens
homines deosque forma commoveat tua.

251. *cultu?* lib.

MEL. And your arrival, Atalanta, is much more welcome to me. But what's the matter. What's the reason for your desire?

AT. So that I can accuse you about the slothful delay of the Court. More than enough time has been spent on feasting and sport. With what excessive luxury was I myself entertained! Therefore it remains for me to express my gratitude with my good right hand. I feel shame and regret at this wantonness, while the boar is devastating the fields of Aetolia, raging against the crops and cattle.

MEL. Noble-minded girl, royal-born Atalanta, your good deeds have more than repaid ours, because you were the first to bring us aid and because our ills are of so great concern to you. Dismiss your concern, tomorrow will end these delays. But why go in this forest alone, so full of terror, full of beasts? The woods has fierce wolves and lions, huge boars and bears, and anything that rages worse than these.

AT. Accustomed to the forest, I am less afraid of its denizens than a source of fear for them. And now I seem to have been away from it a long time. So at first light, bored with inactivity and sleep, I decided to try my bow against your game and indulge my enthusiasm for the hunt, too long interrupted. Nor was my effort fruitless. I laid low a tawny lion wandering beneath the high mountain crest, not that an Aetolian lion seems such a great thing as an Arcadian one.

MEL. Whew! A girl lion-slayer to do the shooting? If you are gripped by such a desire for the hunt, you should chase rabbits, gentle deer, and agile stags, or at most the dire wolf when your noble zeal craves a greater feat. Be prudent and avoid those dangerous animals nature has armed for our destruction. That beauty of yours, which so moves men and

		agita fugaces, fortibus virgo abstine,	
		ne forte laus haec stet tibi magno tua.	285
	AT.	mihi me relinque, sola me novi probe,	
		Meleagre. sic sum, sic ratio vitae exigit.	
		quantum pericli detrahi factis solet,	
		de laude tantum ac gloria auferri puto.	
	PHIL.	at te ipsa praeter faeminae vires nimis	290
		offers labori. potius annorum memor	
		sexusque, rigidam lusibus mentem excute.	
		animum relaxa, propria describit deus	
		officia. calathi faeminam, fusi, colus,	
		et Palladis non tela, sed telae decent.	295
		virum sagittae, spicula, arcus, vulnera,	
		sudor, periculum, labor, pulvis iuvant.	
		hoc esse munus virgini indictum putas	
		ut dura toleret, montibus vitam exigat,	
		sylvestris et truculenta, rectique inscia?	300
		natura mores singulae aetati suos	
		magistra fingit, et suo ducit gradu.	
		matrona frontem tetricam, tristem, gravem,	
		virgo serenam, nobilem, laetam gerat.	
		et ista nunquam forma perpetuo manet,	305
		bonum caducum, temporis donum brevis,	
sig. B 3ᵛ		morbique praeda. nulla transibit dies,	
		quin aliqua vultus spolia formosi auferet.	
	AT.	depone curam quaeso, quam pro me geris.	
		nec ipsa, plus quam par erit, magnis caput	310
		obiicio caeptis, nec pudet me virium.	
		quisquis lacertos sensit, imbelles negat,	
		nec sunt ineptae cursibus plantae pedum,	
		plagamque sanguis insequitur etiam meam.	
		et iis minare, quas movet formae nitor,	315
		et delicatis loquere, queis pulchri nocet	
		iactura colli. strenuas tangunt minus.	
		namque ipsa, quanquam virginum tenero gregi	
		formosa dicar, nomine arridet magis	
		fortis vocari. quam vocant dotem, puto	320
		placere crimen, corporis formae pudet.	
		nunc usta Phaebo colla, perfusae comae	
		ventos sequuntur, nunc in unum simplici	

285. *magni* potius legendum?

gods, makes no impression on them. Girl, hunt the beasts that flee, shun the bold ones, lest perhaps the praise you win cost too great a price.

AT. Leave me to myself, I alone know myself, Meleager. Thus I am, thus the manner of my life ordains. I think that whatever risk is subtracted from my deeds diminishes my praise and glory.

PHIL. But you expose yourself to effort beyond a woman's capacity. Rather, you should be mindful of your age and sex, and dispel this rigid attitude with playfulness. Relax your mind, for the god has set forth our proper duties. Wicker baskets, spindles, the distaff, and looms befit a woman, not Pallas' weapons. Arrows, javelins, bows, wounds, perspiration, danger, hard effort, and dust suit a man. Do you think it a duty enjoined on a girl that she must endure hardships, leading a life in the mountains as a boorish woodland creature, ignorant of what is proper? Mistress Nature creates habits appropriate for each age, guiding us along at her own pace. A matron wears a morose, sad, severe face, a girl a serene, noble, happy one. Beauty itself never endures, it is a transitory good, the gift of a brief moment. It is prey to disease, and no day will pass but that does not somewhat despoil the beauty of a face.

AT. Pray abandon this concern for me. I myself do not risk my head in great undertakings more than is reasonable, nor am I ashamed of my strength. Whoever feels my arms denies that they are weak, nor are my feet unsuited for running. Blood flows when I strike. Threaten those girls who are impressed by beauty's charm, talk to the tender maids who are harmed by the loss of a pretty neck. These things are less important to vigorous women. For myself, even if I belong to the dainty assembly of maidens and am said to be pretty, I take more pleasure in being called stout-hearted. And this ability to please, which people call a gift, I think to be criminal, and I am ashamed of my physical charm. My neck is sunburnt by Phoebus; now my unbound hair flows in the wind, now it is bound

		nodo ligantur, vinciunt alte leves	
		suras cothurni, phaeretra de tergo sonat,	325
		arcumque laeva sustinet fortem manus.	
		iuvat minacem consequi pedibus feram,	
		hyememque duram, et pulverem, et solem, et famem,	
		sitimque saevam perpeti, et culpae otium	
		fugare matrem. qualis in bello furit	330
		pharetrata Amazon, talis in sylvas feror.	
	PHIL.	quid ista prosunt? numquid his armis putas	
		fugari Amorem posse tam levibus deum,	
		qui maria, terras, cumque Styge caelum domat?	
		quicquid deorum, quicquid aut hominum genus,	335
		aut belluarum est, igne tam sacro calet.	
sig. B 4ʳ	AT.	quis iste deus est, quem mihi narras, Amor?	
		nam vos soletis nescio quem dicere	
		regnare puerum, diis gravem ac mortalibus.	
		mihi cum Diana sola virginitas dea est.	340
	MEL.	at ista non est tota virginitas tua.	
		pars una patris, matris est pars altera,	
		pars tertia viri, patriae quarta est tuae,	
		tua sola quinta est. solve quam debes patri	
		matrique partem, coniugi, ac patriae suam.	345
		Atalanta, noli quaeso pugnare omnibus.	
		vincere, nec te ab omnibus vinci est pudor.	
		perire stirpem nemo generosam sinit.	
		generosa stirps, multa te soboles manet.	
		delectet arbor flore, sed fructu magis.	350
		nisi decidisset iste flos matri tuae,	
		flos ubi fuisset, quem facis tanti, tuus?	
		et ecce, plures flosculos coniux dares,	
		impensa multas una virginitas parit.	
	AT.	secreta septis vernat ut in hortis rosa,	355
		pecore remota, vomeri nulli obvia,	
		quam mulcet aura, sol fovet, pluviae rigant.	
		multae puellae, multi eam pueri expetunt.	
		eademque ab ungue carpta, ubi defloruit,	
		nullae puellae, nulli eam pueri expetunt.	360
		intacta sic dum virgo, iucunda est suis.	
		at inquinata corporis casti rosa,	
		ubi virginalem perdidit florem, amplius	
		nec ea puellis grata nec pueris manet.	

with a simple knot. High sandals bind my ankles, a quiver resounds on my back, my left hand clasps a powerful bow. My pleasure is hunting the menacing beast on foot, to withstand the harsh winter, dust, sun, hunger, and savage thirst, and to banish leisure, the mother of evil. As the quiver-bearing Amazon rages in battle, thus am I borne to the forest.

PHIL. What is the advantage of all this? Surely you don't think these insubstantial weapons can rout Love, the god who subdues the seas, earth, heaven, and the Styx? Every one of the gods, of the race of men, of the beasts, burns with his sacred fire.

AT. Who is this god Love you speak about? For you people are accustomed to talk of the reign of some child I know nothing of, harsh to gods and mortals. For me, as for Diana, chastity alone is divine.

MEL. But this chastity is not exclusively yours. One part belongs to your father, a second to your mother, a third to your husband, a fourth to your country, and only a fifth is yours. Pay the parts due your father, mother, husband, and nation. I beg you, Atalanta, do not struggle against everyone. Be conquered, for there is no disgrace in being overcome by the whole world. Nobody permits a noble stock to die out. Your stock is noble, and a large brood awaits you. The tree delights in its flower, but even more in its fruit. Unless your mother's flower had fallen, what would have become of yours, which you value so highly? And reflect, as a wife you would produce many little flowers, and many virginities are acquired at the cost of one.

AT. A hidden rose blooms within a walled garden, far from the herd, exposed to no plough, caressed by the breeze, nutured by the sun, watered by the rains. Many girls and boys seek it. But when it has been plucked by someone's fingers and has lost its flower, then no boys or girls look for it. Thus as long as a virgin remains untouched, she is a delight to her companions. But when the rose of her body's chastity has been sullied, when she has lost the flower of her virginity, she is dear to the girls and boys no more.

MEL. ut vitis agro vidua quae nudo iacet, 365
haud semet unquam tollit, aut mitem educat
sylvestris uvam, at mole deflectens sua,
radice summam prona claviculam implicat,
nulli coloni, nullae eam curant manus,
eadem sed ulmo cum maritata est suo, 370
multi coloni, multae eam curant manus,
intacta sic dum virgo, dum inculta est, statim
senescit, at cum iuncta cunnubio pari est
viro, ac parenti gratior multo emicat,
cunctisque melior prodit. et certe rosam 375
beatiorem, quae manu languet, reor,
naresque pascit interim atque oculos simul,
quam quae senescit frutice. namque ibi mox quoque
iucunda nulli sponte marcescet sua.

AT. quae gravior illa nocte nox caelo exeat, 380
castam puellam quae viro prodit truci,
gremioque matris virginem teneram eripit,
trepidam puellam matris amplexu eripit?
quid peius hostes urbe iam capta patrant?
quod ab hoste peius virgo patiatur nefas? 385

PHIL. quae melior illa nocte nox caelo exeat,
quae miscet animas, et duas unam facit,
natamque matris eripere gremio potest
trepidam puellam matris abducit sinu?
hora quid illa laetius tribuant dei? 390
Atalanta, nescis casta quid praestet Venus.
roga parentes, neve fallaris, tuam
si viva, matrem. iamque testata est satis
quod te pepererit: virgo mansisset, tua
quae iam fuisset vita? quin tu cogita, 395
intacta licet et cruda, quam dulce est tamen
nomen parentis, quamque iucundum foret,
Atalanta si quae parva rideret sinu,
quae te referret ore, vel lactans puer,
cui blandiendo diceres, "o quam tuus 400
et genitor in te fortis," et fortis tamen
pars aliqua matris, miscet ex aequo decus,
et cui iam adulto, facta narrares tua.

---

385. *ad* lib.: corr. Brooke, script. inedit. 402 sq. *decus?...tua?* lib.

MEL. A widowed vine lies alone in a barren field, scarcely ever raising itself, or bearing a single mellow grape-cluster in the woodland, but remains bowed by its own weight, entangling its topmost tendril in its own root, untended by any farmer, by no hand. But when the same vine is wedded to its own elm, many farmers, many hands tend it. In the same way, as long as a maiden is untouched and uncultivated, she quickly grows old. But when she is joined to a husband in a marriage of equality, she shine forth, much dearer to her father, and shows herself better to everyone. And I imagine that a rose is surely happier which droops because of handling, but which in the meantime pleases the nose and eye, than a rose which withers on the bush. For there too it quickly fades on its own, giving pleasure to nobody.

AT. What night can descend in the sky worse than that which gives over a chaste girl to a harsh man, tearing a gentle maiden from her mother's lap, tearing a frightened girl from her mother's embrace? What fouler deed can enemies commit during the sack of a city? What worse thing can a maiden undergo at the hands of a foeman?

PHIL. What night can descend in the sky better than that which joins souls, making one out of two? Can it snatch a girl from her mother's lap and abduct a timid girl from her mother's embrace? What happier thing can the gods grant than this hour? Atalanta, you are ignorant of the superiority of this chaste Venus. Ask your parents. Lest you be deceived, ask your mother, if she is living. She has already given ample proof, since she gave birth to you. If she had stayed a virgin, what would have become of your life? Consider, even if you are fresh and untouched, how sweet is the name of a parent, how pleasant would it be if some tiny Atalanta were giggling at your bosom, having your face, or some nursling boy, to whom you would soothingly say "oh, how your valiant father is in you" (although part of him is his valiant mother, and their glory is blended equally), and to whom you could recount your deeds when he grows up.

AT. quid me ad iugales blandus hortaris faces?
puella sapiens triste vitabit iugum.   405
vel sunt enim plerumque zelotypi viri,
vel dissoluti, vel nimis domini graves.
tum parere, quanti est? quam vel ad vocem horreo!
proinde mecum fugere constitui. prius
mergetur ortu, incipiet occasu dies,   410
paxque ante canibus alta cum damis erit,
quam victa facilem coniugi mentem dabo.
sed nostra ne sint verba suspecta, amputo,
iamque ipsa magis ac solita me facilem dedi.

Exit subirata in regiam.

MELEAGER, PHILEMON

MEL. ut dura cassis undique impenetrabilis   415
iaculis resistit, et gravi sonitu procul
ictus remittit, verba sic nostra excutit.
haud sic abibit. interim spera tuam.

PHIL. ah cur inanem spem tibi frustra facis?
voti facultas nulla contiget tibi.   420

MEL. contiget. et me compotem faciet Venus.
tentabo propius, precibus admotis agam.
et cum reducet crastinum Phoebus diem,
in apri cruore gloriae nostra viam
virtute quaeram, meque ea dignum geram.   425
sin forte nostros pertinax spernet toros,
stat detinere, et si repetat aliquis, manu
raptam tueri.

PHIL.   hospitia violabis furens?

MEL. hospitia violat, hospitem qui deperit?

PHIL. omnem hospitalis Iuppiter raptum vetat.   430

MEL. quam saepe raptum Iuppiter talem probat?

PHIL. opem datura venit.

---

404. *qiud* lib.: corr. Brooke, script. inedit.   414. *mc* lib.: corr. Brooke, script. inedit.

AT. Why are you smoothly urging me to marry? A wise girl avoids the sorry yoke. Men, for the most part, are jealous, dissolute, or harsh taskmasters. Then what is it worth to obey them? I shudder even at the word. And so I have decided to flee by myself. The sun will sooner sunk at its rising, rise at its setting, there will sooner be a deep peace between dogs and deer, than I shall be conquered and offer an agreeable attitude towards a husband. But lest you mistrust my words, I shall cut this short. I have already made myself unusually agreeable. [*Exit into the palace, slightly annoyed.*]

MEL. [*To himself.*] As a sturdy hunting-net, impenetrable in every part, withstands javelins and, with a loud twang, makes them rebound a goodly distance, so she rejects our words. She will scarcely escape thus. In the meantime, hope her to be yours.

PHIL. Ah, why invent this empty hope? You'll never get your way.

MEL. I'll get it, and Venus will make me the master. I'll try her more closely, press her with entreaties. And when Phoebus brings the new day I shall seek a way by my courage, by shedding the boar's blood, and I shall handle myself worthily of her. If perchance she spurns my bed, I have decided to detain her and, if anybody seeks her, to hold her captive in my grasp.

PHIL. In your madness will you violate hospitality?

MEL. Does he violate hospitality, who adores his guest?

PHIL. Jupiter, god of hospitality, forbids all kidnapping.

MEL. How often has Jupiter approved such a kidnapping?

PHIL. She came to bring us aid.

MEL.   at cladem mihi.

PHIL.   feram ut repellat.

MEL.   ipsa mihi maior fera.

PHIL.   quam gravia sint timenda, si rapias, vides.

MEL.   quam gravia sint ferenda, si caream, scio.   435

PHIL.   parente fulget rege.

MEL.   est mihi rex pater,
et imperio, et opibus, et armis praevalens.
est et patri Meleager, et amoris face
Meleager ardens totus, ac plenus deo.
sed tu monere desine, ac scrupulos mihi   440
iniicere vanos. aut erit thalami comes,
aut spes ab alto nostra ruitura est gradu.
iam plura tempus ac meus prohibet pudor.
certamen ingens instat. interea meos
simulabo vultus, spemque consilio regam.   445

CHORVS

o quam nostris truculentus agris
impune furens exultat aper!
rabido fulmen spirat ab ore,
frondesque ipsas spritus urit.
modo crescentes prima segetes   450
proterit herba, modo fleturi
vota coloni matura metit,
spicisque rapit Cererem plenis,
frustra expectant horrea messes.
nunc cum longo palmite faetus   455
sternit gravidos, nunc cum ramis
bacca virentis semper olivae,
cumque racemis eruta vitis
radice iacet. furit in pecudes.
non has pastor fidusve canis,   460
non armentum valeant tauri
servare truces. populi fugiunt,

sig. B 6ʳ

447. *aper?* lib. 461. pro *valeant* vid. Comm. not.

MEL. But also my death.

PHIL. And to repel the beast.

MEL. For me she's the greater beast.

PHIL. You see what heavy things there will be to fear, if you abduct her.

MEL. I know what heavy things I shall have to bear, if I do not have her.

PHIL. She is distinguished by royal paternity.

MEL. My father is also a king, very excellent in power, wealth, and arms. There is one Meleager for his father, and another Meleager who burns wholly by love's fire, filled with the god. But cease giving advice and trying to fill me with meaningless scruples. Either she'll be my partner in marriage, or my hope is to be dashed from its lofty perch. Now the time and my sense of modesty forbid more talk. A mighty combat awaits us. Meanwhile I shall put on a false face, and govern my hope by good counsel. [*Exeunt.*]

CHORUS

Oh, how this ferocious raging boar roam freely in our fields, unpunished! He breathes lightning from his rabid mouth, his breath kindles the very leaves. Now he tramples the rising corn of our early crop, now he lays low the mature hope of our farmers, destined to weep, ravaging the wheat in its mature ears, and in vain our barns await the grain. Now he lays low the swollen clusters together with the long stem, now the fruit of the ever-verdant olive, along with their branches. The uprooted vine lies with its shoots. He savages the cattle. Neither the herdsman nor the faithful dog serve to defend them, nor the bulls to

vix se tutos moenibus ipsis
atque urbe putant. tu, Meleager,
et tu, Theseu, tuque, Atalanta, 465
et vos, procerum lecta caterva,
Calydone ferum pelletis aprum.
iam tibi clades, setiger, instat.
iam Meleagro dabis egregium
caedis honorem, capitisque tui 470
    tergique decus.

save the herd. The people flee, scarce thinking themselves safe behind the very walls, in the city. You, Meleager, you, Theseus and Atalanta, and all you choice band of princes, drive the fierce boar out of Calydon. Now death awaits you, bristly one. Now you will grant Meleager the distinguished honor of your killing, the glory of your head and hide.

- Actus Secundus -

Primo transeunt venatores, e regia ad fanum Dianae, omnes bini.in medio solus incedit aruspex, cum omni apparatu sacrifico, et victima mactanda.

OENEVS, SENEX

<OEN.> par diis superbis gradior, et caelo tenus,
inter tyrannos arduum caput effero.
nam quid feracis annuos terrae loquar
reditus, liquoris copiam Bacchi, horrea 475
sig. B 6ᵛ cumulata Cereris munere, aut pingues deae
latices Minervae? mille quid referam greges
pecudum minorum, mille maiorum meis
armenta in agris? adde quod cingit frequens
faelixque nostrum turba natorum latus. 480
in quot fatigor oscula, et in omnem gregem
dividere patrem? quid quod hunc portum attigi
aetatis, inter perpetua pacis bona?
nec ulla morbi me, vel infortunii
procella, vitae gravior in cursu meae 485
iactavit unquam. fata quae optari queant
meliora, quam quae semper ex voto tuli?
aut quis videtur posse fortunae gradus
ulterior addi? quisve iam noceat mihi?
aut cuius odium? nempe Latona editae. 490
haec, quem deorum tota consensit cohors
semper beatum stare, nec cladem pati,
haec una caepit obstrepere nuper mihi,
et fata verti posse necquicquam putat.
misere verendum est ne gravius aliquid furens 495
Diana statuat. scilicet nostris gravem
immisit agris vindicem cultus aprum
spretique honoris. sed fremat quantum potest,
fremat Diana, cedet in laudes meas
furentis ira. laetus invidia fruar, 500
et vindicem vindicta quam vellem manet.

SEN. magnanime princeps, et domine tantis mihi
colende meritis, comprime affectus, precor,
et quam lacessis cogita. spernis deam,

---

479. *frequens?* lib.

- Act II -

First the hunters cross the stage two by two, from the palace to Diana's shrine. In their midst walks the soothsayer by himself, with all his sacrificial equipment and victims to be killed.

OENEUS, OLD MAN

OEN. I walk along, the equal of the prideful gods, and among other rulers I raise my lofty head to the sky. For what should I say of the yearly returns of my fruitful lands, about my supply of Bacchus' liquor, my barns stuffed with Ceres' gift, or my fat oil of divine Minerva? Why should I mention my thousand herds of lesser animals,[1] my thousand herds of cattle in the fields? Add to these the throng of children swarming around my sides. By how many kisses am I exhausted, and by dividing my paternal attention among such a crew? What that I have attained the harbor of old age among the unbroken blessings of peace? Nor has any storm of illness or misfortune ever tossed me in my life's voyage. What better fate could be hoped for than the one I have ever obtained, in accordance with my wish? Who could hurt me now? Whose hatred? Of course, that of Latona's daughter.[2] This one has lately begun to carp at me, me whom the entire company of gods has agreed should always remain blessed, suffering no hurt. She mistakenly imagines my destiny can be overturned. Unfortunately, it is to be feared lest Diana decide something rather harsh in her rage. In fact, she has sent a boar as a terrible avenger of her rite and scorned honor. But let it rage is at it can, let Diana rage. Her furious wrath will turn out to my credit. Happily, I enjoy her hostility, and the vengeance I would wish awaits this avenger.

O. M. Great-hearted prince, master whom I must honor with all good deeds, I beg you restrain your feelings and consider whom you are insulting. You are spurning a goddess, a

---

[1] Sheep.
[2] Diana.

sig. B 7ʳ

   et praepotentem, quae suo caelo valet,   505
   terraque et Erebo, quaeque per gentes triplex
   numen probavit, usque qua mundus patet.
   ubique praesens colitur in terris dea.
   en hanc lacessis, atque ne facilem putes,
   probavit iram nulla maiorem dea,   510
   nec nisi cruenta morte satiari solet.
   immitis etiam vel levi errori fuit.
   innocuus hoc testetur Actaeon lacer.
   quid illa sceleri faciet, ac menti impiae?
   iamque inchoavit, atque ne pergat, precor.   515

OEN. cui precibus opus est, cum libet, fundas preces,
   mihi nulla voti causa succurrit tui.
   foelix vocor, nam quis neget? faelixque ita
   semper manebo. nulla me miserum dies
   videbit unquam. quis dubitet istud quoque?   520
   copia beatum fecit. en sedeo altior,
   quam cui nocere, velle fac, casus queat.
   atque ut repente multa surripiat mihi,
   multo relinquet plura quam rapuit tamen.
   omnem timorem nostra vicerunt bona.   525
   nam finge posse (sed tamen iam qui potest?)
   sed finge multa copiis demi meis.
   non usque redigar ut miser fiam tamen.

SEN. quo quis superbus extulit sese altius,
   hoc gravius ille ac foedius subito ruit.   530

OEN. decet suprema facere securum bona.

SEN. solent suprema premere securum mala.

OEN. quid est timendum?

SEN.   nempe quod metuas nihil.

OEN. timidi est metuere singula.

SEN.   audacis nihil.

OEN. stulte timetur, causa ubi nulla est metus.   535

---

526. *singe* liber: corr. in Vict. & Albert. Bibl. vol.

very powerful one, mighty in heaven, on earth, in Erebus, who has demonstrated her triple godhead among the nations to the ends of the earth. This goddess, present throughout the world, is worshipped everywhere. You are insulting her and, lest you think her easily placated, no goddess has demonstrated greater wrath. She is not accustomed to being sated by anything less than bloody death. She has been cruel even towards a slight mistake. Unoffending, lacerated Actaeon will attest to that. What will she to do to crime and an impious mind? She has already made a beginning, and I pray she does not continue.

OEN. Offer prayer to the god who requires prayer when you wish. But in my case your wish is groundless. I am called fortunate. Who denies this? Therefore I shall always remain fortunate. No day will ever see me wretched. Who doubts that too? My wealth blesses me. I sit so high that no mishap could harm me, if it wanted. If it should suddenly take much from me, it would yet leave me with more than it took. My prosperity has overcome every anxiety. For imagine this is possible (but who can do so?), still imagine that much is subtracted from my wealth. I shall still not be brought so low as to be unhappy.

O.M. The higher a proud man raises himself, the harder and more shamefully he falls.

OEN. Supreme good fortune will render him secure.

O.M. Supreme misfortunes are wont to oppress the secure.

OEN. What's there to fear?

O. M. The fact that you fear nothing.

OEN. It is the mark of a timid man to fear everything.

O. M.. And of a foolhardy man to fear nothing.

OEN. Fear is foolish, where there is no cause for alarm.

sig. B 7ᵛ   SEN. cum facere miserum sors queat, causa haud deest.

OEN. sum maior ipsa sorte.

SEN.   et in vivis manes?

OEN. rex vivo clarus.

SEN.   nomine hoc magis expave.
graviore turres decidunt casu arduae,
altosque montes crebrius fulmen ferit,   540
et vasta morbo membra maiori patent.

OEN. me subditorum posuit in tuto fides.

SEN. caelestis ira cum premit, ad homines fugis?
quique ipse spernit numen, hunc cives colant?
relligio cultus servat humanos deum.   545

OEN. ingens deorum stat etiam a nobis favor.
quoties opima victima ante aras steti,
et sancta quoties thura congessi focis?
quid quod recepit mensa convivas mea,
et ore nostras saepe gustarunt dapes?   550

SEN. debere superos posse mortali putas,
aut demereri numen officiis potes,
aut tum mereris, cum hospites mensa excipis?
sed fac deos favere: plus tamen unica
Diana noceat laesa quam prosint tibi   555
decem faventes, si tamen faveant decem.
commune superos vinculum generis tenet,
et pariter omnes tangit unius dolor.
nam quisque metuens ne sibi simile accidat,
paena cavendum censet, et iustam probat   560
iram Dianae. nec alii factum deo
fecisse fas est irritum alterius dei.
impune divos Iuppiter sperni vetat.
supplicia moneant: una sit Niobe satis,
nec dignitate nec genere cedens tibi.   565

sig. B 8ʳ   quas illa spreti numinis paenas dedit?
unde illa cecidit, non stat hoc Oeneus loco?
nolo ominari, caelites iterum precor
ut causa similis careat eventu pari.

78

O. M.. Whenever destiny can make you miserable, a cause is scarcely lacking.

OEN. I am superior to destiny.

O. M. And you remain among the living?

OEN. I am alive, a notable king.

O. M. Then feel fear because of this title. Lofty towers collapse with a steeper fall, lightning strikes high mountains more often, and huge frames suffer greater maladies.

OEN. My subjects' loyalty has placed me in a safe position.

O. M. When heavenly wrath oppresses you, do you take refuge among mortals? Should subjects pay homage to a man who himself scorns a god? Piety towards the gods guarantees human veneration.

OEN. I display great devotion towards the gods. How often have I placed fat victims at the altars, how often have I heaped sacred incense on the fires? What about the fact that my table has held banquets for the gods, and they have often tasted my food?

O. M. Do you imagine the gods can be indebted to a mortal, that you can ingratiate yourself with a divinity by such ritual acts, or that you are gaining merit by receiving them as guests at your table? But imagine the gods are favorable. Diana, injured, can work more harm than ten well-disposed gods can help you, if ten are well disposed. A common bond of kinship links the gods, and the pain of one affects them all. For each of them fears lest something similar happen to him, thinks this ought to be forestalled by inflicting punishment, and approves Diana's wrath. Nor is it lawful for one god to undo another's deed. Jupiter forbids the gods to be scorned with impunity. Be warned by previous punishments: let Niobe alone provide ample warning, who was not inferior to you in rank or dignity. What price did she pay for scorning a god? And does not Oeneus occupy the same position from which she fell? I do not wish to play the prophet, and I pray the gods that a similar cause does not engender a similar outcome.

OEN.	ut te senectus timida, necquicquam metu,	570
	expersque veri ludit, ac curis agit!	
	si rueret omne quod vides caelum undique,	
	et ipse ruerem, fateor, et ruerem libens.	
	haud ille miser est, quisquis ex alto cadit,	
	cadente mundo pariter. at magnum facit	575
	Niobe timorem. numquid hic Niobem vides?	
	aut causa par est? illa maledictis deam	
	ultro petivit, me lacessitum queror.	
	ingemere damnis esse tu credis nefas?	

SEN. at te Diana quo lacessivit malo?   580

OEN. delire, nescis? quid quod horrendum meos,
non provocata, misit in fines suem?

SEN.	non provocata? numquid id ducis leve,	
	solenne festo cum sacrum faceres die,	
	cum iam Liaeo vina libares sua,	585
	sua dona Cereri, Palladi latices suos,	
	superosque ad omnes gratia veniret sacri,	
	sine honore solam victimae aut thuris deae	
	aram stetisse, quaeque contemptum tulit,	
	inulta ferret?	

OEN.	scilicet magnum scelus	590
	caruisse sacri honore, cui pars fructuum	
	nulla tribuenda est, quaeque mortales quidem,	
	sed non nocendo, more latronum, beat.	
	quis olea, fruges, vina, lanigeros greges,	
	retulit Dianae accepta? quae sylvas colit	595
	sylvis colatur, quasque venatur feris.	
	parum illa vitae commodis affert boni.	
	sed ecce coniux tristis huc affert gradum,	
	turbata vultu, totus in gestu est dolor.	

sig. B 8ᵛ

OENEVS, ALTHAEA, SENEX

<OEN.> dilecta coniux, cur genae fletu madent?   600
quae tanta vultus causa mutavit tuos?
quid pallor iste? fare quid lacrymae ferant.

---

571. *agit?* lib.

OEN. How timid old age, out of touch with the truth, drives you with its fear and worries! If this heaven you see everywhere were to fall, and I along with it, I confess I should fall gladly. He is scarcely wretched who falls from a high position, if the universe collapses with him. So Niobe creates great fearfulness. You don't see Niobe here, do you? Is the reason the same? She went out of the way to attack the gods with imprecations, I complain that they have injured me. Do you think it sinful to complain of injuries?

O. M. By what evil has Diana harmed you?

OEN. Madman, do you not know? What that she sent this terrible pig against my land, unprovoked?

O. M. Unprovoked? Do you think it a trifling matter that when you were offering solemn sacrifice on that holiday, although you poured libations of his wine to Lyaeus,[1] her gifts to Ceres, and her oil to Pallas, and a festal thank-offering to each of the gods, only this goddess' altar stood without honor or incense, and that, unavenged, she should tolerate the mark of contempt she received?

OEN. To be sure, this is a great sin that she lacked honor, to whom no part of the first-fruits is supposed to be allotted. She scarcely helps mortals by harming them, in the way of robbers. Who offers to Diana out of his harvest of oil, crops, wine, or wooly sheep? She who cultivates the forest is to be worshipped in the forest, with offerings of the beasts she hunts. She scarcely bestows life's useful things.

But see, my wife makes her way here sadly, with a troubled countenance, and pain is in her every motion. [*Enter Althaea.*]

Beloved consort, why are your cheeks drenched with tears? What great thing has changed your countenance? Why this pallor? Tell me the meaning of these tears.

---

[1] Bacchus.

ALTH. exterret animum noctis hesternae metus,
visumque, coniux. luna iam cursum vaga
medium tenebat, maesta cum thalamos meos 605
intrare visa est umbra genetricis mihi,
et bis verendum terque concutiens caput,
"quis dirus," inquit, "nata, te casus brevi,
fratresque geminos, filios olim meos,
sociumque thalami, teque Meleager, premet! 610
horrenda clades, dira pernicies adest."
tum multa secum questa, graviterque ingemens,
"te scire plura, plura me fari vetant
abstrusa fata. si tamen flecti queant,
placa Dianam." dixit, et thalamo exiit. 615
mihi soporem gelidus excussit timor,
artusque subiit horror, ac mentem stupor.
heu quam ruinam fata minantur mihi,
aut quae meorum tanta clades imminet?

OEN. haec causa fletus? per deos, vix tam queo 620
risum tenere. suspitio quaenam mali
tam minima poterit esse, quam si caeperis
misera timere, non statim misere fleas,
et flendo facias maximam? in somnis tibi
haec accidisse visa, quae vigilans times, 625
miraris, et quae timida tecum cogitas?
quaecunque mentem trepida vigilantem gravant,
ea celer, internusque per somnum solet
referre sensus, et sopor geminat metum.
iram Dianae stulta plus aequo times. 630
hinc umbra matris, inde tot somnus tibi
portenta finxit. molliter socrus iacet,
et nocte campus tenuit hesterna sacros
anima beata, qua tibi visam putas.
proinde solitam recipe laetitiam, precor, 635
timore pulso, quem nimis fingis tibi.

SEN. finxisse cupio, ponderis quiddam tamen
habere magni somnia potentum solent.

OEN. aequus potenti ac pauperi somnus venit
mendax virique, forsitan regi magis, 640
quo dormientem maior exagitat metus.
et ipse, quoties talia in somnis tuli

sig. C 1ʳ

610. *premet?* lib.   624. *etflendo* lib: corr. Brooke, script. inedit.

ALTH. Last night's fear terrifies my mind, husband, and a vision. The moon now stood at mid-point in her wandering journey, when I saw my mother's baleful shade enter my chamber. Twice, thrice striking her venerable head she said, "What dire catastrophe will soon torment you, daughter, your twin brothers who were formerly my sons, your husband, and you, Meleager! Horrible slaughter, dire ruin is at hand." Then, making much complaint and groaning heavily, she said "The hidden Fates forbid that you learn more or that I speak further. But, in case they can be swayed, pacify Diana," and left my chamber. Chill terror kept me from sleep, shuddering overcame my limbs, numbness my mind. Alas, with what calamity do the Fates threaten me, what great slaughter impends for my family?

OEN. This is the cause of your weeping? Alas, I can scarcely restrain my laughter. Could there be any premonition of evil so small, but that if you began to dread it in your misery, you should not immediately break out in tears and make it huge by weeping? Are you surprised that the things you fear awake, and timorously brood upon, should have occurred to you in a dream? The fearful things which freight your waking mind, a swift inner sense is accustomed to recall, and sleep doubles your dread. Foolishly you fear Diana's anger inordinately. For this reason your mother's image and sleep created all these portents for you. My mother-in-law lies at peace, and last night her blessed soul, which you thought you saw, kept to its hallowed field. So recover your usual good cheer, I beg you, with that fear banished which you so greatly imagine.

O. M. I hope she imagined it, but the dreams of rulers are wont to be weighty.

OEN. Equally tricksy dreams occur to the powerful and the poor, and possibly more so to royalty, since greater anxiety disturbs them in their sleep. As for me, how often have I

		prodigia quae ridicula tam fecit dies?	
	SEN.	segnis deorum est ira, sed certa est tamen.	
		atque ut securis quo magis retro datur,	645
		et altiore tarda liberatur manu,	
		hoc acriore vulnere ad corpus venit.	
		sic ira superum, quo magis patitur moras,	
		et tardiorem pigra metitur gradum,	
		hoc fortiorem ponit et gravius pedem.	650
	OEN.	ne sponte mulier non satis metuat, senex	
		addat timorem. sed cadat quicquid potest	
sig. C 1^v		accidere, quis me casus infaelix premat?	
	ALTH.	quodcunque fuerit, haud temere credo fuit.	
		aras Dianae petere constitui sacras,	655
		caesis precari victimis numen deae,	
		ut expiatas somnii avertat minas.	
	OEN.	quid ista tandem vult superstitio sibi?	
		cur navigantem torquet in portu metus?	
	ALTH.	tutone regnum stare iam credis loco,	660
		dum vastat ingens patrios fines aper,	
		segetesque adustas sternit, et late fugam	
		edit per agros?	
	OEN.	quicquid impelli potest	
		ac vindicari, num quis id magnum putet?	
		utinam quidem fugare tam possim meis	665
		membris senectam, quam meis agris aprum.	
		sed en, peracto rediit a sacro cohors.	
		florem intueri gentis Argolicae iuvat.	

OENEVS, ARVSPEX, THESEVS, ALTHAEA, MELEAGER, PLEXIPPVS, TOXEVS

	<OEN.>	magnanime Theseu, tuque magnanime comes,	
		et reliqua iuvenum turma, iam votis dies	670
		adest petita, dexteris nunc est opus.	
		sed tu profare, si quid ex sacro deus	
		praescire, aruspex, dederit. an laeta omnia?	
	ARV.	ter magne princeps, patrii columen soli,	

640. *meudax* lib.: corr. Brooke, script. inedit   667. *facro* lib.: corr. Brooke, script. inedit.

experienced such portents in dreams, which the day proved to be foolish?

O. M. The gods' anger is slow but certain, and, just as the farther back someone hauls and axe and the higher he hefts it in his slow hand, the worse the physical wound is inflicted, so the more divine wrath is delayed and the more ponderously its step is measured, the harsher and heavier it lowers its foot.

OEN. Lest perhaps the woman is not insufficiently afraid on her own, let this old man add to her terror. But suppose it happens. What can befalls us, what unhappy calamity might oppress me?

ALTH. Whatever it may have been, I do not rashly believe that it occurred. I have decided to seek out Diana's altars, and with slaughtered victims to beseech her divinity to avert my dream's menaces, now expiated.

OEN. What does this superstition mean? Why should fear drive the sailor into port?

ALTH. Do you believe our kingdom is now on a sound footing, even as this huge boar is devastating our ancestral territory, laying low the withered crops, causing flight through our fields?

OEN. Does anyone think something to be great that can be repelled or punished? Would that I were as able to rout old age from my limbs as this boar from my fields! But see, the throng returns from the completed sacrifice. It is a pleasure to look at the flower of the Aetolian nation. [*Enter the soothsayer, Theseus, Meleager, Plexippus, Toxeus, and the other hunters.*]

Noble-minded Theseus, and you, comrade of this high-minded man, and the rest of this band of youths, the hoped-for day is here, now there is need for your hands. But tell me, soothsayer, if at the rites the god gave us foreknowledge of something. Is everything happy?

S.S. Thrice-great prince, pillar of our ancestral land, I scarcely know whether to grieve or

sig. C 2ʳ

    utrumne doleam nescio, an laeter magis,   675
    nam laeta duris mista perplexe latent.
    apro cruentum laetor instare exitum,
    sic exta monstrant. sed tamen magnus quoque
    quatit horror artus, metuo quid superi parent.

OEN. ostende tandem signa quid sacri ferant.   680

ARV. quod trepida segni lingua cunctatur moram,
    ne tibi animum, rex magne, commoveat precor.
    celare mos est monita sacrorum Iovi,
    horrenda nobis fata cum sciri vetat,
    aut aliquid ingens caelites laesi apparant.   685

OEN. quid istud ingens? fare, sit dubium licet.

ARV. certi quid eloquar? quid effari queam?
    nam versus ordo est. sede nil iacuit sua,
    sed acta retro cuncta. lex pecudis sacra
    remansit utero nulla. mutavit fibras   690
    natura solitas. stipes in mediis focis
    sanguineus arsit, flamma mugitum dedit
    lugubrem, et ara tremuit, ac movit loco.
    nec omen ullis viscerum ostentis queam
    eruere certum, sed tamen triste est, scio.   695

OEN. quid hoc aruspex quod timet, coniux, senex?
    inane quiddam est. si tamen quicquam mali est,
    cras expiabo victima crebra minas.
    vos interim animos erigite fortes, precor.
    en, iste vestras postulat dextras labor,   700
    et dignus in quem tanta desudet cohors.
    ite, spolia referte, titulos vestris novos
    adiicite factis. si foret viridis mihi
    calidusque sanguis, quaeque florenti fuit
    iuventa quondam, nec graves senium gelu   705
    tardaret artus. ite. prohiberet pudor,
    venite dicerem, ipse me primum darem.

sig. C 2ᵛ

    sed fessa virtus robore antiquo caret,
    labantque gressus. qui potest, ibit comes:
    imago nostri et vita Meleager mea.   710
    eum pericli, quicquid est, facio ducem.

THE. venerande princeps, quicquid in nostra manu
    fidei reponis, haud ea spero caedes.
    si quid lacerti, spicula, atque animi queant,

rejoice, for happy things are mixed in with harsh in a perplexing way. I am glad that the bloody death of the boar is at hand, for thus the entrails proclaim. But still great horror makes my limbs shiver, and I fear what the gods may have in store.

OEN. Reveal what the ritual omens portend.

S.S. I beg, king, that you not take amiss the long delay of this timid man's tongue. For it is customary to conceal the omens of Jupiter's rites when the Fates forbid horrible things to be known by us, or when the offended gods give us some great sign.

OEN. What is this great thing? Tell me, even if it be obscure.

S.S. What can I say with certitude? What can I proclaim? For the order of things has been reversed. Nothing remains in its proper place, but everything is driven backwards. No sacred law governs the birthing of your cattle, and Nature has altered the usual entrails. A bloody brand blazed in the midst of the fire, the flame issued a doleful bellow, the altar shivered and moved from its place. I can divine no certain omen in the innards, but it is baleful, I am sure.

OEN. What is this which is feared by the soothsayer, my wife, this old man? It is meaningless. But if there be some evil, tomorrow I shall expiate the threats with bountiful offerings. Meanwhile, I pray, cheer up your brave minds. See, this work requires your hands, it deserves that this great band work up a sweat. Go, bring back the spoils, add new titles to your previous deeds. If only my blood were still fresh and warm, and my youth still what it was in my prime, my heavy limbs not retarded by the chill of old age! Go. I would say "come" if my sense of shame did not prevent me, and I would offer myself as the first to go. But my exhausted virtue lacks its old strength, my steps are halting. But someone who has the ability will go as your comrade, my image, my life, Meleager. I make him the leader of this venture, whatever it is.

THES. Venerable prince, whatever you entrust into our hands, I scarcely think will end in our deaths. If our arms, our spears, our minds have any power, and if the gods' favor

		et placidus adsit numinum caeptis favor,	715
		iam iam triumphum setiger laetum dabit.	
	OEN.	vox digna tali, qualis es, Theseu, viro,	
		virtute macte Graeciae magnum decus.	
		et vos, iuventus reliqua, memores gloriae	
		animis adeste. nemo non aliquo mihi	720
		donatus ibit munere ad patrios lares.	
		sed ecce, tempus in viam ac sylvam vocat.	
		ipse ad penates regios referam gradum.	
	ALTH.	incaepta, iuvenes, dii precor vestra adiuvent.	
		at te parentis si qua, Meleager, tuae,	725
		et vos amantis si qua, germani, manet	
		pietas sororis, parcite in vobis, precor,	
		matri ac sorori. saepe sibi virtus nocet	
		prodiga laboris. cautius pugnae vices	
		inite dubias. nulla sine vobis mea	730
		futura vita est. occidistis, una occidam.	
	MEL.	te nulla, genetrix chara, sollicitam gravet	
		nostrae salutis cura. non hanc maximam	
		pugnam subimus. quaeque nos antehac tibi	
		reduces dedit fortuna, iam reduces dabit.	735
	PLEX.	omnem timorem quaeso deponas, soror.	
		totam cohortem referet actutum deus.	
sig. C 3ʳ	TOX.	germana, nullus anxiam cruciet metus.	
		iam mox reversos ista visura est dies,	
		et ipsa venies in viam laeta obviam.	740
	ALTH.	cupio reversos idque confido fore,	
		etsi repugnet nescio quis animo timor.	

MELEAGER

	comites pericli, qua ratio pugnae placet?	
	quae via iucunda est? hanc mihi visum est sequi.	
	se tota varias scindat in partes cohors.	745
	pars una nemoris hinc et hinc divortia	
	ignota quaerat, seque ad omnes undique	
	obiiciat aditus, pars alia totum nemus	

---

733. *hanc* lib.: corr. Brooke, script. inedit.

smiles on our endeavors, now the bristly one will give us a happy triumph.

OEN. Theseus, that speech is worthy of a man such as you. Be honored for your virtue, great glory of Greece. And the rest of you youths, be present, mindful of your fame. Nobody will return to his ancestral hearth having received no gift from me. But see, the moment summons you to the road, to the woods. I myself shall return to the palace.

ALTH. I pray, lads, that the gods aid your endeavors. If, Meleager, any piety remains in you towards your mother, if, brothers, any piety remains in you towards your loving sister, I beg you spare yourselves for the sake of your mother and sister. Virtue, spendthrift in its effort, often harms itself. Enter cautiously into this adventure's uncertain chances. Without you I should have no life. If you perish, I shall die also.

MEL. Dear mother, let no concern for our safety trouble you. We are entering into no great struggle. Whatever Fortune has given you in the past, it will return to you now.

PLEX. Sister, I beg you dismiss all your fear. Presently the god will return our whole company.

TOX. Sister, let no concern torture you in your anxiety. Today will soon see us returned, and you yourself will happily come out into the road to greet us.

ALTH. I hope and expect that this will come to pass, even if some vague dread struggles in my mind. [*Exeunt all but the hunters.*]

MEL. Comrades in this adventure, what manner of fighting pleases you? What way strikes your fancy? This appears to me the plan to follow. Let one portion scour the unexplored forest nooks, planting itself at every entrance. Let another part encircle the

late coronet. alia per iuga montium
vallesque scandat. per cavos alii specus, 750
atque antra tendant, atque ubi argutum canes
dedere signum, quisque qua clamor vocat
occurrat una, et mutuas iungat manus.
en, si ista vobis ratio venandi placet,
percussa clarum scuta signum praebeant. 755
satis est. at unum restat, ut spolium ferat
apri superbum, qui prior dederit neci.
si pariter ista lege venari placet,
latis apertum spiculis signum date.
recte, peractum est, quisque sibi comitem eligat. 760
Atalanta, mihi te, si placet, sociam dabis,
et parte mecum praelium in eadem geres.
sed ecce, multum ducimus fando diem.
hac hac eamus, qua brevis longum via
compensat iter, haec semita in sylvam feret. 765

CHORVS

sig. C 3ᵛ

o Pax alma, Iovis filia maximi,
quantis regna beas inclyta praemiis,
uti muneribus si bene noverint!
contra, quot misere cladibus afficis,
uti muneribus si male caeperint! 770
huic primogenita est filia Copia,
sed matris petulans filia sobriae,
mollis, blanda, fluens, dedita luxui,
quam ni contineat dextera parcior,
in quodcunque nefas proruit improba. 775
istam subsequitur vana Superbia,
lasciva soboles matre nocentior,
trux, inflata, tumens, effera, gestiens,
contemptrix, nimium semper amans sui,
quam nulla indomitam lora coerceant. 780
hac stirpe Impietas ducit originem,
proles deterior matre Superbia,
cui crista est tumido vertice celsior,
ipsos ausa deos spernere caelites,
semperque in tragicum desinit exitum. 785

768. *noverint?* lib.   770. *caeperint?* lib.

wood, and another climb the mountain crests and valleys. Others should make their way through caves and caverns. Then, when the dogs have given their shrill signal, let everybody run in the direction where the uproar summons, and join forces. If this scheme for hunting pleases you, signify by thumping your shields. [*They do*.] Good. But one thing remains, that the first person to deal the death-blow should bear off the proud boar's trophy. If this hunting-rule pleases you also, give a clear indication by raising your spears. [*They do*.] Right, it's done. Let each man choose himself a companion. Atalanta, if you please, be my partner and share my part of this struggle. But see here, we are wasting much of the day in speech. Let us go this way, where a shortcut reduces the long journey, for this path will lead us into the forest. [*Exeunt*.]

CHORUS

O nuturing Peace, daughter of great Jupiter, how you bless famous kingdoms with your gifts, if they know how to use them well! But how miserably you visit death upon them, if they begin to use them amiss! Her firstborn daughter is Abundance. But this is a headstrong daughter of her moderate mother, soft, smooth, lax, given to luxury. Unless governed by a strict hand, wantonly she plunges into all manner of wickedness. She in turn is followed by vain Arrogance, a lascivious child, more harmful than her mother, truculent, inflated, swollen, bestial, greedy. She is scornful, excessively prone to self-love, whom no reins can restrain. From this stock Impiety derives her pedigree, an offspring worse than her mother Arrogance, whose crest stands higher than her proud neck. She dares scorn the very gods in heaven, and she always comes to a tragic end.

- Actus Tertius -

NVNCIVS, CHORVS

<NVNC.> o laeta fata, placida, memoranda, optima!
o fausta, nivea, prospera! o mites deos,
faciles, benignos! o diem vere diem,
placidamque sortem!

CHOR. quid precor portas novi?
sig. C 4ʳ num caesus aper est?

NVNC. caesus est, ingens iacet. 790

CHOR. quis caedis author? imo si vacat et libet,
ut gesta potius quaeque narrato ordine.

NVNC. est sylva duris quercuum trabibus frequens,
fagisque caelo aequalis, ornisque ardua,
imosque summo prospicit campos iugo, 795
quam nulla ferro laesit, aut coluit manus,
praebet patentem lata planicies viam.
animosa postquam venit huc iuvenum cohors,
pars lora demunt canibus. ast illi moras
patiuntur aegre, et sponte luctantur sua 800
vinclis resolvi. vinculis illi vias
carpunt soluti naribus sylvae invias,
alacres, sagaces. pars graves tendunt plagas,
pars pressa nuper signa rimantur pedum,
reperire cladem quisque praegestit suam. 805
in parte nemoris panditur media specu
vallis profundo. huc proximis rivi solent
pluvialis undae montium labi iugis.
imum lacunae vestiunt salices sinum,
iuncique, et ulvae, vimina, et cannae leves. 810
haec dira sedes, hoc apri stabulum fuit,
immanis apri, terribilis, hirti, trucis.
non maior illo pascuis errat tuis,
Epire, taurus, at minor Siculis solet.
oculi coruscant sanguine, et flammis micant, 815
frons torva rugis, hispida cervix iuba

---

791. *imo = immo* hic et passim   814. *siculis* lib.

- Actus III -

MESSENGER, CHORUS

MESS. Oh happy Fates, peaceful, memorable, the very best! Lucky, fair, and prosperous! Oh kindly gods, gentle and benign! Oh day of days, oh our tranquil lot!

CHOR. Pray, what news do you bring? Is the boar slain?

MESS. He is slain, the huge thing is laid low.

CHOR. Who was responsible for his killing? If you have the time and the will, tell us how each thing in turn was done.

MESS. There is a forest growing thick with beams of oak and beech trees rising up to the sky, filled with mountain ash, overlooking a deep valley from its mountain ridge. No iron has harmed it, no hand has tended it, but its broad clearings offer access. After the bold band of youths had gathered here, part of them kept their dogs under leash. But the dogs could tolerate no delay, and struggled to free themselves of restraint. Unleashed, they followed the forest paths with their noses, eager and knowing. Another part of the band set out heavy nets, while others examined fresh hoofprints. Everyone was eager to play his part in the killing. In the midst of the forest extends a valley in a deep ravine, by which the rainwater is wont to drain off the mountain ridges. Willows grow at the very bottom of this gorge, together with rushes, sedge, osier, and slender reeds. this was the dread home and lurking-place for the boar, the huge boar, terrible, bristling, and fierce. No greater bull than this boar roams your pastures, Epirus, and your Sicilian bull is usually smaller. His eyes blazed, bloodshot, darting fire, his brow was frightful with wrinkles. His neck bristled

	incudis instar, chalibis aut duri riget.	
	setaeque similes spiculis stant ferreo	
	vallo minantes, alba dimanat toris	
sig. C 4ᵛ	stridore vasto spuma, per rictus fluens.	820
	aequatur Indis dentibus vis dentium,	
	mistumque ab ore fulmen et tonitru vomit.	
	excitus antro, talis ac tantus furens	
	medios in hostes fertur, incursu gravem	
	trahens ruinam, sternitur tanto nemus.	825
	repente clamor oritur immensus canum,	
	hominumque cornuumque et ornorum fragor.	
	ille ruit, atque ut quisque se forte obtulit,	
	ictu prementes dissipat gemino canes.	
	hastile primum Echionis missum manu	830
	inane fuit, et vulnere in trunco leve	
	constitit acerno. proximum, nisi robore	
	nimio volasset, tergore haesisset feri.	
	longius it, author cuspidis Iason fuit.	
	ardescit ira setiger, et ignem vomit,	835
	velutique nervo grandis adducto volat	
	impulsa moles, arduas turres petens.	
	sic impete omni fertur in iuvenes aper.	
	cecidisset ictu Nestor oppressus gravi,	
	sed leviter hasta nixus apposita, arboris	840
	insiliit alte quae stetit ramis prope,	
	hostemque celso despicit intus loco.	
	ast ille dentes stipite in querno terens,	
	iam iam ruinam spectat, et caedi imminet.	
	rostroque fortis hausit Orithyae femur.	845
	geminique fratres Tyndari, invictum genus,	
	hastae periti, vulnera dedissent apro,	
	nisi per opaca callidus sylvae loca	
	isset, nec ulli pervias iaculo vias.	
sig. C 5ʳ	sequitur furentem concito Telamon gradu	850
	studioque eundi incautus, arborea cadit	
	radice pronus, dumque eum Peleus levat,	
	Atalanta flexis cornibus celerem expulit	
	arcu sagittam. at illa distrinxit feri	
	sub aure summum corpus, et setas levi	855
	cruore tinxit. erubuit omnis cohors,	
	pudorque vires addit, atque animos viri	
	clamore tollunt. densa telorum volat	
	sine ordine acies, turba coniectis nocet.	

817. *calibis* lib. 831. *levi* liber sed cf. Ov., *Met.* VIII.346

with its shaggy mane, like an anvil or hard steel. His bristles, like spears, stood threatening in a palisade, and white froth dripped over his muscles, drooling from his maw as loudly he grunted. The menace of his tusks equalled that of Indian elephants, and from his mouth he belched mixed thunder and lightning. Goaded from his cave, thus by nature and such in size, he came raging into the midst of his enemies, sowing ruin, and the grove was flattened by such a massive beast. Suddenly the dogs set up a great yowling, there was a clamor of men, trumpets, and birds. The boar came rushing, and as each one chanced to stand in his way he despatched the harassing dogs with his double blow. The shaft first launched by Echion's hand was in vain, and struck a glancing blow in a maple trunk. The next cast would have stuck in the animal's back, if it had not been thrown with excessive force. It carried too far, and Jason was the thrower. The bristly one blazed with anger, belching fire. As when a huge rock is shot by a catapult, aimed at high battlements, thus the boar attacked the youth, with full force. Nestor would perhaps have been felled by his great onrush, but he leaned on his planted spear, vaulted high into the branches of a nearby tree, and peered down on his enemy from this lofty perch. But the boar, whetting his tusks on an oak tree, gravely gashed the the thigh of Orithya's son with his snout. The twin sons of Tyndarus, scions of an indomitable family, skilled at the javelin, would have wounded the boar if he had not cunningly entered the dense brush were no spear could travel. Telamon dashed after the raging boar and, incautious in his movement, tripped on a tree-root and fell. While Peleus was raising him up, Atalanta bent her her bow and shot a swift arrow, but it only grazed the animal behind his ear and dyed his bristles with a trickle of blood. The whole band blushed and their embarrassment lent them strength. The men raised their spirits with a shout. A thick barrage of spears went flying in disorder, and the

> quis fando narret cuncta, tot discrimina, 860
> tot ausa iuvenum clara, tot strages canum?
> sed inter omnes prima Meleagri fuit
> et summa virtus. obviam quoties apro
> occurrit ardens? comminus quoties caput
> offert periclo? nec deest tantis minor 865
> fortuna caeptis, sed favens dextram adiuvat.
> binisque missis, altera in tergo stetit,
> hasta alia fronte. dumque iam volvit minas,
> corpusque in orbem versat, et spumam novo
> cruore fundit, vulnera ingeminans, premit, 870
> hastamque in armos condit adversos apri.
> clamore tota, more venantum, cohors
> exultat, et iam quaeque victricem petit
> tractare dextram dextra. terribilem suem
> tellure multa vix recumbentem undique 875
> mirantur omnes, vixque adhuc tutum satis
> contigere putant, fronte sic torva iacet,
> sic ardet oculis, ore sic toto est minax.
> venabula tamen quisque iam tingit sua.

sig. C 5ᵛ
> hic ordo pugnae, caedis haec series fuit. 880
> ad regiam ipse concitos gressus fero.

VENATORES, MELEAGER, ATALANTA, PLEXIPPVS, TOXEVS

Canunt in scena.

> publicum, cives, celebrate festum,
> occidit frendens aper. ecce torvi
> oris, et tergi spolium cruentum.
> victimas aris date, thura flammis. 885
> tota deducat Calydon superbum
>   laeta triumphum.
>
> o diem laetum peragant coloni,
> tuta iam canas segetes aristis
> proferat tellus, onerata vitis 890
> pampinos fundat gravidos racemis.
> tota deducat Calydon superbum
>   laeta triumphum.

---

861. *iuveuum* lib.: corr. Brooke, script. inedit.

number of missiles ruined their aim. Who can relate everything, all the perils, all the youths' bold deeds, all the dogs killed? But Meleager's virtue was first and foremost. In his ardor, how often did he put himself in the boar's way? How often did he risk his life by fighting at close quarters? Now no lesser fortune proved unequal to such great endeavors, but favorably aided his hand. He throws two spears, of which one plants in the back, the other in the chest. Now, as the boar issues threats, whirls himself in a circle, and pours forth a froth of flesh blood, complaining of his wound, Meleager presses home his attack by planting a spear in the beast's shoulder. After the manner of hunters, the whole company rejoiced with a shout and now everyone wanted to shake the victor's hand. Everybody stood about, admiring the terrible pig barely stretched out over much ground, scarcely thinking it safe to touch it. Thus it lay with its fierce face, thus its eyes glared, thus it was threatening with its great snout. Each man dyed his spears in its blood. This is the sequence of the fight, this is the order of the slaughter. I hasten to the palace. [*Exit, enter the hunters.*]

HUNTERS, MELEAGER, ATALANTA, PLEXIPPUS, TOXEUS

They sing on the stage. [As they enter, Meleager is carrying the boar's hide and head.]

Citizens, celebrate a public holiday, the gnashing boar is dead. See the bloody spoil of its savage head and hide. Give victims to the altars, incense to the fire. Let all Calydon merrily celebrate a proud triumph.

Oh, let our farmers keep a happy holiday, let the earth, now safe, bear long-bearded crops on its cornstalks. Let the laden vine produce bursting grape-clusters on its shoots. Let all Calydon merrily celebrate a proud triumph.

		turba pastorum celebret choreas,	
		fronde velentur iuvenes senesque.	895
		nulla iam pestis pecori minatur,	
		pascuis gramen sine strage carpat.	
		tota deducat Calydon superbum	
		laeta triumphum.	

MEL. generosa Theseu, vosque tantorum inclyti 900
socii laborum, dona quae tantis rear
factis rependi posse? dii certe optima,
virtusque vestra reddet, haud nostrae est opis
paria tribuere. quas tamen grates queo
superis fecundas refero, maiores pater 905

sig. C 6ʳ et tota Calydon solvet. exuviae apri
ex lege nostras interim dono datas
Atalanta, nostri iuris atque animi cape
indicia, et altae signa virtutis tuae,
meumque tecum veniat in partem decus. 910

AT. magnanime Meleager, quid effari queam?
animumne fortem et dexteram bello inclytam,
an liberalem, nescio admirer magis,
suspicio utrumque. quod dabo munus tuo
aequale merito? verba quae digna efferam? 915
sed tu pudori virginis veniam dabis,
quod paria factis verba concipiam minus.
haec pauca referam: sive cum sylvas petam
memorabo sylvis, sive per montes eam
implebo montes, gratiae tantae memor. 920
ubicunque vivam, nullus oblitam tui
meriti videbit, nullus ingratam dies.

PLEX. Toxeu, quid agitur? ista praeripiet viris
insigne honorum? inglorii nos patriam
repetemus? ista sola de nobis domum 925
ibit triumphans, et superbifica manu
spolium per urbes ducet Argolicas apri?

TOX. Plexippe, semper mihi neget reditum deus,
si tale nobis dedecus inuri sinam.
at tu proinde faemina, viriles, age, 930
depone titulos. forma quae nimium tua
istum fefellit, quaeso ne tanti putes
ut capiat omnes. en tuo praeter modum est
amore captus muneris tanti dator.

Let a throng of herdsmen celebrate with dancing, let young and old wear garlands. Now no plague threatens our cattle, let them graze at pasture without harm. Let all Calydon merrily celebrate a proud triumph.

MEL. Noble Theseus, and you, famous partners in such great efforts, what gifts should I think able to repay such great deeds? Surely the gods, and your own courage, have given us splendid things, and our resources are scarcely adequate to repay you fully. However, what rich tokens of thanks I have I shall offer to the gods, and my father and all Calydon will give even greater. Meanwhile, Atalanta, according to our pact, accept these proofs of my authority and of my disposition, emblems of your high virtue, and let a share of my glory be imparted to you. [*He gives her the head and hide.*]

AT. High-minded Meleager, what can I say? I do not know which to admire more, your brave spirit and famous handiwork in battle, or that you are generous. I esteem them both. What gift can I give equal in worth to yours? What fitting words can I utter? But you will forgive a maiden's bashfulness, if I should find words scarcely equal to your gesture. I shall say just this: if I seek the forest, I shall remember you there, if I pass through the mountains, I shall fill them with your praises, mindful of such a great act of favor. Wherever I shall dwell, no day will find me forgetful of your kindness, none will find me ungrateful.

PLEX. [*Aside.*] What's happening, Toxeus? Is she snatching this badge of honor from the men? Must we seek our homeland dishonored? Out of all of us, will she alone go home in triumph, carrying the boar's trophy through the cities of Aetolia in her vainglorious hand?

TOX. [*Aside.*] Plexippus, may the god always refuse me a homecoming if I permit us to be branded with such shame. [*Aloud.*] Come, woman, put down those manly honors. You have bewitched this fellow with your beauty, but I beg you not to overestimate it, thinking that it enchants everyone. The donor of this gift is love-smitten to excess.

sig. C 6ᵛ

MEL. Thestiadae avunculi, quis hic vestris furor 935
incessit animis? spolia meruisse est nefas?
aut mea dedisse cui libet, tantum scelus?
quid torva inanes fronte iactantur minae?
quid me cruento et lumine aspicitis truci?

PLEX. sic collocari munus egregium decet? 940
tanti pericli terror hunc feret exitum?
hanc quisque labem referet ad patrios lares?
haec posteris mandata dedecoris nota,
tanta in cohorte faeminam victoriae
retulisse palmam?

MEL.   scilicet, num vos decet 945
tanta in cohorte avunculos solos, decus
partum nepoti praeripere velle invidos?
an tale facinus gloriae vobis erit?
sed illa spolium referet, et digna est, aprum
quae sauciavit prima, quae virgo, viris 950
virtute par est, genere, factis, dextera.

TOX. horrenda setis terga, et ora haec dentibus
Indis tremenda, faeminae dextram decent?

MEL. invidia vos decuit, et iniustus furor?

PLEX. iustam excitavit magnanimus iram dolor. 955

MEL. at causa nostri iustior doni fuit.

TOX. male collocati muneris?

MEL.   rapti magis?

PLEX. iniusta querimur.

MEL.   iusta raptores probat?

TOX. quae causa iusta?

MEL.   dexterae virtus meae.

PLEX. quid nostra?

MEL.   litis plena, et invidia tumes. 960

MEL. My Thestian uncles, what insanity has invaded your minds? Is it wrong to have deserved the spoils? Or was it such a crime for me to have given them to whom I wished? Why are these empty threats being hurled, with so much frowning? Why look at me with such a bloodthirsty, truculent stare?

PLEX. Is it proper for such an outstanding gift thus to be bestowed? Is this the outcome of the terror we experienced in the face of such danger? Will each of us take back this infamy to our ancestral hearths? Is this brand of shame to be reported to posterity, that a woman carried off victory's palm?

MEL. And I suppose it is proper that out of this entire band only my jealous uncles wish to get their hands on the prize won by their nephew? Will such a misdeed redound to your glory? But let her carry off the spoils. She is deserving because she was first to wound the boar, and she is the equal of us men in courage, breeding, deeds, and the ability of her hand.

TOX. Are this hide, rough with bristles, and this head, fierce with its ivory tusks, suitable for a woman's hand?

MEL. Were jealousy or unjust rage suitable for you?

PLEX. Great-spirited chagrin provoked out legitimate outrage.

MEL. But the grounds for my giving were more legitimate.

TOX. Of a gift given badly?

MEL. Better for it to be stolen?

PLEX. We are complaining about injustice.

MEL. Does justice approve of thieves?

TOX. What are the grounds for this justice of yours?

MEL. The strength of my good right hand.

PLEX. What about our justice?

MEL. It is full of contention, and you are swollen with jealousy.

	TOX.	tua sola virtus?
	MEL.	fateor, auxilium tulit Atalanta.
	PLEX.	nempe contulit magnum.
	MEL.	minus Thestiada uterque.
	TOX.	viribus vestris aper solisne iacuit? ergo quid procerum cohors?
	MEL.	vestrisne cecidit?
sig. C 7ʳ	PLEX.	turpis ut mentem abstulit amoris ardor!

965

MEL. ut furor vestram magis!
sed quid ago, facti ratio reddenda est mei?
placuisse satis est, placuit, et iam perplacet.
mea sunt, dedi, sic libuit, et sic iam libet.

TOX. o turpitudo, et impudens animi furor! 970
Oenida tumide, iam furere pergis palam?
libidini deserviet noster tuae
sanguisque honorque? tantus huc cecidit labor?

MEL. equidem reprimere verba, et audaces malo
poteram domare, sed sibi fraenum mea 975
iniiciet ira. quemque vos linguis modum
non retinuistis, nostra servabit manus.

PLEX. domare poteras? tune? quos? unus duos?
nepos avunculos? virum placidum scias.
libet experiri dexteram et patientiam 980
domitoris huius. pone tu exuvias apri,
nec intuere praemii authorem, nihil
iuvabit ille. pone, vel ferro lues.

Utrique latus subito pugione fodit.

962 et 965. *PEX.* lib.: corr. Brooke, script. inedit.   966. *ardor?...magis?* lib.   975. *peteram* lib.

TOX. Virtue is yours alone?

MEL. I admit that Atalanta helped me.

PLEX. Oh yes, she helped you greatly.

MEL. The sons of Thestius were both less useful.

TOX. Was the boar laid low by your strength alone? What about the band of princes?

MEL. Did he fall by *your* strength?

PLEX. How love's ardor has taken away your wits!

MEL. Rather, how madness has destroyed yours! But what am I doing that I must justify to you? It is enough that I be pleased. This has pleased me, and now it pleases me utterly. These things are mine, I have them, and such remains my will.

TOX. Oh, the shame, the impudent madness of his mind! Proud son of Oeneus, do you now strive to make a public display of your folly? Will our blood and station play the slave to your whim? Has all our effort thus gone for naught?

MEL. For my part, I was able to still your words and subdue you fellows, bold for evil, but my wrath will impose a bridle on itself. My hand will observe the moderation you two have failed to place on your tongues.

PLEX. You were able to subdue us? You? Whom? One against two? A nephew against his uncles? You ought to know I am a man of peace. I wish to test the hand and patience of this tamer of ours. [*To Atalanta.*] You, put down the boar's spoils, nor look to the man who gave you the gift. He will not help you. Put them down, or you will pay the penalty by my steel. (*Meleager suddenly stabs them both in the side with a dagger.*)

MEL.	uterque honoris discite rapaces mei,	
	quid dextra linguae, facta quid distent minis.	985
	sic pereat, atra quisquis invidia tumet.	
	tu spolia recipe parta bis nostra manu.	
AT.	dii paria meritis pretia pro tantis tibi,	
	Meleagre, solvant. quam tamen mallem, minus	
	forent cruenta!	
MEL.	quem locum profugus petam?	990
	ubi me cruento matris aspectu auferam?	
	quae verba nectam? quo feram vultu graves	
	charae sororis caede fraterna minas?	
	qua fronte caedem, qua facinus arte occulam?	
	atque ecce laetum mater huc affert gradum.	995
	hei mihi, tegantur corpora in medio abdita.	

sig. C 7ᵛ

Proiicit pugionem sanguine stillantem.

ALTHAEA, THESEVS, MELEAGER, ATALANTA

<ALTH.> quae digna vestrae merita virtuti feram,
invicta iuvenum turma? victrices iuvat
videre dextras. fama quamprimum ad meas
pervenit aures caedis et victoriae,   1000
ut gratularer in viam memet dedi.
faelici reditum laetus eventu meus
expectat Oeneus. sed quid hoc? quid vis tibi?
quid ora, nate, vertis, et fletu rigas?
quae causa fletus? sicne venientem excipis?   1005
quid maesta vultus tota conticuit cohors?
narrate, fratres. tune quoque, Toxeu, siles?
Plexippe, mutus? quid mali factum est novi?
adeste, fratres, nemo respondet? soror
fratres voco. quid hoc rei? fratres voco.   1010
fratres, ubi estis? sistite in medio palam!
Meleager, ubi fratres? silet, maeret, gemit.
te per tuorum facinorum laudes precor,
Theseu, tuique nominis famam inclyti,
quae causa luctus fare. cur fratres latent?   1015
nihil iis receptis accidere durum potest.

990. *cruenta?* lib. 994. *caedem?* lib. 1002. *faelice* lib. 1011. *palam?* lib.

MEL. Both of you thieves of my honor, learn the difference between my hand and your tongue, between action and threats. Thus let die whoever swells with black envy. [*To Atalanta.*] Take back the spoils, twice bestowed by the gods.

AT. Meleager, may the gods recompense you with just rewards for your kindnesses. But how I would wish they were less bloody!

MEL. As a fugitive, what place should I seek? Where might I remove myself from my mother's bloodthirsty gaze? What words should I contrive? With what appearance should I endure the heavy threats of a beloved sister, about the killing of her brothers? With what countenance, with what art should I conceal this murder, my crime? And see, my mother makes her happy way here. Woe is me, let the bodies lying here in the open be covered. (*He throws away the dagger, dripping blood.* [*Someone conceals the bodies with a cloak. Enter Althaea.*])

ALTH. What things worthy of your courage can I offer, indomitable band of youths? It is a pleasure to see your victorious hands. As soon as rumor of the killing and of your victory reached my ears, I took the road so I might congratulate you. My Oeneus joyously awaits your return with its happy outcome. [*She sees the covered corpses.*] But what's this? What do you mean? Why avert your face, son, and cry? What's the cause of your weeping? Is this how you receive someone who comes to meet you? Why does the entire band remain silent with glum looks? Tell me, brothers. Toxeus, are you silent too? Plexippus, are you mute? What new evil has occurred? Come forward, brothers, will nobody answer? As a sister, I call to my brothers. What is this thing? I am calling my brothers. Where are you, brothers? Show yourselves. Meleager, where are my brothers? He's silent and mournful, he groans. I beg you. Theseus, by the glory of your achievements, tell me the cause of this grief. Why are my brothers hiding? Once I receive them back, no harsh thing can happen.

	THE.	regina, clarum gentis Aetoli decus,
		cur me adgemendae sortis indicium vocas?
		saepe odit ingens indicem cladis dolor.
		verum, cum abire tacita sic nequeant mala 1020
		ut te laterent semper, optarim licet
sig. C 8ʳ		alium doloris indicem faceres tui,
		invita placide verba ut accipias, precor.
	ALTH.	sermone mentem gravius incertam tenes.
		effare, ubi sunt? non amat pietas moram. 1025
	THE.	uterque caesus inter extinctos iacet.
	ALTH.	quod facinus aures pepulit? extinctus iacet
		uterque? Theseu, verba detestor tua.
	THE.	tibi ecce certam faciat aspectus fidem.
	ALTH.	quas misera voces, misera quos gemitus dabo? 1030

planctusque quos? quae verba sint cladi satis?
demissa cerno capita, et imbelles manus,
et ora morte pallida, et vultus truces.
talesne vos aspicio redeuntes soror?
hic est triumphus? festa promissa est dies.   1035
haec illa, tristis, improba, execrabilis?
haec illa nostri cura, crudeles, fuit?
huc crebra, superi, vota redierunt mea?
Plexippe, vultum attolle, vel, Toxeu, tuum.
en osculatur, haeret amplexu soror.   1040
sed heu, querelis tota abit frustra dies.
quaeratur author caedis. incolumes apro
caeso fuisse, nuncius retulit mihi.
differte gemitus, dicite authorem necis.
an fraus, an ensis? casus an fatum fuit?   1045
quid spectat alter alterum? cunctamini?
furit ira in omnes. cur meos, Theseu, fugit
Meleager oculos? ora cur condit sua?
tu, Castor, ede, sed tua, Castor, fide.
tu fare, Pollux, Perithoe, Peleu refer,   1050
Leucippe, Telamon, Nestor, Eurithion, Lelex,

sig. C 8ᵛ Acaste, Phaenix, tuque Laerte impiger,
aut aliquis alter. nil dolor moveat meus?
en quisque gemitus reddit occultos. quid hoc?
quid est silendum? tacita sic abeant mala?   1055
celare stultum est, quod statim fiet palam.

THES. Queen, great glory of the Aetolian race, why ask me for an explanation of this misfortune? Great sorrow often hates the man who reports a death. But truly, since these evils will not disappear if we keep them silent so that you will never learn of them, and although I would prefer that you would make someone else the one to inform you of your sorrow, I beg that you calmly hear my unwilling words.

ALTH. Your mind is even more hesitant than your speech. Tell me, where are they? My duty to them admits no delay.

THES. Both of them are slain, and lie among the dead.

ALTH. What foul deed strikes my ears? Both are dead? Theseus, I detest what you say.

THES. [*Uncovering the corpses.*] Behold, let this sight give you sure proof.

ALTH. In my misery, what shall I say, what wails shall I utter? What words suffice for this slaughter? I see their lolling heads, limp hands, faces pallid in death, their grimaces. Is it thus that I, your sister, see you returning? Is this the triumph? Is this the promised festive day, sad, evil, and hateful? Cruel men, is this what became of my care? Gods, is this how my manifold hopes returned to me? Lift your head, Plexippus; lift yours, Toxeus. See, your sister kisses and embraces you. But, alas, the entire day is vainly squandered on lamentation. Let the murderer be found. The messenger told me they were safe when the boar was killed. Put off your groaning, tell me who committed the murder. Was it by deceit or by the sword? By accident or predestined? Why do they look at each other? Are you delaying? My anger rages against the lot of you. Theseus, why is Meleager avoiding my eyes? Why does he hang his head? You tell me, Castor, but on your oath. You tell me, Pollux, Perithous. Inform me, Peleus, Leucippus, Telamon, Nestor, Eurythion, Lelex, Acastus, Phoenix, and you, industrious Laertes. Or someone else. Does my grief not move you? See, each man groans inwardly. What's this? Why keep silent. Should these evils go away, if kept quiet? Surely this is foolish, since the matter will soon be revealed.

MEL.	me me roga. adsum qui neci fratres dedi!	
	homines deosque testor, et sylvam, et feras,	
	invita tantum facinus admisit manus,	
	et caedis ipse primus exemplum horrui.	1060
	miserere, mater.	

ALTH.   magne regnator poli,
tam lentus audis scelera. vidisti, pater,
nec vindicasti, digna supplicia expetens?
nec adhuc trisulcum dextera telum evolat?
cessas adhuc, iniuste? quin rimas agis   1065
effracta tellus, tuque dominator Stygis,
specus ad imos Tartari sontem rapis,
meritamque paenam infligis? o scelus! o nefas!

MEL.   miserere mater, filium caedis reum
habes fatentem, nec sit idcirco salus   1070
culpam fateri. vincla patiantur manus,
caeci rigente carceris clauder specu,
nihil recuso si licet causam tamen
dicere. peracta quamlibet paenam impera.

ALTH.   o impudentem! causa quae reddi potest   1075
facinore digna?

MEL.   causa dicatur tamen,
quae tollere quidem ut nequeat, imminuat scelus.
miserere, tantum postulo causam audias.

ALTH.   miserere? vix iam misera contineo manus,
quin in capillos involem et vultus tuos.   1080
nil deprecaris? sufficit paene dolor,
noli excitare. desine, ingrate, obstrepis.
Atalanta, fare, causa quae caedis fuit?

AT.   Oenea coniux, Thestii clarum genus,
hoc oro primum, ut concitam mentem domes,   1085
et verba placido pectore accipias mea.
ut gesta res est eloquar. dolor hic tuus,
sed culpa fratrum est, non habet factum hoc scelus.
virtute postquam setiger nati occidit,
spolium superbum tergi, et invidiae capax,   1090
me ferre voluit praemium victor suum.

sig. D 1ʳ

1057. *dedi?* lib.   1076. *Eacinore* lib.: corr. in Vict. & Alb. vol.

MEL. Ask me, me. I am present, who killed your brothers. I call men and the gods, the forests and beasts, to witness that my hand did such an act unwillingly, and I myself was the first to shudder at the example of this murder. Have pity, mother.

ALTH. Great ruler of heaven, how sluggishly you hear of this crime! Father, did you see this and not take vengeance, devising a worthy punishment? Has the forked missile not yet left your hand? Are you still hesitating, unjust one? Earth, why not break asunder and yawn, and you, ruler of the Styx, snatch this sinner to the nethermost caverns of Tartarus, inflicting a deserved punishment. Oh, the crime! Oh, the sin!

MEL. Have pity, mother. You have a son confessing his guilt for the murder. Nor let it be my salvation to confess my guilt. Let my hands endure chains, let me be pent up in the chill cavern of a dark dungeon, I refuse nothing as long as I am allowed to plead my case. When I am done, ordain whatever punishment you desire.

ALTH. Oh, the impudent man! What defense can be offered fit for such a deed?

MEL. Let my plea nevertheless be said, which, although it cannot remove my guilt, may lessen the offense. Have pity. I only ask that you hear my defense.

ALTH. Have pity? In my wretchedness I can scarcely restrain my hands, lest I fly at your hair, your face. You don't beg forgiveness? My grief is scarcely under control, don't arouse it. Cease interrupting me, ingrate. Atalanta, tell me the murder's cause.

AT. Consort of Oeneus, born of Thestius' noble stock, first I beg that you control your aroused mind and hear my words with a calm heart. I shall tell you how the matter occurred. The sorrow is yours, but the guilt lay with your brothers, and no guilt attached to this deed. After the bristly one died by your son's bravery, the victor wanted me to bear off his reward, the proud trophy of the hide, a cause for envy. Your brothers begrudged

	tulere fratres gravius id factum tui,
	et post truces utrinque iactatas minas,
	mihi munus, illi muneris ius auferunt.
	regina, veram caedis en causam tibi.	1095

ALTH. iam iam tonandum est, Iuppiter, caelo tibi,
convolve mundum. tela, Cyclopes, date,
nec cautiore fulmen emittas manu
in hunc vel illam. quisquis ex istis cadit,
merito peribit, non potest in eos tua 1100
errare dextra. num scelere factum caret,
Atalanta? nempe liberat sceleris reum
iudex scelesta. tu mali tanti caput,
materia tute, caedis hic actor fuit.

THE. ah reprime quaeso pectoris fluctum tui, 1105
iram coerce. sint licet nati preces
satis efficaces, sed tamen nostro precor
moveare fletu. quod rogo, cuncti rogant,
pretiumque meritis filio veniam petunt.
moderare tumidum mentis iratae impetum. 1110

ALTH. absiste, Theseu, quaslibet renuo preces.
non ista luctum postulant, ira est opus,
et si quid ira est gravius, et quid tam grave est
quod facinus aequet impium? ulciscar tamen,
ulciscar inquam, dicta firmabit fides. 1115
piget cruentas aspicere saevi manus,
vultusque lanii. sustines coram, impudens,
adhuc morari? non meos oculos fugis?
vos chara, famuli, corpora auferte ocyus.

sig. D 1ᵛ

CHORVS

heu cur superi, fataque semper 1120
fera, Virtuti dominae Invidiam
voluere dari famulam nequam?
non umbra gradum magis insequitur,
quam livor edax magna gerentem.
aspera latam citius feriunt 1125
spicula metam, scutaque crebris
maiora patent obvia plagis,

1099. *in hanc, vel illam* (sic) lib.

this gesture and fierce threats were exchanged by both sides. They stole my gift and his right to bestow it. Queen, there you have the murder's true cause.

ALTH. Now, now, Jupiter, is the time for you to thunder in heaven, enveloping the universe. Cyclopes, provide your weapons. Nor be over-careful where your cast your lightning, at her or at him. Whichever falls will die justly, in their case your hand cannot err. Surely this deed isn't lacking in evil, Atalanta? For this wicked judge absolves the accused of guilt. You are the source of this great evil. You are its grounds, although he committed the murder.

THES. Ah, I pray you restrain this flood within your heart, master your anger. Although your son's entreaties ought to suffice, I beg you be moved by our weeping. What I ask, so do we all. They ask your forgiveness as the reward for his great accomplishments. Control the swollen onrush of your inflamed mind.

ALTH. Leave off, Theseus, I reject any form of entreaty. The situation does not call for mourning, there is need for wrath, for whatever is severer than wrath — and what is so severe that it matches this impious crime? But I shall be avenged, I say I shall be avenged, and my trustworthiness will confirm what I say. I am ashamed to look at the face and hands of this butcher. You bold man, can you still bear to linger in public? Won't you flee my sight? Servants, remove these bodies quickly. [*Exeunt omnes.*]

CHORUS

Alas, why did the gods and the Fates, always savage, decide to give Envy to mistress Virtue as a handmaiden? Our shadow no more dogs our steps than gnawing jealousy clings to him who does great deeds. Sharp arrows more quickly strike the broad target, the larger

scopulosque altos verberat unda.
sic invidiae metaque virtus
et praeda iacet. fulgur montes, 1130
culmina livor summumque petit.
non est monstris tanta domandis
causa timendi, quanta malignis.
non superantur fortibus ausis.
crescente magis virtute fremunt, 1135
nulli dentes parcere norunt.
huic terga daret Virtus monstro,
nisi pulchra foret gloria merces.
haec languentes erigit artus,
haec facit atros spernere morsus. 1140

shields receive more frequent blows, waves beat against the tall cliffs. Thus virtue is target and prey for envy. Lightning strikes mountains, jealousy attacks the summits. Monsters who require subjugation are not such a cause for fear as are men of ill will. They are not conquered by brave deeds. As virtue grows they grumble the more, no teeth know how to be sparing. Virtue would turn her back on this monster in flight, unless glory was her fair reward. This stimulates her languid limbs, this makes her scorn the sharp biting.

- Actus Quartus -

sig. D 2ʳ

NVTRIX SOLA

Candentes carbones in scenam effert.

    quam saevus urit regiam mentem dolor!
    ubi ponet ira pondus, ac fluctus graves?
    nam caedis ex quo patuit admissae nefas,
    similis furenti incessit, ac volvit minas
    Oenea coniux. saeva ut in trepidum pecus   1145
    viduata catulis tygris horrendum fremit.
    nunc ora pallent, ira nunc oculis trucem
    ciet ruborem. vultus est illi modo
    similis minaci nescio quid barbarum
    dirumque, modo quem velle misereri putes.   1150
    cumque illa doleat, propior est irae tamen,
    odioque cumque lacrymas animi ferus
    siccavit ardor, lacrymas fundit tamen.
    atque ut carina, quam mari prensam Affrico,
    hinc ventus, illinc aestus adversam rapit,   1155
    incerta nescit qua magis currat via,
    affectibus regina sic errat suis,
    iraeque ponit invicem ac tollit minas.
    me iussit arae fragmina ac taedas dare.
    "stat," inquit, "aliqua victima fratrum leves   1160
    placare manes, abeat ut praesens dolor."

Accendit ligna in ara, in remotiore scenae parte exstructa.

NVTRIX, ALTHAEA

   <NVT.> atque ecce, demens ipsa prosiliit foras.
       en ut furoris signa lymphati gerit,

sig. D 2ᵛ   et omnis aptum specimen affectus capit!

   ALTH. si quaeris odio quem tuo statuas modum,   1165
       propone fratres. quos egone letho datos
       inulta patiar? liberum hoc ibit scelus?
       fruetur Oeneus filio, ut careat meus
       Thestius utroque? quam melius ambo gemant!
       quonam ista tendit turba Furiarum, inferis   1170

1141. *dolor?* lib.   1149. *minati* lib.   1157. *sicerrat* lib.   1158. *invicim* lib.   1169. *gemant?* lib.

- Act IV -

A NURSE, ALONE

She carries glowing coals onto the stage.

What savage pain burns the queen's mind! Where will her anger discharge its burden, and her great turmoil? For since the time the guilt of this confessed murder has been exposed, Oeneus' wife has paced about like a madwoman, issuing threats, as a tigress, bereft of her cubs, horribly roars against the cowering herd. Now she grows pale, now her wrath makes her eyes glow fiercely red. At one moment her expression that of someone threatening I don't know what kind of dire barbarous act, at the next you'd think she wants to be merciful. When she grieves she is still close to anger, but when the wild ardor of her mind dries her tears with hatred, still she weeps. And as a skiff on the high seas, gripped by the South wind, is borne in one direction by the breeze, another by the tide, so she is uncertain which route to take. Thus the queen wanders in her emotions, thus in turn she sets aside and renews her anger's threats. She bade me place faggots and pine-chips on the fire, saying "Let some sacrifice be placed on the altar to satisfy my brothers' insubstantial shades, so that my present sorrow may depart." [*She kindles the wood on an altar constructed on one side of the stage.*]

And see, dementedly she rushes outside. See how she bears the signs of frantic madness, wholly assuming the symptoms peculiar to this disease. [*Enter Althaea, from Diana's temple.*]

ALTH. If you ask what limit to place on my hatred for you, produce my brothers. Should I allow them to be given over to death without exacting vengeance? Will this crime go scot-free? Shall Oeneus enjoy a son, so that my Thestius might lack the both of his? How better for both to mourn! Where goes this troop of Furies, sent from Hell? Whose

emissa? cuius umbra perfosso venit
cruenta latere? frater est Toxeus, vides?
an sola video? atque ecce Plexippi venit
furens imago. quid sibi fratres volunt?
quid vultis? eia supplicia petitis? dabo.　　　　　　　　　　1175
manes ad imos ire securos licet.
abite, fratres, quid petitis? inquam dabo.
desiste, oro. genibus advolui, dabo.
mihi me relinquite, ista sufficiet manus,
et stipes iste.

NVT.　　　　　　facere quid tandem paras?　　　　　　1180
quonam iste telo tantus utetur dolor?

ALTH.　hunc intuere stipitem, teli est satis,
hic paena abunde est, hic puta vitam ac necem,
Meleager ipse stipite sub isto latet.
quem, cum iacerem pondus enixa impium,　　　　　　1185
ingressa thalamos turba Parcarum meos,
imposuit igni, pariter et fati colo
stamen trahentes. "paria," dixerunt "tibi,
o nate nuper, tempora ac ligno damus."
quo carmine effato, exeunt tectis deae.　　　　　　1190
at ipsa stratis territa exilii meis,
lymphisque sparsi. exinde servatus diu,
servavit illum, proh dolor, nimium diu.

sig. D 3ʳ　hoc sola sensi, coniugem hoc semper meum
celavi, et omnes hactenus visum latet.　　　　　　1195
sed referet eadem quae rapuit olim manus.
nomen sororis perdidi, at matris manet.
vel hoc perempto tam diu cessat manus?

NVT.　regina, clarum familiae lumen tuae,
nefanda matris pectore exturba ocius,　　　　　　1200
quantumque tentas cogita. natum cremas,
pene innocentem, cuius extremus dies
primusque laudes novit, et iuxta deos
cui tota caeso patria acceptam refert
apro salutem. en hunc paras flammis dare.　　　　　　1205
quod stipes omnes iste mortales latet,
an ergo demens credis hoc tantum nefas
omnia videntes posse celari deos?
impune superi facinus occultum sinant:

1204. *paetria* lib.

ghost is this with a stab-wound in his side? It's brother Toxeus, do you see? Or do I alone see him? And look, here comes the furious specter of Plexippus. What do my brothers want? What do you want? Hey, you seek punishment? I shall grant it. You ghosts may go to the Netherworld in confidence. Go away, brothers, what are you seeking? I say I shall give it. Stop, I beg. I have fallen to my knees. I shall give it. Leave me to myself, this hand will suffice, and this log.

NURSE What at last are you preparing to do? What weapon is your great sorrow to use?

ALTH. Look at this log, it is a sufficient weapon. This is punishment in abundance, consider it life and death. Meleager himself lurks within this log. When I lay after giving birth to his unholy mass, a crew of Fates entered my bedchamber and placed this log on the fire, at the same time drawing his life's thread on their distaff. "Oh newborn child," they said, "we give you and this wood the same span of life." Having issued this prophecy the goddesses left the house. But in my terror I sprang up out of my bedclothes and doused it with water. Since then it has long been preserved and has preserved him (oh, the sorrow!) far too long. I alone knew this, I always concealed it from my husband, and until now my vision has been kept from everyone. But the same hand that snatched it up will retrieve it. I have lost the name of sister, but that of mother remains. But with that name lost, why does my hand hesitate so long?

NURSE Queen, bright light of your family, banish these unspeakable things from a mother's heart, think what you are attempting. You are burning your son, almost innocent, all but innocent, whose first and last day have known praise, to whom (next to the gods) our entire nation credited its safety when the boar was slain. Lo, you are making ready to consign him to the flames. Because all mortals are ignorant of this log, are you so foolish as to think that you can conceal such a crime from the all-seeing gods? But suppose the gods should let this secret deed go unpunished. Do you think yourself free of danger, and

	expers pericli credis, ac vacuum metu?	1210
	erras. quid iste conscius facti locus?	
	quid plena mens horrore, diffidens sibi,	
	cuncta expavescens? ipse quid trepidae stupor,	
	pallorque vultus? noctis et somni minae?	
	ut lateat omnes, haud lateat animum tuum.	1215
	hoc mille testes pectore, hic paenae est satis.	
	ecce aderit omni filii extincti loco	
	feralis umbra, cumque nox operit diem,	
	armata facibus veniet, et furiis aget.	
	te per tuorum gloriam, ac patriae decus,	1220
	per iura matrum, per decem mensum grave	
	gestamen uteri, perque natorum oscula,	
	per sceptra regni, per beatorum domos,	
sig. D 3ᵛ	per inferorum posita sceleratis loca,	
	denique per omne quicquid in vita fuit,	1225
	aut est, eritve, pectori gratum, precor,	
	extingue flammas, excidat stipes manu,	
	et te parentem filio mitem refer.	
ALTH.	detinuit aures sermo nequicquam tuus,	
	egone ut inulta perferam tantum nefas?	1230
	mors est pianda morte, funus funere,	
	furor furore, scelere pensandum est scelus.	
	nefanda pleno corruat luctu domus.	
	quid has aniles obiicis nugas mihi?	
	contempsit istas, quae prius sprevit mori.	1235
	cruenta mater, at soror dicar pia,	
	domusque nostra vindicis nomen feram.	
	sumpsisse paenas improbi, et fratrum graves	
	satiassse manes efferar, saltem pia	
	iuvabit animum explesse vindicta meum.	1240
	pietatis iste sufficit titulus mihi,	
	satis iste tumulo ad gloriam inscriptus meo,	
	PIAE SORORIS, IMPIAE MATRIS VIDES,	
	VLTRICIS ALTHAEAE SEPVLCHRVM NOBILE.	
	quid sacra cesso?	
NVT.	nulla te pietas movet?	1245
ALTH.	excede pietas omnis. in fratres tamen	
	maneat sororis, abeat expulsus timor.	
	Odrysia coniux veniat in mentem. soror	

1219. *fariis* lib.

free of fear? You are wrong. what about this place itself, aware of the deed? What about your mind, filled with horror, mistrusting itself, dreading everything? What about your very numbness, the pale cast of your countenance? What about the menaces of sleep and the night? Suppose this act is hidden from everyone: it will not be hidden from your mind. Hence there will be a thousand witnesses in your breast, here is sufficient punishment. Look here, the ferocious ghost of your dead son will be present everywhere, and when night has fallen on the day his savage shade will come, armed with torches, and will hound you with Furies. I beg you by your people's glory, the splendor of your nation, the laws of motherhood, by your nine months' heavy task of bearing him in the womb, by your children's kisses, by the kingdom's scepter, by the dwellings of the Blessed, by the regions of Hell reserved for sinners, and finally by all in your life that was, is, or will be dear to your heart, extinguish the flames, drop the log, and show yourself a gentle mother to your son.

ALTH. Your talk has filled my ears to no good purpose. Should I tolerate such a crime without gaining vengeance? Death must be expiated by death, killing by killing, madness by madness, crime must be repaid by a crime. Let this unspeakable house collapse, full of wailing. Why cast this old woman's foolishness in my teeth? She who previously scorned to die has come to have contempt for these things. I shall be called a bloody mother, but a loyal sister, I shall bear the name of champion of this house. I shall gain a reputation for exacting punishment on a malefactor and for having given satisfaction to my brothers' grim ghosts, and indeed it will give me pleasure to have fulfilled my intention with dutiful revenge. This name gained for piety is enough for me, sufficient for my reputation this inscription on my tomb: "You see the grave of a pious sister, though an impious mother. This is the noble sepulchre of Althaea the avenger." Why am I delaying the rites?

NURSE Does no piety move you?

ALTH. All piety, depart. Let a sister's piety towards my brothers remain, but may all timidity disappear, banished. Let the Thracian consort come to mind. As your sister,

		tua, Philomela, me decet Prognen sequi,	1250
		et causa similis postulat similes manus.	
	NVT.	istane credis victima fratrum graves	
		placare manes? quando in inferias homo	
		impensus homini est? avunculis quando nepos?	
sig. D 4ʳ		a matre quando natus? invidia tuos	1255
		onerare fratres, quos colis scelere, apparas.	
		gratare potius filio genetrix tuo,	
		namque iste vivus sentiat munus tuum,	
		periere fratres.	

ALTH.   sentiant munus tamen.

NVT.   sensu carent.

ALTH.   quin careat is sensu quoque,   1260
per quem carebant?

NVT.   at gravem fratres prius
dedere causam caedis.

ALTH.   at poenam tamen
ille graviorem retulit.

NVT.   at natum necas.

ALTH.   at ille fratres.

NVT.   at minor matre est soror.

ALTH.   mala sorore fateor, at par est pia.   1265
tu quaeris illam, hanc esse me, et dici volo.

NVT.   sis haec et illa.

ALTH.   stulta, qui fieri potest
in hunc et illos?

NVT.   cur tamen in illos magis?

ALTH.   cum par utrinque est, et dubia pietas, licet
eligere utramvis.

NVT.   nec dubia, nec par premit.   1270
nam chariorem fratre quis natum neget?

Philomela, I must imitate Procne, and a similar cause demands a similar deed.

NURSE Do you imagine this victim will satiate your brother's grim shades? When has a man been devoted to the Underworld for the benefit of another man? When has a nephew been sacrificed for his uncles? When has a son been sacrificed by his mother? You seem to be burdening your brothers with odium, whom you worship in this wicked way. Rather, as a mother, rejoice in your son, for he is alive and will appreciate your favor, but your brothers are dead.

ALTH. Yet they will feel my favor.

NURSE They lack feeling.

ALTH. Why shouldn't he also lack feeling, thanks to whom they lack it?

NURSE But beforehand your brothers provided a grave cause for this murder.

ALTH. He nonetheless earned an even graver punishment.

NURSE But he's your son.

ALTH. But they were my brothers.

NURSE But being a sister is a lesser thing than being a mother.

ALTH. I confess a mother is a better thing than a bad sister, but she is equally pious. You search for that mother of yours. This is what I am and want to be called.

NURSE Be the one *and* the other.

ALTH. Foolish woman, who can be pious both to him and them?

NURSE But why more to them?

ALTH. When the claims of both are equal and the claims of loyalty are in doubt, then you can choose whichever you want.

NURSE It is not doubtful, nor do both claims press you equally. Who can deny a son is dearer than a brother?

ALTH.	fortasse fratre, fratribus nemo putet.	
NVT.	nemo est deorum quem furor metuat tuus?	
ALTH.	an non Dianae sacra facturam vides?	
NVT.	facis inimicae?	
ALTH.	sit licet, diva est tamen.	1275
	unam probare, quod paro sacrum, sat est.	
NVT.	an ista pietas impia est.	
ALTH.	pietas tamen.	
NVT.	compesce flammas praecipitis irae, precor,	
	nefasque dirum mente materna excute.	
ALTH.	obstrepere pergis? vile cum nato caput	1280
	mitteris Erebo, nostra ni sacra approbes,	
	et caepta taceas. maximum fieri scelus	
	et ipsa fateor, sed dolor fieri iubet,	
	iamque ipsa nimium segnis in paenam fui.	

sig. D 4ᵛ
Genibus flexus ad aram precatur.

        Stygias sorores, vosque ferales deos   1285
        precor, Chaosque et vulgus inferni Iovis,
        quaecunque fati lege cruciatus pati
        anima iubetur, currat ad nati rogos,
        paenis remissis. poscit hoc vestras sacrum
        manusque opemque. tu quoque e superis, dea   1290
        adsis Diana, te dies haec postulat,
        tibi nulla maior victima offerri potest.

Erigit se.

        ulciscor, ecce ulciscor, et facio nefas,
        et iste nostra viscera cremabit rogus.
        at vos recentes et modo fratres mei,   1295
        sentite manes pignus officii, et pia
        sorore dignas sumite exequias, precor.
        nunc offeruntur. sed quid hoc? non vult manus

1287. *fatilege* lib.

ALTH. Perhaps than one brother, but nobody could imagine he is dearer than two.

NURSE Is there none of the gods whom your madness fears?

ALTH. Don't you see I am going to perform Diana's rites?

NURSE You are preparing rites for our enemy?

ALTH. Even if she is, she's still divine. To show myself acceptable to one goddess, because I am furnishing her rites, suffices.

NURSE But this piety is impious.

ALTH. It is nonetheless piety.

NURSE Douse the flames of your headlong wrath, I beg, and banish this dire wickedness from a mother's mind.

ALTH. Do you persist in making noise? Base woman, you will be sent to Hell together with my vile son, unless you approve my rites and keep quiet about my undertakings. I myself admit that the greatest misdeed is being committed, but my grief bids it occur, and now I am too slothful in wreaking punishment. (*On her knees she prays at the altar.*) I pray to the Stygian sisters, and you savage gods, chaos, and the crew of Zeus of the Underworld, and whatever soul is commanded to suffer tortures by Destiny's law, hasten to my son's pyre, its punishment revoked. This rite requires your hand, your help. You too, Diana, come hither from among the gods above, this day summons you, and no greater victim can be offered to you. (*She raises herself.*) I take vengeance, see how I take vengeance, and this pyre will burn my entrails. But you who were lately my brothers, let your shades feel the pledge of love in this act and, I pray, accept these funeral rites worthy of your pious sister. Now they are offered. But what's this? My hand does not want to

		parere, crescit stipes, ac dextram gravat,	
		flammae recedunt, ignis exhorret nefas.	1300
		ingrata cessas? anime, quid tandem times?	
		incumbe in iras, quid stupes? aude, incipe.	
		poteris nefandam filio mater necem	
		afferre? poteris iniicere vivum rogo,	
		miserum, gementem? potero, perpetiar, sinam,	1305
		dum morte fratrum flebiles umbras queam	
		lenire. poteris? melius ah melius dolor	
		insane loquere. qui regi non vult furor,	
		subire tandem discat invitus iugum.	
		quo rapior? heu me, parcite incaeptis meis,	1310
		matrique, fratres, obsecro veniam date.	
		meruisse fateor cur pereat, et mors placet,	
		sed mortis author displicet, nato parens.	
	NVT.	o mite matris pectus! o quantum tenes,	
sig. D 5^r		natura, regnum! nulla vis maior tua est.	1315
		occidere pavet filium, occidi cupit,	
		caeptumque in ipso limine exhorret scelus.	
	ALTH.	inultus ergo vivet, atque ipsa tumens	
		impunitate sceleris, Aetolam reget	
		gentem superbus? sceptra gestabit manu?	1320
		illi iacebunt exiguus urna cinis,	
		gelidique manes? haud patiar equidem, simul	
		et ille pereat improbus, et una patris	
		regnique vota, ac patriae occasum trahat.	
		utinam cremasset primus infantem rogus,	1325
		idque ego tulissem. munere aetatem meo	
		vixisti ad istam, nunc tamen merito tuo	
		moriere. diri praemium facti cape,	
		animamque partu et stipite erepto datam	
		aut redde matri, aut adde matrem fratribus.	1330
		en horret animus, concutit pectus tremor,	
		artusque torpent. ira discessit loco,	
		et tota mater, fratribus pulsis, redit.	
	NVT.	quin ergo iam feramus hinc alio pedem?	
		minus solent peccare, quibus ansa est procul.	1335
	ALTH.	ignava, metuis? tuta consilia expaves?	
		quid si parares regiam cineri dare?	

1315. *regnum?* lib.   1318. *inulius* lib.

obey, the log swells, weighs down my hand, the flames shrink back, the fire shudders at the crime. Do you hesitate, ungrateful woman? My mind, why be afraid at this late date? Devote yourself to the punishment, why are you paralyzed? Be brave, begin. Could you, a mother, visit an unspeakable death on your son? Could you throw him on the pyre alone, wretched, moaning? I could, I shall bear it, I shall allow it, as long as by his death I can placate my brothers' piteous shades. But could you? Ah, mad sorrow, speak better, speak better. Let your madness, which does not want to be governed, finally learn to bear the yoke against its will. Where am I being carried? Alas for me, brothers, I pray that you pardon my undertakings and forgive a mother. I confess he has deserved death, and his death is pleasing to me; but I am displeased at the one doing the killing, a mother responsible for the death of her son.

NURSE Oh gentle mother's heart! Oh what a kingdom you rule, Nature! No power is greater than yours. She dreads killing her son, although she desires that he be killed, and shudders at the crime she has undertaken at its very outset.

ALTH. Will he therefore live, and proudly govern the Aetolian nation, swollen with the very impunity of his crime? Will he wield a scepter in his hand? Will they lie as a pinch of an ash in an urn, as chill ghosts? For my part, I shall not allow this, let this wicked man die too, let him drag along with him the hopes of his father and kingdom, the collapse of his nation. Would that the former pyre had burned him as an infant, and that I had tolerated it. You lived to this age as a gift from me, but now you must die, your just deserts. Receive your dire deed's reward, and either return to your mother the life given you at birth and by the snatching of the log, or add your mother to her brothers. Lo, my mind shudders, horror strikes my heart, my limbs grow numb. My anger departs its place, and the mother returns wholly, the brothers banished.

NURSE So why should we not go elsewhere? People are less apt to sin when the opportunity is far removed.

ALTH. Coward, are you afraid? Although you are safe, are you terrified at my plans?

       in mille partes distrahere natum? patris
       offerre mensis? cuncta quae fierent palam,
       graviora specie scelera, quam quod iam paras,   1340
       etiam secretum. stipitem demens puta
       rudem cremare, fabulam vanam argue
       dedisse Parcas, error hic mentis fuit
       partu impeditae. stipes hic mortem inferet?
sig. D 5ᵛ   verum cremetur, stipitem ardentem times?   1345
       cupio nequeoque, quod paro factum horreo,
       et pectus unum nomina exagitant duo,
       mater sororque. da locum matri, soror.
       cur non sorori, mater? hinc pietas movet.
       erras, untrinque est, hinc et hinc pietas movet.   1350

   NVT. hanc oro mentem dii tibi servent diu.

   ALTH. incerta quid agam, rapior in varias vices.
       modo mater iram frangit, et ponit minas,
       modo cruda fratrum vulnera occurrunt mihi,
       et tantae imago caedis. atque hic quam vocat   1355
       matrem, sororem cur minus et illi vocent?
       pares vocabunt, rursus increscit dolor,
       et fervet odium. perge, qua ducis, sequar.
       fas omne cedat, pelle faemineos metus
       dum adhuc calescis, dum recens urget scelus,   1360
       animosque silices indue ac ferrum triplex.
       utcunque, fratres, vincitis, at en vincite,
       vosque ipsa pariter et meum munus sequar.

         Meleager, Philemon

   <MEL.> duo me, Philemon, gravia sollicitum tenent
       contraria simul, durus atque ardens amor,   1365
       et matris odium. sed quid hoc? subito caput
       ardet dolore, nec ferunt crines tegi.
       cerebrum repente corripitur aestu gravi,
       flammata facies, igneae lucent genae,
       oculique flagrant. ecce per geminum latus   1370
       descendit alte in viscera et renes calor.

sig. D 6ʳ PHIL. amore nempe totus Atalantae cales.

   MEL. haud ita, Philemon. maius est, maius malum.
       populatur artus flamma, per venas means.
       ardent medullae, iecore siccato fibrae   1375
       pulmonis ardent, ipse distentus tumet,

What if you were preparing to burn down the palace? Tear your son into a thousand pieces? Serve him up at his father's table? All these things which would be done in the open are worse crimes in appearance than what you are now preparing, a furtive deed. In your madness you imagine you are burning a log. Tell that vain story that the Fates gave it, but this was only the hallucination of a difficult birth. Will this log bring death? So let it be burned — are you afraid of a burning log? I want to, I can't, I'm terrified of what I'm preparing to do, and two words inflame my single breast, mother and sister. Yield to the mother, sister. Why not yield to the sister, mother? Thus my piety moves me. You are wrong. Both are true, piety moves me in both directions.

NURSE I pray the gods long keep you in this opinion.

ALTH. Uncertain what to do, I am pulled various ways. Now the mother breaks off her anger and sets aside her threats. Now I think of my brothers' fresh wounds, the image of such a murder. And though he calls me his mother, why should they call me sister any the less? They will both call out to me, and again my grief swells, my hatred boils. Hasten, I shall follow where you lead. Let all considerations of justice disappear, banish your womanly fear while you are still a-boil, while the recent crime impels you, and adopt a heart of flint, be of triple steel. Brothers, by whatever means you prevail with me, see how you do prevail. I shall do the duty that is at once yours and my own. [*Enter Meleager and Philemon out of the palace, on the other side of the stage.*]

MEL. Philemon, two great opposites trouble me at once: my enduring, ardent love and my mother's hatred. But what's this? Suddenly my head burns with aching, my hair cannot bear to be covered. My brain is suddenly overwhelmed by a great burning, my face is inflamed, my fiery cheeks are burning, my eyes are ablaze. Behold, the fire descends down my sides, deep within my guts and bowels.

PHIL. I suppose you are totally afire with love for Atalanta.

MEL. Scarcely that, Philemon. The evil is greater, greater. The flame is ravaging my limbs, with my liver scorched, the fibers of my lungs are burning, while the liver itself is

              ustumque repens sanguinem lambit vapor.
              detrahite vestem corpori, vestis gravem
              intus calorem cohibet. o vastum malum!

PHIL.   paulisper obdura, subita subito cadunt,   1380
           et mox dolorem forsitan vincet sopor.

MEL.   nullum sopori tempus aut spatium dabit
           immensus ardor. alitur et crescit lues,
           et urit intus. qualis Aetnaeo vapor
           exundat antro, talis, en talis furit.   1385
           heu quis relicta Scorpios caeli plaga
           Cancerve torrens viscera exurit mea?
           o ter beati, dubia quos letho dedit
           fortuna belli! morior, et nullo tamen
           transmissus ense. siccine impendi meam   1390
           voluere vitam fata? sic nostram placet
           abiicere mortem, perque tam turpes mihi
           decurrere colos? quo pereo misere modo?

PHIL.   inhibe querelas saltem, et aerumnas preme,
           malisque tantis pectus invictum refer.   1395

MEL.   eheu, quis iste est gloriae finis meae?
           hic fructus operum? summus hic vitae dies?
           huc spes amoris rediit, Atalante, tui?
           utinam cruore saeva lusisset meo
           Oetea pestis! quam prope a fato steti   1400
           nuper decoro! perdidi mortem miser

sig. D 6ᵛ   toties honestam. nam mihi quovis libet
           malo perisse, dummodo ignavus dolor
           vilisque lethum morbus haud mandet mihi.

PHIL.   en, ut supremum non timet lethi diem   1405
           animosa virtus. pessimi authoris pudet.

Althaea stipitem extrahit.

MEL.   quid hoc? recessit morbus, et multum calor
           vires reposuit, nec tamen solitus manet.
           quid esse credam? virus? an potius putem
           me fascinari? an aliquod est aliud nefas?   1410

1376. *arent* lib.   1384. *Aetuaeo* lib.: corr. Brooke, script. inedit.   1386. *scorpius* lib.   1389. *belli?* lib. 1399. *lulisset* lib.   1401. *decoro?* lib.

distended and swollen, and a creeping mist licks at my parched blood. Tear the garments from my body, for my clothing retains the great heat within. Oh, the vast evil!

PHIL. Resist a brief while, for things that suddenly arise end suddenly, and perhaps sleep will soon overcome your pain.

MEL. This immense burning will give no time or occasion for sleep. This bane is nourished and grows, burning me within. As the vapor overflows the cavern of Aetna, thus it rages. Alas, what Scorpio, abandoning heaven's tract, or parching Crab is burning my vitals? Oh thrice blessed, whom the fortunes of war have consigned to oblivion! I die, but pierced by no sword. Thus did the Fates want to expend my life? Are they pleased thus to squander my death and let it pass through such shameful spindles? In what way am I dying in my misery?

PHIL. At least restrain your complaints and stifle your cares, showing an indomitable heart amidst these evils.

MEL. Alas, what end is there for my glory? Is this the fruit of my efforts? Is this my final day? Would that the savage pestilence of Oetea had sported with my blood. How near I lately stood to meeting a glorious fate! So often I have wretchedly avoided a decent death. For I would gladly have perished by any evil, as long as shameful pain and vile disease do not condemn me to death.

PHIL. Behold how his high-minded courage does not fear the day of death. He is ashamed of its most ignoble cause. (*Althaea draws out the brand.*)

MEL. What's this? The disease is abating, the heat has lost much of its of force, and does not remain as it had been. What should I believe this to be? A poison? Or should I rather think myself bewitched? Or is there another kind of evildoing? Is the blood of the

		an ille monstri nuper extincti cruor	
		in me rebellat? illa me forsan lues	
		perempta perdit. has mihi paenas aper	
		infligit, apri vindicat caedem dea.	
		heu parce tandem, parce, tam satis est, dea.	1415
		quid me studentem patriae, ut decuit, gravi	
		persequeris odio? quod nefas in te meum est?	
	PHIL.	quodcunque fuerit, laetor extinctum ocius,	
		deosque supplex ne redeat omnes precor.	

Rursus iniicit.

	MEL.	frustra precaris. urit ecce iterum fibras,	1420
		et rediit ardor. flamma quae aestiferi canis	
		tanta est, leonis terga cum Titan premit?	
		quae tanta Lemnos? quae poli plaga torridi?	
		in ipsa iacter maria et altos gurgites,	
		mediosque in amnes. quis sat est Ister meo	1425
		incendio, aut quis Nilus, aut terram ambiens	
		Oceanus ipse? nulla vis nostros aquae	
		restinguet aestus, omnis arescet liquor.	
	PHIL.	quo gravius istud, hoc erit brevius malum,	
		brevitate gravitas saepe pensari solet.	1430
	MEL.	mediis oberrat, credo, visceribus meis	
sig. D 7ʳ		aper, Philemon, cumque apro centum ferae,	
		venabula, canes, omnia, et nihil est tamen.	
		ignosce tandem mater, has paenas luo	
		utrique fratri. forsan his, licet aestuans,	1435
		irata, minitans, ipsa detractum velis.	
	PHIL.	miser Philemon, tanta Meleagrum premunt,	
		nec iniqua faciunt fata me socium mali?	
	MEL.	sed en, quis iste verberum crepuit sonus?	
		adsunt ab imo Tartaro ultrices deae.	1440
		monstrumque maius, ecce subiiciunt faces	
		Plexippus et Toxeus, et ipsas incitant	
		in odia Furias, et graves poenas docent,	
		stimulantque miras, et nimis lentas vocant.	
		etiamne manes odia post mortem gerunt?	1445

1428. *arescct* lib.

newly-killed monster fighting against me? Perhaps that bane we destroyed is ruining me. The boar inflicts these punishments on me, the goddess takes revenge for the killing of the boar. Alas, spare me at length. Goddess, it is enough. Why persecute me with great hatred when I have been zealous for my country, as I ought? What crime have I committed against you?

PHIL. Whatever it was, I rejoice that it ended quickly, and I humbly pray all the gods lest it return. (*She puts it back in.*)

MEL. You pray in vain. See, again it burns my guts, the heat returns. Is the fire of the heat-bringing dog-star so great, when the sun weighs on the Lion's back? Is Lemnos' fire so great? Or that of the torrid zone? Let me be plunged in the very sea, into deep whirlpools and mid-rivers! What Danube is sufficient for my burning, what Nile, or what world-encircling Ocean? No amount of liquid will quench my burning, all the water will run dry.

PHIL. To the extent this evil is acute, so will it be short. Great force is accustomed to be counterbalanced by brevity.

MEL. Philemon, I think the boar is wandering through my innards, and a hundred beasts with him — spears, dogs, the lot — but it is nothing. At length forgive me, mother. I am paying the penalty to both your brothers. Although you are inflamed, irate, menacing, perhaps you would wish me rescued from these evils.

PHIL. Poor Philemon, such things are oppressing Meleager, and the unfair Fates are not making me a partner in this suffering?

MEL. But behold, what's this sound of whips? The avenging goddesses are here, come from deepest Tartarus. And a greater marvel: see, Plexippus and Toxeus are kindling torches, and are goading on the very Furies to hatred, teaching them heavy punishments. They are urging amazing ones, calling them too slow. Do ghosts nurse grudges even in

		adhuc avunculi in meum vivunt malum?	
		adhuc rebellant? o levem dextram nimis!	
		Megaera, cur me saeva persequeris face?	
		heu parce tandem, sustine Stygias manus,	
		ipsosque mecum comminus sine congredi,	1450
		ut bis sub imos Tartari mittam specus.	
		stringatur ensis, nuda sufficiet manus,	
		in orbe vestrum veniat huc alter mihi.	
		veniat uterque. fugitis ignavi, sequar.	

	PHIL.	quo rapitur amens impetu? heu mentem quoque	1455
		sensumque misero nimius excussit dolor,	
		dolor iste furor est. sequere, quid iam stas miser?	

Aliqua mora sit stipiti cremando, ut in morte Meleagri decorum servetur.

ALTHAEA, NVTRIX

	<ALTH.>	bene est, peractum est. iusta persolvi, satis,	
		satis habet ille. quid ais? in tutum est meos	
sig. D 7ᵛ		mactare fratres? anime, quid subito stupes?	1460
		vindicta parta est. hei mihi, factum execror.	
		quid misera feci? misera iam sero piget.	
		feci. quod unum restat, ac sceleri deest,	
		et ipsa sequere, morte cumuletur nefas.	
	NVT.	regina, cohibe mentis effraenae impetum,	1465
		animum coerce. iam satis sceleri datum est.	

	ALTH.	decreta mors est, pariter et mortis via.	
		cruentus ille pugio in thalamis meis,	
		ille ille mucro, quo iacent fratres, iuvat.	
		hunc dextra poscit, huic decet ferro immori,	1470
		uno perire quam mihi telo placet.	
		gratabor ecce filio tandem meo.	
		laetare Meleager, tuo poenas luam	
		mucrone. mecum est, faciet, ubicunque est, scelus.	
		tu fida nutrix, caepta fac nostra occulas.	1475

1471. *placet?* lib.

death? Do my uncles still live to my destruction? Do they still resist me? Oh my hand, too light! Megaera, why pursue me with your savage torch? Alas, spare me at length, hold your Stygian hand, allow them to come to blows with me, so that I may twice send them to Tartarus' caverns. Let the sword be drawn, bare hands will suffice. Let one of them appear among your throng, let both appear. You flee in your cowardice. I shall follow. [*Exit.*]

PHIL. Where is he rushing at a mad dash? Alas, pain has driven mind and sense out of the poor man. This pain is madness. Follow; why stand here now, wretch? [*Exit.*]

Let there be a delay in burning the brand, so that decorum might be preserved in Meleager's death.

ALTH. It is well, it is done. I have accomplished justice, he has enough, enough. What are you saying? Is it safe to kill my brothers? My mind, why are you suddenly numb? Vengeance has been taken. Alas, I abhor my deed. What have I done in my misery? Wretched, now I am regretful, too late. I have acted. The one thing yet absent from the crime is that you attack yourself. Let this evildoing be crowned by your death.

NURSE Queen, restrain the impulse of your unbridled mind, control your thoughts. Now enough has been devoted to wrongdoing.

ALTH. My death has been decreed, and also my death's manner. I want that bloody dagger in my bedchamber, that blade by which my brothers died. My hand demands it, it is proper I perish by that steel, the one weapon by which I am pleased to die. Lo, I shall finally gratify my son. Rejoice, Meleager. I shall pay the penalty by your blade. He is with me, he shall do the crime, wherever he is. You, faithful nurse, conceal my undertaking. [*Exeunt.*]

CHORVS

quantus irarum cumulus minantum
faeminam versat semel incitatam,
cum dolor fraenum dederit furori!
exulat longe pietas pudorque.　　　　　　　　　1480
mitior Scylla est, simul ac Charybdis,
nulla non illa melior ferarum est.
nulla vis diri gravior veneni.
arcta non illam retinent furentem
vincla naturae, neque iura matris.　　　　　　　1485
nulla tam caeli est violenta clades,
sive descendunt pluviae nivesque
grandini mistae, rapidique venti,
sive cum turres graviore flagrant
fulminis telo, veteresque fagi.　　　　　　　　1490
saevior nulla est pelagi procella,
cum Noto stridens Aquilo minatur,
et fretum venti rapiunt ab imo.
iamque turgescens mare tingit astra,
iamque subsidit, premiturque ad Orcum.　　　1495

sig. D 8ʳ

1479. *furori?* lib.

CHORUS

What an immense number of menacing rages preoccupy a woman when once aroused, after pain has unleashed her madness! Out of control, she is swept along like a whirlwind, piety and shame are banished far away. Scylla and Charybdis are milder, there is no wild beast less gentle than she. No dire poison's power is greater. In her rage Nature's tight bonds do not restrain her, nor the laws of motherhood. No scourge of heaven is more violent, whether rains descend or snow mixed with hail, or swift winds, or when the battlements and ancient beech-trees blaze with the greater weapon of lightning. No sea-storm is more savage, when the howling Nor'easter threatens the North wind and the gales snatch the sea from its bed. Now the swelling sea touches the stars, now it sinks, is thrust down towards the Underworld.

- Actus Quintus -

OENEVS, SENEX

<OEN.> quod ante numquam credidi in rebus meis
potuisse sortem, vixque iam credo mihi
ausam fuisse, pertuli id totum miser.
fortuna, sic est? tanta permissa est tibi
in me tyrannis? sicne versari domum
libuit beatam? pariter extremam placet 1500
incipere, et uno perficere cladem malo?
semel incitata proruis demens dea?
tua ista vero malitia qualis fuit?
periisse natum, pars quota est tanti mali?
rapuisse nihil est, nisi etiam subito occidat 1505
primo in iuventae flore et aetatis bono,
ipso in triumpho laudis et victoriae,
tam singulari flebilis lethi modo,
peiore letho? sic soles rapere improba?

sig. D 8^v   SEN.   miserande princeps, pauca te fidi precor 1510
ut verba famuli mente placata audias.
subito quod obiit natus, haud cecidit male,
haud passus est ille mortis ignavae moras.
quod iuvenis obiit, hoc tulit certe boni,
quod hanc senectae miseriam evasit pigrae. 1515
quod victor, equidem morte faelicem reor.
quo potuit ille tempore extingui magis,
quam curru in ipso gloriae, exuviis ovans,
ipsis in oculis Graeciae palmam ferens?
par ille superis, cui fuit lethi dies 1520
et laudis eadem. quod modum lethi arguis,
laetare potius, titulus accessit novus.
en germanus apri victor ac mortis iacet.
nec imputentur ista fortunae mala.
humana fecit inscitia caelo deam 1525
fortunam, et error numen affinxit sacrum.
non praevidentem si quid adversi opprimat,
id omne sorti ascribitur, vanae deae.
fortuna nulla est, alma nisi prudentia
sit inane nomen. si sit, et curam gerat 1530
caeleste numen, nil temere nobis venit.
quaecunque miseros fata mortales premunt,
ea crede divum nutu et arbitrio regi.

- Act V -

OENEUS, OLD MAN

OEN. That misfortune which I never before thought could exist in my affairs, and which I still can scarcely believe has dared happen to me, I have now fully borne in my misery. Fortune, is this how it is? Is such a tyranny over me allowed you? Has it been your pleasure to overturn a blessed house? Are you equally pleased to begin and complete the ultimate slaughter with a single catastrophe? Once roused, goddess, do you mindlessly hurl yourself at us? What portion of all this evil is it for my son to have died? Is it nothing to have taken him, unless he died suddenly in the first flower of youth, the good time of life, in the very triumph of praise and victory? Wicked goddess, are you thus wont to take your victims by this singular means of piteous death, worse than death?

O. M. Poor prince, I beg that you hear a few words of your faithful servant with a calm mind. Because your son died quickly, he scarcely died a bad death. For he did not experience death's shameful lingering. Because he perished in his youth, he assuredly received this boon, that he escaped the misery of sluggish old age. Because he was a victor, for my part I think him happy in death. When better to pass away than in glory's very chariot, celebrating a triumph with spoils, bearing off the palm in the eyes of Greece? He was equal to the gods, for whom the day of death was the day of glory. And the manner of his dying of which you complain you should rather rejoice in, for this new title of victor came to him. Lo, he lies, a genuine victor over the boar and over death. Nor should these evils be imputed to Fortune. Human ignorance has made Fortune a goddess in heaven, and error has invented her as a divinity. If some reversal oppresses a man who has not foreseen it, this is all ascribed to the false goddess Fortune. There is no Fortune, unless fostering Providence is an empty word. If Providence exists, and is a heavenly divinity, nothing occurs to us at random. Whatever fates oppress us poor mortals, you must believe occur by divine will and judgement.

OEN. fas ergo in ipsos vertere querelam deos,
expostulare facinus ingratum libet. 1535
huc illa, superi, dona redierunt mea?
haec victimarum cura, congesti focis
haec thuris habita est? mensa convivas mea
accepit, en hoc praemium hospitii datis?
ingrata Pallas, et domina frugum Ceres, 1540
et Bacche pollens, vosque dii, quo caeteris
potentiores, hoc magis sceleris rei,
sensistis atque arcere potuistis nefas?
an noluistis? an magis vestrum est scelus?
qui non repellit, cum potest, damnum facit. 1545

SEN. quid? innocentes arguis sceleris deos?
fraena dolorem. numquid id nihili putas,
quod liberarunt patriam tanto metu?
virtutis ecquid filii id credis tui?
erras. deorum viribus cecidit fera. 1550

OEN. minus expulerunt, ut malum maius darent?
aprum abstulerunt, natus ut pereat meus?
hac lege superos petere mortales decet?
haec impetrandi conditio voti datur?
hic mos deorum est? sic opem ferre assolent? 1555
cum saeviunt, et cum iuvant, semper mali,
magis iuvando. summe proh rector poli,
an me quis hominum fata lugentem mea,
miserum, gementem, conspicit? certe dies
haec prima vidit, quodque me cruciat magis, 1560
Diana vidit.

SEN.   pectori tandem impera.
gravi deorum tota iampridem domus
urgetur ira. quid statum impulsum trahis,
et acuis odia?

OEN.   cuius ulterius mala
effluere nequeant, tutus hunc portus tenet. 1565
ita constituto, quis cadere casus potest?
quare ipse superos metuat, aut quare colat?
virumque frustra est, et animi nimis anxii.
absumpsit in me dura sors quicquid potest.
quis tam superbus caelicola quicquam valet 1570
malis meis afferre? iam nec tu potes,
Diana, et adde si quid ad luctum potes.
nato perempto, luce non grata fruor.

OEN. Then it is proper to direct my complaints against the gods themselves. I want to protest their ungrateful wrongdoing. Gods, is this how my offerings are repaid? Is this your concern for my victims, for my altar, choked with incense? My table received you, and this is my reward for hospitality? Thankless Pallas, Ceres, mistress of crops, mighty Bacchus, and you gods, the more powerful you are than others, the guiltier you are of crime. Did you see, were you able to prevent this wrong? Or did you not wish to? Or is this crime more your work? He who does not prevent an injury when he is able, works an injury.

O.M. What? You accuse the blameless gods of crime? Restrain your grief. Do you count it as nothing that they have freed our nation from such terror? Do you credit this to your son's prowess? You are mistaken. The beast fell by the gods' power.

OEN. Did they drive out a lesser evil in order to give us a greater? Did they do away with the boar so that my son might die? Is the rule by which men are to pray to the gods? Is this their condition for granting our prayers? Is this the gods' custom? Are they thus wont to aid us? They are always evil, when savaging us and when helping us, but more in the helping. Bah, great ruler of heaven, does any mortal see me bewailing fate, wretched and in mourning? Certainly this day has seen it first and (what galls me more) Diana has seen.

O.M. At length master your heart. Your household has already been oppressed by the gods' heavy wrath. Why prolong their fixed inclination, whetting their anger?

OEN. Whose misfortunes can flow no greater, reaches the haven in security. With things thus decided, what further calamity can befall? Why should he fear the gods, or why worship them? It is a waste of effort, the sign of an over-anxious spirit. Harsh Fate has done all she can against me. What arrogant divinity can add a jot to my misfortunes? Now neither can you, Diana, add what you can to my grief. With my son dead, the light of day

nam cur supersim? causa cui vitae perit,
is pereat una, mors ei lucro venit. 1575

SEN. quid ipse fatum affligis atque oneras tuum?
concussa nutat, sed tamen constat, domus.
coniux, penates, liberi restant tibi,
restatque regnum. deesse quid credam tibi,
nisi te? parum hoc est, quod rogo, faelix mane. 1580
quisquamne faelix esse noluerit? quid hoc?
cur sponte mortem accersis? hoc quod iam doles,
quantum malorum est? nil adhuc fatum abstulit,
si conferatur, quae tibi restant, bonis.

OEN. nihil abstulerunt fata? nihil est quod fleo? 1585
dolor iste levis est, iam furere par est magis.
coniux, penates, liberi, regnum, omnia,
per me ruant. causa illa, cur starent, iacet
Meleager unus. coniugem, natos, iuvat
patriam, penates, cuncta, congerere in rogum. 1590
haec me patrem regemque dare nato decet,
nec omnia placent. cupio, Meleager, tibi
regale funus ducere, et nihil est satis.
tua vita maior victima quavis fuit.
tua mors ruinis omnium gravior fuit. 1595
sine te meorum, nate, nil dulce est mihi.
egone superstes perfruor regni bonis,
quem te anteisse decuit? ego vivo senex?
tu iuvenis, umbras inter et manes, novas,
sig. E 2ʳ Meleagre, sedes quaeris, expers omnium, 1600
miserabilis, inops, squallidus, nudus, miser,
avunculis invisus, hac vita carens,
ipsisque vitae gaudiis, quibus par fuit
multos per annos regis haeredem frui?
haec ipse capio? tu cares? nec dum paro 1605
ad Tartarum detrudere invisum caput?

SEN. moderare tandem pectoris saevi impetum,
te reprime. non est, ut putas, pietas tuam
abiicere vitam, filii causa tui.
quin illud esse crede pietatem magis, 1610
pia iusta nato facere, et exequias dare.

OEN. quid me parantem, quae refers, facere admones?

1596. *mihi?* lib.

is unwelcome to me. For why do I survive him? When a man's reason for living perishes, so does he, and for him death comes as a boon.

O. M. Why do you yourself aggravate your misfortune, making it heavier? Your house, receiving a blow, is reeling, but still it stands. Wife, household gods, children remain for you, your kingdom remains. What should I believe is lacking for you, unless you yourself? This is a small thing I ask: remain prosperous. Who refuses prosperity? What's this? Why invite death? This which you now lament, how bad is it? So far Fate has taken away nothing at all, in comparison with the good things you still possess.

OEN. Have the Fates taken away nothing? Is it nothing I bewail? This sorrow is a small thing, for it is more reasonable for me to feel outrage. As far as I am concerned, my wife, household gods, children, and kingdom can go to blazes. For the reason why they should remain died together with Meleager. I want to heap wife, children, nation, household gods, everything, on his pyre. I, his father and a king, ought to be giving these things to my son, and all fail to please me. Meleager, I desire to give you a royal funeral, nothing is enough. Your life was more valuable than any offering, your death more catastrophic than the ruination of all. Without you, my child, nothing of mine is sweet. Am I to enjoy all the kingdom's goods as your survivor, who should have preceded you in death? Do I live on, an old man? Meleager, are you, a youth, seeking a home among the shades and ghosts, miserable, forlorn, squalid, naked, wretched, hateful to your uncles, bereft of this life and its joys, which as the royal heir you were entitled to enjoy for many years? Do I myself receive them and you go lacking? Shouldn't I make ready to consign my hateful life to Tartarus?

O. M. Moderate at last the impulse of a wild heart, control yourself. It is not piety, as you imagine, to throw away your life for the sake of your son. Rather, consider it pious to do your duty by your son and give him burial.

OEN. Why admonish me, who am making ready to do that which you mention? I would

unam cremarem regiae ac nati struem.
satis esse credis? urbis atque orbis rogum
instruere vellem, cuncta Meleagro pyram 1615
incenderem. perire tibi, nate, omnia
optare possum, tanta congeries tuum
in funus iret, ut tuos illa queam
levare manes. est quidem minus is miser,
quicunque maesto funeri ac flammis datur, 1620
ardente patriae pariter et mundi rogo.
te tanta ferre iusta, Meleager, decet.

ALTHAEA, OENEVS, SENEX

<ALTH.> me me iuventus Graia, me telis petat.
adhuc labori restat ulterior gradus,
graviorque primo. peior en superest apro 1625
aper interempto, saevior restat fera
primae cruore nata. quid cessant manus?
coite, cives. saxa et incensas faces
iaculetur omnis turba et Aetolum genus.
corripite tela, congerite quicquid furor 1630
iustus ministret, obruite dirum caput.
impune iam nascentur immanes apri,
impune rapient. statis ingrati tamen?

OEN. nescio quod animus maius exhorret nefas.

ALTH. at tu corusco fulminis telo, pater, 1635
matrem scelestam tolle, nec minimum expedi
quo saepe tecta petis et insontes casas,
sed quo cupressos sternis et iuga montium,
aut quo Gigantes montibus quondam pares
cecidere vasti. fulmen hoc dextra evolet. 1640
inusitatum postulat paenam scelus
non usitatum, vindica insolitum nefas.
tam lente cessas? ecquid exaudis, pater?
an otioso cura tibi rerum excidit?
an scelere gaudes? hanc tibi labem elue. 1645

SEN. cor trepidat intus, ista quo vertant timens.

ALTH. sed unde caetus iste processit minax?
aut cui minatur? patria in vultus meos
decurrit omnis, hinc et hinc cives fremunt,
et tota poscit vindicem Calydon suum, 1650
paenasque poscit. me petit ferro pater,

at once burn the pyre of my son and this palace. Do you think that sufficient? I would construct a pyre for this city, for the world, I would burn everything as Meleager's pyre. Son, I am able to hope that everything would perish along with you, that the whole mass would be consumed at your funeral, so that with them I could console your shade. For he is less unhappy who is given over to a funeral and the flames, if his nation and the entire universe are likewise ablaze on the pyre. Meleager, you deserve such rites. [*Enter Althaea.*]

ALTH. Let the young men of Greece seek me, me, with their weapons. This higher step in their effort remains, more serious than the first. A boar survives worse than the slain one, a more savage beast remains, born from the blood of the first. why does your hand hesitate? Gather the citizens. Let the whole throng, the Aetolian race, hurl rocks and kindled torches. Snatch up your weapons, gather whatever your legitimate fury supplies, destroy this dire person. Now let great boars be born with impunity, with impunity may they ravage. But do you stand there, ungrateful?

O. M. My spirit shudders all the more at this unknown evil.

ALTH. But you, father, destroy this wicked mother with the glittering spear of your lightning; shoot not your smallest, with which you strike houses and innocent cottages, but that with which you smite cypress trees and mountain-tops, or that by which the Giants, huger than mountains, once perished. Let this lightning fly from your hand. Novel crime demands novel punishment, avenge this strange misdeed. So sluggishly you hesitate? Do you hear me, father? Does any concern about things exist for you in your leisure? Or do you take pleasure in evildoing? Cleanse this stain on your reputation.

O. M. My heart trembles within, fearing where all this is going.

ALTH. But whence comes this threatening throng? Or whom does it menace? My whole nation hastens into my sight, on this side and that the citizenry mutters, and all Calydon demands its avenger, demands punishment. Father seeks me with cold steel, son seeks me,

		me natus, in me matris armantur manus,	
		soror execratur, odit et frater nefas.	
		iam parce, patria, mox tibi paenas dabo.	

OEN. Althaea, quis te sceleris instigat furor? 1655
quid pugio iste? quidve vociferatio?
sig. E 3ʳ quid imprecata tot tibi dira volunt?

ALTH. en legite, cives, tuque, prae reliquis pater
miser, nefanda. coniuge, stupendum accipe
fatum, meoque scelere prodigium magis. 1660
horreo profari. tu lege, agnosces manum.
ne forte dubites, aut sua careas fide,
scriptum cruore dextra signabit meo,
et hic sigilli pugio implebit vicem,
fratrum, sororis, matris occisor malae. 1665

Furibunda exit in regiam, manentibus maritibus.

OENEVS, SENEX

Syngrapham proiectam tollit senex perlectam. tradit matribus astantibus.

<OEN.> dehisce tellus, tuque tenebrosae potens
dominator aulae, pande Tartareos specus,
et me scelestum coniugis dirae virum
ad Chaos inane merge, et infernam Styga.
ego te peremi, nate, quia matrem dedi 1670
quae te peremit, scelere periisti meo.
vix ipse tantum, vix adhuc credo malum.
Althaea potuit? potuit hoc mater nefas?
at relege: NATVM ALTHAEA MELEAGRVM ABSTVLIT.
hoc credat aliquis? anime, quid factum stupes? 1675
miser vides fecisse, quid fletu vacas?
cur lacrymarum non rigat flumen genas?
quin fles? quid hoc? num siccus haec pateris mala?
iam flere prorsus nequeo, iam lacrymas dolor
absorpsit omnes. cum velis, quantum est mali 1680
non posse fletum exprimere! iam pessundatus,
oppressus, infaelix videor, et iam undique
obsessus omni clade. iam vulnus mihi
sig. E 3ᵛ alte est adactum, iam ferar vere miser.
hoc illud, umbra quod socrus flevit, nefas, 1685

1674. *natum, Althaea, Meleagrum, abstulit?* lib. quasi epistolam haesitans legeret. 1681. *exprimere?* lib.

mother arms her hand, sister curses me, brother abhors my crime. Now spare me, nation, for soon I shall pay the penalty to you.

OEN. Althaea, what criminal madness goads you on? What's this dagger? What's this outcry? What's the meaning of all these imprecations?

ALTH. [*Brandishing a paper.*] Read these unspeakable things, citizens, and you, father more wretched than the rest. Learn this astounding misfortune from your wife, a marvel more than my misdeed. I dread to speak out. You read, you will recognize my handwriting. Lest you be doubtful or disbelieving, my hand will sign this in my blood, and this dagger will perform the office of a seal, the dagger which killed brothers, a sister, and a wicked mother.

[*She throws down the paper and] exits into the palace in a frenzy, the men remaining. The old man picks it up and hands it to Oeneus as matrons stand by.*

OEN. Gape open, earth, and you, mighty lord of the court of darkness, open Tartarus' cavern. Plunge me, criminal husband of a baneful wife, into empty Chaos, down to the infernal Styx. My child, I killed you; because I gave you a mother who murdered you, you have died because of my wrongdoing. I still can scarcely believe such evil. Could Althaea do this? Could a mother do such a crime? But reread it: ALTHAEA KILLED HER SON MELEAGER. Could anyone believe this? My mind, why are you amazed at this deed? Poor man, you see she did, why are you lacking in tears? Why does no river of tears water your cheeks? Why not weep? What's this? Surely you cannot bear these ills dry-eyed? Now I am wholly unable to cry, for sorrow has consumed all my tears. What a great evil, not to be able to weep when you wish! Now I seem to be ruined, oppressed, unfortunate, surrounded now by killing on all sides. Now I have received a deep wound, now in my misery I am truly stricken. This is the evil my mother-in-law's ghost lamented, the evil at

	hoc dudum auruspex horruit, metuit senex.	
	pars illa cladis, quam modo sensi, quota est?	
	votum est sub illa. morte Meleagri nihil	
	potuisse gravius credidi sortem, tamen	
	gradus est. malorum maximum hunc cumulum reor	1690
	quod <me> abhominandum fecit authorem necis	
	Fortuna. cur me non ad aeternas domos	
	pallentis Erebi mitto? num maius nefas	
	adhuc patrandum est? ecquis ulterior gradus?	
SEN.	depone tumidas pectoris saevi minas,	1695
	tibique mortis impiam mentem excute.	
OEN.	quid verba perdis? hoc mihi fixum sedet,	
	quod iam decet fecisse. transcendi mea	
	vivendo fata. vivo adhuc tamen, et diem	
	hominesque non relinquo? sed linquam brevi.	1700
	tamen hoc in istis capio solamen malis,	
	despicere quod iam caelites omnes licet.	
SEN.	absiste tandem. reprime affectus precor	
	animi superbos, iamque pietatem cole.	
OEN.	hunc nostra fructum scilicet pietas tulit,	1705
	ut esse tanto me pium nolim malo.	
	discede pietas pectore ex nostro ocius,	
	discede tandem, dura et infaelix abi,	
	infrugifera, servilis, in natum tamen	
	maneat parentis. in deos plane impium	1710
	iuvat vocari. me colere superos decet	
	miserum, senemque? num senex metuit Iovem?	
SEN.	colendum utrique numen imprimis reor.	

sig. E 4^r

OEN.	miseria vicit iam metus omnes mea,	
	et haec senectae quantula est nostrae mora?	1715
	quam, saeva ne vis raptat, abrumpam mihi.	
	nam quid hic ultra detineo manes meos,	
	aut quae voluptas esse mihi vitae potest?	
	proin, nec ulla vota caelicolis fero,	
	nec si velint nocere, quo possint, habent.	1720
	in me deorum turba iam vires suas	
	exhausit omnes. quid meas frustra preces	

1691. <*me*> supplevi   1703. vel fort. *ah siste* lib.

which the soothsayer shuddered, that the old man dreaded. And what portion of the killing is it of which I have just learned? My desire was for less than that. I had believed no misfortune could be worse than Meleager's death, but there is a further step. I believe it to be the pinnacle of my woes that Fortune made me the abominable instrument of his killing. Why not despatch myself to the eternal halls of pallid Erebus? Surely no greater evil is still to be accomplished? Is there a further step?

O. M. Abandon these bombastic threats of your savage heart, banish this impious thought of death.

OEN. Why waste words? I am determined on this, which I should have done already. Have I outlived my destiny, but am still alive, not yet abandoning daylight and mankind? But I shall depart presently. However, among these ills I take this consolation, that now I am free to despise all the gods.

O. M. Leave off at length. I beg you suppress your mind's arrogant impulses, and begin to cultivate piety.

OEN. This is the fruit my piety has borne, that I do not care to be pious amidst such hardship. Piety, quickly leave my heart, go away at last. Harsh, unhappy, fruitless and servile, go, but let the piety of a father for his son remain. I want to be called impious towards the gods. Should I worship them in my misery, old man? Surely an old man does not fear Jove?

O. M. I think first of all we ought to worship the god.

OEN. Now my misery overcomes all fears, and what a tiny respite is on our old age! And this of I shall rid myself, lest some savage power snatch it. For why delay my shade here any longer, or what pleasure is there for me in life? Therefore I offer no prayers to the gods in heaven, and even if they should wish to harm me to the extent they can, they do not have them. Now the throng of gods have exhausted all their powers against me. Why

perire patiar? quid carent convitio?
detestor omnes, teque, Latona satam,
longe ante reliquos. ecce quas fundo preces, 1725
audite superi. sed quid? Eumenidum cohors
excessit Erebo. propius ac propius, mea
in ora tendit saeva Tisiphone faces,
sudesque in orbem versat, et vulsos coma
tortos in imum coniicit colubros sinum, 1730
flammasque et angues spargit. at tellus labat,
et aula tectis crepuit, et subita ambulat
vertigine domus, titubat, errat sedibus
convulsa propriis, ecce iam nutat minax.
i, profuge, curre, siste, quo vadam miser? 1735
iam nunc ruinam ducit, et lenta mora
eversa lapsu funditus prono cadit.
audite sonitum, tota iam moles meis
incumbit humeris, et caput nostrum obruit.

SEN. remitte inanem pectoris vani metum, 1740
defixa solide vi sua constat domus.

OEN. ecce, alia clades. statuitur medio aureum
caelo tribunal, sedit in paenas meas
frequens deorum curia, et causam petit.
Diana caetum cogit, et questu graves 1745
exacuit iras. causa iam dicta est, nocens
paenae reservor, quaeritur paenae modus.
sententia placet varia: pars Ixionis
vertiginosam Thessali suadet rotam,
pars alia saxum Sisyphi, aut diram senis 1750
famem sitimque Tantali. huic Tytii placet
aeterna volucris, Belidum huic vanus labor.
urget Diana, singulas mites vocat,
deposcit omnes, sola saturari nequit.

SEN. ut animus horret conscios scelerum deos, 1755
et quae meretur, ferre sibi fingit, mala!

OEN. sed ecce, geminus Titan effulget polo,
et gemina duplices extulit Calydon domos.
ubi sum? quid hoc est? en retro soles meant,
conduntque vultus, atra nox profert caput, 1760
miserisque caecum rebus infertur Chaos.
horrenda venti bella cum nimbis gerunt,
omnique parte Iuppiter dirum intonat,
iaculatur ignes, quicquid aut arcu potest,

sig. E 4ᵛ

should I allow my prayers to fail in vain? Why should the gods go without reproof? I loathe them all and you, daughter of Latona, far above the rest. Thus you hear, gods, the prayers I have to offer. But what's this? A crowd of Furies departs Erebus. Tisiphone thrusts her torches in my face, nearer and nearer, whirling her stakes in a circle, and thrusts her smooth snakes, drawn from her tresses, deep within my bosom, scattering her vipers. But the earth quakes, the palace roof creaks, and suddenly the house goes dizzily a-dancing: it shivers, wandering, shaken from its foundations: see how it wavers with menace. Go, flee, run, remain — where should I go in my unhappiness? Now it is falling in ruins and, after a hesitant pause, is overthrown and tumbles headlong to the ground. Hear the noise, as now the entire mass falls about my shoulders, burying my head.

O. M. Dispel this empty fear of your deluded heart, for your home stands solidly, shored up by its might.

OEN. Behold another catastrophe. A golden tribunal is established in heaven, a crowded assembly of gods is sitting for my punishment, demanding my trial. Diana convenes the court and by her complaints she is whetting their powerful wrath. The case has now been tried, and I, guilty, am bound over for punishment as the means of penalty is decided. Various motions are made. One faction urges Thracian Ixion's dizzy wheel; another Sisyphus' rock or the hunger and thirst of old man Tantalus. This one wants Tityus' everlasting bird and the fruitless toil of the Danaides. Diana exhorts them, calling these single punishments mild, demands them all, alone is insatiable.

O. M. How his mind shudders at the gods, conscious of his crimes, and imagines itself to be suffering the ills it deserves!

OEN. But see, a double sun shines in the sky, and a twin Calydon has produced two palaces. Where am I? What is this? Lo, the suns are moving backwards, they hide their faces, dark night raises her head, blind Chaos is added to our miseries. The winds wage horrendous wars against the clouds, and in every direction Jupiter thunders terribly. He

		aut igne patrio, tentat id Phaebi soror,	1765
		frater sagittas praebet, et dextram adiuvat.	
	SEN.	en, ut superbos ultor insequitur deus,	
		et in furorem desinit nimius tumor!	
	OEN.	nunc, anime, persta, rebus audendum ultimis.	
		nunc nunc furentes arma Titanes ferant.	1770
		me duce, secunda bella cum superis gerant.	
		furor, ira, luctus, miseriae vires dabunt.	
		solus Typhoeus expulit caelo deos,	
sig. E 5ʳ		cum se in figuras verterent pavidi novas.	
		pastoris ipse Iuppiter formam induit,	1775
		Bacchus sub hirco latuit, in corvo tuus,	
		Diana, frater. ipsa latuisti improba	
		sub fele, nivea Iuno sub vacca, Venus	
		in pisce tremuit, ibidis plumae deum	
		texere volucrem, quisque sibi metuit miser.	1780
		iamque ecce fugiunt. hoc petam montis iugum	
		aequale caelo, detraham superos polo.	

MATRES CALYDONIDES

quis te furiis deus insequitur,
miserande pater, domuique tuae,
gentique gravis? te, Meleager, 1785
semper flendi sacra cupido est,
tu lachrymarum causa perennis,
tibi perpetuus decidet imber.
nullus flendi sit modus unquam,
quia tanta modum vicit clades. 1790
expedit inter lamenta mori.
    plangite, matres.

hoc continuis egimus horis,
totas noctes totosque dies
misere flendo duximus, ex quo 1795
maesta iacuit frigidus aula.
nec iam solitus nobis satis est
planctus, solitum vincere morem
iuvat. ingeminat saeva dolorem
causa doloris. pede lymphato 1800

1768. *tumor?* lib. 1792. *plangite* lib.: corr. Brooke, script. inedit.

hurls his fires, and whatever she can accomplish with her bow or her father's fire, Phoebus' sister attempts, and her brother provides her with arrows, aiding her hand.

O. M. See how an avenging god pursues the arrogant, and how excessive pride ends in madness!

OEN. Now be persevering, my mind. Now, now let the raging Titans bear arms. With me as captain, let them wage a successful war against the gods. Madness, wrath, grief, and miseries will supply us with strength. Only Typhoeus has driven the gods from heaven when, panic-stricken, they changed themselves into strange shapes. Jupiter himself assumed the appearance of a shepherd, Bacchus hid under the guise of a goat, and your brother, Diana, in the form of a crow. You yourself shamefully hid as a cat, Juno as a snow-white heifer, Venus trembled as a fish, ibis feathers disguised a god as a bird, each poor god feared for himself. Now see how they are fleeing. I shall seek this mountain-top, as high as the sky, I shall pull down the gods from heaven. [*Exit.*]

CALYDONIAN MATRONS

Piteous father, what god pursues you with Furies, harsh towards you and your house? Meleager, my sacred desire is to lament you always, you are a perennial cause for weeping; let there never be a limit to mourning, since your killing exceeded all limits. Meanwhile, death would be a boon. Mourn, mothers.

Thus we have constantly consumed our hours, spending all our nights and days in weeping, since the time he was laid out cold in the gloomy hall. Now even our regular lament is not enough for us, we wish to outdo our usual habit. This savage cause for

sig. E 5ᵛ

    ire per urbem, crine soluto
      ululare decet.

    ingens terrae decus Aetolae,
    columen rerum, spes Calydonis,
    iuvenum gloria, flos, et lumen,   1805
    ille ille apri domitor saevi
    occidit. eheu rumpite vestes,
    pectora duris tundite pugnis.
    gravius nunquam fortuna dedit.
    cui iusta sonent verbera planctu,   1810
    lacerate comas, unguibus ora
    faedate avidis. urbis et orbis
      plangite cladem.

    Meleagre, domus decus Oeneae,
    generosus ubi est ardor, et oris   1815
    decor egregius? periere ista.
    reliquum nihil est praeter luctus
    lachrymasque graves. has pia matrum
    en tibi pleno turba gementum
    gurgite fundit. sed quo nutrix   1820
      confusa ruit?

NVTRIX, MATRES CALYDONIDES

NVT.   eheu beatos premere cum caepit deus,
    simul urget. aliud oritur ex alio malum,
    semperque crescit. quos habent magna exitus?
    o quale superi numen in terris habent!   1825
    quanta est potestas, sive contempti parant
    expetere paenas, sive placati pios

sig. E 6ʳ   beare! quoties remedia videntur dare
    periculis peiora! proh quanti stetit
    aprum necasse? finis alterius mali   1830
    gradum futuro fecit, atque ingens lues
    salute crevit. ecce tot clades dedit
    suina pellis. credere hoc quisquam potest,
    et esse adhuc dubitatur in caelo deos?
    vivax senectus, semper ad luctus novos   1835
    cur me reservas? misera quid matrum cohors
    vestras in unum impenditis lachrymas malum?

1810. *cur* lib.   1828. *beare?* lib.   1829. *peiora?* lib.

sorrow redoubles our anguish. It is proper to go through the city on frenzied foot, wailing with unbound hair.

The great glory of the Aetolian nation, pillar of our fortunes, Calydon's hope, the glory, flower, and light of her youth, this conqueror of the savage boar has fallen. Alas, rend your garments, beat your breasts with clenched fists. Never has Fortune given us worse. For him let rightful blows resound with wailing, tear your hear, disfigure your faces with busy nails. Bewail the catastrophe of our city, of the world.

Meleager, glory of Oeneus' household, where is your noble ardor, the outstanding beauty of your face? They are perished. Nothing is left but mourning and great tears. Lo, this pious throng of mourning mothers pours them forth for you in full flood. But where is the distraught nurse rushing? [*Enter Nurse.*]

NURSE Alas, once the god has begun to oppress the happy he continues. One evil grows out of another, always increasing. What outcome will these great things have? Oh, what authority the gods have on earth! What power they have, whether spurned and ready to exact punishment, or placated and eager to please the pious! How often do they seem to give us cures worse than our predicaments! Alas, what did it cost us to kill the boar? The end of our evil was a step towards a future one, and a great bane grew out of our salvation. See how many killings a boar-hide provoked! Can anyone believe this and still doubt there are gods in heaven? Long-lived old age, why do you always preserve me for new sorrows? Poor band of women, why spend your tears on one evil? Is there no limit to your bewailing

    ecquis perempti filii est flendi modus?
    satis habet ille. vertere hunc luctum decet
    matri patrique.

MAT.   fare quid, nutrix, feras.   1840

NVT. res intus actae, flebiles, miserabiles.

MAT. flebilius aliquid morte Meleagri accidit,
    aut scelere matris?

NVT.   scelere cumulatur scelus.
    regina thalamum ingressa furiali impetu
    mucrone pectus hausit infaelix sibi.   1845

MAT. o triste facinus!

NVT.   hactenus non stat malum.

MAT. quid? an furore percitus ferro Oeneus
    periit, an arce decidit ab alta miser?

NVT. est turris alta, cuius e fastigio
    caelo videtur proxima ostendi via,   1850
    despectat omnem regiae partem domus.
    furibundus hanc conscendit, et tanquam manus
    inferret astris, inde pulsurus deos,
    dissiluit amens, pondere illisum iacet
    deforme corpus. sed quid haec fletu mala   1855
    iuvat indicare? non potest ingens dolor,
    qualisque noster, lacrhrymis vere exprimi.
sig. E 6ᵛ magis stupore cernitur, miseras stupor
    voces cohibeat. perite funestos lares.

CHORVS

    reges, timete numina,   1860
    cavete divos temnere.
    maiora nunquam caelites
    exempla dii mortalibus
    dedere nobis, quam graves

1856. *sacinus* lib.: corr. Brooke, script. inedit. 1848. *periit?* lib. 1855. *quia* lib. 1860. post *reges* non interpunxit lib.

the dead son? He has enough. You should transfer your mourning to the mother and father.

MATRONS Tell us, nurse, what news you bring.

NURSE Piteous, miserable things have occurred within.

MATRONS Has anything more pitiful occurred than Meleager's death, or his mother's crime?

NURSE Crime is piled on crime. The queen entered her chamber at a furious rush and with a blade stabbed herself in the breast.

MATRONS Oh the sad misdeed!

NURSE But the evil does not end here.

MATRONS What? Has Oeneus, driven insane, died by the steel, or has the wretched fallen from his high citadel?

NURSE There is a lofty battlement, and from its pinnacle the way to heaven seems shortest. It looks down on every part of the palace. In his insanity he climbed this and, as if he were grasping at the stars, thence to lash out at the gods, he leapt dementedly, and his mangled corpse lies, dashed to pieces by its own weight. But why betray these evils by weeping? Great sorrow such as ours cannot truly be expressed by tears. It is better perceived in our amazement, let amazement silence our piteous voices. Love this doomed household.

CHORUS

Princes, fear the gods, take care not to scorn them. The gods in heaven have never given us better examples of what great punishments threaten the arrogant. Divine vengeance

paenae superbis imminent. 1865
divina perdit impios
vindicta, tot docti malis.
deos vereri discite.
turres ad astra culmine
se porrigentes arduo 1870
duris relinquuntur Notis,
minisque caeli, et horridis
saevi procellis Affrici.
sternuntur orni montibus,
ipsique montes decidunt. 1875
ferit minora Iuppiter
telo minore fulminis,
et parva parvo. rarius
demissa vallis tangitur.

1877. *malis*, lib.   1880. *arduo*, lib.

destroys the impious, schooled in such evildoing. Learn to fear the gods. Towers reaching to the stars with lofty pinnacles are left as prey to the harsh northerly winds, and the savage storms of the South wind. Mountain-ashes are laid low, the very mountains tumble. Jupiter strikes at lesser targets with a lesser bolt, at humble ones with a small. The lowly valley is more rarely touched.

EPILOGVS AD ACADEMICOS

	haec maesta nostri cantio cygni fuit, 1880

                haec maesta nostri cantio cygni fuit,   1880
                cygnea prorsus, quippe cantanti ultima,
sig. E 7ʳ   placuisse vobis si minus eam senserit.
                excussa si cui lachryma cantando fuit
                vel una, satis est. unica ad laudem est satis
                lachrymula sapiens. iamque Meleagro pia   1885
                solito rogarem iusta faceretis sono,
                Atalanta nisi me, regiae stirpis licet,
                melioris admoneret Atalantae tamen,
                nostraeque, quondam nympha quam Syrinx deo
                Tamesis ad undas inclyto Pani edidit.   1890
                Arcadica cui discedat Atalante loco,
                quantum ipsa cedit Arcadia clarae Angliae.
                quam dura semper nostra Meleagris fuit!
                ah dura nimium, plusque quam vellent sui.
                sic ore grato rigida maiestas micat,   1895
                qua speret ardens, quaque disperet magis,
                qualis Dianae fertur, ubi sylvas petit.
                immanis etiam retulit exuvias apri,
                maioris apri quam tuus, Calydon, fuit.
                cruore setas illa rubefecit levi.   1900
                at nostra totam belluam stravit solo,
                spoliumque victrix abstulit sine sanguine,
                stupenda virgo, bella seu tractet fera,
                seu pacis artes. et tamen tantis deest
                poeta factis? et tamen tanta exteris   1905
                virtus sepulta est, vate quia sacro caret?
                   proinde nostrae plausus Atalantae sonet.
                deinde manibus iusta Meleagro date.

EPILOGVS AD CLARISSIMOS COMITES PENBROCHIENSEM AC LECESTRENSEM

sig. E 7ᵛ

                quicunque sceptro fretus ac solio tumens
                aureus avito spiritus altos gerit,   1920
                nimiumque fidens, caelites temnit deos,
                te videat, Oeneu, videat eversam domum
                modo prepotentem, gentis Aetolae decus.
                hinc quemque par est facere documentum sibi,
                hoc quisque secum reputet exemplum domi.   1925

1893. *fuit?* lib.

EPILOGUE FOR ACADEMICS

This was the mournful song of our swan, all the more swanlike because it is his last tune, if he should sense that it has displeased you. It is sufficient if even a single tear has been provoked by his singing. One small tasteful tear is sufficient for his praise. Now I would request that you perform Meleager's funeral rites with your usual sound of applause, save that Atalanta, albeit born of royal stock, has advised me of a better Atalanta, our very own, whom the nymph Syrinx has borne to the famous god Pan by the waters of the Thames. To her Arcadian Atalanta has yielded place, just as Arcadia herself has yielded to famous England. How harsh our Atalanta has always been to her Meleagers! Ah so harsh, more than her suitors would have wished! Thus unbending majesty shines in her pleasing countenance, because of which the hopeful suitor is all the more ardent and loving. Thus is Diana's majestic beauty supposed to be, when she seeks the forest. She has brought back the spoils of a huge boar, a greater boar than yours was, Calydon. He only reddened his bristles with a bit of blood. But our Atalanta laid low a beast and, as victress, bore off the spoils without bloodshed, a marvellous virgin whether waging harsh battles or plying the arts of peace. But is a poet lacking to recount such deeds? Is her virtue hidden from foreign men because she lacks a sacred bard? So let applause resound for our Atlanta. Then give Meleager his just deserts with your hands.

EPILOGUE FOR THE MOST DISTINGUISHED EARLS OF PEMBROKE AND LEICESTER

Whoever, relying on his scepter and, gilded, swells because of his ancestral throne, arrogant in spirit and overconfident, scorning the gods, let him see you, Oeneus, let him see your overthrown house, lately all-powerful, the glory of the Aetolian race. It is fair for every man to take this as an example for himself, let every one ponder this as a lesson for his own house.

ut nos probetis fabulam, non est opus
iterum rogare, queis semel placuit. satis
actum putamus, si tibi placeat, comes,
comitique comiti, et nobile procerum choro.
si spes Philippus nostra Sidnaeus probet, 1920
ubicunque sedat ille, qui solus novis
favet poetis, ipse vates optimus,
Meleager ipse noster. a verbis meis
triste absit omen, et procul fatis suis
miserandus absit, opto, Meleagri exitus. 1925
   vos quem dedistis antehac nobis, viris
nobilibus istis, nobilem applausum date.

FINIS TRAGOEDIAE

There is no need for us to ask how this play pleases you, since it has pleased you once before. We think it has been enacted well enough if it pleases you, Earls, if it pleases the Earl's companion and this noble gathering of grandees, and if that hope of ours, Philip Sidney, approves, wherever he is seated. He alone bestows favor on novice poets, being himself an excellent bard, being himself our own Meleager. But let there be no sad omen in my words, and I trust Meleager's regrettable end will not be his destiny.

And you who have previously applauded me and these noblemen here, grant your distinguished applause.

THE END OF THE TRAGEDY

Textual Commentary

enutriendum potius puerum, quam tineis blattisque escam relinquendum: This entire passage (which echoes Horace, *Sermones* II.iii 119,*blattarum ac tinearum epulae*) is imitated in the prologue to Robert Burton's *Philosophaster* (written 1607, revised 1615, acted 1617, p.18 Jordan - Smith):

> *emendicatum e nupera scena aut quis putet,*
> *sciat quod undecim abhinc annis scripta fuit,*
> *inter blattas et tineas in hunc diem delituit,*
> *ab authore in aeternas damnata tenebras,*
> *aliorum importunitate nunc in scenam venit.*

Epistle to Essex, *atque ipsi etiam clam me, sed mendose ac perperam educarent*: Gager is evidently referring to the play's unauthorized circulation in manuscript, although no copies survive.

quemadmodum adolescens genui: In fact, Gager was twenty-six when *Meleager* was first performed.

panniculis efformatus: In classical Latin there is no such word as *efformo*. In my translation I assume that this = *deformo* (unless it is a typographical error for that word).

decrevissem tollere: Gager alludes to the Roman custom whereby a father acknowledged a child by picking it up, if he so chose.

fratre tuo Gualtero: Walter Devereux, Leicester's brother, was killed during the siege of Rouen in 1591. Gager recalls their friendship in some lines written in 1596 (poem XXXVIII.106 - 9):

> *Gualterum inprimis (mihi dicere fas sit)*
> *quippe meo propiorem animo. quo candidiorem*
> *nulla tulit tellus, quo non mihi charior alter*
> *contigit, aut cui me fuerit devinctior alter.*

He is also mentioned at poems V.43f., XLII.2, XLVII.10 - 12, and CLIV.

Calendis Ianuarii, MDXCII I. e., January 1, 1593, new style.

Eedes epigram. Richard Eedes (1555 - 1605), a friend and colleague of Gager's, and himself a playwright and poet, was a frequent recipient of Gager's occasional verse. Cf. the initial Commentary note on poem LXXV in Volume III.

For the academic title *Dominus* (employable by all members of the University who had been admitted to the B. A.) see the Introduction to Volume III. For the special Christ Church title *theologus* see Tucker Brooke's "Life and Times," 412.

Notes to pp. 38 - 42.

The point of this epigram is that Gager's play, like its protagonist, would have been doomed to a short life had its author not decided to publish it.

4f. Literally, *ad horae / lumen* means "the light of an hour." Edes may be stressing the words *lumen* and *lux* in this epigram because of Gager's use of light imagery in his dedicatory epistle to Leicester and in the epigram that stands at the head of his address to the academic reader.

Gentili epigram. Alberico Gentili (Albericus Gentilis), a native of Padua and Oxford's Professor of Civil Law, maintained an interest in academic drama and contributed prefatory epigrams to both of Gager's printed volumes. See the description of his support of Gager in the controversy with Dr. John Rainolds in the General Introduction to Volume II, and also poems I and CLXVI in Volume III. There is a biography of Gentili in the *D. N. B.*
I avail myself of the version in C. F. Tucker Brooke's unpublished manuscript (p. 634), slightly modified.

Accio e quivi? Cf. the Commentary note on the phrase *ab Euripide etiam, ac fortasse ab Accio* in Gager's prose introduction *ad Lectorem Academicum* below.

"J. C." epigram. Boas, *op. cit.* 177f., tentatively identified the author of these distichs as Dr. John Case, a Fellow of St. John's College, and formerly a chorister at Christ Church; Gager dedicated a poem to him (CLXVII). See the discussion of this incident in the General Introduction to this volume.

5 Polus was a distinguished Athenian actor of the fifth century B. C., who frequently appeared in Sophocles' tragedies. For the anecdote cf. Aulus Gellius, *Attic Nights* VI.5.

7 The *cothurnus* was the traditional footwear of the tragic actor; the *soccus* was its comic equivalent.

13 There was an old Roman proverb, *omen nomen*, based on the idea that names and words have some mystical portent. In the present instance, the writer playfully suggests that there is some such significance in the fact that the name Meleager contains all but one letter of Gager's own name.

28 There is an untranslatable pun on the two meanings of *carmen*, "magical incantation" and "song."

epigram *ad Lectorem Academicum* 10 He is now a boy because he is going on eleven years old.

prose address to the reader, τὸν Ἑλλάδος κλεινὸν γόνον: Gager cites an anonymous tragic fragment quoted by Aristotle at *Rhetoric* II.23 p.1397^{b}18; this is likely to have been from Antiphon's *Meleager* (for which see below):

Notes to p. 42.

καὶ σὸς μὲν οἰκτρὸς παῖδας ἀπολέσας πατήρ·
Οἰνεὺς δ' ἄρ' οὐχὶ κλεινὸν ἀπολέσας γόνον·;

ἀρηίφιλον: This adjective (in fact a stock Homeric epithet for warriors) is applied to Meleager at *Iliad* IX.550.

Antiphon: The quote is from the tragic poet Antiphon's *Meleager*; Gager found this at Aristotle, *Rhetoric* II.23 p.1399[b]26.

refert Strabo The reference is to Strabo, *Geography* VIII.vi.22, but the geographer is not responsible for this Euhemeristic revision of the myth.

Viriatum Lusitanum Viriatus was a Lusitanian general who opposed the Romans in the Spanish war of 147 - 39, described by such Roman writers as Appian, *Iberike* 60 - 72. Cf. the article at Pauly-Wissowa, *Realencyclopädie der claßischen Altertumswißenschaft* XVII, cols. 203 - 30.

Spartacum gladiatorem He led a slave revolt against Rome in the first century B. C.

Othomanum primum Osman I (1288 - 1326), the dynastic founder of the Ottoman Turks.

Tamburlanem Scytham Marlowe's *Tamburlane Part I* had recently been printed in 1590.

quod et Homerus videtur innuere There is no mention of the burning log in the *Iliad* account.

a quo longe aliter, quod ab Ovidio See the Introduction to this play for a discussion of Gager's sources.

ab Antiphonte See above.

ab Euripide etiam, ac fortasse ab Accio Euripides wrote a lost tragedy on the subject. So did the Roman tragedian Accius, but Gager sensibly hedges his bet, since Accius may or may not have adapted Euripides' original. In a note, Gager refers to the fact that several fragments of Accius' play are preserved by the Latin lexicographer Nonius Marcellus: cf. E. H. Warmington, *Remains of Old Latin* [Loeb Classical Library, Cambridge, Mass. - London, 1936] II.470 - 9.

quaecunque ea fuerit Gager is still unconvinced that she was not some sort of poisoner or witch. This view is not irrelevant, since he models important elements in her characterization after Seneca's witchlike Medea.

tum atrocitate "...there is a suggestion here of the perverted doctrine that tragedy is impressive in proportion to the amount of 'atrocitas' that enters into it..." (Boas, p. 168).

Notes to pp. 42 - 46.

in aves Meleagridas conversae He is referring to the climax of Ovid's version (VIII. 542ff.), in which Meleager's sisters were tranformed into birds called Meleagrides, or guinea-hens.

quasi in piscem This apparently bizarre conclusion is a reference to Horace, *Ars Poetica* 3f., *ut turpiter atrum / desinant in piscem mulier formosa superne*, describing "such a figure as Scylla, in which the hideousness of the whole was increased by the contrast between the beauty of the face and bust and the ugliness of the body." (Edward P. Morris, *Horace, The Satires and Epistles*, Norman, Okla., 1933, repr. 1967, *ad loc.*) Horace is arguing the doctrine that poets should include in any given genre only the things fitting to that the genre, and that any admixture of inappropriate elements serves to create monstrosities. Gager somewhat garbles these lines in such a way as to create an even more incongruous monster that is at once human, birdlike, and fishy, either out of whimsy or because he is quoting inaccurately from memory. His point is that such an ending would be incongruous in a tragedy.

Prologus ad academicos This was the Prologue of the original production. By the time of the revival, with *Dido* behind him, he could no longer claim the special tolerance due a neophyte.

Prologus ad academicos 1ff. Gager also compares a poet to a swan in his non-dramatic poetry, in much the same language. In a poem to his patron Robert Dorset (LXXIV) he writes:

> *est cygno similis, Maecenas chare, poeta:*
> *par vox utrique est, par et utrique color.*
> *fontibus et fluviis, et amaenis gaudet uterque*
> *amnibus, et Pythius gaudet utroque deus.*
> *at nisi cum mitis Zephiri spiraverat aura*
> *candidus extento guttere, cantat olor.*

In slightly modified form, he recycled these lines yet again in his final published poem on the death of Sir Philip Sidney (XXXV):

> *assimulant veteres cigno, Sidnaee, poetam:*
> *par candor, par est suavis utrique sonus.*
> *fontibus et pratis et amaenis gaudet uterque*
> *amnibus, et Phaebo gratus uterque deo.*
> *at nisi cum mitis Zephiri spiraverit aura,*
> *praesagus claro gutture cantat olor.*

10 Cf. Ovid, *Metamorphoses* XIV.430, *carmina iam moriens canit exequialia cycnus*.

Prologus ad academicos 19f. The audience would perceive in these lines an allusion to the Thames, flowing through Oxford.

Argument 23 The speaker draws the spectators' attention to the play's setting: the entire play is enacted before Oeneus' palace. More precisely, from the initial stage direction to Actus II we learn that two "houses" are used to represent the palace and Diana's shrine (as noted by Boas, *op. cit.*, 170), but for the most part the action centers around the former structure.[1]

Argument 56 *Fastus* is most visibly, but perhaps not exclusively, the salient characteristic of Oeneus and of Meleager's uncles.

Prologus ad P. & L. This was the Prologue written for the revival performance.

Prologus ad P. & L. 64 Leicester was Chancellor of the University.

Prologus ad P. & L. 68 I presume that the *baculus* in question was some sort of Chancellor's staff of office.

Prologus ad P. & L. 69ff. This somewhat complex conceit turns on the fact that the dragon was Leicester's emblem, the swan Pembroke's, and that the constellations Draco and Cygnus stand near each other in the sky.

Prologus ad P. & L. 74f. These final lines are addressed to the audience at large.

I.76ff. Even though Gager professes skepticism about the magical or supernatural elements of the Ovidian account in his *Prologus ad Academicos*, his attitude does not keep him from inserting the supernatural machinery traditional in ancient tragedy generally, and of Seneca in particular, in all three of his plays. In the present case, this prologue-like speech, delivered by Megaera, one of the three Furies, caters to the Elizabethan enthusiasm for spectral apparitions. The closest Senecan model is the dialogue between the Ghost of Tantalus and the Fury at the beginning of the *Thyestes*, Other Senecan plays (*Agamemnon*, *Thyestes*) begin with a variant on this idea, the appearance of an angry ghost from the Netherworld, seeking vengeance, and each of these three passages begins with lines that are similar to the first lines of the *Agamemnon*:

> *opaca linquens Ditis inferni loca*
> *adsum profundo Tartari emissus specu.*

Compare the first lines of the Ghost of Agrippina at *Oct.* 593 - 5:

> *tellure rupta Tartaro gressum extuli,*
> *Stygiam cruenta praeferens dextra facem*
> *thalamis scelestis.*

---

[1] For the use of this setting cf. the initial Commentary note on Actus IV. For "houses" in University drama see Bruce R. Smith, *Ancient Scripts & Modern Experience on the English Stage 1500 - 1700* (Princeton, 1988) 74 - 76 and, more generally, the discussion of the "conditions of college drama" in Alan H. Nelson, *Records of Early English Drama: Cambridge* (Toronto, 1989) 2.714 - 22.

Notes to p. 50.

Panniculus begins with the appearance from the Underworld of Cupid, who introduces himself (34 - 6):

> *tandem relicto noctis infernae specu,*
> *ad amoeniores extuli superum domos*
> *pedem Cupido.*

Also, in a poem by Gager (CXXI), *Wulsaei Umbra*, the ghost of Cardinal Wolsey is imagined to return to Christ Church:

> *inauspicata, Tartaro peior, domus*
> *male execranda semper et diris mihi*
> *in te reliqui noctis aeternae loca*
> *Wulsaeus ille extructor infaelix tuus,*
> *clarum galero verticem rubro efferens.*

Appearances by Fury-like creatures are frequent in University tragedies, especially as prologue-speakers. For example, in Actio III of Thomas Legge's *Richardus Tertius* (1579) Furor (Madness personified) speaks the prologue. Likewise, the Prologue to Actio III of Legge's unfinished *Solymitana Clades* is spoken by Vastitas (Devastation personified); Nemesis speaks the prologue, and the Furies constitute the chorus, of Matthew Gwinne's *Nero* of 1603.

In accordance with normal contemporary practice, the "scenes" within each act of *Dido* are numbered in both of Gager's manuscripts (for this practice cf. the initial Commentary note on *Dido* I.i). It may therefore have been the case that he originally employed numbered *scenae* in *Meleager* too, but that they were suppressed by the printer. Each list of speakers inserted in an Actus indicate the speakers in that portion of the Actus, with characters who are present but do not speak usually unrecorded. For practical purposes, this often amounts to a somewhat crude and inexact way of indicating entrances and exits.

I.76 Cf. *noctis aternae plagam* at *Hipp.* 835 and *noctis aeternae plagis* at *Oed.* 393.

I.77 Cf. Vergil, *Aeneid* VI.534 (of the Underworld), *tristis sine sole domos.*

I.78 Cf. *extulit...gradus* at *Oct.* 160.

I.79 Cf. Horace, *Epistulae* I.i.33, *fervet avaritia miseroque cupidine pectus* (and also *fervent...pectora* at Martial IV.lvii.5). For *exundat furor* cf. *Me.* 392 (also at line-end).

I.80 For *crescit rabies* cf. Ovid, *Metamorphoses* III.567.

I.81 Cf. *Me.* 143, *sceptro impotens.*

I.82 Cf. *Ag.* 10, *superba sceptra gestantur manu.*

I.83 For *socia thalami* cf. *Hipp.* 864.

I.83f. There is no verb to go with *Althaea* and *Meleager*: the reader is supposed to supply some such word as *sunt* or *habitant*.

I.84 Cf. Lucan VI.420, *Sextus erat, Magno proles indigna parente*.

I.85 "Jupiter of the Darkness" is of course Pluto. Cf. *H. Oet.* 1705, *nigri .. Iovis*.

I.86 For *iustis precibus* cf. Ovid, *Metamorphoses* I.377 and III.406.

I.87ff. For this prophetic means of indicating the action of the play cf. *Thy.* 40 - 9:

> *fratrem expavescat frater et natum parens*
> *natusque patrem, liberi pereant male,*
> *peius tamen nascantur; immineat viro*
> *infesta coniunx, bella trans pontum vehant,*
> *effusus omnis irriget terras cruor,*
> *supraque magnos gentium exultet duces*
> *Libido victrix: impia stuprum in domo*
> *levissimum sit fratris; et fas et fides*
> *iusque omne pereat. non sit a vestris malis*
> *immune caelum.*

I.87 Cf., perhaps, Statius, *Thebais* VIII.70f.:

> *fratres alterna in vulnera laeto*
> *Marte ruant.*

I.91ff. Cf. *Ag.* 47 - 9:

> *iam scelera prope sunt, iam dolus caedes cruor —*
> *parantur epulae. causa natalis tui,*
> *Aegisthe, venit.*

I.94 For *matris iratae* cf. *Me.* 646.

I.96 Cf. *Oct.* 629 *veniet dies tempusque* and Vergil, *Aeneid* II.324, *venit summa dies et ineluctabile tempus*.

I.97 For *poenas* with forms of *dabo* in the Senecan corpus cf. *H. F.* 843, *H. Oet.* 322, 1973, *Hipp.* 937, and *Oct.* 811.

I.99 Cf. *Thy.* 24, *et penates impios furiis age*.

I.100ff. Cf. *Thy.* 57 - 9:

Notes to pp. 50 - 52.

> dextra cur patrui vacat?
> nondum Thyestes liberos deflet suos —
> et quando tollet?

Cf. also *Panniculus* 47f.:

> et cur tam diu scelere haec vacat
> domus nefando?

I.100 Cf. *Phoen* .342, *miscete cuncta* (also at line-beginning).

I.103 For *evertam omnia* cf. *Me.* 414 (also at line-end).

I.104 Cf. Horace, *Sermones* I.v.54, *Messi clarum genus Osci*, and *Me.* 210, *avoque clarum Sole deduxi genus.*

I.110 For *publico...gaudio* cf. Martial VII.vi.5.

I.111 For *frontem geras* cf. Martial III.xciii.4.

I.113 Cf. *Ag.* 137, *fessus quidem et deiectus et pessumdatus.*

I.117 Gager may have been thinking of Ovid, *Metamorphoses* VIII.547, *interea Theseus sociati parte laboris*, or of Statius, *Thebais* VI.503, *stat sociumque iugi comitesque utrimque laboris.*

I.118 Cf. *sollicitos...tenet* at Ovid, *Fasti* II.727.

I.120f. Cf. *tristis...voces* at Vergil, *Aeneid* XI.840.

I.121 For *sospes est certe parens* cf. *Hipp.* 433.

I.122f. Cf. *Hipp.* 436, *domusque florens sorte felici viget.*

I.123 Cf. *H. Oet.* 441, *miseros facit* (at line-end).

I.128 For *saeva...lues* cf. *Phoen.* 131.

I.130 For *causa gemitus* cf. Ovid, *Metamorphoses* IX.1f.

I.130f. Cf. *Me.* 42f.:

> pelle femineos metus
> et inhospitalem Caucasum mente indue.

I.131 Cf. *Phoen.* 77, *pectus antiquum advoca*, and also *Tr.* 506, *animosque veteres.*

I.133 For *recipe laetitiam* cf. *Oct*. 754.

I.136 Cf. Ovid, *Metamorphoses* XIV.476, *ab agris / pellor*.

I.138 Gager may have been thinking of Vergil, *Aeneid* VIII.202 (of Hercules), *tergemini nece Geryonae spoliisque superbus*.

140 Cf. Lucan X.65, *ductura triumphos*. For *spolia...abstulit* cf. *H. F.* 1154.

142f. For *excidit / virtus* cf. Horace, *Odes*. III.v.29.

I.143 For *robur...pectoris* cf. Ovid, *Tristia* V.xiii.19.

I.144 Cf. *causa subest* at *Thy*. 967.

I.145 Cf. *digna dolore* at Ovid, *Tristia* V.v.64.

I.146 For *miror tamen* cf. Plautus, *Rudens* 1201 (also at line-end).

I.148ff. This is a very shortened equivalent of the list of heroes at Ovid, *Metamorphoses* VIII.301 - 17. For Castor and Pollux cf. *Met.*VIII.301f.

I.149 Cf. *Me.* 89, *Pollux caestibus aptior*.

I.150 For Theseus cf. *Met.* VIII.303. His faithful comrade is Pirithous.

I.151 Cf. *Met.* VIII.317 *nemorisque decus Tegeaea Lycaei*. Gager employs the Greek nominative singular ending *-e* here and at 1905. Cf. his use of *Hecube* for Hecuba at line 10 in the first of his published laments for Sidney (XXVII).

I.153 Oete is a steep mountain on the Graeco-Thracian border; in antiquity, Thracians were noted for their savagery and backwardness.

I.155 For *supplicium* with forms of *dabo* cf. Plautus, *Asinaria* 481, *Cistellaria* 477, Terence, *Eunuchus* 69, *Heauton Timorumenos* 138, and Catullus CXVI.8.

I.157 Cf. *deus arcitenens* (of Apollo) at Ovid, *Metamorphoses* I.441.

I.160 Cf. Ovid, *Amores* II.v.1, *pharetrate Cupido* (cf. also *Metamorphoses* X.525 and *Tristia* V.i.22).

I.161 For *laeta...sata* cf. Vergil, *Aeneid* II.306, *Georgics* I.325, and Statius, *Thebais* VII.275.

I.162 Cf. Vergil, *Aeneid* XI.564, *propius iam urgente*. For *furit intus* cf. Vergil, *Aeneid* VII.464.

Notes to pp. 54 - 56.

I.163 Cf. Martial IV.lxxxvii.3, *quo mireris magis.*

I.166 Cf. *Hipp.* 858, *perplexa magnum verba nescioquid tegunt* (cf. also *Hipp.* 639).

I.167 For *ignosce quaeso* cf. *Oed.* 864. For *impatiens sui* cf. *Hipp.* 372 (also at line-end).

I.168 Cf. *meruisse nefas* at Ovid, *Metamorphoses* IX.372.

I.169 For *nota fraus* cf. *Me.* 181.

I.171f. For *premit / animum* cf. *Ag.* 134f.

I.175 Cf. *quod fuit ante, manet* at Ovid, *Tristia* IV.vi.6, IV.x.30, and V.ii.8 (all at line-end).

I.176 For *nosse...iuvat* cf. Statius, *Silvae* IV.vi.8.

I.179 Cf. *silere pergit* at *Hipp.* 882.

I.180 Cf. *H. Oet.* 1447, *cogis fateri, Tr.* 573, *coacta dices sponte quod fari abnuis* (and also *fari abnuit* at *Hipp.* 883, also at line-end).

I.181 Cf. *Oed.* 708, *ipse ad penates regios referam gradum* and *H. Oet.* 579, *ipsa ad penates regios gressus feram.*

183f. For *tacitis...curis* cf. Statius, *Silvae* V.iii.34. Cf. also *sinat perire* at *Hipp.* 262f.

I.184 For *perire curis* cf. Propertius II.xii.4.

I.185ff. Cf. *Hipp.* 640 - 4:

> *pectus insanum vapor*
> *amorque torret. intimis saevit ferus*
> *penitus medullas atque per venas meat*
> *visceribus ignis mersus et venas latens*
> *ut agilis altas flamma percurrit trabes.*

Throughout the play there is a good deal of fire imagery employed with proleptic irony to describe Meleager's love. This is all suggested by Ovid, *Metamorphoses* VIII.325f:

> *optavit renuente deo flammasque latentes*
> *hausit.*

I.189 The phrase *populatur artus* occurs in the Nurse's description of the lovesick Phaedra's symptoms at *Hipp.* 377.

I.190 For *pudet fateri* cf. *H. F.* 1147 (also at line-beginning). Cf. also *Hipp.* 190, *ferre quod subiit iugum*.

I.191 Cf. Horace, *Epodes* xvii.21, *fugit iuventas et verecundus color*. Did Gager write *color* rather than *calor*?

I.192 For *gratia nostra* cf. *Oed.* 692.

I.193 Cf. Terence, *Eunuchus* 312, *nervos intendas tuos*. For *digna fide* cf. Lucan VI.543 and Juvenal, *Satire* XV.118.

I.199 For *pectus indomitum* cf. *H. Oet.* 155 and Statius, *Thebais* XI.714. For *pectus...domet* cf. Seneca, *Oedipus* 927f.

I.200f. Cf. *Hipp.* 230 - 2:

> *exosus omne fenimae nomen fugit,*
> *immitis annos caelibi vitae dicat,*
> *conubia vitat.*

I.201 Cf. *caelibis...tori* at *H. F.* 245 (cf. also *Ag.* 185)

I.202 Gager was evidently thinking of *Tr.* 250, *iuvenile vitium est regere non posse impetum*.

I.202f. Cf. *Ag.* 203, *frena temet et siste impetus*.

I.203 For *frustra* with forms of *cupio* cf. Catullus LXIV.260, Propertius I.vii.19, Martial X.xviii.2 and XII.lxi.4.

I.204 Cf. *fata vetant* at Lucan X.485, Statius, *Achilleis* I.81, *Thebais* III.316, V.179, and IX.254.

I.205 *Causa doloris* is common in Latin poetry: Vergil, *Aeneid* IX.216, the Vergilian *Ciris* 336, Propertius I.xvi.35, II.xxxiii(a).21, Ovid, *Amores* I.xiv.14, II.vi.10, *Ars Amatoria* III.599, *Fasti* VI.746, *Heroides* xv.119, *Metamorphoses* I.509, I.736, XIII.748, *Remedia Amoris* 572, 726,*Tristia* III.viii.32, IV .iii.33, Martial X.xli.3, and Juvenal, *Satire* IX.90.

I.206 For *hinc pallor* cf. Statius, *Thebais* III.564.

I.207 Cf. *silvas...colebat* at Ovid, *Metamorphoses* XI.146.

I.208 Cf. *nescit...amare* at Propertius II.xxx(b).34 and *nescistis amare* at Ovid, *Ars Amatoria* III.41.

Notes to pp. 56 - 58.

I.209 Cf. *conubiis...sociare* at Vergil, *Aeneid* VII.96.

I.212 For *cannam...levem* cf. Ovid, *Ars Amatoria* I.554 and *Metamorphoses* XIV.515.

I.213 Cf. Ovid, *Metamorphoses* XV.169f.:

> *utque novis facilis signatur cera figuris*
> *nec manet ut fuerat nec formam servat eandem.*

I.216 For *ferrum uritur* cf. Lucan IV.578 and Statius, *Thebais* VI.397.

I.218 Cf. *ardens..face* at *Ag.* 119 and *ardescit face* at *Hipp.* 681.

I.220 For *Herculeus labor* at line-end cf. Horace, *Odes* I.iii.36 and *H. Oet.* 1453. Cf. also *H. F.* 1316.

I.222 For *mutet animum* cf. Terence, *Phormio* 774.

I.222f. For *pari...odio* cf. *Oct.* 49.

I.223 For *precibus* with forms of *flecto* cf. Vergil, *Aeneid* II.698, Ovid, *Metamorphoses* XI.439, and Statius, *Silvae* IV.i.34. For *flecti potest* cf. *Thy.* 200.

I.224 For *fera est* cf. Ovid, *Ars Amatoria* III.735, *Fasti* V.540, *Metamorphoses* VII.782, *Tristia* III.v.36, *H. Oet.* 17, 236, 1215, and Martial, *Spectacula* XIII.8.

I.225 For *genus omne profugit* cf. *Hipp.* 243. For *careo* with the genitive the *Oxford Classical Dictionary* cites Terence, *Heauton Timorumenos* 400, but cf. also *Hipp.* 243, *paelicis careo metu.*

I.227 For *quae placeat* cf. Plautus, *Captivi* 180, *Poenulus* 1417, Ovid, *Fasti* VI.2, and Statius, *Thebais* XII.172.

I.228 For *patria tellus* cf. *Tr.* 602.

I.229 Cf., perhaps, Ovid, *Heroides* xvii.253, *apta magis Veneri, quam sunt tua corpora Marti.*

I.230 For *rudis est* cf. *Ag.* 995 (also at line-beginning).

I.231ff. Cf. Ovid, *Metamorphoses* VIII.318 - 21:

> *rasilis huic summam mordebat fibula vestem,*
> *crinis erat simplex, nodum conlectus in unum,*
> *ex umero pendens resonabat eburnea laevo*
> *telorum custos, arcum quoque laeva tenebat;*

Notes to pp. 58 - 60.

> *talis erat cultu, facies, quam dicere vere*
> *virgineam in puero, puerilem in virgine possis.*

I.237f. Cf. *Me.* 549f.:

> *spiritu citius queam*
> *carere, membris, luce.*

I.239 Cf. *Oct.* 903f.:

> *sin caede mea cumulare parat*
> *luctus nostros.*

Cf. also Ovid, *Heroides* xx.167, *gravior mihi morte repulsa est.*

I.240 Cf. *Hipp.* 268, *incubat menti furor.*

I.241 Cf. *Ag.* 250, *animam...trucem.* For *virginis saevae* cf. *Oct.* 974f.

I.242 Cf. Statius, *Thebais* IX.593f.:

> *ut forte iugis longo defessa redibat*
> *venatu.*

I.243 For *casus dedit* cf. *Tr.* 506 (also at line-end), and also *Hipp.* 426f., *dedit / tempus locumque casus.*

I.244 Cf. Vergil, *Aeneid* VI.894, *facilis datur exitus.* Cf. also *praestat...Venus* at Ovid, *Heroides* xv.213.

I.245 Cf. the Commentary note on 243.

I.248 Cf. Ovid, *Ars Amatoria* I.712, *da causam voti* (cf. also Martial IV.lxxvii.4).

I.249f. Cf. *Thy.* 899f.:

> *iam satis mensis datum est*
> *satisque Baccho.*

I.252 Cf. *gratia...rependatur* at Ovid, *Metamorphoses* II.694.

I.252f. For *pudet / pigetque* cf. Terence, *Adelphoe* 392.

I.254 For *agros* with forms of *vasto* cf. Vergil, *Aeneid* VIII.8, Statius, *Thebais* III.576 and IV.297.

Notes to p. 60.

1.255 In Seneca the epithet *magnanimus* is applied to a man five times (*H. F.* 310 and 647, *Oed.* 294, *Phaed.* 869, *Phoen.* 182), but never to a woman. Evidently, then, the characteristic designated by this word is a distinctly a masculine one. For *regia stirpe edita* cf. *Phoen.* 320.

1.256 For *gratiam...parem* cf. Plautus, *Mercator* 999 and Terence, *Eunuchus* 719. Cf. also Plautus, *Miles Gloriosus* 670, *huius pro meritis ut referri pariter possit gratia.*

1.259 For *tantaeque...curae* cf. Vergil, *Georgics* III.112 and Statius, *Thebais* V.625.

1.260 In the Introduction to this play we have seen that Boas asserted that *Meleager* adheres strictly to the Unities. But the play does not conform to the rule that the action should take place within a single day: this line and also 423 establish that Actus I occurs on the day before the hunt. Likewise, the Matrons state that they have lamented each day and night since the death of Meleager (1793f.), which indicates the passage of a significant amount of time.

Cf. Terence, *Hecyra* 467, *sed eam iam remittet*. For *moram* or *moras* with forms of *tollo* cf. Ovid, *Heroides* iv.147, *Metamorphoses* XIII.556, Propertius III.xiii.14, Seneca, *Phoen.* 458, and Lucan I.281.

1.261 Cf. *loca plena metus* at Ovid, *Metamorphoses* IV.111 and *Tristia* III.xi.10.

1.262 Cf. *Metamorphoses* XIV.10, *variarum plena ferarum.*

1.265 Cf. *Hipp.* 922, *silvarum incola.*

1.265f. Cf., perhaps, Plautus, *Curculio* 45, *minus formidabo.*

1.266 For *maior metus* cf. *Me.* 516.

1.270f. Cf. Ovid, *Remedia Amoris* 199, *venandi studium cole.*

1.271 For *labor vanus* cf. *Hipp.* 182, Martial X.lxxxii.7 and XIV.xlviii.2.

1.272f. For *fulvum...leonem* cf. Vergil, *Aeneid* II.722, IV.159, Ovid, *Fasti* II.339, *Metamorphoses* I.304, X.551, Germanicus, *Aratea* 149, and Statius, *Thebais* I.397.

1.272 Cf. *Oed.* 808, *nivoso sub Cithaeronis iugo.*

1.273 Cf. *stravit...leonem* at Martial, *Spectacula* xv.5.

1.275ff. This speech is modelled on Ovid, *Metamorphoses* X.535 - 49:

> *per iuga, per silvas dumosaque saxa vagatur*
> *fine genus vestem ritu succincta Dianae*
> *hortaturque canes tutaeque animalia praedae,*

> *aut pronos lepores aut celsum in cornua cervum*
> *aut agitat dammas; a fortibus abstinet apris*
> *raptoresque lupos armatosque unguibus ursos*
> *vitat et armenti saturatos caede leones.*
> *te quoque, ut hos timeas, siquid prodesse monendo*
> *possit, Adoni, monet, "fortis" que "fugacibus esto"*
> *inquit; "in audaces non est audacia tuta.*
> *parce meo, iuvenis, temerarius esse periclo,*
> *neve feras, quibus arma dedit natura, lacesse,*
> *stet mihi ne magno tua gloria. non movet aetas*
> *nec facies nec quae Venerem movere, leones*
> *saetigerosque sues oculosque animosque ferarum.*

1.275 Cf. *feri...leonis* at *Hipp.* 327."

1.279 For *facinus* with forms of *audeo* cf. Plautus, *Pseudolus* 542 and Terence, *Eunuchus* 959.

1.280 For *generosus ardor* cf. *Oct.* 54 (also at line-beginning).

1.281 Cf. *Oct.* 498f., *in caedem...armauit manus*.

1.282 For *nimium potens* cf. Vergil, *Aeneid* VI.870, Ovid, *Metamorphoses* III.293, and Seneca, *Hipp.* 330, 609, and 1114 (all Senecan examples at line-end).

1.283 Cf. Vergil, *Aeneid* VII.473, *hunc decus egregium formae movet*, and *Tr.* 1144, *hos movet formae decus* (*forma movet* is also found at Statius, *Silvae* II.i.139 and *Thebais* X.752).

1.286 For *mihi me relinque* cf. *Me.* 969 (also at line-beginning).

1.287 Although the proper vocative *Meleager* is sometimes employed, the form *Meleagre* appears enough (cf. also 989, 1600, 1814) that it is best left undisturbed by an editor. For *ratio vitae* cf. *Oed.* 696.

1.291f. Cf. *Hipp.* 443f.:

> *potius annorum memor*
> *mentem relaxa.*

1.292 For *mentem...rigidam* cf. Ovid, *Heroides* iii.96.

1.293f. Cf. *Hipp.* 451 - 3:

Notes to p. 62.

> *propria descripsit deus*
> *officia et aevum per suos ducit gradus:*
> *laetitia iuvenem, frons decet tristis senem.*

I.294 Gager was evidently thinking of Vergil's Camilla, who did not adhere to this prescription. Cf. *Aeneid* VII.805f.:

> *non illa colo calathisve Minervae*
> *femineas adsueta manus.*

I.295 The pun on *tela / telum* is untranslatable. Cf. *Hipp.* 103, *Palladis telae vacant*.

I.298ff. Cf. *Hipp.* 463 - 5:

> *hoc esse munus credis indictum viris,*
> *ut dura tolerent, cursibus domitent equos*
> *et saeva bella Marte sanguineo gerant?*

I.303f. Cf. the Commentary note on 293f.

I.305 Cf. Propertius II.28.57f. (traditional lineation):

> *nec forma aeternum aut cuiquamst fortuna perennis:*
> *longius aut propius mors sua quemque manet.*

I.306ff. Cf. *Hipp.* 761 - 3:

> *anceps forma bonum mortalibus,*
> *exigui donum breve temporis,*
> *ut velox celeri pede laberis!*

Cf. also *ib.* 770 - 2:

> *ut fulgor teneris qui radiat genis*
> *momento rapitur nullaque non dies*
> *formosi spolium corporis abstulit.*

I.308 For *vultus...formosi* cf. Ovid, *Amores* II.i.37.

I.309 Cf. Vergil, *Aeneid* XII.49f.:

> *quam pro me curam geris, hanc precor, optime, pro me*
> *deponas letumque sinas pro laude pacisci.*

I.312 For *sensit...lacertos* cf. Ovid, *Metamorphoses* IV.555.

I.313 For *plantae pedum* cf. Vergil, *Aeneid* VIII.458 and XI.573.

I.314 Cf., possibly, *sanguis...sequitur* at *Aen.* III.333.

I.317 For *minus* with forms of *tango*, cf. Ovid, *Ars Amatoria* II.684 and *Fasti* VI.274.

I.318ff. Cf. Ovid, *Metamorphoses* V.580 - 5:

> sed quamvis formae numquam mihi fama petita est,
> quamvis fortis eram, formosae nomen habebam,
> nec mea me facies nimium laudata iuvabat,
> quaque aliae gaudere solent, ego rustica dote
> corporis erubui crimenque placere putavi.

I.318 Cf. *virginum...greges* at *H. F.* 478.

I.322ff. This picture of Atalanta plying her vocation is inspired by Vergil's description of Venus disguised as a huntress at *Aeneid* I.314 - 20:

> cui mater media sese tulit obvia silva,
> virginis os habitumque gerens et virginis arma,
> Spartanae, vel qualis equos Threissa fatigat
> Harpalyce volucremque fuga praevertitur Hebrum.
> namque umeris de more habilem suspenderat arcum
> venatrix, dederatque comam diffundere ventis,
> nuda genu nodoque sinus collecta fluentes.

I.324f. Cf. further *Aen.* I.337f.:

> virginibus Tyriis mos est gestare pharetram
> purpureoque alte suras vincire coturno.

I.325 *Pharetra de tergo sonat* appears calculated to recall *Iliad.* I.46, ἔκλαξγαν δ' ἄρ' ὀϊστοὶ ἐπ' ὤμων χωομένοιο.

I.327 Cf. *Hipp.* 110, *iuvat excitatas consequi cursu feras.*

I.328 For *hymemque duram* cf. Vergil, *Georgics* IV.239 and Ovid, *Tristia* III.x.44.

I.328f. Cf. *Tr.* 583, *et famem et saevam sitim.*

I.329f. *Culpae otium...matrem* may be inspired by the English "idle hands are the Devil's playthings": in *Ulysses Redux* Gager amuses himself and his audience by working into the text several Latinized versions of vernacular proverbs and saws.

I.330 Cf. *furere...bello* at *Phoen.* 484.

Notes to pp. 64 - 66.

I.332 For *quid ista prosint?* cf. *H. F.* 249.

I.332f. For *armis...levibus* cf. Ovid, *Tristia* III.xii.19.

I.334 For the idea cf. *Hipp.* 352f.:

> vindicat omnem
> sibi naturam; nihil immune est.

Cf. also, perhaps, Propertius II.xxvi(c).52, *hic deus et terras et maria alta domat.*

I.336 For *igne...sacro* cf. Germanicus, *Aratea* 394 and *Me.* 842. Cf. also *Hipp.* 191, *igne tam parvo calet.*

I.341ff. The source of this argument is Catullus, LXII.62 - 4:

> *virginitas non tota tuast, ex parte parentumst:*
> *tertia pars patris est, pars est data tertia matri,*
> *tertia sola tua est.*

I.348 For *perire* with forms of *sineo* cf. Ovid, *Heroides* xxi.60 and Seneca, *Hipp.* 262.

I.355ff. The next part of the debate is based on the dialogue about marriage between the choruses of youths and girls in Catullus LXII. The present speech is closely modelled on lines 40 - 9:

> *ut flos qui in saeptis secretus nascitur hortis,*
> *ignotus pecori, nullo convulsus aratro,*
> *quem mulcent aurae, firmat sol, educat imber,*
> *iam iam se expandit suavesque exspirat odores;*
> *multi illum pueri, multae optavere puellae:*
> *idem cum tenui carptus defloruit ungui,*
> *nulli illum pueri, nullae optavere puellae:*
> *sic virgo, dum intacta manet, dum cara suis est;*
> *cum castum amisit polluto corpore florem,*
> *nec pueris iucunda manet, nec cara puellis.*

I.365ff. Likewise, this speech is based on the similar rejoinder in Catullus, *ib.* 51 - 60.

> *ut vidua in nudo vitis quae nascitur arvo,*
> *numquam se extollit, numquam mitem educat uvam,*
> *sed tenerum prono deflectens pondere corpus*
> *iam iam contingit summum radice flagellum;*
> *hanc nulli agricolae, nulli coluere iuvenci:*
> *at si forte eademst ulmo coniuncta marita,*
> *multi illam agricolae, multi coluere iuvenci:*

Notes to p. 66.

> *sic virgo dum intacta manet, dum inculta senescit;*
> *cum par conubium maturo tempore adeptast,*
> *cara viro magis et minus est invisa parenti.*

Compare Gager's description of a widow at poem CXXXII.1f.:

> *quae modo vitis eram laetis faecunda racemis*
> *nunc iaceo sterilis funere facta tuo.*

I.377 For *oculos* with forms of *pasco* cf. Terence, *Phormio* 85, Lucretius II.419, Ovid, *Amores* III.ii.6, and Juvenal, *Satire* VI.0x21.

I.379 Ovid uses forms of *marcesco* at *Epistulae ex Ponto* I.v.45 and II.ix.61.

I.380ff. Cf. Catullus, *ib.* 21 - 5:

> *Hespere, quis caelo fertur crudelior ignis?*
> *qui natam possis complexu avellere matris,*
> *complexu matris retinentem avellere natam,*
> *et iuveni ardenti castam donare puellam.*
> *quid faciunt hostes capta crudelius urbe?*

I.386ff. Cf. Catullus, *ib.* 26 - 31:

> *Hespere, quis caelo lucet iucundior ignis?*
> *qui desponsa tua firmes conubia flamma,*
> *quae pepigere viri, pepigerunt ante parentes,*
> *nec iunxere prius quam se tuus extulit ardor.*
> *quid datur a divis felici optatius hora?*

I.391ff. Cf. *Panniculus* 295 - 7:

> *Hippolyte, nescis quod fugis vitae bonum,*
> *Hippolyte, nescis; atque ideo certe fugis.*
> *roga maritos, et homines simul et deos.*

I.391 For *casta...Venus* cf. *Hipp.* 237, Martial II.xxxiv.4, VI.xlv.2f., and X.xxxiii.4.

I.393 For *satis* with forms of *testatus* cf. Germanicus, *Aratea* 250 and Statius, *Silvae* IV, proem 18.

I.397 For *nomen parentis* cf. Ovid, *Epistulae ex Ponto* IV.ix.134 and *Phoen.* 225.

I.398 Cf. Ovid, *Metamorphoses* IV.516, *deque sinu matris ridentem.*

I.398f. Cf. Vergil, *Aeneid* IV.328 - 30:

Notes to pp. 66 - 68.

> *si quis mihi parvulus aula*
> *luderet Aeneas, qui te tamen ore referret,*
> *non equidem omnino capta ac deserta viderer.*

I.400ff. Cf. *Hipp.* 659f.:

> *est genitor in te totus et torvae tamen*
> *pars aliqua matris miscet ex aequo decus.*

I.404 For *qui blandiendo* cf. *Hipp.* 134 (also at line-beginning).

I.404 For *iugales...faces* cf. *Ag.* 158, *Herc. Oet.* 339, and *Hipp.* 597.

I.405 For *puella sapiens* cf. Ovid, *Metamorphoses* X.622. Gager was possibly thinking of Catullus LXIII.32f.:

> *veluti iuvenca vitans*
> *onus indomita iugi.*

I.409ff. For this *topos*, listing various impossibilities or *adynata*, cf. the expression of gratitude at Vergil, *Eclogue* i.59 - 63:

> *ante leves ergo pascentur in aethere cervi,*
> *et freta destituent nudos in litore piscis,*
> *ante pererratis amborium finibus exsul*
> *aut Ararim Parthus bibet aut Germania Tigrim,*
> *quam nostro illius labatur pectore vultus.*

Gager subsequently used this same device in one of his published laments for Sidney (poem XXXIV.116 - 9):

> *desinet ergo lupum prius agna timere, columba*
> *accipitrem, piscisque amnem dediscet amarae,*
> *quam tua pastorum labatur cura medullis,*
> *quam calamo taceare meo.*

I.416 For *gravi sonitu* cf. Lucretius VI.285.

I.417 For *verba...excutit* cf. *Tr.* 575.

I.418 For *sic abibit* cf. Catullus XIVA.16 and Ovid, *Ars Amatoria* III.60.

I.419 For *inanem spem* cf. Vergil, *Aeneid* X.627, X.648, and Ovid, *Metamorphoses* VII.336.

I.420 Cf. *Hipp.* 877, *leti facultas nulla continget tibi.*

I.421 For *compotem* or *compotes* with forms of *facio* cf. Plautus, *Captivi* 41, 218, and *Hipp.* 710.

I.422 For *precibus admotis agam* cf. *Hipp.* 635.

I.423 This line is suggested by such lines as Ovid, *Metamorphoses* III.149f.:

> *altera lucem*
> *cum croceis invecta rotis Aurora reducet*

and Vergil, *Aeneid* XI.913f.:

> *ni roseus fessos iam gurgite Phoebus Hibero*
> *tingat equos noctemque die labente reducat.*

For *crastinum...diem* cf. Plautus, *Mostellaria* 881, *Stichus* 635, and Propertius II.xv. 54.

I.424f. Cf. Vergil, *Aeneid* XII.913, *quacumque viam virtute petivit.*

I.425 Cf. *dignum gerant* at *Phoen.* 333 (also at line-end).

I.426 Cf. *H. F.* 350, *fore ut recuset ac meos spernat toros.*

I.427f. For *manu* with forms of *raptus* cf. Vergil, *Aeneid* XII.901, *Georgics* III.32, Ovid, *Fasti* III.504, *Heroides* vi.14, *Metamorphoses* IV.496, *H. F.* 341, and Martial V. xxxvii.11.

I.428ff. As this dialogue shifts into stychomythic exchanges, it gravitates into the orbit of Senecan scenes in which a bad ruler, contemplating a crime, is questioned by an advisor or underling: cf. *Oct.* 846ff., *Thy.* 204ff., and *Tr.* 327ff.

I.431 I. e., how often has Jupiter committed such acts himself (as in the episode of Europa and the bull)?

I.436 Cf. *Me.* 168, *rex meus fuerat pater.*

I.437 Gager was possibly thinking of Statius, *Thebais* V.305, *insula dives agris opibusque armisque virisque.*

I.438f. For *face* with forms of *ardeo* cf. *Ag.* 119, *Hipp.* 681, and *Oct.* 119.

I.439 For *deo* with forms of *plenus* cf. Lucan VI.708 and IX.564.

I.442 For *alto...gradu* cf. Vergil, *Aeneid* IV.685, Ovid, *Ibis* 485, and *Oct.* 501. Again, in view of Oeneus' fate this line seems imbued with proleptic irony.

Notes to pp. 70 - 72.

I.443f. Cf. Ovid, *Metamorphoses* VIII.327f.:

> *nec plura sinit tempusque pudorque*
> *dicere: maius opus magni certaminis urguet.*

I.445 For *consilio* with forms of *rego* cf. Terence, *Eunuchus* 58 and *Tr.* 359.

Actus I chorus As is often the case in Senecan tragedy, the identity of the chorus is not stated explicitly but is, at best, left to be inferred by the reader. At V.1792ff. there is a lyric passage delivered by some Calydonian matrons who are onstage throughout the Actus. Unlike other lyric intrusions within some of Gager's acts, this is not a song so much as an extra choral passage, albeit one not used to demarcate an act division. These matrons next engage in dialogue with the Nurse, and then the Actus ends with another chorus. We may possibly think that this group of matrons is a secondary chorus (for which there is precedent in the *Hercules Furens* and the *Hercules Oetaeus*), but it is simpler and more straightforward to assume that this is the play's principal chorus.

This passage is written in anapestic dimeters, rounded off by a single anapestic metron scanned as an Adonic.

I.446 - 464 These lines are a close adaptation of Ovid, *Metamorphoses* VIII.289 - 99:

> *fulmen ab ore venit, frondes afflatibus ardent.*
> *is modo crescentes segetes proculcat in herba,*
> *nunc matura metit fletura vota coloni*
> *et Cererem in spicis intercipit: area frustra*
> *et frustra exspectant promissas horrea messes.*
> *sternuntur gravidi longo cum palmite fetus*
> *bacaque cum ramis semper frondentis olivae.*
> *saevit et in pecudes: non has pastorve canisve,*
> *non armenta truces possunt defendere tauri.*
> *diffugiunt populi nec se nisi moenibus urbis*
> *esse putant tutos.*

The closest Senecan analogy is probably the chorus at *Oed.* 110ff. describing the afflictions suffered by Thebes, already quoted in the initial Commentary note on *Oedipus* I.

I.461 I do not understand the purpose of the subjunctive *valeant* in what appears to be a straightforward declarative statement (and cf. *possunt* at *Met.* VIII.287), and is translated as such.

II.472ff. For a similar picture of prosperity cf. *Thy.* 225 - 31:

> *est Pelopis altis nobile in stabulis pecus,*
> *arcanus aries, ductor opulenti gregis,*
> *cuius per omne corpus effuso coma*
> *dependet auro, cuius e tergo novi*

> *aurata reges sceptra Tantalici gerunt;*
> *possessor huius regnat, hunc tantae domus*
> *fortuna sequitur.*

II.474ff. Cf. Ovid, *Metamorphoses* VIII.273 - 5:

> *Oenea namque ferunt pleni successibus anni*
> *primitias frugum Cereri, sua vina Lyaeo,*
> *Palladios flavae latices libasse Minervae.*

II.479ff. Cf. *Tr.* 959ff.:

> *modo turba felix latera cingebat mea,*
> *lassabar in tot oscula et tantum gregem*
> *dividere matrem.*

II.496 By a metrical slip *st* fails to create positional lengthening. It will be noticed that such errors (there is also one at IV.1659) almost always involve the consonantal combinations *sc* or *st*, and this same phenomenon can be observed in other contemporary Anglo-Latin poets such as Thomas Legge and Matthew Gwinne. Possibly there was some phonological basis for such errors.

II.502ff Gager's designation of this character merely as the Senex imitates the introduction of a like-named character (who is in fact Astyanax' tutor) in Seneca's *Troades*.

II.506 Diana was sometimes portrayed with three-headed statues also and was, as we have just seen, sometimes identified with Hecate. For the phrase *triplex Diana* cf. Ovid, *Heroides* XII.79.

II.513 Cf. the Commentary note on *Oedipus* I.10f.

II.516ff. Echoes of Ovid. *Met.* VI.193 - 200 show that Gager drew some of his inspiration for Oeneus' characterization from another mythological character destroyed by Diana for offending her, Niobe:

> *sum felix (quis enim neget hoc?) felixque manebo*
> *(hoc quoque quis dubitet?): tutam me copia fecit.*
> *maior sum quam cui possit fortuna nocere,*
> *multaque ut eripiat, multo mihi plura relinquet.*
> *excessere metum mea iam bona. fingite demi*
> *huic aliquid populo natorum posse meorum:*
> *non tamen ad numerum redigar spoliata duorum,*
> *Latonae turba, qua quantum distat ab orba?*

II.531f. Both of these lines echo *Oed.* 386, *solent suprema facere securos mala*.

II.539ff. This philosophy praising the humble man is typically Senecan. Cf., for example, the choral sentiments at *Ag.* 87ff. and *Hipp.* 1123ff. Like the present passage, these are indebted to Horace, *Odes.* II.x. 6 - 16:

> *auream quisquis mediocritatem*
> *diligit, tutus caret obsoleti*
> *sordibus tecti, caret invidenda*
>   *sobrius aula.*
>
> *saepius ventis agitatur ingens*
> *pinus et celsae graviore casu*
> *decidunt turres feriuntque summos*
>   *fulgura montis.*
>
> *sperat infestis, metuit secundis*
> *alteram sortem bene praeparatum*
> *pectus.*

The reference to *turres* in this admonition displays proleptic irony in the light of the manner of Oeneus' subsequent death.

II.543 Cf. *H. Oet.* 441, *caelestis ira quos premit, miseros facit.*

II.560f. Cf. Ovid, *Epistulae ex Ponto* I.viii.96, *iustam subprimat iram.*

II.564 Cf. the Commentary note on *Oedipus* I.12f. (for the significance of this allusion to Niobe, cf. the Commentary note on II.516ff. above).

II.558 Cf. Vergil, *Aen.* 9.138f. *nec solos tangit Atridas / iste dolor.*

II.563 Cf. Ovid, *Metamorphoses* VIII.739f.:

> *pater huius erat, qui numina divum*
> *sperneret et nullos aris adoleret odores.*

II.573ff. In writing 574 Gager may have had in mind *Thy.* 927 *ex alto culmine lapsum*. In any event, note the use of proleptic irony here too.

II.584ff. Cf. Ovid, *Met.* VIII.272 - 8:

> *Oenea namque ferunt pleni successibus anni*
> *primitias frugum Cereri, sua vina Lyaeo,*
> *Palladios flavae latices libasse Minervae;*
> *coeptus ab agricolis superos pervenit ad omnes*

> *ambitiosus honor: solas sine ture relictas*
> *praeteritae cessasse ferunt Latoidos aras.*

II.596f. There is an untranslatable pun on the two meanings of *colo*, "cultivate" and "worship."

II.600 Cf. *Hipp.* 1121, *cur madent fletu genae?* and *Oct.* 692, *cur genae fletu madent?*

II.601f Cf. *Oct.* 710f.:

> *Quae subita vultus causa mutauit tuos?*
> *quid pallor iste, quid ferant lacrimae doce.*

II.603f. This portentious dream is suggested by that of Andromache in Seneca's *Troades*. Thus Andromache also begins (435f.):

> *hic proprie meum*
> *exterret animum, noctis horrendae sopor.*

II.607. Cf. Ovid, *Metamorphoses* II.49f.:

> *qui terque quaterque*
> *concutiens inlustre caput.*

II.616f. Likewise, after Seneca's Andromache reports her vision of the dead Hector in a dream, she says (*Tr.* 457f.) *mihi gelidus horror ac tremor somnum excutit.*

II.635f. Cf. *Oct.* 754f.:

> *recollige animum, recipe laetitiam, precor,*
> *timore pulso redde te thalamis tuis.*

II.644ff This speech embroiders on Juvenal, *Satire* XIII.100 *ut sit magna, tamen certe lenta ira deorum est.*

II.655ff. Cf. *Oct.* 756 - 8:

> *delubra et aras petere constitui sacras,*
> *caesis litare victimis numen deum,*
> *ut expientur noctis et somni minae.*

II.670f. Cf. *Oct.* 693f.:
> *certe petitus precibus et votis dies*
> *nostris refulsit.*

II.674ff. This passage, with its dire portents, is inspired by the sacrifice scene in Seneca's *Oedipus*, in which Manto describes the sinister behavior of the fire on the altar

Notes to p. 88.

and the equally sinister aspect of the of the victims' entrails to her blind father Tiresias (303ff.).

II.675 Cf. *Ag.* 579, *utrumne doleam laeter an reducem virum?*

II.676 Cf. *Oed.* 208, *ubi laeta duris mixta in ambiguo iacent.*

II.679 Cf. *Ag.* 508, *tenet horror artus.*

II.680 Cf. *Oed.* 384f:

> *quid ista sacri signa terrifici ferant*
> *exprome.*

II.682 Cf. *Oed.* 528, *coacta verba placidus accipias precor.*

II.683ff. Contrast *Oed.* 331f.:

> *solet ira certais numinum ostendi notis.*
> *quid istud est quod esse prolatum volunt*
> *iterumque nolunt et truces iras tegunt?*

II.686f. In the same way, in the prototype scene in Seneca's *Oedipus*, Manto says to Tiresias (328), *quid sit, parens, effare,* and he responds (328 - 30):

> *quid fari queam*
> *inter tumultus mentis attonitae vagus?*
> *quidnam loquar?*

II.688f. Cf. *Oed.* 366f.:

> *mutatus ordo est, sede nil propria iacet,*
> *sed acta retro cuncta.*

II.689ff. Compare Manto's description of the entrails' sinister aspect at *Oed.* 353 - 83.

II.691ff. Surely this is intended as a proleptic foreshadowing of the burning of the *stipes* that will later destroy Meleager.

II.692f. Cf. *Oed.* 383, *immugit aris ignis et trepidant foci.*

II.703f. Cf. *Oed.* 298f.:

> *si foret viridis mihi*
> *calidusque sanguis,*

II.707 The meter guarantees that the printer did not omit *ni* before *prohiberet*, but this word must be supplied by the reader.

II.708f. Cf. *Hipp.* 846f.:

> *sed fessa virtus robore antiquo caret*
> *trepidantque gressus.*

II.718 Cf. *Me.* 226, *decus illud ingens Graeciae et florem inclitum.*

II.731 Here is a fine example of Gager's use of proleptic irony. *Occidistis, una occidam* can be translated "if you die, I shall die too," and also, prophetically, "if you commit murder, I shall kill too."

II.732f. Cf. *Hipp.* 438, *namque anxiam me cura sollicitat tui.*

II.742 Cf. *Me.* 294, *repugnat precibus infixus timor.*

II.743 Gager may have been thinking of *Ag.* 234f.:

> *tu nos pericli socia, tu, Leda sata,*
> *comitare tantum*

II.763 Note the imitation of *Tro.* 758f.:

> *non vacat vanis diem*
> *conterere verbis.*

And cf. *Oedipus* 184ff.

Act II chorus The meter is lesser Asclepiads.

II.766 For *Pax alma* cf. Tibullus I.x.67.

II.783f. Cf. Juvenal, *Sat.* 4.70 - 2:

> *et tamen illi*
> *surgebant cristae. nihil est quod credere de se*
> *conterere verbis.*

Gager reemployed this expression at *Panniculus* 2.

III.786ff. In Seneca, Messengers tend to make melodramatic entraces. There is no Senecan example of a Messenger entering bearing glad tidings, but the Messenger's entrance lines at *Tr.* 1056ff. present an equivalent of the present passage that is very similarly structured:

> *o dura fata, saeva miseranda horrida!*
> *quod tam ferum, tam triste bis quinis scelus*
> *Mars vidit annis?*

In several Senecan tragedies a Messenger delivers his news to the Chorus: cf. *Me.* 879ff., *Oed.* 915ff., *Thy.* 615ff. and also *Oct.* 780ff.

III.793ff. So far, Gager has displayed remarkable independence of Ovid's version of the myth. Indeed, he has had to, since the Ovidian version is on the whole not the kind of prototype which any dramatist could follow closely. But a major element of Gager's model consists of a protracted set-piece describing the hunt and the killing of the boar (*Metamorphoses* VIII.392 - 424), and the present messenger speech follows that passage closely. Gager makes two important changes. For brevity's sake he excludes many of Ovid's descriptions of various hunters' failed attempts to kill the boar; for some less obvious reason he also suppresses any suggestion that the outcome of the hunt is dictated by Diana's behind-the-scenes intervention.

III.798 - 810 Cf. *Met.* VIII.329 - 37:

> *silva frequens trabibus, quam nulla ceciderat aetas,*
> *incipit a plano devexaque prospicit arva:*
> *quo postquam venere viri, pars retia tendunt,*
> *vincula pars adimunt canibus, pars pressa sequuntur*
> *signa pedum, cupiuntque suum reperire periclum.*
> *concava vallis erat, quo se demittere rivi*
> *adsuerunt pluvialis aquae; tenet ima lacunae*
> *lenta salix ulvaeque leves iuncique palustres*
> *viminaque et longa parvae sub harundine cannae.*

III.813 - 22 Cf. *Met.* VIII.282 - 9:

> *misit aprum, quanto maiores herbida tauros*
> *non habet Epiros, sed habent Sicula arva minores:*
> *sanguine et igne micant oculi, riget ardua cervix,*
> *et setae similes rigidis hastilibus horrent*
> *stantque velut vallum, velut alta hastilia setae;*
> *fervida cum rauco latos stridore per armos*
> *spuma fluit, dentes aequantur dentibus Indis,*
> *fulmen ab ore venit, frondes afflatibus ardent.*

III.823 - 34 Cf. *Met.* VIII.340 - 8:

> *sternitur incursu nemus, et propulsa fragorem*
> *silva dat; exclamant iuventes praetentaque forti*
> *tela tenent dextra lato vibrantia ferro.*
> *ille ruit spargitque canes, ut quisque furenti*

Notes to p. 94.

> *obstat, et obliquo latrantes dissipat ictu.*
> *cuspis Echionio primum contorta lacerto*
> *vana fuit truncoque dedit leve vulnus acerno;*
> *proxima, si nimiis mittentis viribus usa*
> *non foret, in tergo visa est haesura petito:*
> *longius it; auctor teli Pagasaeus Iason.*

III.835 - 8 Cf. *Met.* VIII.355 - 60:

> *ira feri mota est, nec fulmine lenius arsit:*
> *emicat ex oculis, spirat quoque pectore flamma,*
> *utque volat moles adducto concita nervo,*
> *cum petit aut muros aut plenas milite turres,*
> *in iuvenes certo sic impete vulnificus sus*
> *fertur.*

III.839 - 56 Cf. *Met.* VIII.365 - 82:

> *forsitan et Pylius citra Troiana perisset*
> *tempora, sed sumpto posita conamine ab hasta*
> *arboris insiluit, quae stabat proxima, ramis*
> *despexitque, loco tutus, quem fugerat, hostem.*
> *dentibus ille ferox in querno stipite tritis*
> *imminet exitio fidensque recentibus armis*
> *Eurytidae magni rostro femur hausit adunco.*
> *at gemini, nondum caelestia sidera, fratres,*
> *ambo conspicui, nive candidioribus ambo*
> *vectabantur equis, ambo vibrata per auras*
> *hastarum tremulo quatiebant spicula motu.*
> *vulnera fecissent, nisi saetiger inter opacas*
> *nec iaculis isset nec equi loca pervia silvas.*
> *persequitur Telamon studioque incautus eundi*
> *pronus ab arborea cecidit radice retentus.*
> *dum levat nunc Peleus, celerem Tegeaea sagittam*
> *inposuit nervo sinuatoque expulit arcu.*

III.841ff. In describing Nestor's escape, both Ovid and Gager mean to indicate that he employed his spear much as a modern vaulter uses his pole.

III.845 This minor hero's name was Hippasas, son of Eurytides and Orithya (cf. *Met.* VIII.371).

III.857 - 9 Cf. *Met.* VIII.388 - 90:

> *erubuere viri seque exhortantur et addunt*
> *cum clamore animos iaciuntque sine ordine tela:*

Notes to pp. 96 - 98.

III.862 - 71 Cf. *Met.* VIII.414 - 19:

> *at manus Oenidae variat, missisque duabus*
> *hasta prior terra, medio stetit altera tergo.*
> *nec mora, dum saevit, dum corpora versat in orbem*
> *stridentemque novo spumam cum sanguine fundit,*
> *vulneris auctor adest hostemque inritat ad iram*
> *splendidaque adversos venabula condit in armos.*
> *gaudia testantur socii clamore secundo*
> *victricemque petunt dextrae coniungere dextram*
> *immanemque ferum multa tellure iacentem*
> *mirantes spectant neque adhuc contigere tutum*
> *esse putant, sed tela tamen sua quisque cruentat.*

III.882ff. This song contains a variant on Sapphic stanzas: five rather than three hendecasyllables followed by an Adonic.
This song, with its refrain of *laeta triumphum*, is calculated to remind the spectator of a song sung in a Roman victory procession with its refrain *io triumphe*: cf. Horace, *Odes* IV.ii 49f., *Epodes* ix.21-3, and Ovid, *Metamorphoses* I.560f. At the same time, the triumphal chorus at *H. F.* 875ff. is comparable in a general way.

III.882 Cf. *Thy.* 970f.:

> *festum diem, germane, consensu pari*
> *celebremus.*

III.886f. etc For *superbum...triumphum* cf. poem XXIII.43f.

III.900ff. This entire scene, including the killing of Meleager's uncles, is loosely based on Ovid, *Met.* VIII.425 - 44

III.904ff. Cf. *Met.* VIII.426f.:

> *"sume mei spolium, Nonacria, iuris,"*
> *dixit, "et in partem veniat mea gloria tecum."*

III.918ff. Cf. Gager's second eclogue on the death of Sir Philip Sidney (poem XXXIV.119f.):

> *seu montibus errem,*
> *seu sylvis, Daphnin sylvae, montesque sonabunt.*

And also his *Aegloga ad Matthaeum* (poem CL.73 - 5):

> *per valles seu sit eundem*
> *seu montes, nomen valles montesque loquentur.*
> *cantibus implebo sylvas.*

III.921f. Cf. *Ulysses Redux* 131f.:

> nulla me oblitum tui
> arguerit unquam, nulla non gratum dies.

And Gager's second poem to Dr. Harbert Westphaling, CXLIII.41f:

> omnia polliceor, tanti me nulla videbit
> oblitum meriti degeneremve dies.

And also his *Aegloga ad Matthaeum*, CL.68f.:

> omnia profiteor, nec me lux ulla videbit
> immemorem.

II.926f. Cf. *H. F.* 59f.:

> de me triumphat et superbifica manu
> atrum per urbes ducit Argolicas canem.

III.930f. Cf. Ovid, *Met.* VIII.433ff.:

> "pone age nec titulos intercipe, femina, nostros,"
> Thestiadae clamant, "nec te fiducia formae
> decipiat, ne sit longe tibi captus amore
> auctor."

III.938 Cf. *Tr.* 467, *fronte sic torva minax.*

III.939 Gager may have remembered Vergil, *Aen.* X.447, *lumina voluit obitque truci procul omnia visu.*

III.952f. Cf. Ovid, *Met.* VIII.429f.:

> protinus exuvias rigidis horrentia saetis
> terga dat et magnis insignia dentibus ora.

III.965f. Cf. *H. Oet.* 823f.:

> "resistite" inquit, "non furor mentem abstulit,
> furore gravius istud atque ira malum est."

III.984f. Cf. *Met.* VIII.438f.:

> "dixit, raptores alieni," dixit, "honoris,
> facta minis quantum distent."

Notes to pp. 104 - 106.

III.988f. Cf. *Thy.* 530f.:

> *di paria, frater, pretia pro tantis tibi*
> *meritis rependant.*

III.990ff. Meleager's shame and chagrin imitate that of Hercules at *H. F.* 1321f.:

> *quem locum profugus petam?*
> *ubi me recondam quave tellure obruar?*

III.992f. Cf. *H. F.* 329, *saevus ac minas vultu gerens.*

III.995 Compare the entrance cue at 598, *sed ecce coniux tristis huc affert gradum.* Gager invariably marks each entrance with a heavy cue; at least on the character's initial entrance, he is identified for the benefit of the audience. This is a technique not always used by Seneca.

III.997ff. The way Althaea learns of the murder of her uncles is engineered differently than in Ovid (cf. *Met.* VIII.445 - 50).

III.1004 Cf. *H. Oet.* 985, *quid ora flectis?* and *Me.* 937, *ora quid lacrimae rigant(?)*

III.1012 Cf. *Tr.* 615, *maeret, illacrimat, gemit.*

III.1015 Cf. *Tr.* 166f.:

> *quae causa ratibus faciat et Danais moram,*
> *effare.*

III.1017 Cf. *Hipp.* 900, *gentis Actaeae decus*, and cf. also *Tr.* 876, *Me.* 227f., and *Oct.* 535.

III.1023 Cf. *Oed.* 528, *coacta verba placidus accipias precor.*

III.1026 For *inter extinctos iacet* cf. *Tr.* 603.

III.1027 For *quod facinus aures pepulit?* cf. *H. F.* 415.

III.1030ff. Cf. *Thy.* 1036 - 9:

> *quas miser voces dabo*
> *questusque quos? quae verba sufficient mihi?*
> *abscisa cerno capita et avulsas manus*
> *et rupta fractis cruribus vestigia.*

III.1036 Cf. *Phoen.* 223, *nefandus, incestificus, exsecrabilis.*

III.1039f. Cf. *Hipp.* 585 - 8:

> terrae repente corpus exanimum accidit
> et ora morti similis obduxit color.
> attolle vultus, dimove vocis moras:
> tuus en, alumna, temet Hippolytus tenet.

III.1041 Cf. the similar abrupt change of mood at *Oedipus* 184ff. and, as for that passage, cf. *Tro.* 758f.:

> non vacat vanis diem
> conterere verbis.

III.1055 For *tacita sic abeant mala* cf. *H. F.* 1186.

III.1061ff. Althaea's speech echoes the horror expressed by Hippolytus when he realizes Phaedra is making advances at him, at *Hipp.* 671 - 81:

> magne regnator deum,
> tam lentus audis scelera? tam lentus vides?
> et quando saeva fulmen emittes manu,
> si nunc serenum est? omnis impulsus ruat
> aether et atris nubibus condat diem,
> ac versa retro sidera obliquos agant
> retorta cursus. tuque, sidereum caput,
> radiate Titan, tu nefas stirpis tuae
> speculare? lucem merge et in tenebras fuge.
> cur dextra, divum rector atque hominum, vacat
> tua, nec trisulca mundus ardescit face?

Cf. also poem XXIII.53f.:

> maior trisulco fulmine Iuppiter
> sternet rebelles,

III.1071ff. Cf. *Me.* 461 - 4:

> nihil recuso. dira supplicia ingere:
> merui. cruentis paelicem poenis premat
> regalis ira, vinculis oneret manus
> clausamque saxo noctis aeternae obruat:

III.1080 Cf. Terence, *Eunuchus* 648, *ut ego unguibus facile illi in oculos involem venefico!* and *ib.* 859f., *vix me contineo quin involem in / capillum.*

Notes to pp. 108 - 14.

III.1090 I do not find the phrase *invidiae capax* in any of the major classical poets, but it appears at Thomas Legge, *Richardus Tertius* II.ii 2306.

III.1096ff. Cf. *Thy.* 1077 - 9:

> *tu, summe caeli rector, aetheriae potens*
> *dominator aulae, nubibus totum horridis*
> *convolve mundum,*

III.1106ff. Cf. *H. F.* 1272 - 4:

> *sunt quidem patriae preces*
> *satis efficaces, sed tamen nostro quoque*
> *mouere fletu.*

III.1109 Cf. *H. F.* 1265f.:

> *memoranda potius omnibus facta intuens*
> *unius a te criminis veniam pete.*

III.1110 Cf. *Hipp.* 255, *moderare, alumna, mentis effrenae impetus.*

III.1115 Cf. Thomas Legge, *Richardus Tertius* I.ii.iv.1 740, *mox prisca firmavit fides.*

III.1123f. For a similar image, cf. Gager's youthful *Susanna* 24f.:

> *sequitur velut umbra cupido*
> *foeda pudicitiam.*

III.1130 Cf. Horace, *Odes.* II.10.12f.:

> *feriuntque summos*
> *fulgura montis.*

Act III chorus This passage is written in anapaestic dimeters.

Actus IV The staging of the entire play, and particularly of the present scene, is inspired by that of Seneca's *Medea*, in which two doors in the *scaenae frons* represent Medea's house and the Corinthian royal palace. In the sacrifice scene of that play (670ff.), a Nurse first enters and expresses her alarm about Medea's distraught condition. Then Medea enters and, with the Nurse a reluctant onlooker, performs an unholy sacrifice with prayers to the powers of the Underworld, employing an altar temporarily set up before her house, and poisons the fatal robe to be given to Creusa. In Ovid (*Metamorphoses* VIII.451ff.), Althaea produces the log, puts it on the burning altar with a brief invocation to the Furies, and then delivers herself of a long speech in which her resolve momentarily wavers (481ff.). While much of what she says in that speech is adapted by Gager, he assimilates the action to that of the *Medea*'s sacrifice scene, save that here the Nurse is given a more important role and displays greater independence in judging Althaea's actions. But at the same time, Althaea's vacillation is modeled on Medea's hesitancy in a subsequent part of Seneca's play, where she wavers in her determination to commit the same crime: the killing of her children (893ff.).

The stagecraft of the present scene is modeled on the Senecan one, with the burning of the log occurring on one side of the stage, in front of the temple of Diana mentioned at Ovid, *Met.* VIII.445. Meanwhile, Meleager and Philemon stand before the palace. Thus the audience can simultaneously witness the burning and its effect on Meleager. And while Althaea is falling into the role of Seneca's Medea on her side of the stage, on the other side Meleager is similarly displaying the symptoms and reactions of Hercules in the *Hercules Oetaeus* as he is being consumed by Deianira's poisoned robe. Both characters speak many lines and phrases distinctly reminiscent of the characters they imitate.

IV.1141ff. Cf. *Met.* VIII.465 - 74:

> *saepe metu sceleris pallebant ora futuri,*
> *saepe suum fervens oculis dabat ira ruborem,*
> *et modo nescio quid similis crudele minanti*
> *vultus erat, modo quem misereri credere posses.*
> *cumque ferus lacrimas animi siccaverat ardor,*
> *inveniebantur lacrimae tamen, utque carina,*
> *quam ventus ventoque rapit contrarius aestus,*
> *vim geminam sentit paretque incerta duobus,*
> *Thestias haud aliter dubiis affectibus errat*
> *inque vices ponit positamque resuscitat iram.*

This speech is constructed as a parallel to *Me.* 670ff., in which the horrified Nurse describes Medea's angry condition.

IV.1142 Cf. *Me.* 670f.:

> *immane quantum augescit et semet dolor*
> *accendit ipse vimque praeteritam integrat.*

IV.1143 Cf. *Me.* 391f.:

> *quo pondus animi verget? ubi ponet minas?*
> *ubi se iste fluctus franget? exundat furor.*

IV.1145ff. Cf. *Me.* 858 - 65:

> *flagrant genae rubentes,*
> *pallor fugat ruborem.*
> *nullum vagante forma*
> *seruat diu colorem.*

Notes to pp. 114 - 16.

> *huc fert pedes et illuc,*
> *ut tigris orba natis*
> *cursu furente lustrat*
> *Gangeticum nemus.*

IV.1161 (stage direction) According to Boas, *op. cit.* 172f., "...there were two 'houses,' apparently on opposite side of the stage, the Palace and Diana's temple. At the opening of this Act the Nutrix enters with burning coals, and...the stage-direction... suggests an inner stage which could, when the action so required, be curtained off. Here takes place the dialogue between Althaea and the Nutrix..." But the word *remotiore* means "at a remove from Meleager and Philemon" and does not warrant the conclusion that the burning of the log was meant to be played as an interior scene. Such an understanding is excluded by the Nurse's description of Althaea coming outdoors at 1162.

IV.1162ff. For this entrance cue, cf. *Me.* 738f.:

> *sonuit ecce vesanu gradu*
> *canitque.*

III.1163 Cf. *Me.* 386, *furoris ore signa lymphati gerens.*

III.1164 Cf. *Me.* 389, *omnis specimen affectus capit.*

IV.1165ff. Cf. *Me.* 397 - 9:

> *si quaeris odio, misera, quem statuas modum,*
> *imitare amorem. regias egone ut faces*
> *inulta patiar?*

IV.1168f. Cf. *Met.* VIII.486f:

> *an felix Oeneus nato victore fruetur,*
> *Thestius orbus erit? melius lugebitis ambo.*

IV.1170 Cf. *Me.* 958, *quonam ista tendit turba Furiarum impotens?*

IV.1171ff. Cf. *Me.* 963 - 70:

> *cuius umbra dispersis venit*
> *incerta membris? frater est, poenas petit:*
> *dabimus, sed omnes. fige luminibus faces,*
> *lania, perure, pectus en Furiis patet.*
> *discedere a me, frater, ultrices deas*
> *manesque ad imos ire securas iube:*
> *mihi me relinque et utere hac, frater, manu*
> *quae strinxit ensem.*

IV.1175ff. Cf. Matthew Gwinne's *Nero* (1603) sig. K 2r:

> *o parce, mater: at petis poenas, dabo,*
> *requiris a me, an verius de me? dabo.*

IV.1180 For *facere quid tandem paras* cf. *Thy.* 266.

IV.1181 Cf. *Thy.* 258, *quonam ergo telo tantus utetur dolor?*

IV.1182f. Cf. *Thy.* 279f.:

> *bene est, abunde est: hic placet poenae modus*
> *tantisper.*

IV.1185ff. Cf. *Met.* VIII.451 - 9:

> *stipes erat, quem, cum partus enixa iaceret*
> *Thestias, in flammam triplices posuere sorores*
> *staminaque inpresso fatalia pollice nentes*
> *"tempora," dixerunt, "eadem lignoque tibique,*
> *o modo nate, damus." quo postquam carmine dicto*
> *excessere deae, flagrantem mater ab igne*
> *eripuit ramum sparsitque liquentibus undis.*
> *ille diu fuerat penetralibus abditus imis*
> *servatusque tuos, iuvenis, servaverat annos.*

1195 This line reminds us that Althaea's essential predicament is that she is confronted with the contradictory duties of a mother and of a sister, a situation which produces her vacillation throughout this scene. In seeing her quandary in these terms, Gager takes his cue from *Me.* 779f.:

> *piae sororis, impiae matris, facem*
> *ultricis Althaeae vides.*

IV.1199f. Cf. *Hipp.* 129f.:

> *nutrix Thesea coniunx, clara progenies Iouis,*
> *nefanda casto pectore exturba ocius.*

Although this line does not directly imitate one in Seneca, cf. the types of greeting cited in the Commentary note on 1017 above.

IV.1202f. For *cuius extremus dies / primusque laudes novit*, cf. *H. Oet.* 315f.

IV.1209 Cf. *Hipp.* 151, *latere tantum facinus occultum sinet?*

Notes to pp. 118 - 20.

IV.1210f. Cf. *Hipp.* 146, *tutum esse facinus credis et vacuum metu. / erras.*

IV.1211 Cf. *Thy.* 632, *quis hic nefandi est conscius monstri locus?*

IV.1214 For *noctis et somni minae* cf. *Oct.* 758.

IV.1216 Cf. *Me.* 1008, *est poenae satis.*

IV.1218f. Cf. *Thy.* 23f.:

> *detestabilis*
> *umbra, et penates impios furiis age.*

IV.1221ff. In Ovid the argument is Althaea's own. Cf. *Met.* VIII.499f.:

> *mens ubi materna est? ubi sunt pia iura parentum*
> *et quos sustinui bis mensus quinque labores?*

IV.1226f. Cf. *Hipp.* 103f.:

> *nefanda casto pectore exturba ocius,*
> *extingue flammas.*

IV.1231f. Cf. Ovid, *Met.* VIII.483 - 5:

> *ulciscor facioque nefas. mors morte pianda est,*
> *in scelus addendum scelus est, in funera funus.*
> *per coacervatos pereat domus inpia luctus!*

IV.1237 Cf. *Thy.* 542, *regni nomen impositi feram.*

IV.1245f. Cf. *Thy.* 248f.:

> SATELLES   *nulla te pietas movet?*
> ATREVS   *excede, Pietas.*

IV.1247 Cf. *Me.* 900, *fas omne cedat, abeat expulsus pudor.*

IV.1249ff. The wicked Thracian king Tereus had married Procne and they had a s(Itys. He raped her sister Philomela and cut out Procne's tongue so she would not bl; Procne retaliated by killing Itys and serving him to her husband. Then the entire family v transformed into various sorts of birds. Cf. Robert Graves, *The Greek Myths* (New Yo 1955) § 46.

IV.1251 Cf. *Thy.* 276f.:

> *causa est similis: assiste et manum*
> *impelle nostram.*

IV.1253ff. Cf. *Tr.* 298 - 300:

> *quando in inferias homo est*
> *impensus hominis? detrahe inuidiam tuo*
> *odiumque patri, quem coli poena iubes.*

IV.1278f. Cf. *Hipp.* 165f.:

> *compesce amoris impii flammas, precor,*
> *nefasque.*

And also *ib.* 404, *compesce tela, fratribus ferrum excute.*

IV.1280f. Cf. *Oed.* 521f.:

> *mitteris Erebo vile pro cunctis caput,*
> *arcana sacri voce ni retegis tua.*

IV.1282f. For *maximum fieri scelus / et ipsa fateor, sed dolor fieri iubet* cf. *H. Oet.* 330f.

IV.1285ff. This extended invocation of Underworldly powers is suggested by Ovid, *Met.* 481f.

> *Eumenides, sacris vultus advertite vestros!*
> *ulciscor facioque nefas.*

At the same time, cf. Medea's great invocation to the gods at *Me.* 740ff., which begins:

> *comprecor vulgus silentum vosque ferales deo*
> *et Chaos caecum atque opacem Ditis umbosi domum,*
> *Tartari ripis ligatos squalidae Mortis specus.*

IV.1285 For *Stygias sorores* cf. Statius, *Thebais* X.833 and XI.415.

IV.1286 Cf. the Commentary note on I.85.

IV.1288f. Cf. *Me.* 743, *supplicis, animae, remissis currite ad thalamos novos.*

IV.1296 *H. F.* 370, *pignus hoc fidei cape*, is perhaps comparable.

IV.1299f. Cf. *Thy.* 986f.:

Notes to pp. 124 - 26.

> *sed quid hoc? nolunt manus*
> *parere, crescit pondus et dextram gravat.*

IV.1301f. Cf. *Me.* 895 *quid, anime, cessas? sequere felicem impetum.*

IV.1305ff. Cf. *Tr.* 563 - 5:

> *potero, perpetiar, feram,*
> *dum non meus post fata victoris manu*
> *iactetur Hector.*

IV.1309 Cf. *Tr.* 747, *subeat iugum* and *Hipp.* 135, *subiit iugum.* Cf. also *Me.* 189f.:

> *regium imperium pati*
> *aliquando discat.*

IV.1310ff. Cf. *Met.* VIII.491 - 3:

> *fratres, ignoscite matri!*
> *deficiunt ad coepta manus. meruisse fatemur*
> *illum, cur pereat. mortis mihi displicet auctor.*

IV.1314 Cf. *H. F.* 1126, *pectus o nimium ferum!*

IV.1315 Cf. *Thy.* 549, *nulla vis maior pietate vera est:*

IV.1318ff. Cf. *Met.* VIII.494 -8:

> *ergo inpune feret vivusque et victor et ipso*
> *successu tumidus regnum Calydonis habebit,*
> *vos cinis exiguus gelidaeque iacebitis umbrae?*
> *haud equidem patiar. pereat sceleratus et ille*
> *spemque patris regnumque trahat patriaeque ruinam!*

IV.1331ff. Cf. *Me.* 926 - 8:

> *cor pepulit horror, membra torpescunt gelu*
> *pectusque tremuit. ira discessit loco*
> *materque tota coniuge expulsa redit.*

IV.1334 For *referamus hinc alio pedem* cf. *Tr.* 516.

IV.1337 Cf. *Ag.* 108, *tuta consilia expetis.*

IV.1346ff. Cf. Medea's description of her divided heart at *Me.* 939ff.

Notes to p. 126.

IV.1347 Cf. *Met.* VIII.464:

> *et diversa trahunt unum duo nomina pectus.*

IV.1352ff. Cf. *Met.* VIII.506 - 11:

> *et cupio et nequeo. quid agam? modo vulnera fratrum*
> *ante oculos mihi sunt et tantae caedis imago,*
> *nunc animum pietas maternaque nomina frangunt.*
> *me miseram! male vincetis, sed vincete, fratres,*
> *dummodo, quae dedero vobis, solacio vosque*
> *ipse sequar!*

IV.1357f. Cf. *Me.* 953:

> *rursus increscit dolor*
> *et fervet odium, repetit invitam manum*
> *antiqua Erinys. ira, qua ducis, sequor.*

IV.1359 For *fas omne cedat* cf. *Me.* 900, and for *pelle faemineos metus* cf. *Me.* 42.

IV.1361 Cf. *Me.* 43, *et inhospitalem Caucasum mente indue,* and also Horace, *Odes* I.iii.9, *aes triplex.* Cf. also *Ulysses Redux* 1064, *saxumque fibris indue, ac ferrum triplex.* One of these lines seems echoed at Matthew Gwinne's *Nero* (1603), sig. H 4[r]:

> *accingere anime, Caucasi rupes feras*
> *inhospitalis indue, et ferrum triplex.*

IV.1364ff. Gager's elaborate representation of Meleager's suffering and death presents a strong contrast to the brief description in Ovid (*Met.* VIII.515 - 25).

IV.1355ff. For the ensuing passage cf. *Met.* VIII.515 - 7:

> *inscius atque absens flamma Meleagros ab illa*
> *uritur et caecis torreri viscera sentit*
> *ignibus ac magnos superat virtute dolores.*
> *quod tamen ignavo cadat et sine sanguine leto,*
> *maeret.*

IV.1373 Cf. *Hipp.* 697, *maius haec, maius malum est.*

IV.1374ff. Compare the description of Hercules' symptoms at *H. Oet.* 1220 - 32:

> *sanguinis quondam capax*
> *tumidi igne cor pulmonis arentes fibras*
> *distendit, ardet felle siccato iecur*

Notes to pp. 126 - 28.

> totumque lentus sanguinem avexit vapor.
> primam cutem consumpsit, hunc aditum nefas
> in membra fecit, abstulit pestis latus,
> exedit artus penitus et costas malum,
> hausit medullas. ossibus vacuis sedet;
> nec ossa durant ipsa, sed compagibus
> discussa ruptis mole conlapsa fluunt.
> defecit ingens corpus et pesti satis
> Herculea non sunt membra — pro quantum est malum
> quod esse vastum fateor, o dirum nefas!

IV.1384 Cf. *H. Oet.* 1429, *longus dolorem forsitan vincet sopor.*

IV.1386f. Cf. *H. Oet.* 1218 - 20:

> heu qualis intus scorpios, quis fervida
> plaga revulsus cancer infixus meas
> urit medullas?

IV.1389f. Cf. *H. Oet.* 1165f.:

> morior nec ullus per meum stridet latus
> transmissus ensis.

IV.1390ff. For the general tenor of this and Meleager's next speech. cf. *H. Oet.* 1170 - 3:

> sine hoste vincor, quodque me torquet magis
> (o misera virtus!) summus Alcidae dies
> nullum malum prosternit; inpendo, ei mihi,
> in nulla vitam facta.

IV.1396ff Cf. Ovid, *Met.* VIII.518f:

> quod tamen ignavo cadat et sine sanguine leto
> maeret et Aencaei felicia vulnera dicit.

IV.1397 Cf. *H. Oet.* 1171, *summus Alcidae dies.*

IV.1399f. Cf. *H. Oet.* 1192f.:

> utinam meo cruore satiasset suos
> Nemeaea rictus pestis.

For the idiomatic phrase *ludo cruore* cf. *Tro.* 560.

IV.1401f. Cf. *H. Oet.* 1205f.:

>   *perdidi mortem, ei mihi,*
> *totiens honestam.*

IV.1403f. Besides the Ovid passage quoted in the Commentary note on 1366ff., cf. *H. Oet.* 1410 - 2:

> *vel scelere pereat, antequam letum mihi*
> *ignavus aliquis mandat ac turpis manus*
> *de me triumphat.*

IV.1405f. Cf. *H. Oet.* 1201 - 9:

> *viden ut laudis conscia virtus*
> *non Lethaeos horreat amnes?*
> *pudet auctoris, non morte dolet.*

IV.1407f. Cf. *H. Oet.* 307f.:

> *quid hoc? recedit animus et ponit minas;*
> *iam cessat ira.*

IV.1408 Cf. *H. Oet.* 20, *et hydra vires posuit.*

IV.1409 *Virus* is a word repeatedly used in the *Hercules Oetaeus* for the poison put on the robe given Hercules (536, 565, 719, 914, 916, 1396, all suggested by *Me.* 778, *qui virus Herculeum bibit*).

IV.1412f. Cf. *Oed.* 107f.:

> *illa nunc Thebas lues*
> *perempta perdit.*

IV.1426f. Cf. *H. Oet.* 1005f.:

> *quid me flagranti, dira, persequeris face,*
> *Megaera?*

IV.1420f. Cf. *H. Oet.* 1277f.:

> *urit ecce iterum fibras,*
> *incaluit ardor.*

IV.1423ff. Cf. *H. Oet.* 1362 - 8:

> *quae Lemnos ardens, quae plaga igniferi poli*
> *vetans flagranti currere in zona diem?*

> *in ipsa me iactate, pro comites, freta*
> *medios in amnes — quis sat est Hister mihi?*
> *non ipse terris maior Oceanus meos*
> *franget vapores, omnes in nostris malis*
> *deficiet umor, omnis arescet latex.*

IV.1423 Lemnos is a volcanic island in the Aegean.

IV.1425 The Danube.

IV.1430 Cf. Matthew Gwinne's *Nero* (1603), sig. P 2ʳ: *si longa, levia: brevia, si gravia.*

IV.1431 Cf. *H. Oet.* 1359, *errare mediis crede visceribus meis.*

IV.1439ff. This speech resembles, in a very general way, that of the insane Hercules in Seneca's *Hercules Furens* as he has hallucinatory visions, takes up his bow, and kills his children (*H. F.* 976ff.).

IV.1439 For *verberum crepuit sonus* cf. *H. Oet.* 1002.

IV.1440 The Furies. Cf. *H. F.* 86f.:

> *adsint ab imo Tartari fundo excitae*
> *Eumenides.*

For *Ultrices deae* cf. *Me.* 13.

IV.1447 Cf. *Tr.* 956, *adhuc rebellat? o manum Paridis leuem.*

IV.1448 Cf. the Commentary note on 1421f.

IV.1452ff. For *stringatur ensis* cf. *Hipp.* 706 and *Thy.* 26. More generally, cf. *H. Oet.* 1399 - 1401:

> *estne adhuc aliquid mali*
> *in orbe mecum? veniat huc. aliquis mihi*
> *intendat arcus: nuda sufficiet manus.*

IV.1455f. Cf. *H. Oet.* 1402f.:

> *ei mihi, sensus quoque*
> *excussit illi nimius impulsos dolor.*

IV.1457 For *dolor iste furor est* cf. *H. Oet.* 1407.

IV.1457 (stage direction) Boas (*op. cit.* 173) admires this direction. "Even though the hero's death takes place behind the scenes, neo-Senecan decorum requires that it should not be unbecomingly hurried. The Christ Church audience may, however, have been grateful for this concession to their sensibilities, for it made a pause before the culminating horrors of the last Act." Gager evidently had some such understanding, but one is obliged to wonder if the sensibilities of University audiences were really any more squeamish than those of their London counterparts. Certainly some dramas written for academic performance (e.g. Thomas Legge's *Solymitana Clades*, Matthew Gwinne's *Nero*, Thomas Alabaster's *Roxana*) would tend to suggest a quite different verdict.

IV.1458ff. This speech contains a couple of ingredients from the climactic scene of Seneca's *Medea*: But Gager employs these elements in his own way: once Medea begins her career as an infanticide she shows no more than momentary remorse.

IV.1458 For *bene est, peractum est*, cf. *Me.* 1019, and also *Oed.* 998, *bene habet, peractum est: iusta persolvi patri.*

IV.1462 For *quid misera feci?* cf. *Me.* 990.

IV.1463 For *unum restat* cf. *Me.* 37 and 498.

IV.1465 Cf. *Hipp.* 156f. (spoken by the Nurse to Phaedra):

>*moderare, alumna, mentis effrenae impetus,*
>*animos coerce.*

IV.1466 Cf. *Thy.* 899, *iam satis mensis datum est.*

IV.1467 At *Hipp.* 258ff. the words *decreta mors est* are spoken by Phaedra at the beginning of a speech in which she contemplates suicide. For *mortis via* cf. his *Ag.* 1031.

IV.1468ff. Cf. *H. Oet.* 868f.:

>*utinam esset, utinam fixus in thalamis meis*
>*Herculeus ensis: huic decet ferro inmori.*

IV.1475 For *tu fida nutrix* cf. *Me.* 568 (also *o fida nutrix* at *Hipp.* 432).

Act IV chorus This passage is written in hendecasyllables. It takes its inspiration from the first stanzas of the chorus at *Me.* 579ff.:

>*nulla vis flammae tumidique venti*
>*tanta, nec teli metuenda torti,*
>*quanta cum coniux viduata taedis*
>   *ardet et odit;*
>*non ubi hibernos nebulosus imbres*

Notes to p. 136.

> *Auster advexit properatque torrens*
> *Hister et iunctos vetat esse pontes*
>   *ac vagus errat;*
> *non ubi impellit Rhodanus profundum,*
> *aut ubi in rivos nivibus solutis*
> *sole iam forti medioque vere*
>   *tabuit Haemus.*
> *caecus est ignis stimulatis ira*
> *nec regi curat patiturve frenos*
> *aut timet mortem; cupit ire in ipsos*
>   *obvius enses.*

IV.1479 Cf. *Hipp.* 736, *fugit insanae similis procellae.*

Actus V Almost all the action in this Actus is of Gager's own invention. In Ovid (*Met.* 526ff.) we are only told that Althaea kills herself and that Oeneus is prostrate with grief, complaining that he is lived too long, and that the citizenry of Calydon, most particularly his sisters, lament Meleager's passing.

Unlike some others of Gager's invented characters, his Oeneus is not modelled on some figure out of classical literature. Although there are some elements of Ovid's Niobe in him (cf. the Commentary note on II.516ff.), Oeneus far surpasses Niobe or anyone else in his outspoken and virtually monomaniacal loathing of the gods.

V.1510f. Cf. *Hipp.* 183f.:

> *pauca, o parens magnanime, miserandae precor*
> *ut verba natae mente placata audias.*

V.1510 Cf. *H . F.* 198, *venit ad pigros cana senectus.*

V.1520f. Cf. *H. Oet.* 104f.:

> *par ille est superis cui pariter dies*
> *et fortuna fuit;.*

V.1524 Gager may have been thinking of *Hipp.* 144, *nam monstra fato, moribus scelera imputes.*

V.1525ff. Cf. Gager's poem *de Fortuna* (CVII — cf. also his *de Cupidine*, CIII):

> *stultitia primo posuit in caelo deum*
> *fortunam, et error numen affinxit sacrum.*
> *non paevidentem si quid adversi premit*
> *id omne sorti ascribitur vanae deae.*
> *fortuna nulla est, si quid in terra uspiam*
> *prudentia regat, si sit et curam gerat*

caeleste numen. quicquid est factum undique
nutu dei id tu factum et arbitrio puta.
sapiens supremi est pectus et regnum Iovis.
haud ille quoties fulmen emittit manu,
aut premere miseros clade mortales parat,
id ante nobis aperit aut mentem indicat.

Both these passages take their inspiration from *Hipp*. 195 - 7:

deum esse amorem turpis et vitio favens
finxit libido, quoque liberior foret
titulum furori numinis falsi addidit.

Cf. also *Oct.* 557 - 65:

volucrem esse Amorem fingit immitem deum
mortalis error, armat et telis manus
arcuque sacras, instruit saeva face
genitumque credit Venere, Vulcano satum.
vis magna mentis blandus atque animi calor
Amor est; iuventa gignitur, luxu otio
nutritur inter laeta Fortunae bona.
quem si fouere atque alere desistas, cadit
brevique vires perdit extinctus suas.

Cf. also *Panniculus* 186ff.

V.1530 Cf. Horace, *Odes*. I.xvii. 41, *aut virtus nomen inane est*, and Ovid, *Heroides* x.116 and *Ars Amatoria* I.740, *nomen inane fides*.

V.1546 Cf. *Hipp.* 721, *Venerem arguamus*.

V.1547 For *fraena dolorem* cf. *H. Oet.* 277.

V.1548 Cf. *Phoen.* 642, *libera patriam metu*.

V.1557ff. Cf. *H. Oet.* 1275 - 7:

flentem, gementem, summe pro rector poli,
me terra vidit, quodque me torquet magis,
noverca vidit.

V.1562f. Cf. *Oct.* 257f.:

gravi deorum nostra iam pridem domus
urgetur ira.

Notes to pp. 138 - 42.

V.1563 Cf. *H. Oet.* 884, *quid domum impulsam trahis?*

V.1573 For *luce non grata fruor* cf. *Oct.* 105.

V.1581 Cf. *Thy.* 445, *miser esse mavult esse qui felix potest?*

V.1586 Cf. *Me.* 115, *levis est dolor.* Cf. also poem LXI.11f.:

> *nam quid dolor? ah minus iste*
> *sufficit, et nostra est multo moderatior ira.*

V.1597 Cf. *Oed.* 687f., *regni bonis / fruor.*

V.1599 Cf. *inter umbras* at *Me.* 621, *Oed.* 584, *H. Oet.* 1196, 1157, *Oct.* 139 and 598.

V.1600ff. Cf. *Me.* 20f.:

> *per urbes erret ignotas egens*
> *exul pavens invisus incerti laris.*

V.1606 For *invisum caput* cf. *Thy.* 188. Cf. also line 229 of Gager's youthful *Susanna*, *invisumque caput detrudat ad Orcum.*

V.1607 Cf. *H. F.* 974f.:

> *pectoris sani parum*
> *magni tamen compesce dementem impetum.*

V.1627 For *cessant manus* cf. *H. F.* 615, *Me.* 417, *Tr.* 309, but especially *H. Oet.* 872, which stands in a passage upon which this speech is largely based.

V.1628f. Cf. *H. Oet.* 871f.:

> *coite, gentes, saxa et immensas faces*
> *iaculetur orbis,*

and also *H. Oet.* 319 - 21:

> *domusque soceri prima et Aetolum genus*
> *sternetur omne, saxa iam dudum ac faces*
> *in te ferentur.*

V.1630 For *corripite tela* cf. *H. Oet.* 873.

V.1631 Cf. *H. Oet.* 227f. *dirum caput / obruere*, and for *dirum caput* also *Oct.* 861 and

Thy. 244.

V.1632 Cf. *H. Oet.* 875, *impune iam nascetur indomitum malum.*

V.1635 Cf. *Oed.* 1029, *corrusca...tela.* This speech is patterned after *H. Oet.* 1077 - 85:

> *tu, summe caeli rector, aetheriae potens*
> *dominator aulae, nubibus totum horridis*
> *convolve mundum, bella ventorum undique*
> *committe et omni parte violentum intona,*
> *manuque non qua tecta et immeritas domos*
> *telo petis minore, sed qua montium*
> *tergemina moles cecidit et qui montibus*
> *stabant pares Gigantes, hac arma expedi*
> *ignesque torque. vindica amissum diem.*

V.1645 Cf. *Hipp.* 893, *labem hanc pudoris eluet noster cruor.* Cf. also poem CVI.11f.:

> *sustines, tellus, luem*
> *gestare tantam?*

V.1647 Cf. *H. Oet.* 1017f., *minax / unde iste coetus?*

V.1649f. Cf. *H. Oet.* 1118f.:

> *hinc et hinc populi fremunt*
> *totusque poscit vindicem mundus suum.*

V.1651f. Cf. *Oed.* 872f.:

> *me petat ferro parens,*
> *me gnatus, in me coniuges arment manus.*

V.1655ff. Cf. *Hipp.* 1156 - 8:

> *quis te dolore percitam instigat furor?*
> *quid ensis iste quidve vociferatio*
> *planctusque supra corpus invisum volunt?*

V.1658ff. Gager was fond of the dramatic device of the letter, and used it again in *Panniculus*. In the present case the source of the idea is not obvious.

V.1659 Another line where *st* fails to make positional lengthening: cf. the Commentary note on II.496.

Notes to pp. 144 - 46.

V.1666ff. Cf. *Oed.* 688 - 70:

> *dehisce, tellus, tuque tenebrarum potens,*
> *in Tartara ima, rector umbrarum, rape*
> *retro reversas generis ac stirpis vices.*

And also *Hipp.* 1238f.:

> *dehisce tellus, recipe me dirum chaos,*
> *recipe, haec ad umbras iustior nobis via est:*

For *dehisce tellus* cf. also *Tr.* 519.

V.1667 Cf. *Tartari...specu* at *Ag.* 2.

V.1669 Cf. *Thy.* 1007 - 9:

> *non ad infernam Styga*
> *te nosque mergis rupta et ingenti via*
> *ad chaos inane regna cum rege abripis?*

V.1670 For *ego te peremi* cf. *Hipp.* 1250. Cf. also *Oed.* 1045, *matrem peremi: scelere confecta est meo.*

V.1672f. Cf. *Me.* 117f.:

> *vix ipsa tantum, vix adhuc credo malum.*
> *hoc facere Iason potuit(?)*

V.1675 Cf. *H. Oet.* 843, *quid, anime, cessas? quid stupes?*

V.1677 Cf. *Tr.* 409 - 11:

> *quid, maesta Phrygiae turba, laceratis comas*
> *miserumque tunsae pectus effuso genas*
> *fletu rigatis?*

V.1678 For *siccus* = "dry-eyed," cf. *H. Oet.* 1269, *siccus aerumnas tuli.*

V.1679f. Cf. *H. Oet.* 1667f.:

> *nec lacrimas dolor*
> *cuiquam remisit.*

V.1687 Cf. *H. F.* 1191, *cladis tuae pars ista quam nosti quota est!*

V.1689f. Cf. *H. F.* 208f:

> > *finis alterius mali*
> *gradus est futuri.*

And *Thy.* 746f.:

> > *sceleris hunc finem putas?*
> *gradus est.*

V.1690 Cf. *Hipp.* 1119, *equidem malorum maximum hunc cumulum reor.*

V.1695f. Cf. *H. Oet.* 927f.:

> *depone tumidas pectoris laesi minas*
> *mortisque dirae expelle decretum horridum.*

V.1697ff. Cf. Ovid, *Met.* VIII.330, *foedat humi fusus spatiosumque increpat aevum.*

V.1697 Cf. *Phoen.* 140, *quid perdis ultra verba?*

V.1701 Cf. *Oct.* 70, *totque malorum breve solamen.*

V.1707f. Cf. *Thy.* 249f.:

> *excede, Pietas, si modo in nostra domo*
> *umquam fuisti.*

V.1712 The adjective *infrugiferus* is not in the classical lexicon.

V.1717 Cf. *Phoen.* 234f:

> > *quid hic*
> *manes meos detineo?*

V.1722f. Cf. *Thy.* 720f.:

> *stetit sui securus et non est preces*
> *perire frustra passus;*

V.1726f. Cf. *H. F.* 86f.:

> *adsint ab imo Tartari fundo excitae*
> *Eumenides.*

More generally, these and the following lines echo part of the speech of hallucinating Hercules at *H. F.* 982 - 6:

Notes to p. 148.

> *flammifera Erinys verbere excusso sonat*
> *rogisque adustas propius ac propius sudes*
> *in ora tendit; saeua Tisiphone, caput*
> *serpentibus vallata, post raptum canem*
> *portam vacantem clausit opposita face.*

V.1728 Tisiphone, like Megaera, was one of the Furies. In the next line her "stakes" are the handles of her torches.

V.1732ff. Another stage madman, Pentheus in Euripides' *Bacchae*, imagined he saw his palace collapsing in a similar earthquake. Interestingly, although at least one modern commentator on the *Bacchae* (E. R. Dodds) assumed that an earthquake actually occurs in that play, a close reading of Euripides' text shows that there is much to be said for Gager's understanding that this is no more than Pentheus' hallucination, since words for seeming and appearing are used repeatedly in the passage immediately following. Although the text does not make this clear, the same is probably true of Atreus' vision of the earthquake and collapse of the palace at *Thyestes* 262ff. And how could such an event have been represented on the stage? Hence this passage cannot fairly be alleged as evidence that Seneca was not writing with stage production in mind.

The passage in question is *Thy.* 262 - 5:

> *imo mugit e fundo solum,*
> *tonat dies serenus ac totis domus*
> *ut fracta tectis crepuit et moti lares*
> *vertere vultum.*

V.1737 Cf. *Ag.* 912, *eversa domus est funditus*.

V.1740 Cf. *Hipp.* 435f.:

> *metus remitte, prospero regnum in statu est*
> *domusque florens sorte felici viget.*

V.1746 Cf. *Hipp.* 1059, *hic se illa moles acuit atque iras parat*, and *Tr.* 834, *tunc quoque ingentes acuebat iras.*

V.1747 Cf. *Oed.* 31, *cui reseruamur malo?* and *Thy* 279, *hic placet poenae modus.*

V.1748ff. A list of some of the famous sinners suffering punishment in the Underworld. Ixion was condemned to spin forever on a fiery wheel for having sought to rape Hera. For similar catalogues cf. *H. F.* 750 - 8:

> *rapitur volucri tortus Ixion rota;*
> *cervice saxum grande Sisyphia sedet;*
> *in amne medio faucibus siccis senex*
> *sectatur undas, alluit mentum latex,*

Notes to p. 148.

> *fidemque cum iam saepe decepto dedit,*
> *perit unda in ore; poma destituunt famem.*
> *praebet volucri Tityos aeternas dapes*
> *urnasque frustra Danaides plenas gerunt;*

And *Me.* 744 - 9:

> *rota resistat membra torquens, tangat Ixion humum,*
> *Tantalus securus undas hauriat Pirenidas,*
> *[grauior uni poena sedeat coniugis socero mei]*
> *lubricus per saxa retro Sisyphum solvat lapis.*
> *vos quoque, urnis quas foratis inritus ludit labor,*
> *Danaides, coite: vestras hic dies quaerit manus.*

And *Oct.* 621 - 3:

> *poenasque quis et Tantali vincat sitim,*
> *dirum laborem Sisyphi, Tityi alitem*
> *Ixionisque membra rapientem rotam*

V.1750 Sisyphus was condemned to roll a hill uphill forever as punishment for having revealed Zeus' secrets.

V.1751 Tantalus boiled his son Pelops and fed him to the gods. Therefore he was punished with eternal hunger and thirst. Tityus was a giant who tried to rape Artemis. His punishment was to be pegged out on the ground while vultures perpetually gnawed his liver.

V.1752 I.e., the Danaides, who murdered their husbands and were condemned to carry water eternally in leaky buckets.
Cf. *Hipp.* 182, *cedit in vanum labor.*

V.1757ff. Double vision, whereby two suns are seen in the sky, is a symptom exhibited by such Greek tragic characters as Pentheus and the protagonist of Euripides' *Heracles*. But the immediate model is the raving Cassandra in Seneca's *Agamemnon* (726 - 9):

> *ubi sum? fugit lux alma et obscurat genas*
> *nox alta et aether abditus tenebris latet.*
> *sed ecce gemino sole praefulget dies*
> *geminumque duplices Argos attollit domus.*

V.1759ff. Similarly, the present hallucination is based on that of Hercules, as he begins to go mad in the *Hercules Furens* (939 - 44):

Notes to pp. 168 - 50.

> sed quid hoc? medium diem
> cinxere tenebrae. Phoebus obscuro meat
> sine nube vultu. quis diem retro fugat
> agitque in ortus? unde nox atrum caput
> ignota profert? unde tot stellae polum
> implent diurnae?

V.1762 Cf. *Me.* 940, *ut saeva rapidi bella cum venti gerunt.*

V.1763f. Cf. *Me.* 531f.:

> nunc summe toto Iuppiter caelo tona,
> intende dextram, vindices flammas para.

V.1768 Cf. *Oct.* 792f.:

> hinc urit animos pertinax nimium favor
> et in furorem temere praecipites agit.

V.1770f. Cf. *H. F.* 967f.:

> bella Titanes parent,
> me duce furentes;

V.1772f. Cf. *Oct.* 175f.:

> NVT. natura vires non dedit tantas tibi.
> OCT. dolor ira maeror miseriae luctus dabunt.

V.1773ff. For the giant Typhoeus' assault on heaven, with the results described here, cf. Ovid, *Metamorphoses* V.319 - 31. The god who transformed himself into an ibis was Mercury.

V.1782ff. For the argument that these matrons comprise the play's chorus, see the Commentary note on the Act I chorus.
The inspiration for this chorus is Ovid, *Met.* VII.526 - 8:

> alta iacet Calydon. lugent iuvenesque senesque,
> vulgusque proceresque gemunt, scissaeque capillos
> planguntur matres Calydonides Eueniae.

This passage recalls the long lamentation by Hecuba and the chorus at *Troades* 67 - 164, and also Alcmena's lament for the dead Hercules. Like the present passage, both are written in anapaestic dimeters rounded off by an occasional Adonic.

V.1786 Cf. *Thy.* 953, *flendi miseris dira cupido est.*

V.1788 Cf. *Thy.* 950, *imber vultu nolente cadit.*

V.1789 Cf. *Tr.* 812, *nullus est flendi modus.*

V.1793 Cf. *Tr.* 68f:

> *hoc continuis*
> *egimus annis, ex tuo tetigit &c.*

V.1797f. Cf. *Tr.* 97 *solitum flendi vincite morem* and 115 *non sum solito contenta modo.*

V.1799f. Cf. *Tr.* 78, *sed nova fletus causa ministrat.*

V.1800 Cf. *Tr.* 34 (of Cassandra), *ore lymphato furens.*

V.1802 This Adonic is resolved.

V.1803 Cf. *Me.* 226, *decus illud ingens Graecia.*

V.1804 Cf. *Tr.* 124, where Priam is lamented as *columen patriae* (and also *Oct.* 126, where Britannicus is called *columen augustae domus*).

V.1807f. Cf. *Tr.* 104 - 8:

> *cadit ex umeris vestis apertis*
> *imumque tegit suffulta latus;*
> *iam nuda vocant pectora extras;*
> *nunc, nunc vires exprome, dolor.*
> *Rhoetea sonent litora planctu.*

V.1808 Cf. also *Tr.* 114, *pulsu pectus tundite vasto.*

V.1811 For *lacerata comas* cf. *Tr.* 100f.:

> *solvimus omnes lacerum multo*
> *funere crinem*

and also *Tr.* 409 - 11:

> *quid, maesta Phrygiae turba, laceratis comas*
> *miserumque tunsae pectus effuso genas*
> *fletu rigatis?*

and *Oct.* 327 - 9:

Notes to pp. 152 - 54.

> *scindit vestes Augusta suas*
> *laceratque comas*
> *rigat et maestis fletibus ora.*

In his descriptions of ritual mourning, Seneca never mentions mutilation of the face, but cf. *Tr.* 120 - 3:

> *tibi maternis ubera palmis*
> *laniata iacent. fluat et multo*
> *sanguine manet quamcumque tuo*
> *funere feci rupta cicatrix.*

V.1813 Cf. the Adonic *plangite natum* at *H. Oet.* 1864.

V.1820 For a similar transition from a choral passage to an eyewitness narrative delivered to the chorus, cf. *Hipp.* 989f.:

> *sed quid citato nuntius properat gradu*
> *rigatque maestis lugubrem vultum genis?*

V.1822f. Cf. *H. Oet.* 713f.:

> *semel profecto premere felices deus*
> *cum coepit, urget. hos habent magna exitus.*

V.1823 Cf. *Tr.* 427, *exoritur aliquod maius ex magno malum.*

V.1825 The closest parallel in the Senecan corpus is *Oct.* 911, *nullum Pietas nunc numen habet.*

V.1833f. Cf. *Me.* 433f.:

> *remedia quotiens invenit nobis deus*
> *periculis peiora.*

V.1830f. Cf. the Commentary note on 1694f.

V.1838 Cf. the Commentary note on 1799.

V.1839f. Cf. *Tr.* 130f.:

> *vertite planctus; Priamo vestros*
> *fundite flletus, satis Hector habet.*

V.1842 Cf. *Tr.* 784, *flebilius aliquid Hectoris magni nece.*

V.1844 Cf. *Oedipus* 147, *furibunda thalamos intrat.*

Notes to p. 154.

V.1847 For *furore percitus* cf. *H. F.* 852.

V.18449ff. The manner of Oeneus' death was evidently suggested to Gager by Ovid, *Metamorphoses* V.288 - 93, in which Pyreneus hurled himself off the tower of his palace while attempting to rape the Muses:

> *vimque parat, quam nos sumptis effugimus alis.*
> *ipse secuturo similis stet arduus arce*
> *"qua" que "via est vobis, erit et mihi," dixit, "eadem"*
> *seque iacti vecors e summae culmine turris*
> *et cadit in vultus discussisque ossibus oris*
> *tundit humum moriens scelerato sanguine tinctam.*

At the same time, Oeneus' attempt to storm heaven is suggested by the ambition expressed by the insane Hercules at *H. F.* 961 - 73:

> *en ultro vocat*
> *omnis deorum coetus et laxat fores,*
> *una vetente. recipis et reseras polum?*
> *an contumacis ianuam mundi traho?*
> *dubitatur etiam? vincla Saturno exuam*
> *contraque patris impii regnum impotens*
> *avum resolvam; bella Titanes parent,*
> *me duce furentes; saxa cum silvis feram*
> *rapiamque dextra plena Centauris iuga.*
> *iam monte gemino limitem ad superos agam;*
> *videat sub Ossa Pelion Chiron suum,*
> *in caelum Olympus tertio positus gradu*
> *perveniet aut mittetur.*

And the following description of Oeneus' fall and disfiguring death imitates the similar one of Astyanax in the *Troades* (114 - 7):

> *confundit imam pondus ad terram datum;*
> *soluta cervix silicis impulsu, caput*
> *ruptum cerebro penitus expresso. iacet*
> *deforme corpus.*

1856ff. Cf. the Commentary note on *Dido* 279f.

Act V chorus Unlike Attic or Senecan tragedies, each of Gager's plays end with a full-blown chorus rather than with a brief choral *Schlußwort*. Evidently he thought that one should be able to draw a moral from a play, as from a fable (cf. *Dido*, Epilogue 1217, *nunc quisque reputet quid sibi hinc referat boni*). Now he spells it out. For the particular moral of this chorus, cf. the Commentary note on II.539ff.

The meter is iambic dimeters.

Notes to p. 156.

V.1869ff. Compare *Hipp.* 1123ff.:

> quanti casus, heu, magna rotant!
> minor in parvis Fortuna furit
> leviusque ferit leviora deus;
> servat placidos obscura quies
> praebetque senes casa securos.
>   admota aetheriis culmina sedibus
> Euros excipiunt, excipiunt Notos,
> insani Boreae minas
> imbriferumque Corum.
> raros patitur fulminis ictus
> umida vallis:
> tremuit telo Iovis
> Caucasus ingens Phrygiumque nemus
> matris Cybeles: metuens caelo
> Iuppiter alto vicina petit.

And also *Ag.* 87ff.:

> licet arma vacent cessentque doli,
> sidunt ipso pondere magna
> ceditque oneri fortuna suo:
> vela secundis inflata Notis
> ventos nimium timuere suos;
> nubibus ipsis inserta caput
> turris pluvio vapulat Austro,
> densasque nemus spargens umbras
> annosa videt robora frangi;
> feriunt celsos fulmina colles,
> corpora morbis maiora patent,
> et cum in pastus armenta vagos
>   vilia currant,
> placet in vulnus maxima cervix:
> quidquid in altum Fortuna tulit,
>   ruitura levat.
> modicis rebus longius aevum est:
> felix mediae quisquis turbae
>   sorte quietus
> aura stringit litora tuta
> timidusque mari credere cumbam
> remo terras propiore legit.

Both of these choruses are indebted to Horace, *Odes.* II.10. 6 - 16, quoted in the Commentary note on II.539ff.

Epilogue I, 1889f. This mythological allusion to Anne Boleyn and Henry VIII is far from inappropriate. Gager repeated it in the new prologue he wrote for the production of *Rivales* for the Queen's visit in September, 1592.

Epilogue I, 1891 Cf. the Commentary note on 151.

1902f. "The allusion to the Queen's treatment of her wooers, including Leicester, is unmistakable" (Boas, *op. cit.* 177).

1900ff. "If, as appears to be the case, [the Prologue and Epilogue *ad Academicos*] were written for the first performance of the play, the 'bellua' is probably the Jesuit conspiracy, headed by Campion and Parsons, against Elizabeth in 1581" (Boas, *loc. cit.*).

1933ff. "Gager doubtless wished to pay a special tribute to a distinguished son of the 'House,' but it is curious that he should single out Sidney as the only favourer of new poets, and that after his untimely death the ill-omened reference to *Meleagri exitus* should have been made public": Frederick S. Boas, *Sir Philip Sidney* (London, 1955) 171.

RIVALES

Introduction

hen in his *Palladis Tamia* of 1598 (sig. Oo 3ᵛ) Francis Meres enumerated those English playwrights whom he held to be "our best for tragedy" and "our best for comedy," he produced the following list for the latter category: "Edward Earl of Oxford, Dr. Gager of Oxford, Master Rowley...Master Edwards, one of her Majesty's chapel; eloquent and witty John Lily; Lodge, Gascoigne, Greene, Shakespeare, Thomas Nash, Thomas Heywood, Anthony Munday, our best plotter; Chapman, Porter, Wilson, Hathway, and Henry Chettle."

Most likely *Rivales* earned Gager his place in this company, although the possibility cannot quite be excluded that Meres was thinking of the tragicomic *Ulysses Redux*. Perhaps surprising is the fact that such a compliment was earned by Gager's only unqualified comedy, and by a play that the author himself did not think fit to print.[1] To be sure, *Rivales* must have enjoyed a considerable reputation both because of the number of its revivals and because of the stellar occasions on which it was produced. On the strength of his highly successful and influential trilogy *Richardus Tertius*, Meres included Gager's Cambridge contemporary Thomas Legge in his tragedy list. Gager and Legge were the two most prominent University playwrights, and Meres may have wanted to maintain an evenhanded balance between the two Universities, linked to a similar balance between the two dramatic genres. Thus Gager's name may have been placed in the comedy list as a counterweight to Legge's inclusion in the one for tragedians. But then, why exclude Gager's name from the list of "our best for tragedy?" Among University playwrights, after all, he was unusual for working in both genres. The answer may that Meres wanted to highlight the importance of the one playwright he admired above all others, whose name uniquely stands in both lists, William Shakespeare.

Rivales was first performed at Christ Church on June 11, 1583, in connection with the visit of a Palatine nobleman: the details of this memorable occasion are described in the Introduction to *Dido*. The play also received two revival performances. The first was on February 7, 1592, as part of the Shrovetide performances, sandwiched in between *Ulysses Redux* and *Panniculus* in what, it will be argued in the General Introduction to Volume II, was an attempt at producing a thematically integrated trilogy. The second revival was on Sunday, September 24 of the same year, when *Rivales* and Leonard Hutton's *Bellum Grammaticale* (for which Gager contributed a prologue and epilogue)[2] were performed as part of the entertainment for a Royal visit.[3] Appended to the printed text of *Ulysses Redux* is a prologue for *Rivales* that in its first lines alludes to a second performance. Obviously, this was written to be delivered in connection with the Shrovetide revival. Likewise appended to the printed *Meleager* is a prologue in which Apollo addresses the Queen before the September performance.

Rivales is a lost play. The only evidence for its contents consists of allusions elsewhere

---

[1] In "Life and Times" (416) Tucker Brooke speculated that Gager destroyed the manuscript out of chagrin for the way Rainolds had savaged the play.
[2] Printed here as Volume II, Appendix I.
[3] The circumstances of this visit are described by Boas, *op. cit.* 252 - 6.

in Gager's works and quotations and allusions provided by various parties in connection with the Gager-Rainolds-Gentili controversy about the legitimacy of academic drama, described in the General Introduction to Volume II. In view of the play's historical importance, it seems worthwhile to collect here such of this material as appears to shed light on the play's contents.[1]

What may fairly be inferred from this evidence? Possibly not as much as first appears. Certainly, *Rivales* dealt with rustic wooing. The title implies that this wooing involved rivalry. It is equally beyond doubt the play contained a scene featuring some riotously drunken sailors, to which Gager's antagonist Dr. John Rainolds took particular exception. Could the plot have had to do with rustic swains and sailors competing for the same love-objects? Then too, if Rainolds is to be trusted (cf. no. 10), the play also contained some situation of actual or attempted adultery.

One of the characters was a braggart warrior. The evidence appears to (and perhaps does) present three more circumstantial details about the play. Gager seems to say that one of the characters was named Mopsus (cf. no. 3 below). But might he not be using the name figuratively, meaning "a rustic sort of fellow, such as Vergil's Mopsus"? At one point (cf. no. 7) Rainolds states that a character was named Phoedra, or perhaps Phaedra. He may have been right, but we must bear in mind that Phaedra was a character in another play at least partly written by Gager, *Panniculus*, produced on the same occasion that provoked Rainolds' indignation; at another point (no. 8) Rainolds professes not to know the name of any of the female parts in *Rivales*. It therefore seems possible that something has gone wrong in the text of his letter.[2] Finally, the evidence seems to suggest that the play contained panders or bawds (cf. no. 4, line 443, and no. 10). But in his anti-theater polemics Rainolds employs the term "bawd" very frequently and very loosely to designate any stage-character of whose morality he disapproves, and at one point explicitly proposed to extend this broad usage to the Latin words *leno*, *lena*, and *lenocinium*.[3] It is therefore possible that when Gager put the word *lena* in Momus' mouth he was making fun of this linguistic mannerism of Rainolds rather than testifying that *Rivales* contained such a character. On the other hand it is undeniable the *lena* and the *leno* are stock types in Roman comedy no less than the *miles gloriosus*.

Boas' remarks on the play are worth quoting:

> The introduction by Gager into his comedy of a burlesque of rustic love-making is remarkable, for though in *Gammer Gurtons Nedle* and in *Misogonus* country personages and scenes appear, there is no extant play, English or Latin, written in this country before 1583 which brings amorous yokels on the stage. That the wooers in *Rivales* were such, and not conventional pastoral figures, is made

---

[1] Few of Rainolds' rather copious allusions to *Rivales* are included here, since he provides little factual information beyond what can be gleaned from Gager's own writings. At this point is worth advising the reader that, by his own confession, Rainolds had neither seen nor read *Rivales*, and by his testimony his knowledge of the play is based solely on what he had been told about it by an unnamed mutual friend of himself and Gager.

[2] The possibility can probably be excluded that Rainolds meant that the comedy contained a Phaedra-like woman who tried to seduce a son or stepson. Surely the somewhat prudish Gager too would have considered such a situation shockingly inappropriate for a comedy.

[3] *Th'Overthow of Stage-Players* (Middelburg, Holland, 1599, reprinted London - New York, 1972) p. 107.

additionally plain by the way in which he emphasizes the piquancy of their representation by members of a cultured society, or 'cyvill men.".. .Gager's mariners would evidently have been fit shipmates for Stephano and Trinculo...

Tucker Brooke added:[1]

> [*Rivales* was] precisely contemporary with the earliest comedies by the "university wits," Lyly's *Campaspe and* Peele's *Arraignment of Paris*, and the allusions to it in the Gager - Rainolds correspondence indicate that, though in Latin, it was probably a clearer reflection of English life and manners than any of the vernacular plays of the period.

Because of his involvement with the Polish Pfalzgraf's dramatic entertainment, Gager's friend George Peele must have remembered *Rivales* when he came to write his own *The Old Wives Tale* (printed 1595, but acted ca. 1590). Elements in that play that were in all probability reminiscent of *Rivales* were the humous look at life in an English country village, and also the character of the braggart warrior Huanebango, since there is testimony that *Rivales* contained a similar figure.

John Sanford of Magdalene College wrote a fine cycle of lyric poems to be read at a banquet for the members of Elizabeth's Privy Council present on this occasion. These were subsequently printed by Joseph Barnes under the title *Apollonis et Musarum* εὐκτικὰ εἰδύλλια.[2] The idea of this cycle is that Apollo and the Muses, expelled from Greece, have found their way to Oxford, where they make a new home. Then they individually praise the Queen and offer greetings to Burghley, Essex, and the other grandees present. It would appear that the conceits used by Sanford and by Gager in this special prologue were coordinated by prearrangement. Perhaps "Oxford as home of Apollo and the Muses" was the chosen theme for Elizabeth's visit. For a similar coordination of imagery in courtly poetry and pageantry in the case of the marriage of Prince Frederick of the Rhine and Princess Elizabeth cf. the Introduction to Volume III.

---

[1] "Life and Times," 416.
[2] Reprinted by Charles Plummer (ed.), *Elizabethan Oxford* (Oxford, 1887) 277 - 299.

1.

PROLOGVS IN *RIVALES* COMAEDIAM

semel acta, rursus fabula in scenam redit.
iterumne? mors est ergo, non comaedia,
bis posita crambe. quaeso responsum tamen
accipite nostrum. quae semel vere placent,
decies placebunt, pulchra bis dici queant.   5
haec ergo pulchra est? absit a nostro procul
iactantia grege, sed, quia haec vobis semel
perplacuit, ideo digna nobis denuo
visa est reponi. vos penes scenae optimae
censura vera est, quam reformidat chorus,   10
colitque noster, et colere semper decet.
et ecce, rediit illa post annos decem,
Ulyssis instar. nam quotusquisque hic sedet,
qui sciat eandem? sed penitus eadem venit.
minus apparata forsan. at comaediam   15
recitare nullam non placuit, ullam minus.
novam invenire difficile, dicam, fuit?
an noluimus? an non fuit certe otium?
an aliquid aliud? casus an fatum fuit?
lucrum putate, fabula quod hodie exiit,   20
tam prodit aegre, pene tam non prodiit.
   utcunque fuerit, consulite quaeso boni.
ridicula bis prolata rideri solent.

2.

APOLLO προλογίζει AD SERENISSIMAM REGINAM ELIZABETHAM 1592

saltus relinquens clara Woodstockii iuga,
venatione fessus, ac dammis satur,
et iam necandis tempore exacto feris,
meis reviso nobilem Musis domum.
   sed unde tanta sedibus nostris nova
successit hospes? ore quam sese ferens!   5
quae celsitudo! quanta maiestas adest!

1.1. *Woodstochii* liber 2. titulus *SEREMISSIMAM* lib. 5. *ferens?* lib. 6. *celsitudo?...adest?* lib.

1.

PROLOGUE TO THE COMEDY *RIVALES*

Having been acted once before, this comedy returns again to the stage. Again? Therefore it's the death of us, not a comedy, it's a twice-baked cookie. But I pray you hear my reponse. Things that truly please once will give pleasure ten times. Fair things can be said twice. So are these things fair? Let boasting be far removed from our troupe, but since these things once gave you delight, they strike us as worthy of being put back on the stage. The decision about what is a good play is entirely your choice, of which our chorus stands in awe, and which our poet cultivates, as he always should. And see, Ulysses-like, this play has come back after ten years. And as often as it settles here, who is to know if it is the same? But it returns entirely unchanged, although perhaps less well appointed. But we don't want to perform no comedy, and even less to perform any at all. Should I say it was hard to invent a new one? Or that we didn't want to? Or that we didn't have the leisure? Or anything else? Was this accident or destiny? Count it your blessing that any kind of comedy is being put on; it was produced with difficulty, it almost wasn't produced at all. However it happened, I pray you to think well of it. Funny things twice produced customarily get a laugh.

2.

APOLLO ADDRESSES A PROLOGUE TO HER MOST SERENE MAJESTY, QUEEN ELIZABETH, 1592

Leaving the famous ridges of Woodstock's forest, worn out by the hunt and having had my fill of venision, the time for slaying the beasts now spent, in the company of the Muses I have revisited this noble house. But whence has this new guest approached our dwelling? With what a countenance she bears herself! What loftiness! What majesty is upon her! Are

genus esse divum credo, nec vana est fides.
tune illa Elisa, nympha quam Syrinx suo
Tamesis ad undas pulchricoma Pani edidit?
tune illa es, annos ante quae bis iam decem   10
et sex, ad istos prima venisti lares?
ipsam esse memini, pristinum agnosco decus.
  regina salve virgo, terrarum dea,
caelique cura, saeculi ac mundi stupor.
o singulare pectoris studium tui!   15
iterumne tibi delubra Musarum sacra
subire placuit, et tui, dignum tuo
utinam absolutum, adire monumentum patris?
bis hospes, et bis grata venisti, mihi
Phaeboque, Graiisque, Musisque, omnibus.   20
utque aliqua merito gratia habeatur tuo,
soccum Thalia comicum ornabit tibi.
  laetare quaeso, diva, sceptrique inclyti
repone pondus, et supercilium grave.
iocosa laetos Musa tibi ludos dabit.   25

3.

hesterna Mopsum scena ridiculum dedit.

4.

hesterna qualis exiit camaedia?   440
amata sine rivale, *Rivales*, suis,
bis cocta crambe, morsque, non comaedia.
quam blanda morum lena pravorum fuit!
parumne vitia sponte iam pollent sua,
nisi prostitutis vim quoque theatrum afferat?   445
laetitia nisi prorumpat in lasciviam,
sub specie inani carminum, et facundiae?
disertiorem scena num quenquam dedit,
aut doctiorem? num bonum vatem extulit?

you Elisa, whom the fair-haired nymph Syrinx bore to her Pan by the waters of the Thames? Are you she who first came to this hearth six and twenty years ago? I recall that you are she, I recognize your pristine glory. Hail, virgin queen, goddess of this world, special charge of heaven, wonder of our times, our world. Oh, the singular zeal of your heart! Has it pleased you to reenter this sacred shrine of the Muses, and approach this monument to your father (and would that it were perfect and worthy of a father of yours)? You have twice come as a guest, twice welcome to myself, Phoebus, to the Fates, Muses, to us all. And that some measure of our gratitude may be paid to you, for your benefit Thalia will don the comic slipper. Pray be happy, divine lady, and lay aside the weight of your famous scepter, your grave mein. The playful Muse will furnish you with amusing jokes.

3.

Yesterday the stage gave you ridiculous Mopsus.

4.

What kind of comedy was produced yesterday? *Rivales*, loved without a rival by its supporters, a twice-baked cookie, a death, not a comedy. How pleaant was that bawd with her depraved morals. Wasn't she sufficiently rife with her own vices, without having to fill the theater full of whores, unless fun turned into wantonness under the guise of pointless songs and jokes? Hasn't the stage given us a playwright more eloquent and learned? Hasn't it produced a good poet?

5.

In *Riuales*, what *Cato* might not be delyted to see the fonde behaviour of cuntrye wooinge, expressed by cyvill men, or the vanytye of a bragginge soldier? by the spectacle of the drunken mariners(?)

6.

Rivales fond, & amarous; mariners beastly dronken.

7.

...as your *Rivales*, in which some of the wooers perhaps kissed *Phoedra*.

8.

Hee would not haue his youth to counterfeit a womans voice: you procure *Minerva*, *Penelope*, *Euryclea*, *Antinoë*, *Eurynome*, *Hippodamia*, *Melantho*, *Phaedra*, the *Nurse*, the *Nymph*, besides I know not whom in the vnprinted *Comedie*, to bee played by yours.

9.

If they shuld not as much as salute *Terence*, the finest Comicall Poet, for purnes of the Latin toung in *Tullies* judgement: much lesse should they be made will acquainted with *Plautus*; and lesse yet with *Rivales*.

10.

quin et ipse, quum fabularum, quales Terentianae sunt, verbis factisque inhonestis et improbis aspersae, actores pronuntias iure improbari, sententiam meam astruis. nam *Ulysses Redux*, *Hippolytus*, et *Rivales* (de quibus amici tui Momus hanc quae nobis est litem excitavit) non minus illis vitiis laborant, quam nonnullae, immo *Rivales* multo magis, quam ulla Terentii. itaque licet quaedam addas refutatu forsan non indigna, ut quod mimos asseris habitu muliebri egisse personam viri, lenonis, adulteri, temulenti, ne temulenti in *Rivalibus* eorum similes videantur; et Theophrasti exemplo, qui in schola docens, ita omnes gestus rei, quam tractabat, congruentes adhibuit, ut exerta lingua labra circumlinxerit quum heluonem describeret, histrioniam oratori concludas esse necessariam.

10.

Indeed, you yourself strengthen my opinion when you declare that the actors of plays, such as Terence's which are stained with shameful and vile words and deeds, are justly condemned. For *Ulysses Redux*, *Hippolytus*, and *Rivales* (about which the Momus of your friend incited this dispute between us) suffer no less from these faults than some of Terence's plays, nay *Rivales* much more. And granted that you add certain things, perhaps not undeserving of refutation, as when you assert that mimes, in female costume, performed the part of a man, of a procurer, of an adulterer, of a drunkard, in order that the drunkard might not seem similar to them in *Rivales*. With the example of Theophrastus, who taught in school and allowed every gesture appropriate to the matter which he treated, so that the extended tongue licked his lips when he described the glutton, you demonstrate that the dramatic art is necessary for the orator. [trans. Markowicz]

Textual Commentary

1.

Source: *Ulysses Redux*, sig. F 2ʳ.

3 Cf. Juvenal, *Sat.* VII.154, *occidit miseros crambe repetita magistros*. More appositely, note that Erasmus glosses the phrase *crambe bis posita* with the word *mors* in his *Adages*.

4ff. These lines embroider on Horace, *Ars Poetica* 365, *haec placuit semel, haec deciens repetita placebit*.

13. Gager has a general program of inserting both overt and covert reference to his other works in his prologues and epilogues, thus weaving them together into a kind of intertextual network.

15f. *Minus apparata* presumably means that the expenditure on the 1592 performances was less than that spent on the original production of *Rivales* and *Dido*. But according to Gager in his letter to Rainolds, the three Shrovetide productions cost a total of thirty pounds, not a paltry sum.

19 *Casus an fatum fuit?* echoes Althaea's question at *Meleager* 1045.

21 This must refer to some incident familiar to the audience, but unknown to us.

2.

Source: *Meleager*, sig. F 6ʳ.

1 Woodstock, a town ten miles from Oxford, was the site of a royal hunting lodge. Compare the way Gager creates a neoclassical Oxonian setting by weaving local placenames into his eclogue *Daphnis*, written on the death of Sir Philip Sidney (poem XXXIV), a poem which begins:

> *pastorem pastor Daphnim Melibaeus acerbo*
> *funere correptum Shotoveri in vertice flebat,*
> *Daphnis ubi curare greges in valle propinqua,*

Notes to pp. 228 - 30.

> *Cherwelli ad ripas, piscosique Isidis undas*
> *dignari solitus quondam.*

3 From the insistence with which Gager refers to Christ Church as *domus* here and elsewhere, we may observe that it had already aquired its traditional nickname, "The House." Cf. also his repeated reference to "owre House" in his letter to Rainolds printed in Volume IV.

5ff. Note the echo of *Dido* 465ff. (in turn, of course, based on Vergil).

8f. Note the echo of *Meleager* 1893f.

9f. Gager had already employed this pretty conceit about Henry VIII and Anne Boleyn at *Meleager* 1879f.:

> *quondam nympha quam Syrinx deo*
> *Tamesis ad undas inclyto Pani edidit.*

10f. For Elizabeth's 1566 visit to Oxford, cf. Boas, *op. cit.* 98 - 108. That visit too had been the occasion for Christ Church dramatic performances.

18 His original foundation, Cardinal College, was dissolved after Cardinal Wolsey's downfall. Then it was refounded as Christ Church by Henry VIII: see the Commentary note on CXX.20ff. in Volume III.

22 Thalia was the Muse of poetry.

25 For *iocosa Musa* cf. Ovid, *Tristia* I.354.

3.

Source: Prologue to *Dido*, line 5.

4.

Source: Lines 440 - 9 of Momus' epilogue to *Panniculus*.

442 Momus is of course echoing lines 2f. of the February, 1592 prologue (no. 1 above).

5.

Source: Letter of William Gager to Dr. John Rainolds, July 31, 1592, (printed here in Volume IV).

6.

Source: Letter of Dr. John Rainolds to William Gager, July 10, 1592, printed at *Th'Overthow of Stage-Plays* p. 20.

7.

Source: Rainolds to Gager, May 30, 1593, printed *ib.* p. 36.

8.

Source: The same, printed *ib.* p. 122.

9.

Source: The same, printed *ib.*, p. 127.

10.

Source: Letter of Dr. John Rainolds to Professor Alberico Gentili, June 10, 1593, *Th'Overthrow of Stage-Plays* edited and translated by John Marcowicz, *Latin Correspondence by Alberico Gentili and John Rainolds on Academic Drama* (Salzburg Studies in English Literature: Elizabethan and Renaissance Studies 68, Salzburg, 1977p. 165f.,) 22 - 5.

Theophrasti exemplo A sidenote by Rainolds says *Athenae, li. 1*, i.e., Athenaeus, *Deipnosophistae* I.21.

DIDO

Introduction

ronically, *Dido* has received more scholarly attention than any other Gager play. Printed repeatedly, edited twice, translated into both English and German, *Dido* has nevertheless been accounted his weakest work. Boas[1] thought it hastily cobbled together to serve a pressing necessity, and explained the mechanical fidelity with which it follows its Vergilian model in terms of the speed with which it had to be written, just as the author himself offered this speed as an excuse in his Epilogue (1216). In April 1583 Albertus Alasco, Palatine Pfalzgraf of Stadia in Poland, arrived in England on a state visit. On May 13, the Earl of Leicester, Chancellor of the University, wrote to the Vice-Chancellor:[2]

> The Queen's Majestie hath willed me to signifie unto you that the Palatin Lasky the nobleman that is nowe out of Polonia mindeth shortly to come downe to see the universitie of Oxford, and that her highnes pleasure therefore is that he be receaved of you with all the curtesy and solemnitie that you may. I minde myself to accompanie him thither: the time we appoint to be there shalbe on mondaye the xth daye of June, and there to remaine that daye all tuesdaye and all wednesdaye and on Thursdaye morning to depart. You must use all solemnitie of disputation, orations, and readings as you did at her majesties being with you...I doo thinke it fittest for him to lie in Christ Church.

The visit came off as planned,[3] and was memorable, as is recorded in Raphael Holinshed's *Chronicles of England, Scotland, and Ireland*:[4]

> Touching the interteinement which he [the Pfalzgraf] had at Oxenford, and how the vniuersitie did congratulate his comming, it is somewhat worth the noting...On the east gate wherat he entered, stood a consort of musicians, who for a long space made a verie sweet harmonie, which could not but moove and delight;
>
> > *inscia plebs populusque arrectis auribus astat*
> > *dulciferumque rudi suscipit aure melos.*
>
> All up the high street vnto saint Maries church, on either side the waie, were decentlie marshalled scholars in their gownes and caps, batchelors and maisters in their habits and hoods. At saint Maries the orator of the vniuersitie (notable in his

---

[1] Cf. his seminal discussion of the play, *op. cit.* 179 - 91. The assessment is found on p. 183.
[2] British Library ms. Twayne xvii, fol. 170, cited by Boas, *ib.* 179. As with all contemporary English documents, abbreviated words are spelled out in full.
[3] Save that in the event the Pfalzgraf was rather upstaged by one of the members of his party. See John Bossy, *Giordano Bruno and the Embassy Affair* (New Haven, 1991), 22 - 7.
[4] [London, 1807 - 8, repr. New York, 1965] 4.507f. *Rivales* was performed on the evening of June 11, and *Dido* on the following night.

facultie) presented him a booke, in which were closelie couched verie rich and gorgeous gloues. From thense he marched to Christs church, where he was whilest he abode in the vniuersitie most honourablie interteined. And the first night being vacant, as in which he sought rather rest in his lodging than recreation in anie academicall pastimes, strange fire works were shewed, in the great quadrangle besides rockets and a number such maner of deuises. On the second daie, his first dinner was made him at Alsoules college, where (besides dutifull receiuing of him) he was solemnelie satisfied with scholerlie exercises and courtlie fare. This night and the night insuing, after sumptuous suppers in his lodging, he personaly was present with his traine in the hall, first at the plaing of a pleasant comedie intituled Riuales; then at the setting out of a verie statelie tragedie named Dido, wherein the queenes banket (with Eneas[1] narration of the destruction of Troie) was liuelie described in a marchpaine patterne, there was also a goodlie sight of hunters with full crie of a kennell of hounds, Mercurie and Iris descending from and to an high place, the tempest wherein it hailed small confects, rained rosewater, and snew an artificiall kind of snow, all strange, maruellous, and abundant.[2]

Most of the actors were of the same house, six or seauen of them were of saint Iohns, and three or foure of other colleges and hals. His second dinner the third daie was at Magdalen college, with oratorie welcoming and bountifull feasting. His third dinner the fourth daie at New college. The eloquent speech in Greeke Latine and Dutch with his own vnstudied answer theruunto, and all other before rehersed, are not to be omitted: nor the publike philosophie, physike, and diuinitie disputations, in all which those learned opponents, repondents, and moderators, quitted themselues like themselues, sharplie and soundlie, besides all other solemne sermons and lectures. At afternoone the fourth and last daie, he went towards Woodstocke manour, and without the north gate by the waie he was invited vnto a banket at saint Iohns college, where the gates and outward wals ouercouered with thousands of verses, and other emblematicall poetries then offered him, argued their hartie goodwils: but his hasting to his iournies end caused him not to tarie the delicat banket: yet onelie staieng the deliuerie of a sweet oration and his owne quicke wittie replie thereunto, he departed immediatlie, acoompanied for a mile or two with the most of those reuerend doctors and heads of houses all on horssebacke, where the orator againe gaue him an orators farewell. And this is the summe of his interteinement, not deliuered in such sort as the dignitie of the same requireth; howbeit sufficient for a sudden remembrance.

At first sight *Dido* is a straightforward adaptation of Vergil, a form of innocent academic entertainment. But this is not quite the whole story. A work of imaginative fiction is a cultural artifact. Transplanted into the context of a different society, it can acquire a very different import, entirely unforeseen by its original author. Certainly this axiom is true of the present play, for in the specific context of Elizabethan England the story of Dido becomes

---

[1] An error: in the play the narration is by Ascanias.
[2] William Percy writes in his *Aphrodisial*, "also a showre of Rose-water and confits, as was acted in Christ Church, in Oxford, in Dido and Aeneas." (Huntington Library ms. HM 4, fol. 126). Brooke, "Life and Times" 417, observes that Percy did not matriculate at Oxford until 1589. So this is a description cribbed out of Holinshed (the language is very similar) and not an independent eyewitness account.

fraught with new meaning.

In a society ruled by a queen, the Dido story acquires extra contemporary significance. The parallel Gager had drawn between the virgin huntress Atalanta and Elizabeth in the first Epilogue of *Meleager* is superficial and unilluminating. Not so the parallel he now draws between Dido and Elizabeth. The fact that Dido is often called by her alternative name Elisa may partially be explicable in terms of metrical convenience, but the insistence with which this word is used is scarcely accidental.[1] Note, for example, the way this name is highlighted as the final word of several stanzas of the Hymn of Iopas in Actus II, in which the queen's nobility and hospitality are praised. As Boas observed (cf. the Commentary note on this passage) this is a song carefully crafted to draw a parallel between Dido's kindly reception of Aeneas and the hospitality accorded the Polish Pfalzgraf by Elizabeth. But Boas could have added that this song is much more than an exercise in courtly flattery. It serves to point up the deeper parallels between the two queens for the benefit of any spectator who cared to think about them. The play's message is that a woman is fit to govern. We are shown an initial portrait of a queen piously presiding over a well-governed kingdom, and administering just laws. And the woman is, if not a virgin, at least the next best thing, a prudently chaste widow.

The play refers to another similarity between Dido and Elizabeth. Dido was a colonist who had founded a successful city, and Elizabeth was going into the colonization business herself. Line 1243 of the Epilogue seems to contain an allusion to the claiming of Newfoundland in the previous year. More generally, Gager was writing against the background of rising enthusiasm for American exploration and settlement, and he was admirably situated to hear about this ferment, since another Christ Church student was that great advocate and historian of oceanic exploration, Richard Hakluyt.

But of course such comparisons between Dido and Elizabeth do not exhaust the subject. The fuller "subtext" of the Dido story is that a woman is fit to govern as long as she keeps a tight rein on her passionate female nature. But going off the rails by yielding to erotic impulses is a formula for ruin. For a regnant queen, chastity is a necessity. In case the contemporary relevance of this implicit comparison is insufficiently obvious, Gager drives it home in the Epilogue (1244f.):

> *dignata nullo coniuge Sychaeo tamen,*
> *animumque nullus flectat Aeneas suum.*

["But she has not condescended to marry any Sychaeus, and may no Aeneas sway her affections!"]

Thus the Dido story points directly to one of the central political problems of Elizabeth's reign. In view of this, we cannot take a dismissive view of *Dido*, no matter how quickly it was dashed off. *Dido*'s original audience can scarcely have viewed the play as a pallid rehash of a classical model.

The audience's interest must have been further stimulated by the element of lavish spectacle. Boas may have overstated the case in describing *Dido* as "a curious blend of a

---

[1] I mean, of course, within the context of *Dido* only: many poets, writing in the vernacular as well as in Latin, referred to Elizabeth as Elisa or Eliza with no intention of drawing any comparison with Dido. For Elizabeth under this name cf. E. C. Wilson, *England's Eliza*, Cambridge, Mass., 1939.

Senecan tragedy and a pageant,"[1] for this assessment manages to overlook the fact that interest in stunning visual effects is very much a characteristic of Senecan drama. There is undoubtedly a strange discrepancy between the impressive stage effects described by Holinshed and *Dido*'s exceedingly laconic stage directions. But, despite one minor factual error noted above, there is no reason for thinking that Holinshed embellished on the truth. Indeed, if he erred at all, his mistake is likely to have been in the other direction. For he does not mention such additional features as the ghost apparition in Actus III, the singing nymphs in the same Actus, and the sacrifice scene in Actus V. These are all points where further interesting visual effects could have been introduced.

We can gain some idea of the lavishness of the production from an account record quoted by Boas[2] which mentions the very considerable sum of £86 18 s. 2 d. for "the chardges of a Comedye and a Tragedye and a shewe of fireworks as appeareth by the particular bille of Mr. Vice Chauncelor, Mr. Howsone, Mr. Maxie, and Mr. Pille."[3]

There is much truth in Boas' description of *Dido* as being pageant-like. Certainly, the play contained a fair amount of extra-textual material, which which helps account for the short length of the text. After Actus II, scena ii the stage directions call for a *pompa larvalis*, indicating that some sort of masque occurred at this point. Actus III, scena i begins with a stage direction *transitur ad venationem* and the direction *redeunt a venatione* occurs at the end of scena iii of the same Actus. It was at these points that the audience was given "a goodlie sight of hunters with full crie of a kennell of hounds," as described by Holinshed.[4] These could have been simple processions across the stage, but again these events could have been used as pretexts for masquing. At the very minimum, these stage directions indicate a fair amount of dumb-show (to which must be added the celestial descents of Mercury and Iris mentioned by Holinshed, which must have used some sort of *deus ex machina* device).[5]

It is likely that *Dido* was also graced by instrumental music. The normal choruses of a neoclassical tragedy are supplemented by other lyric passages, choral or solo, performed within acts. The fact that Gager's act-ending choruses are often divided into quasi-stanzas of unequal length does not encourage the idea that they were meant to be sung. But lyric passages interpolated into acts are written in balanced stanzas, which strongly suggests that they represent the texts for songs, and Iopas' hymn in Actus II and the song of the nymphs in Actus III. Dido's words (432) *interea laeto personet cantu domus* has been interpreted as a cue for a moment of instrumental music before the entrance of Dido's advisers, and when she commands (1022f.) *ordire, vates, carmen effare, insolens / ad hosce ritus* it looks as if the sacrifice scene may have meant to be performed against a suitably weird musical background. And, of course, if Actus II and III did contain masquing, instrumental

---

[1] *Op. cit.* 189.
[2] *Op. cit.* 180. As I write the volume in the *Records of Early English Drama* series pertinent to Oxford has not yet appeared.
[3] To give some idea of the scale of this expenditure, in 1584 Convocation lent Joseph Barnes £100 to go into the printing business, and by his death in the next century he had only managed to repay £80. It cost nearly as much to put on two plays and a fireworks show as it did to found the Oxford University Press!
[4] A bear may also have been produced onstage: cf. the Commentary note on 610.
[5] While an undergraduate at Trinity College, Cambridge, Dr. John Dee had designed a similar device for a 1546 performance of Aristophanes' *Peace*, doubtless to facilitate the ascent of the giant dung beetle in the first scene of the play. Cf. Richard Deacon, *John Dee* (London, 1968) 17.

managed to accommodate this contemporary taste.

Dido must have been written very quickly.[1] Word of the Pfalzgraf's projected visit reached Oxford on May 13, the play was performed on June 12, and sufficient time must have had to be allowed for part-copying and rehearsal. The suggestion has been made[2] that Gager had already had the work underway before he knew of the forthcoming visit, but a line in the Epilogue (1216), *et scriptam et actam tempus excuset breve*, surely refers to the haste with which author and performers had to work.[3]

Fredrick Boas' assessment of *Dido* is mordantly negative:[4]

> [It] makes the impression of having been 'sharked up' hastily for the occasion, and Gager must bear the discredit, if he is the sole author, of perverting, with the minimum of purely verbal change, the god of the Virgilian hexameters into the base metal of his neo-classical iambics. Nevertheless, in the selection and arrangement of the material from the first and fourth books of the *Aeneid*, and in the incidental additions made to it, *Dido* shows the practiced hand of its author.

We ought to rate it considerably higher, for two reasons. First, as already suggested in the General Introduction, the imitative nature of *Dido*'s dependence on a single literary model may differ from Gager's working method in his other plays in degree, but it does not differ in kind. We have already seen that in the *Meleager* he appropriates Ovid's speeches where he can, and he goes considerably farther in this direction in the *Ulysses Redux*. The entire first half of that play, and some scenes in the second, follow Homer no less closely than *Dido* follows Vergil.

Didi is a more impressive piece of work than Boas allowed. If you want to account the closeness with which Gager followed Vergil a sign of haste, you of course may. But much more important is the fact that the overall effect of the play is impressive. Gager's fidelity to Vergil was only possible because the narrative in Book IV of the *Aeneid* (with some material taken from Book I) makes such an excellence source for a tragedy. Indeed it should: Vergil was well aware of Attic tragedy and this part of the *Aeneid* smacks more than a little of the stage. Book IV has an appropriate central figure, a genuinely tragic subject, plenty of dramatic situations and effectively rhetorical speeches, an interesting element of divine interference, and mounts to a highly melodramatic climax. Gager did not deviate very far from Vergil in order to produce a well constructed and highly effective play, precisely because he did not have to.

This does not mean that changes are not introduced. The ways in which *Dido* differs from its Vergilian model can be divided into two categories. First, the added elements of spectacle, masquing, and song already noted. To this category can be added scenes which

---

[1] This does not discount the possibility that Gager had already been contemplating a dramatization of the subject. That the story of Dido exerted a powerful attraction for him is shown by a remark in his oration *Eloquentiae Encomium* delivered on January 17, 1585: *sed tamen quis est qui si quartum illum Aeneidos librum legerit, ut in nimis saepe laetitia fit, ita prae summa animi delectatione non abeat in lacrhymas?*

[2] J. W. Binns, "William Gager's *Dido*," *Humanistica Lovaniensia* 20 (1971) 168f.

[3] Binns, *ib.* 169, writes "Lines such as Iopas' salutation of Aeneas...which in the event gained in significance through the presence of Prince Alasco at the performance need not necessarily have been written with his visit in mind: they fill a dramatic function within the play," which is unconvincing in view of the explicit Epilogue.

[4] *Ib.* 183.

are introduced for their entertainment value, such as Ascanias' demonstration of Trojan topography, and the charming monologues of Cupid and Mercury. Second, ways in which the tragedy gravitates into the orbit of Senecan tragedy. At least one scene with no Vergilian precedent is added: the appearance of the Ghost of Sychaeus at the beginning of Act III, modeled on the prologues of Seneca's *Agamemnon* and *Thyestes*.

Some scenes having a Vergilian basis are recast, insofar as is possible, so as to resemble specific episodes from Seneca's plays or at least generic Senecan scenes. The interview between Anna and Dido, in which Anna urges the queen to succumb to her love (Actus II, scena v), is rather reminiscent of Senecan *domina-nutrix* scenes in general, and particularly of the scene in which the Nurse urges Phaedra to yield to her love of Hippolytus (*Hippolytus* 85ff.). Dido's sacrifice in Actus V, complete with its tremendous invocation to gods, supernatural beings, and natural forces, bears a distinct resemblance to the sacrifice scene in Seneca's *Medea* (740ff.); but of course there is already plenty of Medea in Vergil's Dido, for the Roman poet was fully conscious of the comparisons that could be drawn between the two spurned and vengeful heroines. There is even a kind of resemblance in form (although scarcely in specific content) between the dialogues between Aeneas and Achates in Actus III and between Aeneas and Ilioneus in Actus IV, and various dialogues between Senecan tyrants and their ministers or henchmen, insofar as Gager's dialogues too are employed to reveal the inner workings of Aeneas' mind.

Dido is partially preserved in Gager's autograph notebook, now possessed by the British Library (A). Specifically, this manuscript contains the Prologue, Argumentum, Actus II, Actus III, and the Epilogue. Why did he not copy the entire play? Various speculations have been adduced,[1] of which the most interesting is that advanced by Boas, that Gager only troubled himself to write out the parts of the play he had contributed, and that the rest is by a different hand. This theory is not implausible, since the speed with which *Dido* had to be written might have required a collaborative effort.[2] It gains further plausibility when one reflects that, speaking *grosso modo*, the portions of the play most liable to accusations of servile dependence on the Vergilian model are precisely those parts not copied into A.

Boas' theory can be put in stronger terms. In describing this manuscript in the Introduction to Volume III, it will be argued that, since Gager was a great one for recycling bits and pieces of his unpublished poetry in his printed poems and plays, a bit of *post hoc propter hoc* reasoning is probably not amiss: he maintained this file of unpublished stuff to be able to borrow from it as the need arose, so that he would never again be put under the pressure to work as quickly as he had in the case of *Dido*. If so, his omission of large parts of *Dido* from that manuscript is fully comprehensible: as a conscientious autoplagiarist, he thought it unethical to appropriate another man's work, so that there would be no point in copying out these parts of the play. On the other hand, his fair copy of *Dido*, identified here as B,[3] was obviously executed for some quite different purpose, where a similar omission of a collaborator's work would not have made sense.

It is possible to put the multiple authorship theory to the test by doing a bit of stylometric analysis. For this purpose, analysis of meter is especially useful since metrical technique affords plenty of opportunity for the display of personal tastes, idiosyncratic mannerisms

---

[1] By Boas, *op. cit.* 183, and Binns, *op. cit.* 168.
[2] A good parallel, written for a similar purpose, is the comedy *Alba* composed for performance at Christ Church during the visit of King James in 1605. One of the collaborators on that play was Robert Burton.
[3] See below for Gager's responsibility for this manuscript.

(not always conscious ones), and levels of competency, and because the results of such analysis are readily quantifiable. Let us, then, compare the first hundred iambic lines undoubtedly by Gager (the Prologue, Argument, and Actus II, lines 267 - 320) with the first hundred iambic lines possibly by a second hand (Actus I, 38 - 137), for convenience identifying these groups as I and II respectively. Now, let us consider some statistics. First, in I there are 70 lines containing one or more resolutions,[1] while in II there are only 38. In I there are 18 lines having multiple resolutions, in II only 7. Even more interesting is an analysis of the distribution of resolutions into the first five feet of the line:

	1	2	3	4	5
I	18	21	9	9	26
II	22	0	3	1	20

Stylometric analysis need not be carried any farther, because these figures already delineate two radically different metrical techniques. In the parts of the play undoubtedly his, Gager uses resolutions copiously, freely introducing them into all possible feet. But in Actus I the technique is far more conservative, and tends to limit resolution to the first and fifth feet. A reluctance to employ them in the second and fourth may be understandable, but the low number of third-foot resolutions is truly remarkable. This lower frequency of resolution may be taken as an index of personal technique and preference, not necessarily of lesser adroitness. But it is worth recording that *Dido* contains several metrical solecisms (false quantities, failure to apply positional lengthening before a double consonant, etc.): cf. the Commentary notes on 783, 795, 972, 1083, 1193, and 1195. While these errors may be explicable as signs of haste, it is noteworthy that they all occur in portions of the play that, according to the theory of multiple authorship, are not Gager's, and so they perhaps are indications of a less sure metrician.[2]

I have already quoted a document recording that a large sum of money was furnished for "the chardges of a Comedye and a Tragedye and a shewe of fireworks as appeareth by the particular bille of Mr. Vice Chauncelor, Mr. Howsone, Mr. Maxie, and Mr. Pille." We happen to have (in the Christ Church accounts) a receipt signed by one of the recipients of this money, "Received by me George Peele the XXVIth day of May anno 1583 at the handes of Mr Thomas Thornton Treasurer the some of XX^{li} I say the some of twenty pounds [signed] Geo. Peele."[3] Presumably this money was to pay for the stage, scenery, costumes, special effects, and the like.

---

[1] For the purpose of this analysis I include among resolutions situations (such as the word *maria*) where the foot can or cannot be scanned as a disyllable by synaeresis. Whether or not this is a wise policy, since I am applying it to both text-groups, I very much doubt that the overall outcome is affected.

[2] To be sure, a few similar slips occur in some of Gager's other works. But they scarcely occur with similar frequency.

[3] (Christ Church Disbursement Books, 1582 - 3 volume.) The most detailed study of Peele's involvement with the production of *Dido* is David H. Horne, *The Life and Minor Works of George Peele* (New Haven, 1952) I.57 - 64 (who gives a facsimile of the document just quoted on p. 63). From this the reader can glean interesting information about the way Christ Church Hall was employed as a theater.

Horne[1] suggested that:

> Both [Emmanuel] Maxie and [John] Houson were almost exactly contemporaneous with Peele and may have formed, together with Peele, [Leonard] Hutten, Gager, and [Richard] Edes (who was one of the Proctors at the time of Alasco's visit), the nucleus of a dramatic society. All but Peele were in residence at Oxford in 1583, only Peele being called in from outside, perhaps because he alone was familiar with London and particularly with the business of acquiring theatrical materials such as would be needed for properties and effects. It may be that Peele had not yet moved his wife and family to London, and was spending a portion of his time in Oxford, and that this is why his name occurred to Convocation. More likely, however, his dramatically inclined friends needed help and thought of their schoolmate, who for two years had been gaining theatrical experience in London.

The claim has been made that Peele (a former member of Christ Church, who had taken his M. A. in 1579 but did not depart Oxford until 1581) returned from London in June of 1583 to assist in the forthcoming dramatic production.[2] But we have just seen a document placing him in Oxford towards the end of the preceding month. This is only nine days after the Chancellor's letter was read in Convocation, where money was allocated and a committee was established to supervise the coming festivities.[3] This *ad hoc* committee must have selected Gager as the playwright soon thereafter (doubtless on the strength of *Meleager*'s recent success), so Peele was on the scene only a week or so after Gager began composition of the plays. He was present in plenty of time to assist by lending technical advice and to supervise the early stages of preparation.

Why issue Peele the £20 so early? Work could also begin on the construction of whatever scenery, stage machinery, etc., was used, and props and costumes could be assembled.[4] For such matters, the presence of a someone familiar with the latest resources of the London theaters would be highly useful. And Peele was present, functioning in the capacity of technical advisor, while *Dido* was being written. For a play with so much stage spectacle, consultation about the feasibility of stage effects would obviously have been important, so in that sense *Dido* may be regarded as a collaborative effort. Peele may or may not have been the second author. If Tucker Brooke is right in identifying him as the author of the anonymous mini-epic *Pareus* published in 1585,[5] this work would serve to show that he was capable of serving as *Dido*'s second author. But of course evidence that Gager was not the sole author scarcely goes to prove that Peele was his collaborator, and so Horne was judicious to conclude that "the exact assignment of Peele in the production remains obscure." As he also wrote,[6] "...if we believe all the literary historians who have published

---

[1] *Loc. cit.*
[2] So the biographical sketch in the *Dictionary of National Biography* XV.671.
[3] Boas, *op. cit.* 179f.
[4] The May 17 Convocation authorized the construction of *theatra...pro ludis theatricis*. Horne, *op. cit.* 64 suggested that the money "was most likely advanced because [Peele] had to buy materials which required ready cash, presumably in London." All that Peele would have had to do was issue bulletins to London indicating what was needed. We probably do not have to imagine him shuttling back and forth personally.
[5] *Pareus* will be discussed in the General Introduction to Vol. III of this series.
[6] *Op. cit.* 87.

'discoveries' concerning Peele, he wrote most of the anonymous plays of the period and had a hand in some of Shakespeare's," and one should be very hesitant to add to the roster. If Gager needed help in completing *Dido* in a race against time, other potential helpers were scarcely lacking. Nevertheless, the idea that Peele may have been his collaborator remains a tantalizing possibility.

But if we were to seek another possible collaborator, we would not have far to look. At this time Christ Church contained a second playwright, Richard Eedes, who had produced a tragedy *Caesar Interfectus*, probably at the same time Gager's *Meleager* was acted, in 1582, and so in 1583 was every bit as distinguished as Gager (although he would write no more plays). In view of the short notice on which dramatic entertainment produced, it would be somewhat strange if no help were asked from Eedes, especially because he was Gager's senior by three years and the particular friend of the Dean of Christ Church, Dr. Tobie Mathew.[1] Eedes' sole surviving Latin poem of any length, the *Iter Boreale*, written in this same year, reveals him to be a vigorous and talented writer but an occasionally shaky metrician, capable of committing such solecisms as introducing false scansions and ignoring elisions. So perhaps *Dido* was co-authored by Eedes, or even written in committee. Gager never claimed to be fully responsible for *Dido*, and none of his contemporaries attributed it to him. All we can say, on the showing of the portions preserved in his commonplace book, is that he was the play's principal mastermind.

A final point perhaps deserves notice. A diary entry of Dr. John Dee, the Queen's astrologer, for June 15, 1583, reads:[2]

> Abowt 5 of the clok cam the Polonian Prince Lord Albert Lasky down from Bissham, where he had lodged the night before, being returned from Oxford whihter he had gon of purpose to see the universityes, wher he was very honourably used and enterteyned. He had in his company Lord Russell, Sir Philip Sidney, and other gentlemen.

On the basis of this statement Binns[3] argued that Sidney had perhaps been present at Oxford for the performances of Gager's plays, and of course Sidney was present for the revival production of *Meleager* in 1585. Hence the question deserves to be asked, if only to be dismissed, whether Sidney meant to include Gager in his blanket condemnation of English dramatists in the *Defense of Poesie* (III.38ff. Fueillerat). The *Defense* was not printed until 1595, and was written in response to Stephen Gosson's *The School of Abuse* (1579); as such, it was probably composed before its author became familiar with any of Gager's work (the common opinion is that it was written in 1581 or at most 1582). To be sure, the only recorded tradition of Sidney's opinion of Gager is a statement by Anthony à Wood that he esteemed his character and learning, and his literary abilities are conspicuously unmentioned. Nevertheless, it would seem very dangerous to come to any conclusion that Sidney disdained his dramatic output, and one would hope that *Meleager*, and

---

[1] See the Commentary note on poem CXXXVII.1f. in Volume III, where his satiric *Iter Boreale* is described.
[2] Quoted by Baumann-Wisseman, *op. cit. infra* 18 from J. O. Halliwell (ed.), *The Private Diary of John Dee* (Camden Society, 1st Series XIX, London, 1842) p.20.
[3] *Op. cit.* 170f., but cf. the more negative assessment of Frederick S. Boas, *Sir Philip Sidney* (London, 1955) 170.

perhaps also *Dido*, caused Sir Philip to revise his opinion of the contemporary theater sharply upward.[1]

One further question deserves consideration. In my Commentaries on *Meleager* and *Ulysses Redux*, I show that there is reason for thinking that Gager was familiar with the trilogy *Richardus Tertius* by his Cambridge contemporary, Dr. Thomas Legge. This is not surprising, since *Richardus* was the best known and most influential academic drama yet written. As such, it survives in more manuscripts than any other unprinted University play, a couple of which are owned by Oxford libraries.[2] If unprinted Cambridge drama exerted influence on Oxford plays, it might be thought, similar influence could conceivably have worked in the opposite direction. The production of *Dido* created something of a splash. Could it have come to the attention of a Cambridge student who wrote his own *Dido* play not long thereafter? For it is generally agreed that *The Tragedy of Dido Queen of Carthage* was at least begun by Marlowe during his University days.[3] In general, it is easy to exclude any such possibility, Marlowe's play is conceived along quite different lines.[4] Only one significant point of comparison exists. At the end of both plays Anna commits suicide, a development not indebted to Vergil. The reasons are quite different: Gager's Anna kills herself out of grief for her sister's death, while Marlowe's Anna does so because of the death of her lover Iarbas. Nevertheless, one might possibly reason, Marlowe might have known of Anna's suicide as handled by Gager and decided to supply a superior motivation, and one calculated to heighten the tragic effect. But it is far from certain that Marlowe did not hit on this idea independently.

✳ ✳ ✳

Dido is represented by two manuscripts. British Library Add. ms. 22583, fols. 34^v - 44^r, designated here as **A**, is Gager's autograph ms. containing the Prologue, Argument, Actus II, Actus III, and the Epilogue. The entire play is preserved by the Christ Church ms. 486, which may be called **B**.[5] Walter Hiscock suggested that **B** is also an autograph, an

---

[1] On the other hand, a word of sympathy has been spoken for his uncle Leicester: "His failure to command Latin, contrasted with Elizabeth's linguistic brilliance and with Cecil's careful scholarship, must have been a cause of embarrassment to him on such occasions as his visits to the universities when he had to endure Latin tragedies, comedies, and disputations for days on end": Eleanor Rosenberg, *Leicester, Patron of Letters* (New York, 1952) 142f.
[2] Bodleian Library Tanner ms. 306, folios 42 - 62, and Bodleian Library ms. Lat. Misc. e 16.
[3] The work was not published until after his death, and Nash's claim that he helped write it is notoriously difficult to evaluate. Nobody has ever discovered convincing internal evidence showing this play to have been a collaborative effort.
[4] There is at least nothing overt in the latter's play that invites the reader to draw any kind of comparison between Dido's situation and that of Elizabeth: the heroine, for example, is never called by her alternative name of Elisa. And, even though Marlowe may well have written some or all of his play at Cambridge, it lacks the prologue and epilogue virtually obligatory for an academic drama, in which he could have pointed up such a comparison, had he wished.
[5] Photographically reproduced in *William Gager, Oedipus (Acted 1577 - 1592), Dido (Acted 1583), Prepared with an Introduction by J. W. Binns* (Renaissance Latin Drama in England, First Series, vol. 1, Hildesheim - New York, 1981); both the manuscript and the photographic reproduction are unpaginated. Boas, *op. cit.* 167 wrote that this manuscript "is not improbably the 'book' used at the actual performance." This is sheer

identification questioned by Binns.[1] **B** is executed in a very beautiful Italic script. Our single manuscript of Gager's long poem on the Gunpowder Plot, *Pyramis* (British Library ms. Royal 12 A LIX, dated 1608, identified as **D** in this edition), is written in a very similar hand, in all probability the same one. This suggestion may seem difficult to accept if you compare these mss. with that of **A**, executed in a much more cursive and casual hand. But by comparison with signatures of Gager in Christ Church account books, Tucker Brooke, the editor of *Pyramis*, has suggested that this is an autograph copy.[2] This suggestion receives support from the elegiac couplet written at the front of the Dyce copy of the *Meleager* quarto (poem CXCVI in Volume III),[3] which closely resembles both **B** and **D**. While minor differences do exist,[4] the close resemblance of **B**, **D**, and the Dyce epigram virtually guarantees that they are all work of the same man: if you think any of them is an autograph, they you must think the same of all of them. This conclusion receives further confirmation from a document undoubtedly written in Gager's own hand, his holographic last will and testament (printed here in Volume IV). Although this will lacks the laborious copperplate formality of **B** and the *Pyramis* manuscript, and employs ligatures, scrupulously avoided in those manuscripts, a number of letter shapes are identical in all three documents, or nearly so.[5]

Dido first saw the light when Dyce printed the text of **A** in his edition of Marlowe.[6] A transcript of **B**, together with a collation against **D** and English translation, was published by Binns in 1971,[7] and a quite faulty transcript of **B** was published by Roberts-Baytop (unaware of Binns' work) in 1974.[8] In 1981 Binns oversaw, and supplied the Introduction for, a photographic reproduction of **B**.[9] More recently, the work has appeared with an introduction, text (which, save in a very few places, reproduces that of Binns), German translation, and commentary, by Baumann and Wissemann.[10] It will therefore be appreci-

---

speculation: there is nothing about this manuscript (a very formal fair copy) to suggest it was employed for the purpose.

[1] Walter George Hiscock, "Plays 1548 - 1945," in *A Christ Church Miscellany* (Oxford, 1946) 171f. (this is doubted by Binns, *op. cit.* 172 n. 8).

[2] *William Gager's Pyramis* (Transactions of the Connecticut Academy of Arts and Sciences 32, 1936) 250 - 349. Cf. pp. 252f. for a photographic reproduction of the first two pages of the manuscript. The most striking peculiarity of this manuscript is perhaps that the word *causa* is always written *caussa* (a spelling not encountered elsewhere), but surely this and a couple of other orthographic anomalies do not suffice to cast severe doubt on the proposition that it is a holograph.

[3] Now part of the Dyce Collection of the British National Library.

[4] For example, the Dyce couplet uses a closed *e* while the *Pyramis* manuscript uses an open, Greek-style *e*.

[5] This raises an obvious question: if both manuscripts are holographs, why do they present variant readings? The probable answer is supplied by **A**, in which Gager made a number of small revisions in *Susanna* and his translations, although these were written years earlier. He was one of those authors who could not resist the temptation of tinkering with his work as he copied it out.

[6] The Rev. A. Dyce, *The Works of Christopher Marlowe* (London, 1865) III.391 - 7.

[7] Binns, *op. cit.* 167 - 254.

[8] A. Roberts-Baytop, *Dido, Queen of Infinite Literary Variety: The English Renaissance Borrowings and Influence* (Salzburg Studies in English Literature, Elizabethan & Renaissance Studies No. 25, Salzburg, 1974) 37 - 94. Cf. the appraisal of Baumann - Wisseman, *op. cit. infra.* 28 - 30, n. 48.

[9] *Vide supra.*

[10] Uwe Baumann and Michael Wissemann, *William Gager, Dido Tragoedia, Herausgegeben, übersetzt, eingeleitet und kommentiert* (Bibliotheca Humanistica 1, Frankfurt a. M. - Bern - New York, 1985). Their deviations from Binns are itemized on p. 28 n. 48. Save for an emendation necessary to correct the meter at 222, their alterations amount to correction of typographical errors (605, 1067, 1116) or introduction of

ated that Binn's edition is the only significant contribution to the establishment of the text.

This edition not entirely satisfactory. Binns doubted that **B** is an autograph manuscript, so according to this logic his decision to base his text on that manuscript was indefensible: he ought to have used **A** when available, filling in from **B** when it is not, and to have preferred **A**'s readings when the two manuscripts are in disagreement. But he clung to **B** through thick and thin. Baumann and Wissemann, undisturbed by this questionable editorial policy, were content to reproduce his text save in a very few details.

This is no mere quibble, for there are a number of points where **B** deviates from **A** in ways large and small: leaving aside from many details of punctuation[1] and orthography, the two manuscripts present an impressive number of different readings (prologue inscription, 1, 36, II.i speaker list, 283, 310, 362, 365f., 429 and following scene-division in **A** only, 479, 499, 504, 563, III.ii speaker list and initial stage direction, stage direction after 553, 607, 609, 621, 630, 661f., 707, 725, 1216, 1226, 1238, 1241, and 1243). The great majority of these divergences involve situations where the **A** reading is equally acceptable in terms of sense, syntax, and meter. In making this private and hastily written copy Gager probably omitted some material by simple mistake: a stanza is left out of one chorus (580ff.) and two lines are accidentally skipped (728, 1235), as is one stage direction. And there are a very few places where text readings in **A** are impossible. At 283 *aerumnis* is not an acceptable substitute for *extremis* (the context calls for an adjective, not a noun). 707 *et hinc* merely substitutes the preceding word, and cannot stand because it deprives the line of a necessary syllable. *Magnus* at 609 might give one a moment's pause, since *etiam* would be easier understood with *maior*, but the objection is probably not fatal, and would Gager be saying that there might be some *greater* love affair afoot in Tyre at the moment? At 661 **A**'s reading is acceptable, since Gager also uses the vocative form *Aeneas* at 884.[2]

In parts of the play not covered by **A**, **B** contains a number of palpably erroneous features that must be put right by emendation, most notably at 52, 185, 222, 773, 794, 858, 1024, 1033, 1089, 1106, and 1151.[3] These are all minor slips of the pen, that scarcely cast doubt on the proposition that **B** is an autograph copy.

Faced with two autograph copies differing in many particulars, what is an editor to do? For once, he may very pardonably find himself in the position of Housman's donkey, hopelessly standing midway between two haystacks. In the event, the considerations preponderate which favor following **A** when it is available and **B** only when it is not. To be sure, the errors in **B** noted in the previous paragraph are by themselves insufficient to greatly disparage that manuscript's value, and it might be thought that the more carefully prepared copy is preferable. And Binns elsewhere suggested[4] "some of the surviving manuscripts [of academic plays] are so beautifully written that they may well be presentation copies given to distinguished visitors to help them follow the play in Latin." Certainly **B** is a handsome enough manuscript to fall in this category, but this interesting idea is no more than speculation (albeit a considerably more reasonable one than that this was a performance copy). **B** could also be a fair copy presented by the author to his college

---

unnecessary changes where the received text is perfectly acceptable (85, 267, 450, 480).

[1] But the differences in punctuation are interesting enough to warrant detailed examination in an Appendix.

[2] In Binns' transcript, 1217 *hunc* would also be wrong. But the true reading is *hinc* with an undotted *i*.

[3] Additionally, I have already listed places where metrical faults seem attributable to the (presumably second) author's own haste or carelessness, not to copying mistakes.

[4] *Intellectual Culture* 139.

library at some indefinite time. But, as shown in the Introduction to Volume III, Gager began his literary notebook no later than September 1583, while no estimate can be made about the date of **B**. Thus, since **A** version is demonstrably executed soon after *Dido*'s writing, while **B** is not, there is no choice but to follow **A** where available.

Dido Tragaedia

acta in Aede Christi Oxoniae

publice academicis recitata

pridie idus Iunii
1583

Dido, a tragedy

acted at Christ Church, Oxford

peformed for the Univerisity

June 12
A. D. 1583

DRAMATIS PERSONAE

PROLOGVS	ASCANIVS
VENVS	IOPAS
CVPIDO	ANNA
HANNO	NYMPHAE
MAHARBAL	MERCVRIVS
ILLIONEVS	SYCHAEI VMBRA
TROIANI	NVNCIA <ANCILLA>
ACHATES	BARCE
AENEAS	IRIS
CHORVS	EPILOGVS

DRAMATIS PERSONAE

PROLOGUE	ASCANIVS
VENUS	IOPAS
CUPID	ANNA
HANNO	NYMPHS
MAHARBAL	MERCURY
ILLIONEUS	GHOST OF SYCHAEUS
TROJANS	A MAID, SERVING AS MESSENGER
ACHATES	BARCE
AENEAS	IRIS
CHORUS	EPILOGUE

PROLOGVS IN *DIDONEM* TRAGAEDIAM

A p.64 (in B paginae non numerantur)

res quaeque varias invicem patitur vices,
et ipsa gratam varietas formam parit.
quae saepe fiunt illa cui placeant diu?
vicissitudo semper oblectat magis.
hesterna Mopsum scena ridiculum dedit, 5
hodierna grandem scena materiam dabit.
levis in cothurnum vertitur soccus gravem.
nec gratiora laeta sunt maestis tamen,
nec amara quovis melle delectant minus.
tulit omne punctum tristia admiscens iocis, 10
ridere forsan aliquis ad fletum potest,
idemque magna flere laetitia potest.
iucunditates lachrimae summas habent.
magna est voluptas flere ubi nihil est mali.
tantum benignas quaeso vos aures date, 15
et argumentum, si placet, totum eloquar.

ARGVMENTVM

huic Dido clarum fabulae nomen facit.
hic ipsa ad horas regna moderatur duas.
urbs ista Libyci est magna Carthago soli.
Iunonis odio per tot Aeneas freta 20
iactatus, istis applicat terris ratem.
benigna tectis excipit Dido hospitem.
sed ante nato chara prospiciens Venus,
(Tyrios bilingues quippe est ambiguam domum

p. 65   et adhuc furentis odia Iunonis timet) 25
Cupidinem sollicita lascivum rogat,
ut ora pueri sumat Ascanii puer,
uratque tacita regium pectus face.
gerit ille morem, deperit Eliza hospitem.
instigat Anna, nemore venatur, dolo 30
Iunonis atrum nymbus involvit diem,
iunguntur antro. monitus Aeneas parat
abire Libya. rescit abituri fugam
regina, queritur, obsecrat, saevit, furit.
immotus ille navigat, iussu Iovis. 35

prologum et argumentum habet A   1. *fragiles* pro *varias* B   22. *Dido hospitem excipit* B ante corr.

PROLOGUE TO THE TRAGEDY *DIDO*

Everything undergoes shifting changes, and variety itself imparts a pleasing aspect. How can things which often occur continue to please? Change always provides greater enjoyment. Yesterday the stage gave you silly Mopsus, today it will offer serious matter. The comic slipper turns into the tragic buskin. But happy things are no more welcome than the sad, and vinegar's no less pleasant than honey. The comic writer who mixes sorrowful matters in with his jokes spoils the point, but somebody can laugh so hard he cries, and in the same way great joy can produce tears. Crying is highly pleasurable. There's great delight in weeping — when nothing's wrong. I only ask that you lend me your kindly ears and, if it please you, I shall set forth the plot.

ARGUMENT

Dido lends her famous name to this play, and for a couple of hours this place will be her kingdom. This is the great city of Carthage, belonging to the land of Libya. Aeneas, so often wave-tossed by Juno's wrath, lands his ship here. Kindly Dido grants him hospitality in her palace. But loving Venus, caring beforehand for her son (since this is the uncertain home of the double-tongued Tyrians and she is still concerned about the ire of raging Juno), anxiously asks of wanton Cupid that the lad assume the guise of Ascanius and singe the royal breast with his stealthy torch. He obeys, Elisa dotes on her guest. Anna goads her on; they go hunting in the forest; by Judo's contrivance a cloud darkens the day; they are joined in a cave. Aeneas, warned, makes ready to leave Libya; the queen finds out about the departing man's flight; she complains, she begs, she rants, she rages. Unmoved,

Elisa, magicos rite constructa pyra
simulata cultus, propria dextra occidit.

---

36. *at Dido* pro *Elisa* habet **B**

he sets sail at Jupiter's command. But Dido builds a pyre, pretends to perform magic writes, and dies by her own hand.

- Actus Primus -

scena i

VENVS, CVPIDO

VEN.	dilecte fili (filium ni te meum	
	pudet vocari, filio quando meo	
	tuoque fratri cernis infensos deos)	40
	si quid parentis cura contemptae movet,	
	si cura fratris ulla disiecti manet,	
	si quid iacentis casus, orantis preces	
	valent (valentque plurimum spero) mihi	
	pariterque fratri te pium praesta tuo.	45
CVP.	quid impetrare, mater, id verbis studes,	
	quod impetrare filio debes tuo?	
VEN.	odium cruentae Palladis sensit meus	
	Anchise natus, cum per incensos lares	
	ignesque Troiae patrios ferret deos,	50
	aliam coactus quaerere atque alibi domum.	
	odio Minervae maius excepit malum.	
	Iunonis ira saevit, ah saevit nimis	
	etiam in iacentem, nec satis censet sua	
	prohibere terra, quaerat ut sedes novas,	55
	sed urget omnes eius in caedem deos.	
	qui fraena ventis ponit et laxat, deus	
	maria ciebat Aeolus, misit Notum,	
	misit procellis Africum crebrum suis,	
	totumque ab imis sedibus volvit mare.	60
	proinde vires excita tandem tuas,	
	dolore te dolere non dubito meo.	
CVP.	addis volenti calcar et stimulos mihi.	
	tuus est, videre quid velis fieri, labor.	
	mihi fas, capessam iussa, tu iubeas modo.	65
	manus ista tela mittet invitis deis.	

actus I deest de A 52. *odium* B 53. 65. vel *capessere* legere possis: vid. Comm. not.

- Act I -

scene i

VENUS, CUPID

VEN. My beloved child (unless you are ashamed to be called my child, since you see the gods are hostile to me and to my son, who is your brother), if you are moved by any concern for your spurned mother, if any concern remains for your ruined brother, if the humbled one's catastrophe or your begging mother's prayers have any influence with you (and I hope they have great influence), show yourself loyal to me and to your brother.

CUP. Mother, why seek to obtain with your words that which you have a right to obtain from me, your son?

VEN. My child by Anchises experienced savage Pallas' wrath when he carried his ancestral gods through the burning homes and the fires of Troy, forced to seek a new home elsewhere. And he suffered an evil greater than Minerva's anger. The wrath of Juno rages. Ah, it rages greatly at him even now that he has been prostrated. Nor does she think it enough to forbid him his land, so that he must seek a new homeland. She also urges all the gods to kill him. Divine Aeolus, who imposes and loosens his reins on the winds, stirred up the seas. He sent Notus, the South wind, he sent Africus, the Southwest wind, swollen with his storms, and boiled up the sea from its deep beds. Therefore exert your powers, for I do not doubt you are grieved by my sorrow.

CUP. You apply your spurs and goads to a willing person. Your job is to decide what you want to be done. It is permissible for me to act. I shall follow your orders, just command me. My hand will shoot these darts, though the gods be unwilling.

VEN.	gere quaeso morem, quid velim paucis scies.
	postquam quievit ventus, et pelagi fragor
	cecidit, ad illa se recepit littora
	quae prima vidit. vidit et Libyae solum. 70
	trabes ut aptet, sistit hic laceras rates,
	reficitque quicquid fregerat ponti furor.
	ad littus illud ambulanti illi obviam
	Tyriae sub ore virginis memet tuli.
	aliudque fingens, quaero de causa viae 75
	virique casu (quae tamen noram prius),
	simul ad Elizae regiam monstro viam.
CVP.	quae spes Elizae? quippe Iunoni favet.
VEN.	favet, sed illud antevertit Iupiter,
	in urbe ne quid fiat Aeneae mali. 80
CVP.	utinam profecto, suspicor Paenos tamen.
VEN.	quid suspicare? misit in terras suum
	Atlante natum, corda qui Paenis fera
	mollire possit, reddat et Tyrios meis
	magis hospitales. nescio quo se tamen 85
	Iunonis ira vertet, hospitii domus
	suspecta debet esse cui Iuno praeest.
	proinde flammis cinge reginam novis,
	dolisque falle. fac sit Aeneae mei
	amore capta, sic erit Dido magis 90
	amica nostris, sic erit Iuno magis
	placata Teucris.
CVP.	quo placet fallam modo?
VEN.	adverte. Elizae gratus Aeneas erit.
	trahetque captus vocibus blandis moram,
	sociumque Achatem mittet ad naves, ferat 95
	ut huc Iulum, spem patris solam sui,
	et dona regum rapta ab Iliacis rogis.
	referas ut ora dulcis Aschanii velim,
	notosque vultus induas pueri puer,
	ut cum suo regina te excipiet sinu 100
	inter paratas exteris lautas dapes,

VEN. Please obey, hear briefly what I want. After the wind grew calm and the sea's commotions subsided, he came to the first shore he saw. And he saw the land of Libya. In order to fit new planks, here he beached his damaged ships and repaired whatever the ocean's rage had shattered. And I, disguised as a Tyrian maiden, put myself in his way as he walked along the shore. Pretending another concern, I asked the reason for his journey and about the man's misfortune (although I knew these things beforehand), and at the same time I showed him the way to Elisa's palace.

CUP. What hope lies in Elisa? She is devoted to Juno.

VEN. She supports Juno, but Jupiter has taken precautions lest any evil befall Aeneas in the city.

CUP. Would that this might be so! Nevertheless I mistrust the Phoenicians.

VEN. Why be mistrustful? He has sent down to earth his child, the offspring of Atlas, to soften the Phoenicians' hard hearts and render them more welcoming to my people. But I do not know where Juno's wrath will turn itself, and a house of hospitality ruled by Juno must be held suspect. So surround the queen with novel fires, beguile her with your wiles, enthrall her with love for my Aeneas. Thus Dido will be friendlier to our race, thus Juno will be more appeased regarding to the Teucrians.[1]

CUP. In what way does it please you that I bewitch her?

VEN. Pay attention. Aeneas will be grateful to Eliza and will be detained by her pleasant speech. He will send his companion Achates to the ships to fetch Iulus, sole hope of his father, and also royal gifts, snatched from the pyres of Troy. I want you to assume the guise of sweet Ascanius and, a boy yourself, to take on the lad's familiar appearance, so that when the queen takes you on her lap during the banquet laid for the strangers, kisses

---

[1] The Trojans.

	cumque osculatur, cum dat amplexus tibi,	
	spires amorem et ignis inspires facem.	
CVP.	quid vero Iulo fiet?	
VEN.	Idalium super	
	montem recondam, et blandulo somno premam,	105
	ne forte nostris medius occurrat dolis.	
CVP.	factum putato, mater, ut fieri cupis,	
	simulabo vultus quos iubes, fallam dolo,	
	fallam veneno, spiritu mittam faces	
	etiam in medullas, facibus Aetnaeis pares.	110
	non ipse terris maior Oceanus meos	
	extinguet ignes, non dabit flammis modum	
	regina caeli, quamlibet venti deum	
	accersat, omnes promat et ventos simul.	
	sed quid moramur? regia en Dido exiit.	115

scena ii

DIDO, HANNO, MAHARBAL

DI.	nisi me perire fata voluissent prius,	
	ut pulsa regno quaererem regno locum,	
	minus beata dicerer, nusquam mea	
	Carthago staret. lapsus illustrem facit,	
	meusque faelix casus in casu fuit.	120
	nunc est videndum qui mihi constans status	
	in urbe fiat, quomodo faciam deos	
	adhuc faventes, semper ut faveant mihi.	
HAN.	quibus obtinetur artibus regnum potens	
	iis tenetur. prima quae fecit deos	125
	pietas faventes servat, id praesta modo.	
	quod praestitisti, nosque securos facis.	
	quanquam timere fecerit praesens malum.	

---

115. *faciam brevi* post *moramur?* scriptum tum deletum B | post hunc v. *ut linquat aras eius et faveat tuis*. scriptum tum deletum B

and embraces you, you may breathe love into her and kindle her torch.

CUP. What will happen to the genuine Iulus?[1]

VEN. I shall hide him up on Mt. Ida and wrap him in pleasant sleep, lest he blunder into the midst of our trickery.

CUP. Mother, consider your wishes already done. I shall feign the appearance you command, I shall beguile her by my trickery; with my potions, I shall breathe fire into her very marrow, torches equal to those of Etna. Ocean himself, greater than the lands, will not extinguish my fires. The queen of heaven will put no limit on my flames, even if she should summon the god of the winds and he should let forth all his gales at once. But why are we delaying? See, Dido is leaving her palace. [*Exeunt. Enter Dido.*]

scene ii

DIDO, HANNO, MAHARBAL

DI. Unless the Fates had previously wished to destroy me, so that I, an exile forced to seek a site for my kingdom, should be called less blessed, my Carthage would not stand. A reversal makes one fortunate, and my happy condition is founded on my misfortune. Now I must see how my position in the city can be made constant, how I can induce the gods who have favored me until now to support me always.

HAN. A kingdom is maintained by the same arts that gained it. Just show that piety that has made the gods favor you. Because you displayed it, you render us secure. However, a present evil has made us fearful.

---

[1] Ascanius.

DID.	malum? quod illud?	
HAN.	quod frequens vulgo sonat.	
DID.	quod illud inquam?	
MAH.	littus ad nostrum ferunt	130
	venisse naves, sive tempestas eas	
	adegit illuc, sive (quod potius reor)	
	venere fines Marte praedari tuos.	
DID.	et hoc et illud quicquid est metuo quidem.	
	quin sciscitatum mittimus causam viae?	135
HAN.	nihil necesse est, ecce venerunt tuam	
	vel experiri gratiam notam tuis,	
	vel experiri viribus quantum potes.	

scena iii

DIDO, ILIONEVS, TROIANI

DID.	quid hoc? quid iste vester ingressus, viri?	
	quae causa turbae? qui? quibus tandem locis	140
	venistis? aut quem quaeritis? nunquid meum	
	patere littus navibus, terram viris	
	nec impetrata, nec rogata (quod sciam)	
	venia putatis omnibus? nunquid solum	
	probatis? hospites an hostes vos putem?	145
	an utrosque? nempe saepe confundi solent.	
	referte paucis, absit a iussis mora.	
IL.	regina Dido, cui novam summus deum	
	concessit urbem condere et gentes feras	
	fraenare regni legibus iustis tui,	150
	nos te per undas flatibus vecti vagis	
	Troes rogamus. parce crudeli rates	
	violare flamma, parcito generi pio,	
	propiusque fautrix rebus afflictis veni.	
	non nos penates venimus Libycos fero	155
	populare ferro, non is incessit furor,	

DI. Evil? What's that?

HAN. The evil the people are talking about.

DI. What's that, I say?

MAR. Ships have come to our coast, either because a storm has driven them hither or (as I am inclined to believe) because they have come here to despoil your people in war.

DI. Whether it is the one or the other, I am still afraid. Why don't we send someone to learn the reason for their voyage?

HAN. There's no need. See, they have come, either to experience your favor, well known to your own people, or to try your strength. [*Enter Ilioneus and some other Trojans.*]

scene iii

DIDO, ILIONEUS, TROJANS

DI. What's this? Why make this entrance, men? What's the reason for this throng? Who are you? From what regions do you come? Or whom are you seeking? Do you think that my shore and my land are open to ships and their crews although, as far as I know, no permission has been sought or granted? Are you testing our land? Should I think of you as guests or enemies? Or as both? For sometimes the two become confused. Answer briefly, let there be no delay in obeying my commands.

IL. Queen Dido, whom the chief of the gods has allowed to found a city, to restrain the wild peoples with your realm's just laws, we Trojans, carried over the waves by the capricious winds, beseech you. Refrain from burning our ships with the cruel flame, have mercy on our pious race. As our protectress, be friendly to us in our adversity. We have not sailed here to ravage Libyan homes with the savage steel; that madness does not inspire

non ille victos ardor in praeceps tulit.
   antiqua tellus (Italam gentes quidem
vocant minores), terra proventu ferax,
rebusque certe bellicis quondam potens,   160
inter remotas hinc procul gentes iacet.
   hanc nos petentes obruit fluctu maris
nimbos Orion turbidos secum ferens,
totoque quassas dispulit naves freto.
   pauci marinis fluctibus pulsi tuas   165
intramus oras, rebus adversis opem
a te petentes. prohibet hospicium tuae
tua gens arenae: quod tuae gentis genus?
quae terra morem tam potest dirum pati?
   humana si nil vota tam duros movent,   170
sperate saltem caelitum iustas manus
fandi et nefandi vindices saevos fore.
   rex ipse nostrae classis Aeneas fuit
virtute belli clarus, et pacis simul.
quem si tuentur fata, si vitam trahit   175
nec adhuc silentes tetigit inferni lacus,
dubitare noli, quicquid impendis, metes,
neque paenitebit sis quod officio prior.
   quanquam nec omnis Troia cum Troia fuit
extincta. sunt in Siciliae regno viri   180
Troia profecti nominis clari, suum
rex ipse Acestes iactat a nostris genus.
   tantum rogamus liceat ut classi trabes
aptare, sylvis stringere et remos tuis,
ut vel recepto rege cum sociis viae   185
Latium petamus, fata quo monstrant iter,
vel spe relicta vasta Sicaniae freta
repetamus. illic rebus afflictis dabit
spem rex Acestes noster et nostris favens.

TROIANI OMNES

quid ille solus orat, oramus simul.   190

DI.   Teucri, timorem pellite, et curas graves.
      novitate regni cogor hunc morem sequi.
         quis nescit urbem? nescit Aeneadum genus?

---

185. *incepto* B: *recepto* scripsi ex Virg., *Aen.* II.553 (vid. Comm. not.)

us, that zeal does not compel us, who have suffered defeat. There is an ancient land (the younger races call it Italy), a fruitful country, once powerful in war, lying far from here among the remote nations. While we were seeking it, Orion overwhelmed us, bringing his roiling clouds, and he scattered our broken ships over the entire sea. We few, driven over the sea-surge, have come into your territory, seeing help from you in our adversity. Your nation forbids us the hospitality of your sands. What kind of people is this? What land tolerates such a custom? But if no human prayers can move such hard-hearted people, at least you may expect that the just hands of the gods, those avengers of rights and wrongs, will be savage. Aeneas himself was the admiral of our fleet, distinguished by his virtue alike in war and peace. If the Fates protect him, if he lives and has not reached the silent lakes of the Underworld, do not doubt that whatever you sow you will reap. Nor will you have cause for regretting that you are the first to perform hospitality's duty. However, not all of Troy was destroyed along with Troy. In the kingdom of Sicily there are men of distinguished name, come from Troy, and their king himself, Achates, boasts that he is born of our stock. We only ask that we be permitted to fit planks to our fleet, to hew oars from your forests, so that, recovering our king, we with our comrades on this expedition may search for Latium, by the route the Fates reveal. Or, abandoning hope, we shall revisit the immense Sicilian Strait where, as our king, Achates will restore courage to us in our adversity, being our patron.

ALL THE TROJANS What he alone begs for, we all request.

DI. Teucrians, dismiss you fear, your heavy concerns. I am compelled by my kingdom's newness to adopt this policy. Who is unfamiliar with your city, with Aeneas' lineage? Who

quis nescit ignes, bella, virtutes, viros?
non corda sic obtusa gestamus, neque 195
tam sol remotos vertit a Tyriis equos.
quocunque cursum flectitis, Troes, meis
opibus iuvabo, vos et auxilio meo.
quod si manere vultis hic mecum, domus
et urbis usum liberum vobis dabo. 200
mihi nulla Paeni, nulla Troiani nota
distincta fiet, lege constabunt pari.
utinamque certe vester Aeneas Noto
simili fuisset actus in terram meam.
mittam per omne littus, et quaeram quibus 205
aut ille sylvis lateat, aut erret locis.

scena iv

ACHATES, AENEAS, DIDO

ACH. o nate diva, quid manes? confer pedem.
socios receptos, omnia in tuto vides.
abest Orontes solus, hunc medio mari
fusum per undas vidimus.

AEN.   recte mones. 210
adeamus ergo principem. coram tibi
quem quaeris adsum Troius Aeneas, maris
ereptus undis, quae solum Libyae secant.
o sola nostris casibus princeps favens,
et sola praestans rebus afflictis opem, 215
quae, quos reliquit improbus Danaum furor
ignisque Troiae, quos mari fractos vides
terraque, egenos omnium hospicio beas.
nec urbe solum, sed domo socias tua.
dignas referre gratias non est opis, 220
regina, nostrae, nec potest quicquid manet
in orbe Troiae consequi tantum bonum.
tibi dii potentes (si dei curant pios
minus potentes, si valent iustae preces,
si possit ullus esse iusticiae locus) 225
meritis rependant praemia (ut debent) tuis.
quae te tulerunt laeta mundo saecula,

199. *meum* B ante corr.   200. *liberum usum* B ante corr.   222. *Troiae in orbe* corr. in *orbe in Troiae* B: sic Baumann-Wissemann

does not know about your burning, your wars, your virtues, your men? Our hearts are not so ignorant, the sun does not avert his horses so far from us Tyrians.[1] Whatever direction your journey takes, Trojans, I shall support you with my resources and aid. But if you choose to remain here with me, I shall grant you he freedom of my home and city. I shall make no distinction between Phoenicians and Trojans, they will enjoy equal laws. Would that the same North wind had also driven Aeneas to my land! I shall send along my entire shore, seeking in what forest he is hiding, in what place he wanders. [*Enter Achates, followed by Aeneas, on one side of the stage.*]

scene iv

ACHATES, AENEAS, DIDO

DI. Why hesitate, goddess-born? Move ahead. You see your comrades receiving hospitality, everything in a safe condition. Only Orontes is missing, and we saw him bobbing in the waves in mid-ocean.

AEN. You advise me rightly. So let's approach the queen. [*They cross over to Dido's side of the stage.*] I whom you seek am present, Aeneas of Troy, rescued from the waves which batter Libya's shores. Oh queen, who alone supports us in our misfortune, who alone aids us in our adversity, with your hospitality you bless us, the survivors of the Danaans'[2] evil fury, whom you see shattered by land and by sea, lacking everything. You do not just share your city with us, but also your home. Oh queen, we have not the resources to pay you adequate thanks, nor is whatever remnant of Troy still existing in the world able to assemble such great wealth. May the mighty gods (if the gods care for pious men who are helpless, if just prayers count for anything, if there is any place for justice) repay you for your merits, as they should. What happy centuries gave birth to you in this

---

[1] Tyre was the mother city of Carthage.
[2] The Greeks.

      tantique talem qui dederunt principes?
      donec profundum flumina in pontum cadent,
      dum terra pascet arbores, stellas polus,   230
      tuas tuique nominis laudes canam.
      et una vestri reddit oblitum dies
      et una nostri. quando me reddis meis
      (quos esse salvos laetor, amplector lubens)
      mihi me deesse malo quam laudi tuae.   235

DI.   quis te per ista casus insequitur mala?
      quae vis et oras cogit immanes sequi?
      generis et urbis nomen agnosco tuae.
      Sidona Teucer cum veniret, rettulit
      et hostis hostes laude non parva tulit,   240
      ductumque dixit Teucer a Teucris genus.
      quare subite vos meam, iuvenes, domum.
      per non minores me quidem similis tulit
      fortuna casus, et tamen regnum dedit.
      mala passa, rebus laeta succurro malis.   245

AEN. morem geremus, nobilis Dido, tibi.

CHORVS

      fertur incerto pede sors in altum.
      tollit, et rursus premit, ima summis
      aequat, in partem levis hanc et illam.
      addit afflictis mala rebus, urget   250
      quos videt pronos, sequiturque partem
          deteriorem.

      fata cum fatis inimica pugnant,
      sunt in hac causa superi faventes,
      sunt in hac causa superi furentes,   255
      nec premunt omnes pariter nec adsunt
          omnibus omnes.

      est in extremis mora nulla rebus.
      quod nequit peius fieri, recedit.
      spem dat afflictis sine spe fuisse,   260
      et salus victi sine spe salutis
          dicitur esse.

world, what great parents produced such a daughter? As long as rivers pour into the fathomless sea, as long as the land bears trees, the sky stars, I shall sing praises of you and your name. On the same day I shall forget you and myself. Since you give me back to my people (and I rejoice that they are safe, I embrace them gladly), I would rather fail myself than be failing in your praise.

DI. What evils follows you through all these misfortunes? What power compels you to pursue those wild shores? I know full well your city's name, your lineage. When Teucer came to Sidon, he brought report of you and, though an enemy, piled no small praises on his foes. Teucer said his pedigree was derived from you Teucrians. So enter my home, young men. A similar destiny brought me through no smaller misfortunes, but granted me a kingdom. Having experienced evils, I gladly succor you in your adversity.

AEN. Noble Dido, we obey. [*Exeunt omnes into the palace.*]

CHORVS

On unsteady foot, our fortune is born aloft. It raises us up, casts us down again, makes the highest and lowest to be equal, fickle towards both this side and that. It adds woes to us in our adversity, burdens those whom it sees laid low, following the worse course.

Hostile fates struggle against fates: the gods are friendly in this cause, savage in that They neither oppress all equally, nor are uniformly favorable to all.

There is no respite for us in our extremities. What can grow no worse eases. To be without hope encourages the afflicted, and the lack of any hope for salvation is said to be the salvation of the vanquished.

nox diem, solem nebulae reducunt,
laeta succedunt ubi dura cedunt.
heu fuit clamor pelagi, sed intus   265
    io triumphat.

Night brings back the day, clouds the sun, and happy things come when hardships recede. Alas, the ocean was in upheaval, but, oho, he rejoices inside.

- Actus Secundus -

A p. 65

scena i

DIDO, AENEAS, ASCANIVS FALSVS

DI. quin, hospes, ista missa faciamus magis.
     olim iuvabit quod fuit durum pati
     meminisse, curas interea menti excute.
     instructa dapibus mensa nos eccum manet.   270
     accumbe quaeso. Bacchus aerumnas levet.
       magnanime princeps, si foret suasum tibi
     quam gratus aulam veneris nostram advena,
     nec non Iulus pariter, et comites viae,
     non dico Troia penitus excideret tibi   275
     sedesque patriae, laetior certe fores.

AEN. regina, gentis candidum sydus tuae,
     non lingua nostri pectoris sensum explicet,
p. 66 non vultus animum. laetitia gestit levis,
     ingens stupescit, seque non capiens silet.   280
     quis tam benignae verba reginae satis
     vultusque placidos referat, et miseris fidem
     opemque nostris rebus extremis datam?
     quis apparatus regios digne efferat
     luxusque tantos? ista meditantem tua   285
     promerita, si me cogites, laetum putes.

DI. non ista tanti agnosco quae memoras bona.
     equidem esse cupio, fateor, et spero assequi
     ut non Elisae pigeat Aeneam hospitis.
     sed cur Iulus tristior spectat dapes?   290

ASC. urbs ista Troiae praebuit speciem mihi,
     animumque misero subiit aspectu dolor.
     quae nocte genitor retulit hesterna altius
     hic breviter oculis subiici videas tuis.

DI. Iule, quaeso repete fortunam Ilii.   295

Actus II et III habet A   index personarum. ASCANIVS FALSVS A, ASCANIVS B   283. *extremis* B,
aerumnis A

- Act II -

scene i

DIDO, AENEAS, THE FALSE ASCANIUS

DI. Come, friends, let us dismiss these things. Someday it will be pleasant to remember what was hard to experience, but meanwhile banish cares from your mind. Behold, a feast awaits us. Recline yourselves, I beg you. Bacchus will lighten your cares. Great-hearted prince, if you were convinced how welcome you are as a guest coming to our court, and Iulus likewise and also your comrades, I shall not say that you would entirely forget Troy and your ancestral home, but you would surely be happier.

AEN. Queen, shining star of your people, my tongue cannot express what is in my heart, my visage cannot express what I think. A trifling happiness eagerly expresses itself, but a great one is dumbfounded, cannot control itself, and is silent. Who can describe the words of this kindly queen, her placid countenance, the faith and help she gives us wretched people in our misfortune? Who can properly describe this royal splendor, all this magnificence? If you think of me, think of me as joyfully pondering your merits.

DI. I do not value highly these merits of which you speak. But I must confess that I desire, and hope I am achieving, that Aeneas is not ashamed to have Elisa as his hostess. But why is Iulus staring at his meal in sorrow?

ASC. That city of Troy showed me its image, and at the doleful sight sorrow came over my mind. What my father told you last night at greater length, you may see here put briefly before your eyes.

DI. Iulus, pray retell the fate of Troy.

[*At this point servants hold up a platter containing a map executed in marzipan. Iulus stands before it, pointing out its individual features.*]

ASC. hanc esse Troiam finge quam patera vides.
      hac Simois ibat fluvius, hic densis sita est
      mons Ida silvis, hac stetit Tenedos via,
      hac Cilla, Chrise, quaeque circuitu undique
      urbes minores dirutae bello iacent.   300
      hic mille ratibus hostium statio fuit.
      hic castra, campus inter hic pugnae iacet.
      hos esse magnos Pergami muros puta,
      haec porta Scaea est, Hector hac solitus ferox
      turmas in aciem ducere. hic Priami lares,   305
      hic patris, illic steterat Anchisae domus.
      hic parte muri diruta, insidiis equi

A p. 67   ingens in urbem panditur mediam via.
      hic caepta caedes. plura quid fari queam?
      post multa tandem funera et strages ducum   310
      sic est Sinonis fraude, sic Danaum face
      incensa, sic est in leves cineres data.

DI.   o quam stupendi specimen ingenii datum!
      o te beatum prole generosa patrem,
      et te parente filium tali editum.   315
      divinam, Iule, sequere naturae indolem.
      laudes parentis bellicis opto tibi,
      senemque precor aetate transcendas avum.
      et hoc amoris osculum pignus cape.

ASC. quin oscularis filium, genitor, tuum?   320

HYMNVS IOPAE

quod tibi nomen tribuam deorum?
sive te Martem, Lyciumve Phaebum,
Herculem seu te Iove procreatum
    dicere fas est,

sive digneris titulo minore,   325
teque mortalem placeat vocari,
(at deum certe poteris videri
    sanguine cretus)?

310. habet *virum* pro *ducum* B   313. *datum?* A B

ASC. Imagine this dish you see to be Troy. Here went the river Simois, here is located Mount Ida with its thick forests, in this direction lie Tenedos, Cilla, Chryse, the circle of outlying towns ruined in the war. Here was the harbor for our enemies' thousand ships, here were the camps, with the battlefield lying between. Imagine that these are Pergamum's[1] high battlements; this is the Scaean gate out of which warlike Hector used to lead his squadrons to battle. Here was the house of Priam, here my father's, there dwelt Anchises. Here is a portion of the wall pulled down, and by the trick of the horse a great avenue is opened into the middle of the city. Here the killing has begun. How can I say more? After all the deaths, the slaughter of captains, thus by Sinon's deceit and the Danaans' torches the city is turned into insubstantial ash.

DI. Oh, what an example of amazing ingenuity is offered here! Oh father, happy to have such a noble offspring — and you, son, blessed son of such a parent! Iulus, you must be true to your nature's divine character. I hope you will reap praises like those of your warlike father, I pray you surpass the span of your aged grandfather. Receive this kiss as the pledge of my love.

ASC. Father, why don't you kiss your son too? [*They drink a cup, while Iopas sings.*]

THE HYMN OF IOPAS

What god's name should I attribute to you? It is right to call you Mars, or Lycian Phoebus, or Zeus-born Hercules?
Or do you claim a lesser title, if it you please you to be called a mortal (but surely you can be seen to have an admixture of divine blood)?

---

[1] Troy's.

quas tibi dicam celebremve laudes?
quo mihi fas est resonare plectro? 330
quod decet tanto memorare carmen
    principe dignum?

splendor heroum, patriaeque lumen
inclytum, salve, generisque prisci.
non tua nostras tetigit carina 335
    gratior oras.

p. 68

sis licet tantus superesque nostri
pectoris captum, tamen est Elisa
maior, o hospes nimium beate
    hospite Elisa. 340

est minor nemo nisi comparatus,
neve te dici pudeat minorem.
nil videt nostrae simile aut secundum
    orbis Elisae.

Cynthiae qualis nitor inter astra, 345
talis in terris decor est Elisae.
ecce cui gratus patria relicta
    veneris hospes.

proximas illi tamen occupasti
nominis laudes, sequerisque iuxta, 350
proximos illi tibi vox Iopae
    cantat honores.

vinciant pictae cyathos coronae,
nobili Bacchus statuatur auro,
maximi fiant strepitus per aulam, 355
    iussit Elisa.

hospes illustris tibi gratulamur,
iam iuvat longos geminare plausus,
en tibi laetae volitant per ampla
    atria voces. 360

What praises should I pronounce, or celebrate you with? With that plectrum may I strike my lyre? What song should I bring to mind worthy of such a prince?

Hail, glory of heroes, famous light of your nation, of your ancient line. No ship has ever attained our shores more welcome than yours.

But though you are so great and overwhelm my heart's understanding, Elisa is yet greater, oh guest so fortunate to have Elisa as hostess.

Nobody is any lesser, save in comparison to her, nor should it shame you to be called the lesser. The world sees nothing like or equal to our Elisa.

As Cynthia shines among the stars, such is our Elisa's splendor on earth. See, happy guest, to whom you have come when you left your homeland.

But you gain a reputation second only to hers, you follow close behind, and Iopas' voice sings your praises next to hers.

Let decorated garlands encircle the cups, let Bacchus be placed in the noble gold, let great shouts ring through the hall. Thus orders Elisa.

We salute you as a noble guest. Now it is pleasing to redouble our lengthy praises, now our happy voices ring through this great hall.

scena ii

DIDO, AENEAS

	DI.	dux magne Teucrum, quae tibi placeant dapes?	
	AEN.	nec hae nec illae, sed placent cunctae mihi. epulas in epulis, in cibis quaero cibos, et copia meum tanta delectum impedit.	
A p. 69	DI.	non ista Priami regna. quis Catharginis hospitia Troiae conferat quondam tuae? sed tenuis aures pepulit hic rumor meas quaedam fuisse fata secreta Ilii. quaenam illa fuerint, hospes, exponas precor.	365
	AEN.	regina, variis illa numerantur modis. in his reponi Troili laethum solet, scissumque Scaeae limen, atque Helenus sacer, Rhesique equorum raptus, et Pirrhus simul. sed prima Troiae fata memorantur duo: flavae sacratum Palladis signum deae, et cum sagittis arcus et pharetra Herculis.	370 375
	DI.	quod hoc Minervae quaeso simulacrum fuit?	
	AEN.	cum dives Asiam regeret, et muros novi extrueret Ilus Ilii, festo die cecidisse caelo fertur, hic illuc means, colum sinistra, spiculum dextra tenens, habituque toto bellicam referens deam. obstupuit Ilus, consulit Phaebum pius. consultus ille, tale responsum dedit. "in hoc ruina stabit et Troiae salus. servate tectis, urbe cum vestra, deam. ablata, secum tollet imperium loci." ast Ilus arcem Palladi sacram extruit, caeleste tuto collocat signum loco, additque vigiles. nec quidem haeredi minor pervenit inde cura, Laomedon, tibi.	 380 385 390

362. *hae nec* A, *hae, ne* B   365. *non* pro *quis* habet B   366. *fecerim paria* pro *conferat quondam* habet B

scene ii

DIDO, AENEAS

DI. Great captain of the Teucrians, what dishes would delight you?

AEN. Neither this one nor that one: they're all delightful. I am given serving upon serving, dish upon dish, and the huge amount obstructs my pleasure.

DI. This is not Priam's kingdom. What Carthaginian would ever compare his hospitality with that of your Troy? But this faint rumor has struck my ears, that there were certain prophecies about Ilium. I beg you, guest, to tell me what they were.

AEN. Queen, they are accounted variously. Among them are customarily reckoned Troilus' death, the breaking of the Scaean gate, Helenus the priest, the abduction of Rhesus' horses, and also Pyrrhus. But the chief portents for Troy are remembered as being two, the statue consecrated to fair-haired Pallas, and Hercules' bow together with its arrows and quiver.

DI. What, pray tell, was that statue of Minerva?

AEN. When wealthy Ilus governed Asia and built walls for his new Ilium, this is said to have dropped out of the sky on a festival day, in a striding pose, holding a distaff in its left and and a spear in its right, showing the goddess in full battle-dress. Ilus, amazed, piously consulted Apollo. The god, being asked, gave the following response. "In this thing will rest both Troy's ruin and her salvation. Protect the goddess under your roofs, along with your city. If she is taken away, she will take with her your dominion over this place." So Ilus built a consecrated shrine for Pallas, placed the heaven-sent statue in this safe place, and set guards upon it. Nor, Laomedon, were you less careful as his heir. But, alas, it was

		at heu parum servata sub Priamo fuit.	
		hoc ipsa voluit Pallas, ex illo die	
		quo forma victa est Paridis arbitrio, furens.	
	DI.	quis machinator facinoris tanti extitit?	395
p. 70	AEN.	furtis Ulisses aptus et natus dolo	
		dum per cloacas abditam quaerit viam.	
	DI.	quin et secundum Pergami fatum explica.	
	AEN.	arsusrus illo natus Alcmena rogo	
		quo victor astra petiit, et superum domos,	400
		"Paeante genite," dixit, "hoc munus cape."	
		arcumque dono pariter et pharetram dedit	
		gravidam sagittis: arguunt tela Herculem.	
	DI.	quis hoc Pelasgis aperuit fatum deus?	
	AEN.	et hoc et illud proximum Phaebo caput	405
		monstravit Helenus, ipse fatorum mora.	
		hic captus Ithaci fraude sic Danais sacra	
		resolvit ora, Delio plenus deo.	
		"en hic sagittis restat Alcidae labor	
		supremus, illum fata rapuerunt licet,	410
		at interesse gloriae haeredem iubent.	
		nec minima tanti pars erit facti Hercules.	
		non ante Troia poterit aequari solo	
		Priamique regnum, quam Philoctetes gravi	
		serpentis ictu saucius, Lemno exulans	415
		in castra veniat, ut ducum strage edita	
		cruore arundo madeat Herculea Phrygum.	
		ne quid geratur arduum, dempto Hercule."	
		en ista Troiae summa fatorum fuit.	

Pompa larvalis.

403. *supremus* corr. in *sagittis* A

not preserved in the reign of Priam. This Pallas herself decided, in her outrage, beginning on the day she was bested in the contest about beauty, by judgment of Paris.

DI. Who was the contriver of such a misdeed?

AEN. Ulysses, prone to deceit, born to trickery, as he sought his furtive way through the city's sewers.

DI. Explain Pergamum's second fate.

AEN. When Alcmenus' victorious son[1] was about to burn on the pyre, seeking the stars and the gods' dwelling place, he said "son of Poeas,[2] accept this gift." As a present he gave him his bow, and also his quiver, heavy with arrows. These weapons showed him to be Hercules.

DI. What god revealed this destiny to the Pelasgians?[3]

AEN. Helenus, consecrated to Phoebus, himself an obstruction to Destiny's fulfilment, pronounced this and the other doom. Captured by the Ithacan's deceit, he revealed these things to the Danaans while possessed by the god. "Lo, this final undertaking depends on Alcides'[4] arrows. Even though the Fates have snatched him, they ordain that his heir share in this glory. Hercules will play no small part in this achievement. Troy and the kingdom of Pergamum cannot be laid low before Philoctetes, wounded by the serpent's heavy bite and now an exile on Lemnos, comes to your camp, so that in the slaughter of their captains Hercules' arrows will be drenched with Phrygian[5] blood. Let no arduous task be undertaken, now that Hercules is dead." And this is the sum of the prophecies concerning Troy. (*Enter a procession of masquers.*)

---

[1] Hercules.
[2] Philoctetes.
[3] The Greeks.
[4] Hercules'.
[5] Trojan.

scena iii

DIDO

DI. rector deorum Iupiter et hominum sator, 420
(nam iura te loquuntur hospitibus dare),
si rite pateram solitus hanc Belus tibi

p. 71 implere vino, et quisquis a Belo minor,
hanc esse Tyriis pariter et Teucris diem
iucundam, et huius posteros olim, velis 425
meminisse nostros. Bacche, laetitiae dator
adsis, et alma Iuno iam Phrygibus bona.
et o faventes esto vos Tyrii precor.

Libat Iovi.

scena iv

DIDO, ASCANIVS

ASC. regina, tandem quaeso tollantur dapes.
satis epularum, luxui satis est datum. 430
inambulando membra relevemus precor.

DI. mos tibi geretur, tollite ministri ocius.
interea laeto personet cantu domus.
nos inferamus regiis hortis gradum.

scena v

MAHARBAL, HANNO

MAH. ut vereor, Hanno, quem ferent ista exitum 435
hospitia! si (quod omen avertat deus)
quod saepe factum, iamque ne fiat precor,
si deperiret hospitem Dido novum,
quae bella, quas hae nuptiae turbas darent?

scena iv. novam scaenam non recognovit B: vid. Comm. not.   429. v. et indicium actionis desunt de B
436 *hospitia?* B

scene iii

DIDO

DI. Jupiter, governor of the gods and father of mankind, they say you ordain the laws of hospitality. If Belus[1] and his descendants have duly filled a cup for you, let today be a happy one for Tyrians and Trojans alike. Grant that his posterity and also ours will remember it. Bacchus, giver of happiness, be present, and also motherly Juno, already kindly to the Phrygians. And, o Tyrians, I ask you to be favorable.

She pours a libation to Jupiter.

scene iv

DIDO, ASCANIVS

ASC. Queen, I ask that at lest these dishes be cleared. Sufficient feasting and luxury have been provided. I beg you, let us ease our limbs in walking.

DI. Your wish will be granted. Servants, remove this stuff quickly. Meanwhile, let this house ring with glad music. We shall stroll in the royal garden. [*Exeunt. Enter Mahabal and Hanno.*]

scene v

MAHARBAL, HANNO

MAH. Hanno, how I fear all this hospitality will lead to ruin! If, as often happens (but may the god avert this omen!) Dido falls in love with our foreign guest, as often happens, what wars, what riots will this marriage engender?

---

[1] Her father.

	HAN.	at tu, Maharbal, quem tibi fingis metum? 440
nolo oscitantem, nolo prudentem nimis.
quae bella vates (illa fac nubat) canis?
	MAH.	tantumne Iarbas dedecus inultum feret
furens adhuc amore? quod Libyae duces
quos illa toties sprevit, impune hospitem 445
in regna recipi, despici indiginas sinent?
p. 72	HAN.	si tu, Maharbal, exigi miserum putes
licito iuventam ducat ut vacuam toro
regina, pollens opibus, aetate integra,
tuove potius nubet arbitrio an suo? 450
an magis Iarbae? lege si tali velim
rex esse, moriar. coniugem nolo eripi,
nolo imperari, gravius hoc multo reor.
nam quas Iarbae, quas refers regum minas?
ducente Tyrias Troico turmas duce, 455
Carthago clarum gentibus caput efferet.
	MAH.	at subeat animo quae sit hospitibus fides
habenda: Theseus doceat Ariadnae malo,
Iason Medeae. trita peregrinis fuga est.
	HAN.	ah ne duorum scelera sint culpa omnium. 460
sed maesta vultus exiit Dido foras.
at nos secreto tecta repetamus gradu.

scena vi

DIDO, ANNA

	DI.	quae me, Anna, dubiam somnia exterrent, soror!
quis iste nuper sedibus nostris novus
successit hospes? ore quem sese ferens! 465
quam fortis alto pectore, armisque inclytus!
equidem, soror, (nec vana credentis fides)
genus esse divum credo: degenerem arguit
animum timor. quot ille perpessus mala
terra marique! bella quae gessit ferox! 470

450. *arbitrio nubet* B ante corr.   465. *ferens?* B (sed cf. Virg., Aen. IV.11)   463. *soror?* B   465 sq. *ferens?...inclytus?* B   470. *marique?...ferox?* V (sed cf. Verg., Aen. IV.14)

HAN. Maharbal, what fear are you imagining? I don't like anybody to be careless, nor yet over-cautious. Suppose she marries — what wars do you prophesy?

MAH. Could Iarbas, still burning with love, tolerate such a great unavenged wrong? Will the princes of Libya, so often spurned by her, allow this guest to be received in her realm while the native-born are rejected?

HAN. Maharbal, if you should think it a terrible thing for those empty youths to be thrust aside, so that our queen, powerful in her resouces, a mature woman, should make a marriage, then do you think she marry according to your wishes or to her own? Would you prefer her to obey Iarbas? If I could be king according to such an arrangement, I'd rather be dead. I don't want Dido as his consort to be thrust aside or ordered about. I think that would be much worse. What threats of Iarbas or the princes are you speaking about? With a Trojan at the head of the Tyrian army, Carthage will hold her head up proudly among the nations.

MAH. But think how guests' faith is to be regarded. Let Theseus teach you by Ariadne's injury, Jason by Medea's. Foreigners' desertion is commonplace.

HAN. Ah, the wickedness of two men should not convict them all. But Dido is coming outside, wearing an unhappy look. Let us steal indoors. [*Exeunt. Enter Dido and Anna.*]

scene vi

DIDO, ANNA

DI. Sister Anna, what dreams terrify me in my doubtful state! Who is this strange guest newly come to our home? What distinction he has in his looks! How brave with his deep chest, famous for his prowess at war! Sister, I believe he is born of the gods. Nor is this an idle belief of the gullible, for fear betrays the low-born spirit. How many hardships has he undergone by land and sea! How many battles has this warlike man fought! If I had not

p. 73

        si non sederet in animo fixum mihi,
        ne cui iugali lege sociari velim,
        postquam mariti morte deceptam mei
        amor fefellit primus, et taedae mihi
        si non perosae penitus ac thalami forent,   475
        huic forsan uni cederem culpae libens.
        sed vel dehiscat ante mihi tellus precor,
        vel pater ad umbras fulmine omnipotens agat
        pallentis umbras Erebi et infernam Styga,
        quam tua resolvam iura, te violem, pudor.   480
        me primus ille qui sibi iunxit, meos
        abstulit amores, habeat is secum, et suo
        servet sepulchro. nemo levitatem arguat.

AN.   o chara magis hoc lucis aspectu soror,
        semperne maerans caelibem vitam exiges?   485
        nunquamne Veneris pignora et licitos thoros
        dulcesque natos noveris? id tu putas
        curare manes? esto, nulli aegram viri
        flexere quondam, non tua spretus Tyro
        nobilis Iarbas, gentis et Libyae duces,   490
        et quos abundans Africa triumphis alit.
        etiamne amori sola pugnabis deo?
        nec quorum in arvis degis in mentem venit?
        hinc Marte gens invicta Getuli truces
        Numidaeque cingunt, hinc regio squalens siti   495
        et vasta Syrtis, inde Barcaei fremunt
        late furentes. bella quid dicam Tyro
        iam nascitura? quid graves fratris minas?
        Iunonis equidem et caelitum auspiciis reor
        huc detulisse Dardanas ventum rates.   500
        germana, quam tu, quam brevi, hanc urbem tuam
        quae regna cernes surgere Aenea duce!

p. 74   comitante Teucro milite, ut se Punica
        nomenque terris gloria attollet tuum!

DI.   non ista nostrum quae refers animum latent.   505
        et iam fatebor, Anna: post miserum mei
        fatum Sichaei, et caede fraterna impie
        sparsos penates, solus hic sensus meos
        flexit, animumque cardine labantem impulit,
        primasque flammae veteris agnosco notas.   510

---

479. *horrendam* pro *infernam* habet B   502. *duce?* A (cf. *Aen.* IV.48 sq.)   504. *nomen per orbem* pro *nomenque terris* habet B

made up my mind firmly that I do not want to marry, after Love had previously cheated me by my husband's death, and if marriage torches and the bridal chamber were not hateful to me, perhaps I would yield to sin gladly for this one man. But I pray that the earth would swallow me up beforehand, or that the almighty Father with his lightning would bring me to the shades, the shades of pallid Erebus and the infernal Styx, before I break your laws and do injury to you, Modesty. Let that man who married me before and stole my heart keep me with him, let him keep me in his tomb. Let nobody accuse me of inconstancy.

AN. Oh sister, dearer to me than the sight of day, are you always going to lead a celibate life in mourning? Are you never to have known the pledges of Venus, the lawful pleasures of the bed, sweet children? Do you think that shades cares about this? I grant you, no men have previously moved you in your misery, not noble Iarbas, scorned in your Tyre, nor the princes of Libya and the men nourished by Africa, rich in victories. Are you now going to be the only one to struggle against love's god? Does it not occur to you whose land you inhabit? This land is surrounded by the fierce Gaetuli, indomitable in war, and by the Numidians. On this side is a land parched by thirst and the vast Syrte. From the other direction the Barcaeans shout defiance at us, raging over great distances. Why must I speak of the wars impending for Tyre? Why mention your brother's horrible threats? I think the wind drove the Dardanian[1] ships here according to the will of Juno and the gods. Oh sister, imagine what city, what manner of kingdom will quickly arise here, with Aeneas our prince! With the Teucrian soldiers as allies, how Punic glory will extol your name throughout the world!

DI. That which you say does not escape my attention. And now I shall confess, Anna, after the sad death of my Sychaeus and the impious scattering of my household by my brother's slaughter, this man alone has moved my feelings, has unhinged my tottering mind, and now I acknowledge the first signs of that old flame. But doubtful timidity and

---

[1] Trojan.

        sed dubius animum distrahit nostrum timor
        pudorque. voti quam mei spem das, soror?

AN.   germana, tantum posce tu veniam deos.
        sacris litatis, hospiti indulge novo.
        causas morandi necte dum pelago gravis   515
        desaevit hyemis ira, dum quassae rates,
        dum non sereno murmurant venti polo.

DI.   satis est. amori subdis ardenti faces.
        laxabo fraena. stultus excedat pudor.
        cras demereri victima crebra deos   520
        pacemque in extis quaerere statutum est mihi.
        tibi vacca, Cereri, pariter et Baccho cadet.
        longe ante reliquos sacra Iunoni feram,
        cui coniugalis vincla sunt curae thori.

CHORVS

eheu, Dido, miseret nos tui.   525
o ignarae vatum mentes.
quid iuvat aras tangere supplicem?
nulla iuvabunt vota furentem.
excedit intus flamma medullas,
tacitum vivit pectore vulnus.   530
   Dido miseris uritur ignibus,
totaque vurens vagatur,
missa qualis cerva sagitta,
quam procul inter Cressia fixit
nemora incautam pastor, et inscius   535
medio liquit pectore ferrum,
maerens sylvas illa petit fuga
lateri stridens haeret arundo.
nunc per muros demens hospitem
secum Aeneam ducit Elisa.   540
nunc Sydonias ostentat opes
urbemque novam. cupit effari
et mox media voce resistit.
nunc Iliacos audire expetit
illa labores, nunc convivia   545

513. *deos?* B: sic Binns

bashfulness trouble my mind. What encouragement can you offer my desire, sister?

AN. Sister, just ask the gods' forgiveness; having offered sacrifices, entertain your foreign guest. Manufacture reasons for his delay, while winter's heavy wrath now rages against the sea, while their ships are shattered, while the winds are howling in a sky now unserene.

DI. It is sufficient. You kindle my ardent love. I shall loosen the reins, let foolish shame depart. Tomorrow I shall ingratiate myself to the gods with plentiful victims. I have made up my mind to search for peace in sacrifice. A heifer shall fall for you, Ceres, and also one for Bacchus. By far the first, I shall offer to Juno, who is concerned for marriage bonds. [*Exeunt.*]

CHORUS

Alas, Dido, we are sorry for you. O ignorant minds of prophets! What use is there in grasping the altar in supplication? No prayers will help her in her amorous rage. Fire smoulders in her marrow, a secret wound lives in her heart.

Dido is scorched by piteous fires, she roams throughout the city in her frenzy like an arrow-stricken hind shot unexpecting from afar in some Cretan glade by a shepherd who, unawares, leaves the steel implanted in mid-breast. In her frenzy she seeks the woods, but the whirring arrow sticks in her flank.

Now frantic Eliza escorts Aeneas along the battlements. Now she displays her Sidonian wealth, her new city. She craves to speak, but her voice soon catches in mid-utterance. Now she begs to hear about Ilium's agonies, and now, at day's waning, she seeks

eadem quaeret labente die.
   non iam caeptae surgunt turres,
non exercent iuvenes arma,
non iam bello tela recondunt
portusque parant. cessant opera,   550
pendent altae murorum minae.
o quis superum tanta clemens
peste furentem solvat Elisam?

renewed feasting. Not now are rising the towers she has started. The youths are not now practising at arms, nor are they storing up weapons for battle or making ready the harbors. They tarry at their work, the high pinnacles of the walls suspended. Oh, which merciful one of the gods will give raging Elisa surcease from her great malady?

- Actus Tertius -

scena i

Transitur ad venationem.

SICHAEI VMBRA

SI. tellure scissa, per vias saxo asperas
maestum Sichaeus Tartaro gressum extuli, 555
atram sinistra praeferens taedam novis
thalamis Elisae, coniugis quondam meae.
nam quae sub imas fama mihi terras venit?
amore Teucri furere Didonem hospitis?
in media recipi regna peregrinum? loco 560
viri esse? quo me? quo meas lachrymas feram?
si iam Sichaeus excidit penitus tibi,
si iam secundos expetis, Dido, thoros,
nullosne Libya, quos ames, gignit duces?
misero beata, perfido nubes pia? 565
regina profugae? Troico Tyria viro?
genus omne Phrygium fecit invisum Paris.
hic rapuit, iste deseret vagus hospitem.
absiste, Dido. rara in hospitibus fides
erratque ut ipsi. prodidit patriam suam. 570
prodet alianam, coniugem quanto magis?
secum penates avehat, Latium petat.
at tu, Megaera, pectus hoc furiis age,
perure. satis est. caveat Aeneas malum.
quin intus abeo? stabo et arcebo nefas. 575

Exit in regiam.

descriptionem actionis habet B   563. *secundos, Dido, moliris toros* B

- Act III -

scene i

They cross over the stage on the way to the hunt.

GHOST OF SYCHAEUS

The earth has split and I, Sychaeus, have made my sad way by avenues rough with rock out of Tartarus, bearing before me in my left hand a gloomy torch for the new bridal-chamber of Elisa, once my wife. For what rumor reached me, deep underground? That Dido is raging with love for her Teucrian guest? That a stranger was admitted into the midst of her realm? That he occupies her husband's place? Where should I go? Where should I take my tears? Dido, if now Sychaeus has completely left your mind, if now you are undertaking a second marriage, has Libya produced no princes whom you might love? Will you, a fortunate woman, marry this wretch, a pious woman marry a traitor? A queen marry a fugitive? A Tyrian woman marry a Trojan? Paris rendered the entire Phrygian race hateful. He kidnapped his hostess, this wanderer will abandon his. Refrain, Dido. Loyalty is rare in guests and guests' faith wanders just as they do. He forsook his fatherland. He will forsake a foreign country — and how much more a wife? He carries his household gods with him, seeking Latium. But you, Megaera, attack this breast with your furies, make him burn. It is enough. Let Aeneas guard against wrongdoing. Why should I not go within? I shall stay and ward off this evil. [*Exit into the palace.*]

p. 77

scena ii

Tempestas Iunonis.

NYMPHARVM PLANCTVS

Nymphae canunt in scena.

        eheu querulos fundite planctus,
        terite insertis pectora palmis,
        eheu dicite Tyriis omen
           venit acerbum.

        resonet tellus, reboet caelum,   580
        iterent ripae gemitus nostros,
        ululent silvae, referant montes
           et mare reddat.

        heu hyminaeos, heu male iunctos,
        heu connubium, quale nec aevum   585
        vidit priscum, nullaque nascens
           hora videbit.

        non cessabit nemorum questus,
        nos quoque nymphae fletum dabimus,
        atque ex imis maesta cavernis   590
           ingemet Echo.

scena iii

CVPIDO VERVS

Exeat e nemore.

        bene est, abunde est. exitum nacti sumus
        matris repertum fraudibus, partum meis.
        amavit? etiam amore bacchata est, novo

---

descriptio actionis. *Tempestas* **B**   indicium chori. NYMPHAE PLANGENTES **B**   descriptionem actionis non habet **B**   580 - 3. vv. desunt in **A**   scena iii. indicium scenae non habent mss.: sic Binns

scene ii

Storm caused by Juno.

THE NYMPHS' LAMENT

Nymphs sing on the stage.

Alas, pour out your wail, beat your breast with your hands. Proclaim, alas, that an evil omen has come to the Tyrians.

Let the earth resound and heaven echo, let the river banks redouble our laments, let the forests howl and the mountains and oceans resound.

Alas for the wedding, alas for the evil marriage, alas for this wedlock such as no former age has seen, no future hour will witness.

The glades' lament will not cease, we nymphs shall also weep, and sad Echo will groan from within her deep caverns.

scene iii

CUPID, UNDISGUISED

Coming out of the forest.

It is good, it is fulfilled. We have achieved the outcome planned by my mother's wiles, encompassed by mine. Has she fallen in love? She is drunk with love, she has caught

flagravit igne, nec levi pretio stetit 595
tenuisse Iulum genibus et gremio levem.
insuave retuli suavium, dulci osculo.
cum lusit illa ludicro, lusi dolo.
bibit? recepi. aspexit? et vultum intuli.
vocavit? aderam. mulsit? implevi sinum. 600
vafer fefelli simplicem, astutus piam.
et iam reliqui perditam, quamvis putet
abiisse curam penitus. et coniux Iovis
genitrixque nostra, manibus ad speciem datis
pepigere faedus. nuptiis dicunt diem, 605
in nemora mittunt, imbribus caelum rotant,

p. 78 et hanc cavernam nuptiis statuunt locum.
mox ducet extra coniugem sponsus suam.
sed nos in urbem magnus etiam num labor
accersit. aliquis semper in Tyriis amat. 610

Redeunt a venatione.

scena iv

MERCVRIVS SOLVS

Caelitus dilapsus.

facunda proles maximi superum Iovis,
matrisque Maiae, nuntius velox deum,
corusca summi templa deserui aetheris.
quis hic locus? quae zona? quas terras premo?
utrumne votum visa decipiunt meum, 615
an ista Libya est? ista Carthago nova?
ni fallor, ipsa est: urbis agnosco notas.
Didonis hoc est regiae limen domus,
hic delinitus ductor Aeneas Phrygum
moratur, ille causa veniendi fuit. 620
nec vile quisquam munus hoc nostrum putet,
quod huc et illuc pervolem nutu Iovis.
sancte colendum est numen in terris meum.
legatione caelitum fungi grave est,
nec nisi valenti munus ingenio datur. 625

607 *et* pro *atque* habet B   609. *magnus* A, *maior* B: vid. Comm. not.   sc. iv descriptionem actionis habet A   621. *nostrum hoc munus* B ante corr. (*nostum munus hoc* scripsit Binns)

fire with a new flame, it has cost her dearly to dandle little Iulus on her knees and lap. With my mouth I return her kiss with one of my own, which is something other than just a pleasantry. While she plays with me sportively, I have tricked her with my fraud. She drank? I cadged a sip. She gazed at me? I turned my face to her. She called? I appeared. She caressed me? I perched in her lap. A rascal, I deceived this simpleton, shrewdly I tricked the pious woman. Now that she is destroyed I have left her, although she fancies her cares completely departed. And now Jupiter's consort and my mother have made a specious pact. They fix a day for the marriage, send the lovers into the forest, set the sky a-whirling with rain, and appoint this cavern the place for the wedding. Soon the bridegroom will lead out his bride. But some great task is summoning me to the city. Somebody in Tyre is always falling in love. [*Exit.*]

They return from the hunt.

scene iv

MERCURY, ALONE

Descending from heaven.

I, the eloquent son of Jupiter, greatest of the gods, and of my mother Maia, the gods' swift messenger, have left the shining precincts of the lofty air. What's this place? What region? On what land do I alight? Does this sight cheat my desire, or is this Libya? Is this the new Carthage? Unless I am mistaken, this is it. I recognize the city's features. Here's the threshold of Dido's palace. Here the Phyrgians' leader Aeneas lingers, bewitched. He is the reason for my arrival.

Let nobody imagine this duty of mine is an easy one, flying hither and thither at Jove's command. My godhead is to be held in reverence throughout all the lands. Doing the gods' errands is serious business, only to be entrusted to someone quite clever. Whether I

seu petere terram, seu fretum supra placet
volare, rapido flamine alarum vehor.
tum quanta virgae, quam potens virtus meae?
hac pallidi animas evoco Ditis domo,
hac pariter alios mitto ad infernam Styga. 630
induco somnos, rursus hac somnos fugo,
et pressa morte lumina resigno gravi.
hac fretus aequor transeo, ventos agens
nubesque moti turbidas trano aetheris.
    sed ecce quisnam regia gressum extulit? 635
ipse est Achati iunctus Aeneas suo.

scena v

MERCVRIVS *ad Aeneam*

Carthaginis tu moenia excelsae locas
urbemque nunc uxorius pulchram exstruis
rerum tuarum oblite, regnique immemor.
hominum deumque rector, et mundi arbiter 640
qui numine polos torquet et terras suo,
celeres per auras ipse me iussit tibi
mandata ferre. quid struis? qua spe teris
Libycis in oris otia, et terris tibi
fato negatis? quo tuae spectant morae? 645
si nulla rerum fama tantarum movet,
nec ipse proprium laude moliris super
tua laborem, subeat Ascanius tibi,
et spes Iuli respice haeredis tui,
cui iam Latini regna debentur soli. 650
arcesne Latias invides nato pater?
non alma talem te mihi dixit Venus,
nec vindicavit ideo bis Graium dolis,
sed qui frementem regeret Italiam fore,
a sanguine alto proderet Teucri genus, 655
orbique iura victor et leges daret.
legationis summa nostrae est, naviga.

630. *alias* B, fort. recte

choose to travel by land or fly over the waters, I am borne by the rapid flash of my wings. What is the power, the virtue of my wand? With it I summon souls out of wan Dis, with it I despatch other men to the infernal Styx. I bring sleep, again I banish it, I unseal eyes shut by grim death. Trusting in my staff I come over the sea, I skim along driving winds and clouds roiling with aetherial turbulence.

But look, who's coming out of the palace? It is Aeneas, accompanied by his friend Achates [*Enter Aeneas and Achates.*]

scene v

MERCURY, TO AENEAS

You are building walls for lofty Carthage and constructing a fine city in devotion to your wife, forgetful of your own affairs, unmindful of your kingdom. The ruler of gods and men, the universal judge who makes the heavens and earth spin by his command, has bid me convey to you his orders, coming through the swift breezes. What are you building? What hope makes you waste your time lingering in Libya, in lands forbidden you by your destiny? What's the point of your delays? If the reputation of your great accomplishments fails to move you, and you do not wish to achieve great glory for your effort, at least think of Ascanius, consider the hopes of your heir Iulus, to whom is bequeathed domination over the land of Latium. Do you, a father, begrudge your son these citadels? Your mother Venus did not tell me you are such a man, nor for this did she twice rescue you from the Greeks' deception, but because you were a man who would govern unruly Italy, who would propagate the Teucrians' ancient blood-line and, as a victor, give laws to the world. This is the sum of my mission: set sail. [*Exit.*]

scena vi

AENEAS, ACHATES

AEN.	horrore quatior totus et mentem pavor
	concussit ingens, atra nox oculos subit,
	facilemque verbis denegat lingua exitum. 660
	sed quid profari, quid loqui, Aeneas, potes?
	aut unde fas est? huc et huc animus mihi
	variusque rapitur, qualis Euripus solet
	fluere et refluere septies uno die.
	tanto deorum attonitus imperio iuvat 665
	abire, et istas deserere terras fuga.
	sed te furentem quo mihi affatu licet
	ambire, Dido? quem mihi vultum induam?
	quae prima sumam verba? quae causa est satis?
	incertus animi versor in varias vices, 670
	sic ut carinam media sulcantem freta
	hac rector illac unda transversam rapit.
	restitue fluctus, Iuno, iam Lybicos mihi.
	levior in illis ira praelusit tua.
	quicunque saevo maria transitis deo 675
	amate fluctus, credite experto mihi.
ACH.	magnanime Troum ductor, et captae unicum
	patriae levamen, comprime affectus precor
	teque obsequentem nuntio praebe Iovis.
	minus elegendum est cum duo occurrunt mala. 680
AEN.	sic est, Achates. at quis hic iudex erit?
ACH.	Iove imperante te tamen iudex latet?
AEN.	at hospitalis Iupiter prohibet fugam.
ACH.	iter institutum cur fugam turpem vocas?
AEN.	sic praedicabit fama.
ACH.	sed falsa et levis. 685
AEN.	tamen est timenda levior.

661 sq. *sed quid profari poteris Aenea miser? / aut unde poteris?* B

scene vi

AENEAS, ACHATES

AEN. I am wholly shaking with fear. Terror strikes my mind, dark night comes over my eyes. My tongue permits no easy expression of my words. But what could you say, Aeneas, what can you utter? How would it be proper for you to defend yourself? My shifting mind is snatched hither and thither, as the Euripus changes its current seven times in a day. Amazed by such a divine command, I must be off, abandoning this land in flight. But with what discourse can I mollify you, Dido, as you rage at me? What face can I put on? What words should I say first? What excuse is sufficient? Uncertain in my mind, I am pulled in different directions, like a ship in mid-ocean, as the steersman guides it in one way, the tide in another. Juno, restore the tide that brought me to Libya. Your anger fell more lightly on them, by way of a rehearsal. Whoever has crossed the sea because of a god's anger, love the storms — take it from one who knows.

ACH. Great-hearted leader of the Trojans, sole support of our captive nation, I beg you to calm your emotions and make yourself obedient to Jupiter's herald. When two evils occur, the lesser is to be chosen.

AEN. That is so, Achates. But who is to be the judge?

ACH. When Jupiter is doing the bidding, does the judge's identity elude you?

AEN. But Jupiter, god of hospitality, forbids flight.

ACH. Why do you call our ordained journey a disgraceful flight?

AEN. Thus rumor will portray it.

ACH. But rumor is false and fickle.

AEN. But is to be feared in her fickleness.

	ACH.	at superi magis.	
	AEN.	at chara Dido est.	
	ACH.	veniat in mentem tibi Ascanius.	
	AEN.	etiam magna Carthago venit.	
p. 81	ACH.	num terra fatis debita Italia est minor?	
	AEN.	via longa pelago.	
	ACH.	Iupiter monstrat viam.	690
	AEN.	at saeva Iuno.	
	ACH.	materia laudis tuae.	
	AEN.	at cuncta Elisae debeo, classem, meos, vitamque Iuli.	
	ACH.	quas decet grates age.	
	AEN.	omnis habeatur gratia, ingratum arguet.	
	ACH.	promerita perdit qui satis grato exprobrat.	695
	AEN.	amat.	
	ACH.	sequetur forsan.	
	AEN.	insanit.	
	ACH.	fuge.	
	AEN.	at obsecrabit per fidem misero datam, per hospitia, per lachrymas, per dexteram, per omne quicquid dulce mihi secum fuit.	
	ACH.	tu pariter obsecra per Ascanii caput, per dira superum monita, per fatis tibi promissa Latii regna, per gentes novas. obsiste lachrymis iamque te intractabilem durumque praebe fortis, auresque obstrue, vocesque miseras perfer, obdura, excute,	700 705

ACH. But the gods are to be feared more.

AEN. But Dido is dear to me.

ACH. Think of Ascanius.

AEN. I am also thinking of great Carthage.

ACH. Is the land of Italy, owed you by the Fates, any the lesser?

AEN. The voyage is long.

ACH. Jupiter shows the way.

AEN. But Juno is savage.

ACH. This is matter to build your reputation.

AEN. But I am indebted to Elisa for everything — my ships, my men, Iulus' life.

ACH. Thank her appropriately.

AEN. Let every thanks be offered her, it will prove me an ingrate.

ACH. The man who reproaches a grateful man loses his moral standing.

AEN. She loves me.

ACH. Then perhaps she'll follow you.

AEN. She's out of her mind.

ACH. Then flee.

AEN. But she will beg me by the faith she showed me in my misery, by her hospitality, her tears, our pledge, whatever was sweet to me while I was with her.

ACH. Beg her in turn by the head of Ascanius, by the gods' dire warnings, the kingdom of Latium granted you by destiny, your new nations. Restrain your tears, and courageously show yourself to be hard and intractable, stop your ears, endure her miserable

	ut alta quercus, quam simul facto impetu	
	Boreae valentes hinc et illinc flatibus	
	eruere certant, haeret haec scopulis tamen,	
	quantumque ad auras vertice erigitur suo,	
	radice tantum extenditur in imam Styga.	710
AEN.	satis est, Achates. vincat imperium Iovis.	
	et te deorum sancte, quisquis eras, sequor.	
	o placidus adsis quaeso, cursumque adiuves,	
	et astra caelo dextera placato feras.	
ACH.	at Mnestea Coanthumque rectores iube	715
	ut arma taciti colligant, classem instruant,	
	ex urbe socios ad suas cogant rates,	
	novique causam fronte consilii tegant.	
	interea tu dum nesciat Dido furens	
	tantosque amores non putet rumpi suos,	720
	aditum experire, quaeque fandi tempora	
	idonea, rebus quis modus dexter tuis.	
AEN.	te cura, Achates, classis armandae manet.	
	homines deosque testor, et sanctam fidem,	
	me, Elisa, terris cedere invitum tuis.	725

Aeneas ad regiam, Achates ad naves.

CHORVS

o quam velox est fama malum	
celeri versans mobilitate!	
improba vires auget eundo.	
primo semper parva timore	
postea sese tollit in auras,	730
graditurque solo, mox caput inter	
nubila condit.	
odiis illam stimulata deum	
Caeo, ut perhibent, Enceladoque	
tulit extremam Terra sororem	735
pedibus celerem, levibusque alis,	
monstrum horrendum, cui quot plumae	
corpore, tot sunt oculi subter,	

707. sic B, *et hinc et hinc* A   725. *Dido* pro *Elisa* habet B   descriptio actionis habet B   728. v. deest de A

complaints, withstand them, shake them off. Be like a lofty oak which, when the northerly winds strike it from this side and that, striving to uproot it with their blasts, still clings to the rocks, and just as high as it thrusts its top into the air, equally deep it plunges its roots down to deepest Styx.

AEN. Enough, Achates. Let Jupiter's command convince me. And you, whichever holy god you were, I obey. I pray, be with me in your kindness, aid my journey, bring me propitious stars in a sky made placid by your hand.

ACH. But order the captains Mnester and Cleanthus to gather up weapons with stealth. Let them prepare the fleet, muster their shipmates from the city to their boats, but keep straight faces, concealing the reason for this new plan. In the meantime, while Dido in her ardor is still ignorant, not believing that her great love is being broken off, you must attempt a meeting, deciding the suitable moment for an interview, what approach is propitious for your affairs.

AEN. The care remaining for you, Achates, is to arm the fleet. I call men and the gods, also holy Faith, to witness that, Dido, I leave your land against my will.

Exit Aeneas to the palace and Achates to the ship.

CHORUS

Oh, how swift an evil is Rumor, plying her business with great speed! Shameless, she gathers strength as she goes. At first always small out of timidity, afterwards she surges upward, striding over the land, and soon raises her head to the clouds.
They say that Earth, provoked by her hatred of the gods, gave birth to her as the younger sister of Coeus and Enceladus, swift of foot, with gossamer wings, a horrid monster. As many as there are feathers on her body, such is the number of eyes beneath

>   tot sunt linguae, totidemque sonant
>   ora, tot avidas subrigit aures.   740
>   noctu caeli medio pervolat,
>   nec declinat lumina somno.
>   custos summi culmina tecti
>   turresque altas tenet interdiu.
>   garrula magnas territat urbes,   745
>   nuntia ficti, nuntia veri.
>   haec multiplici voce replevit
>   populos gaudens, infecta simul
>   et facta canens. scilicet hospitem
>   venisse novum, sanguine Teucro,   750
>   cui se Dido dignetur viro
>   iungere, nunc se luxis hiemem
>   ducere totam regni immemores.
>   haec dea passim faeda per urbes
>   Libycas hominum fundit in ora.   755

p. 83 (at line 747)

752. pro *luxis* vid. Comm. not.

them, such is the number of tongues, such the number of speaking mouths, such the number of greedy ears perked up.

She flies through the midnight sky, nor do her eyes close in sleep. Sometimes as warden she perches on the high housetops or the lofty battlements. Garrously she terrifies great cities, announcing the false, announcing the true.

With her manifold voice she rejoices in filling the ears of entire peoples, singing things done, singing things left undone. She sings that a strange guest has come, a man of Teucrian blood, whom Dido has seen fit to marry. Now they have spent the entire winter in luxury, unmindful of government. The foul goddess has poured this news into men's ears throughout the cities of Libya.

- Actus Quartus -

scena i

DIDO

proh facinus ingens, fallor! obtestor deos
omnes deasque, vos et infernam Styga
Erebique fluctus, quicquid est rerum undique,
si quid nefandi sceleris admissum est. dolo
et amore casto victa Phaenissa occidi.   760
quid facio, quo me confero? abrepta impetu
aestuque mens indomita constringi nequit.
ubi est? abiit heu tam cito? libet alloqui,
libet experiri misera. quo misera feror!

scena ii

DIDO, AENEAS

DI. periure, tantum posse sperasti scelus   765
     latere, tantum posse simulari nefas?
     Didone fugere nec salutata paras?
     non dextra nuper iuncta, non mutua fides,
     amor iugalis, non maritalis torus,
     moritura nec te funere cruento tenet   770
     Phaenissa Dido? an sidere hiberno paras
     aptare classem, cum gravis nimbus Notus
     et raucus altas Aquilo contorquent nives,
     Lybicasque arenas Auster et Syrtes agit?
     crudelis, an si Pergama Hectorea forent   775
     nec arva peteres alia, et ignotas domus,
     peteres per undas Pergama, et saevum mare?
     mene fugis? an sum digna quam fugias? per has
     nunc oro lacrhimas, per tuam dextram precor
     (cum nil relictum est aliud, et regnum meum   780
     famamque in arcto stare et ancipiti sciam)

Actus IV et V desunt de A   764. *feror?* B (sed cf. Sen., *H. F.* 1012 et Ps. - Sen., *H. Oet.* 909)   773. *contorquet* B

- Act IV -

scene i

DIDO

Oh, the monstrous crime! I'm deceived! I call all the gods and goddess to witness, and you, infernal Styx and waters of Erebus, everything that exists in the world, if such a foul crime has ever been committed. I, a defeated woman of Phoenicia, am undone by his treachery and my chaste love. What am I doing? Where do I go? My mind, never conquered before, is swept away by passion and ardor, cannot restrain itself. Where is he? Has he gone, alas, so quickly? I want to speak with him. In my misery, I want to put him to the test. Where am I being driven in my unhappiness? [*Enter Aeneas.*]

scene ii

DIDO, AENEAS

DI. Deceiver, did you expect that such an outrage could be could be kept secret, such a crime could be concealed? Are you preparing to abandon Dido without having said farewell? Are you not bound by the recent pledge of our clasped hands, the faith we shared, our conjugal love, our wedding couch? Are you not bound by Phoenician Dido, about to die a bloody death? Are you making ready a voyage under a winter sky, when Notus the North wind, heavy with clouds, and blustering Aquilo the Northeast wind stir up the deep snow, when Auster the South wind drives the Libyan sands of Syrte? Cruel man! Even if Hector's Pergamum still stood and you were not seeking other lands and unknown homes, would you search for Pergamum through the waves and the savage sea? Are you fleeing me? Do I deserve your flight? Now I beg you by these tears, I pray by the pledge you gave (since nothing else is left me, and I know my reign and reputation are jeapordized

per coniugales sceleris ultores deos,
per spes Iuli, per mei sceptrum imperii
tuamque vitam, perque iam cineres meos,
si merita quicquam, sive te pietas movet, 785
si triste fatum, sive violati decus
pudoris, aut si dulce tibi quicquam fuit
Didonis, immanem exuas mentem precor.
miserere nostri, gratiam meritis refer.
utcunque (si quis est adhuc precibus locus) 790
en haec suprema vota Didonis cape.
te propter omnes Africae et Nomadum duces
odere. eundum propter egregium decus
celebrisque fama qua prior caelum attigi
extincta cum pudore semianimis iacet. 795
cui me remittis, hospes? hoc unum mihi
nomen relictum est coniuge amisso, cui
me deseris? quis spolia de nobis feret?
sed si qua proles ante tam tristem fugam
de te foret suscepta, quae vultum tuum 800
et te referret, si quis Ascanius mea
luderet in aula, cuius aspectu meum
solarer animum — "en habuit hos vultus meus
quondam maritus, talis Aeneas fuit,
sic celsus humeris, sic tulit fortes manus" — 805
florens vigeret sorte faelici domus.

AEN. parere precibus cupio me fateor tuis,
regina, nec enim merita dicendo queam
numerare, nec si fata monstrabunt viam,
immemor Elisae dicar aut regni tui. 810
pro me licebit pauca, sed vera eloqui.
regina, non hanc tegere speravi fugam,
ne finge, furto nec maritales faces
prae me ferebam, tale nec faedus inii.
si fata vitam dicere auspiciis novis, 815
aut sponte curas gerere paterentur mea
Troiae reliquias colerem, et eximiae domus
Priami manerent. nomen aut patriae suum
Phrygibusque victis redderem, et sparsos darem
cives reductos Hectori, Priamo, mihi. 820
nunc sorte Phaebi ductus Italiam sequor.
Italia patria est, uxor, imperium, salus.

783. vid. Comm. not.   786. *sive tristem* B ante corr.   795. vid. Comm. not.   812. *speravi tegere* B ante corr.

and hangin the balance), by the gods who avenge crimes against marriage, by your hopes for Iulus, by the scepter of my realm and your life, and now also by my own ashes — if you are moved by my good deeds, my piety, my sad fate, or the beauty of my decorum, now violated, if anything about Dido was sweet to you, abandon this monstrous fancy. Have pity on me, repay me for my kindnesses.

But be this as it may, if there is any room for entreaties, hear Dido's final wish. Because of you, all the princes of Africa and the Numidians despise me. For the sake of this same man, my outstanding glory, the widespread fame by which I was extolled to heaven, is now annihilated along with my shame, a half-dead thing. Who are you handing me over to, guest? (This one word is left for me to call you by, now that I have lost my husband.) To whom are you abandoning me? Who will despoil me? But if I had any children by you before your sad escape, who would recall you and your appearance, if I had an Ascanius playing in my hall, at whose sight I could console my mind, saying "see, my husband used to look like this, thus was Aeneas, thus he was high in the shoulders, thus he held his strong hands," my house would have flourished with happy fortune.

AEN. Queen, I confess I wish I could comply with your wishes, nor do I have the eloquence to count up the good things you have done for me. Nor, if the Fates show me the way, let me be said to be unmindful of Elisa, or of your realm. It is rightful to say few things in my defense, but true ones. Queen, I have not hoped to conceal my departure. Do not imagine such. Neither did I carry the marriage-torches before me fraudulently, nor enter into such a disgraceful pact. If the Fates were to let me lead my life under new auspices or let me choose what to care about, I would tend the remnants of Troy, Priam's palace would be standing. Or I would restore the reputation of my country and the defeated Phrygians and return our scattered citizens to Hector, to Priam, to myself. Now, led on by Phoebus' decree, I am seeking Italy. Italy is my my nation, wife, dominion, salvation. If

Carthago si te detinet et arces novae
Phaenissa cum sis, invides Latium mihi?
externa regna quaerere et nobis licet. 825
quam saepe tristis umbra genitoris meis
offertur oculis, membra cum solvit quies
dulcisque fessum corpus oppressit sopor!
quam saepe tristis intrat in thalamos meos
imago patris admonens celerem fugam! 830
quin puer Iulus debito fatis solo
frustratur, ipse caelitum interpres, Iove
nuncius ab alto missus in terras (caput
utrumque testor) per leves auras tulit
mandata. vidi lumine in aperto deum 835
haec intuentem moenia, atque hausi auribus
dulcem loquelam, iussa supremi Iovis.
remitte planctus, sit querelarum modus.
non sponte, non iniussus Italiam sequor.

DI. non diva genetrix, perfide, nec author tibi 840
stirpis nefandae Dardanus, sed te Sinis
aut quis Procustes genuit, et tygres ferae
per inhospitalis Caucasi rupem asperam
aluere. primos redit ad authores genus,
feramque stirpem degener sanguis refert. 845
quid misera faciam? misera quid primam querar?
fletune nostro gemuit aut lachrimis meis
reflexit oculos? an madent fletu genae?
precibusne victus cedit? hoc instar mihi
magni fuisset muneris. quid iam potest 850
pro me esse? nusquam tuta consistit fides.
ego hunc egentem, littore eiectum meo
patriaque pulsum nuper accepi, et malis
tot me levamen, denique et regnum dedi.
proh facinus ingens! vatem et insontes deos 855
praetendit. augur Phaebus, infensus pater
Lyciaeque sortes debitum regnum avocant.
Maia quin illa genitus interpres Iovis
horrida per auras iussa Mercurius tulit.
haec cura superos, hic deos urget labor, 860
forsan quietos. oro, nec teneo tamen.
i, sequere ventis, regna per fluctus pete,
per maria terram debitam fatis tibi.

828. *sopor?* **B**   830. *fugam?* **B**   841. *Scinis* **B**   858. *quin illa Maia* corr. in *quin Maia illa* **B**, quod autem cum re metrica haud quadraret

Carthage and your new citadels hold you here, since you are Phoenician, why begrudge me Latium? I too may seek a foreign empire. How often has the sorrowful shade of my father presented itself to my eyes when sleep has relaxed my linbs and sweet slumber has overcome my exhausted body! How often has my father's baleful image come into my bedchamber, urging swift flight! My boy Iulus is cheated of the land bequeathed him by the Fates. The very messenger of the gods, the herald sent to earth by Jupiter on high (I swear this by both our heads), delivered this command. I saw this god in broad daylight as he was contemplating these walls, I heard his pleasant discourse with these ears, the orders of Jupiter almighty. Cease your lamentations, let there be a limit to reproaches. I do not seek Italy of my own will, I am not unbidden.

DI. No goddess was your mother, traitor, nor was Dardanus the founder of your wicked race. Some Sinis or Procustes sired you, wild tigers nursed you on a harsh crag of the inhospitable Caucasus, your character reverts to its first ancestors, your base blood betrays your savage pedigree.

[*Aside.*] What should I do in my unhappiness? In my misery, what should I complain of first? Did he groan at my weeping, turn his eyes to me when I cried? Or has he wet his cheeks with tears? Has he yielded, overcome by my entreaties? This would be a great gift for me. What can help me? Loyalty has never stood on a firm foundation. Lately I took in this needy man, cast up on my shore, exiled from his country. I gave my all to him as consolation for his misfortunes, and finally gave him my realm. The monstrous outrage! He offered as an excuse the oracle, the unoffending gods. Soothsaying Phoebus, his hostile father, the Lycian oracles summon him to his kingdom. The son of Maia, indeed, the messenger of Jupiter, Mercury, carried these horrid commands through the skies. This concern of his, this effort, claims that the gods support it, although perhaps they are indifferent. I am begging him, but I am not holding on to him.

[*Aloud.*] Go, follow the winds, seek your kingdom by crossing the waves, the ocean to

confido, (si quod vota si valeant preces)
paenas daturam sceleris et brevibus vadis 865
scopulisque fixum, aut inter elisas rates
caput exerentem, me vocaturum. sequar
flammisque nigris adero, non unquam tibi
defuerit umbra, teque perpetuo obruam
defuncta luctu. facinorum paenas lues 870
nec me latebunt, perfide. extincta audiam
veloxque ad umbras fama perveniet meas.

scena iii

AENEAS, ILIONEVS

AEN. an sic reliquit, abiit et celeri fuga
vocem antevertit, saeva ne questum parem
audiret? o si penetret in teneras dolor 875
absentis aures. unus en cogit deus,
deusque prohibet alter Aeneam Tyro
abire, utrumvis non datur iussum sequi.
te, te, Cupido, sequerer et sequerer libens
sed urget aliud maius edictum Iovis. 880
Elisa, comites, memet, Ascanium, omnia
laetus relinquam, si Iovi fiat satis
fatoque. non est culpa discessus mea.

IL. nisi tibi pectus ferreum, Aeneas, foret,
animusque multis undique obductus malis, 885
has ferre lachrimas durus, has poteras preces
negare? quid hic haesitas? Dido rogat
et Dido merita est. quid fugis, quidque expetis
revolvat animus. quaeris Italiam? Tyrus
offertur, ingens dabitur imperium tibi. 890
magnum relinques nec minus tutum. nova est
promissa coniux? Dido coniugium novum
regemque facere spondet. an nescis deos
haec invidere regna Troianis, et hoc
quodcunque nobis sidus obtulerit boni 895
animo maligno ferre? dum tutus potes
istis morare sedibus, metuo deos
Teucris iniquos. quod petit Dido leve est,
praestare Teucris dulce solamen tibi.

the land promised you by the Fates. If prayers and entreaties have any power, I am confident that you will pay the penalty for this outrage, grounded on shoals and reefs, or bobbing your head among your smashed hulls, crying out for me. I shall follow. I shall be there with black fires, my ghost will never leave you. When I am dead, I shall oppress you with my ceaseless lamentation. You will pay the penalties for your crimes, traitor, nor will they be hidden from me. In death I shall hear of them, swift Rumor will visit my shade. [*Exit.*]

scene iii

AENEAS, ILIONEUS

AEN. Has she left me thus, departing and by her swift flight avoiding my response, lest in her rage she hear my equal complaint? Oh, if my sorrow could reach the absent woman's gentle ears! See how one god compels Aeneas to leave Tyre, while another forbids me, and I can follow the bidding of neither. Cupid, I would follow you, and follow you gladly, but Jupiter's greater command compels me. Elisa, I should gladly abandon my comrades, myself, Ascanius, everthing, if this would satisfy Jupiter and my destiny. This departure is not my fault. [*Enter Ilioneus, overhearing this speech.*]

IL. Aeneas, if you did not have a heart of steel, a mind everywhere calloused by many evil experiences, would you be hard enough to bear her tears, could you deny her prayers? Why hesitate here? Dido asks you, Dido has earned it. Your mind is pondering why you are departing, what you are seeking. Are you looking for Italy? Tyre is being offered, a huge empire will be given you. You are leaving a great one, no less safe. Is a wife promised you? Dido has pledged you a marriage, promised to make you a king. Are you unaware that the gods begrudge us this Italian kingdom, that they begrudge whatever good thing our star has offered? As long as you can, stay safely in this place. I fear the gods, ill-disposed towards the Teucrians. What Dido asks is a simple thing, to offer support to the Teucrians and to you.

AEN.	solus repugnat precibus infaelix dolor.	900
	habuere Teucri numen infensum antea
	cum Troia staret, nunc tamen superis sat est.
	sunt aequiores, Pergama in cineres data
	non negligenda caelitum iussa admonent.

IL. doluere Teucri non minus laesam fidem   905
     quam spreta divum numina. extinctus Paris
     non negligendum faedus hospicii docet.

AEN. at appetitu cessit effreni Paris
     ego deorum iussus imperium sequor.

IL. idem est utrique crimen et Paridi et tibi.   910

AEN. non animus idem est. velle concludit scelus,
     nocens vocatur sponte quicunque est nocens.
     invitus abeo, stat Iovis iussum exsequi.
     sermone nullo nostra retinetur fuga.

scena iv

ANNA, DIDO

AN. regina, quamvis plura quam fas est loquar,   915
     et lingua fraeno fundat excusso sonos
     non expetitos, admove vigiles tamen
     aures sorori. grata tibi quondam fuit
     Anna, atque adhuc me cura sollicitat tui.
     quid te ipsa torques? quid malis offers volens 920
     animam dolentem? si neque imperio potest
     Libiae teneri, si tuos spernit preces,
     despicit amores, fallit intactam fidem,
     potius ubivis regnet Aeneas precor
     quam clara nequam serviat Dido duci.   925
     male retinetur quem tu retines malo.

DI. amitto, simul est noster amissus pudor.

AN. est impudica quae datam frangit fidem,
     non quae tuetur.

927. v. om., add. marg. B

AEN. Only her unhappy sadness opposes me with its entreaties. Previously, when Troy was standing, the Teucrians had a god for an enemy, but now the gods are satisfied. They are better disposed. But the burning of Pergamum warns us the gods' decrees are not to be ignored.

IL. The Teucrians have been grieving over the breaking of faith no less than the spurning of divine decrees. The death of Paris teachers that pacts of hospitality are not to be ignored.

AEN. But Paris died because of his unrestrained greed. I, having been commanded, am obeying the gods' behest.

IL. You and Paris are guilty of the same thing.

AEN. Our motives are not the same. Wanting makes the crime. He is called guilty who does wrong of his own will. I am leaving unwillingly. I have made up my mind to obey Jupiter's command. Our departure will not be obstructed by any argument. [*Exeunt. Enter Anna and Dido.*]

scene iv

ANNA, DIDO

AN. Queen, although I am going to say more than is proper, and my unbridled tongue will say things you have not requested, lend an attentive ear to your sister. Anna was once pleasing to you, and concern for you still troubles me. Why torture yourself? Why willingly expose your grieving soul to evils? If he cannot be retained in your Libyan dominion, if he spurns your prayers, despises your love, abuses the faith you have not broken, then I urge you, let Aeneas play the king anywhere at all rather than have famous Dido be this prince's slave in vain. He is badly retained whom you retain to your own harm.

DI. I am losing him, and that the same time my shame is lost.

AN. A woman is shameless when she breaks a pledge she has given, not a women who

DI.	noster est fractus pudor.	
	meone an eius crimine hoc refert parum.	930

AN. an esse sacrum culpa coniugium potest?

DI. secreta cum sint pacta quis testis sciat?
quid quod negavit?

AN. audio Iliacam fidem,
agnosco Paridem. sed maritales dei
pronubaque Iuno testis.

DI.	haud metuo deos.	935
	me fama terret, fama vix vero favet.	

AN. quis te pudoris arguet laesi?

DI. rogas?
qui rapuit.

AN. orbem profugus ignotum petit.

DI.	hoc est quod urit. quid moras nectis, soror?	
	levis est amor qui capere consilium potest.	940
	unum est quod oro, non vacat vanis diem	
	conterere verbis.	

AN. loquere, perficiam lubens.

DI.	iam classe pelagus splendet, et Teucri undique	
	littore relicto maria properantes petunt.	
	per transtra fusus navita implorat deos,	945
	ut aura plenos fortior tendat sinus.	
	remi apparantur, instant Aeneas fugae	
	omnisque nimium longa properanti est mora.	
	sperare tantum misera si potui malum	
	et ferre potero, restat ut supplex petas	950
	hostem superbum. non ego antiquum decus	
	potentis Asiae Pergama in cineres dedi,	
	non triste patris funditus bustum erui,	
	cineresve sparsi. dicta quid in aures mea	
	dimittere negat? hoc det extremum mihi	955
	solumque amanti munus. expectet fugam	
	facilesque ventos. non peto dulces thoros	
	et coniugales, non ut amittat potens	
	pulchrumque Latium, quod tamen solum licet,	

preserves it.

DI. My shame is ruined. It scarcely matters whether the fault is mine or his.

AN. But can sacred matrimony be a crime?

DI. When vows are made in secret, what witness is there to know of them? What if he denies them?

AN. I have heard of Trojan faith, I am aware of Paris. But there are marriage-gods, and Juno, protectress of marriage, is your witness.

DI. I scarcely fear the gods. Rumor terrifies me, for Rumor scarcely favors the truth.

AN. Who is accusing you of breaking faith?

DI. You ask? The man who stole it.

AN. As a deserter, he is seeking an unknown world.[1]

DI. This is what makes me burn. Why delay me, sister? It is a trifling love that can heed advice. There is only one thing I ask you, I do not have time to waste the day in conversation.

AN. Speak, and I shall gladly comply.

DI. Now the sea gleams with his fleet, and everywhere the Teucrians hasten in search of the high seas, leaving behind the shore. Arrayed on their benches, the sailors beseech the gods that a stiff breeze fill their sails. They fit their oars, Aeneas urges on the departure, any delay is too long for him in his haste. If I in my unhappiness have been able to see this great catastrophe coming and bear up under it, all that is left is for you to approach our haughty enemy in supplication. I was not responsible for burning Pergamum, glory of mighty Asia. I did not overthrow his father's sad pyre or scatter his ashes. Why does he refuse to hear my words? Let him give this final gift to me, his lover. He may look forward to escape and favorable winds. I am not asking for sweet marriage, not that this mighty

---

[1] And therefore will not be here to bear false witness against you.

	tempus moramque cupio, ut aerumnas levem.	960
	ito, ito, celera. perage mandatum, soror.	
AN.	iussa haud morabor, conferam ad naves gradum.	

CHORVS

o auspiciis Pergama primis
vanae fidei, tum cum superos
astus merito fraudavit suo   965
   Laomedontis.

cur antiquas querimur fraudes?
peperit nobis hora recentior
monstrum maius. cur documenta
quaerimus extera? Tyrias oras   970
tetigit propior culpa, domestica
   fraude stupemus.

nusquam fidei remanet candor,
maculis atris sordet ubique.
docuit fallax hospes in hospitem,   975
docuit fallax Tros in Tyriam,
docuit fallax vir in uxorem,
qualem fidei praestat honorem
   Dardana tellus.

petiit superos, terras liquit,   980
simplex probitas, impia vestibus
eius tegitur dissimulatio.
o si redeat rursus ab astris
   candida virtus.

971. vid. Comm. not.

man forego his Latium. I just desire what is possible, a delay so I might ease my sorrow. Go, go quickly, sister, do as you are told.

AN. Being given this task I shall not delay. I shall go to the ships. [*Exeunt.*]

CHORUS

Oh Pergamum, devoid of faith from your first foundation, then when the cunning of Laomedon cheated the gods of their rightful reward.

But why should we complain of ancient deceits? A more recent time has produced for us a greater outrage. Why seek foreign evidence? A crime involving ourselves has affected our Tyrian shores, we are astonished by fraud here at home.

Faith's sincerity does not endure, everywhere it is smirched by foul stains. The treacherous guest shows with his hostess, the treacherous Trojan shows with the Tyrian woman, the treacherous husband shows with his wife, how greatly the Dardanian land honors faith.

Straightforward probity has deserted the earth, seeking the gods. Impious deceit clothes herself in probity's garments. Oh, if simple virtue would return from the stars!

- Actus Quintus -

scena i

NVNCIA ANCILLA

o quanta torquet regiam mentem lues! 985
quam dira pestis exedit! quamque intimis
habitat medullis! nulla nec restat quies
nec spes quietis, luce nec tenebris silet.
quin errat amens, ingemit, stridet, furit.
et nisi querelis non vacat. memori fugam 990
frequens retractat mente, talique intonans
sermone linguam solvit: "en expes, inops.
deserta, quid agam? num sequar solitos procos
irrisa? Nomadum coniuges supplex petam
hos ante dedignata? an Iliadum sequar 995
extrema fata, quos opibus auxi meis?
quis me superbis (velle fac) ratibus Phrygum
accipiet? olim perfidos nosti dolos.
quin morere sicut merita es, et ferro insitos
averte luctus." talibus noctem trahit 1000
diemque dictis, iamque componi pyram
spondamque iussit, baltheum, ferrum, institam,
diadema, sceptrum, quicquid Aeneas dedit
profugus, in unum coniici. magicis parat
lenire mentem ritibus. nempe Aethiops 1005
qua parte solis proximi sentit iubar,
Massyla vates, inquit, hos docuit modos
fraenandi amorem. credimus, bustum damus,
bustoque quicquid illa mandavit prius.
atque ecce demens proripit sese foras. 1010

---

985. *lues?* **B**   986. *exedit?* **B**   987. *medullis?* **B**

- Act V -

scene i

A MAID, SERVING AS MESSENGER

Oh, what a plague tortues the queen's mind! What a dire pestilence consumes her! How it clings to her inmost marrow! No peace remains for her, no hope of peace, neither by day nor by night does she find repose. Pacing about, out of her mind, she groans, hisses, rages, as no time for anything but complaints. She often recalls his flight in her memory, giving voice to such speech: "See, I am hopeless, helpless, abandoned. What shall I do? Pursue the same old suitors, to my derision? Shall I humbly seek a Nomad husband, although previously I scorned them? Or shall I share the Trojans' ultimate destiny, whom I have helped with my resources? Who will permit me — would that this would happen! — onto the Phyrgians' proud ships? Dido, you have already experienced their perfidious wiles. Rather, die as you deserve, use the steel to end your deep grief." With such outbursts she drags out her nights and days. Now she gives orders for there to be built a pyre and bier, for her baldric, sword, robe, diadem, scepter, whatever Aeneas the refugee has given her, to be heaped together. She is preparing to ease her mind with magic rituals. For she says that an Ethiopian from the region which feels the radiance of the nearby sun, a Massilan prophetess, has taught her this way of restraining her love. We believe her, build the pyre, and put on it whatever she has commanded. And now see, the frenzied woman rushes outside. [*Exit. Enter Dido from the palace, accompanied by Barce and priests. As they talk, an altar is set up on the stage.*]

scena ii

DIDO, BARCE NVTRIX

DI. dilecta Barce, cuius amplexae meum
ulnae maritum saepe sunt, testor deos
tuumque dulce caput, et hanc aram, mea
non sponte fieri quod vides. regnat dolor
quaeritque tutum qua datur cunque exitum.   1015
hinc posse luctum spero leniri meum.

BAR. o fiat utinam, posse quod fieri putem
negemve dubito. te tibi reddat furor,
nobisque, et omnes exuat vires precor.

DI. quin tu remotum in parte seducta locum   1020
capesse. sola cantibus linquar meis.
  ordire, vates, carmen effare, insolens
ad hosce ritus. utere insueto gradu
habituque, qualem Colchidis dicunt statum.
  silentis Erebi vulgus, infandum genus   1025
umbraeque pavidae, tuque squalentis Stygis
ferale numen, coniugis raptor tuae,
tricepsque rictum Cerbere expandens trucem,
altaeque tenebrae noctris, et nunquam satis
Hecate triformis dicta, et immensum chaos,   1030
informe pondus, quamque tergeminam vocant
Diana, noctis conscia, et iudex mali
adeste. tristes noctuae et dirae stryges
et Hydra, cuius Herculem attrivit diu
iterata cervix, tuque vix manibus dei   1035
superate Python tetra serpentum lues
adeste. vos qui colitis aethereas domos
quocunque diffugistis, acciti his sacris
adeste. montes, flumina, et venti, lacus
amnesque, valles, maria, et herbarum genus,   1040
quotquot viretis flore mortifero simul
adeste. vestras postulate carmen manus.
abigendus amor est. ferte subsidium, graves
auferte curas, quaestubus finem date.

24. *Colchidos* B (nisi *apud Colchidos* intellegendum a lectore)

scene ii

DIDO, BARCE THE NURSE

DI. Darling Barce, who often held my husband in your embrace, I swear by the gods and your sweet head, and by this altar, what you see is not being done of my volition. Sorrow rules me, it is always seeking a safe outlet. I hope my grief can thus be assuaged.

BAR. Oh that it could, for I am hesitant whether I should think this is possible or deny it. Let madness give you back to yourself and to us, and I pray that it lose all its powers.

DI. Then hasten yourself to some remote place. Let me alone for my incantations. Seer, begin your strange chant for the ritual. Use your outlandish gait and dress, such as they say is customary for the Colchians.

Crew of still Erebus, you silent race, fearful shades, and you, wild spirit of gloomy Styx, abductor of your own wife, and three-headed Cerebrus with your ghastly grin, shades of deepest night, triform Hecate, never sufficiently invoked, infinite Chaos, you shapeless mass, and you Diana whom men call triform, a partner of night and judge of evil, be you present. Baleful night owls, dire screech owls, Hydra, whose multiple neck Heracles snapped long ago, and you, Python, foul bane among serpents, scarce overcome by a god's hands, be present. You who inhabit heaven's palaces, wherever you have fled, be present, summoned to these rites. Mountains, rivers, winds, lakes, torrents, valleys, oceans, all manner of plants flourishing with death-dealing flowers, be present also. My incantation requires your handiwork. Love is to be banished. Bring me your aid, remove my heavy cares, put an end to my complaints.

BAR. dent oro finem. fluctuans cesset dolor 1045
aestumque ponat animus indocilis pati
tantam malorum pondus.

DI. en clamor meas
percellit aures, et ferit mentem stupor.
tremisco. gelidum concipit pectus metum,
horrore quatior, sic tygres orbae furunt. 1050
   iam vela pandunt remiges, pontum secant
Tyriumque nudant littus, Aeneas fugit.
proh sancte sancte Iupiter nunquam nimis
vocande, regnis advena illudet meis?
an sic abibit? lecta quin sequitur cohors 1055
ex urbe tota, et improbas quassat rates,
ducesque laniat? ite, quid statis? moram
removete, flammas ferte, cursuque impigro
volate, remos agite. sed quorsum loquor
furiosa? qua sum parte? quae rabies premit 1060
versatque pectus? sortis, o Dido, asperae
o miseranda Dido. fata iam tangunt tua
tetigisse decuit antea. en dextram piam
fidemque patrios cui tulit secum deos
humerisque patrem subiit ingratis senem. 1065
   num stulta raptum corpus haud potui dare
in frustra centum, et gurgite invisum caput
obruere? socios manibus haud potui meis
diripere? Iulum patriis escam novam
offerre mensis? dubius at belli exitus 1070
fuisset. esto. nunquid habuissem metus
moritura? castra facibus implessem meis
forumque. facibus his pater, natus, genus
periisset omne. memet extremum super
egomet dedissem.

BAR. fervidos seda impetus. 1075
compesce gemitus. qua iuvat, fallax eat.
Tyro recedat. magica virtus id sapit
ut mente careas peius? insiste obsecro
iramque cohibe.

DI. fiat. ad sacrum voca
Annam sororem, dic lavet corpus suum 1080
pecudesque coram sistat et vitta insuper

1064. *qui* B 1065. *subiit patrem* B *ante corr.* 1079. *cohibe?* B

BAR. Indeed, I pray they make an end. Let this wavering anguish cease, may your mind set aside its passion, your mind untrained to bear such a weight of woes.

DI. And now a roaring strikes my ears, stupor siezes my mind. Chill dread grips my breast, I tremble with horror. Thus rage tigresses in their bereavement. Now the oarsmen are spreading their sails, cleaving the sea, leaving bare the Tyrian coastline, and Aeneas flees. Oh holy, holy Jupiter, whom one cannot invoke overmuch, will this foreigner mock my realm? Will he thus depart? Is a squadron hand-picked from the whole city pursuing, smashing his wicked ships, killing his captains? Go — why are you hesitating? Abandon your delay, bring fire, fly at full speed, ply your oars.

But why am I speaking in my rage? Where am I? What madness overcomes me, oppressing my heart? Oh Dido, Dido, piteous for your harsh fate! Now your destiny touches you, it should have touched you long ago. See his pious trust and loyalty: he carried with him his ancestral gods, he bore his aged father on his ungrateful shoulders! I was foolish — was I unable to cut his body into a hundred pieces, sink his hateful head in the sea? Could I not have ripped apart his shipmates with my own hands, served up Iulus as a novel dish at his father's table? But war's outcome would have been doubtful. Let it be so. On the brink of death, surely I would not have been afraid? I would have filled his camp and its center with my torches. By those torches would have perished father, son, the whole race. And I would have offered myself as the final victim.

BAR. Calm your burning ardor, stifle your groans. Let the deceiver go where he wishes Let him depart Tyre. Is this the power of your magic, that you lose your mind all the worse? Persevere, I beg you, restrain your wrath.

DI. Let it be so. Summon my sister Anna to the rite. Tell her to bathe her body, produce

ornet capillos. tuque venienti comes
accede, Stygio vota iam solvam deo.

BAR. regina, monitis Anna parebit tuis,
aderitque Barce.

Exit Barce.

DI. sacra num dixi Iovis? 1085
namque expianda sacra cum terra audiet,
pontusque et aether, audiet Ditis domus,
et quicquid uspiam est sceleris odio mei
capietur. o sol qui veheris axe arduo,
aurate Titan, conscia incaepti mei 1090
germana et eadem coniugi coniux Iovi,
ululata triviis Hecate, et Eumenides ferae,
et vos Elisae vindices superi piae
audite, moriens ultimas fundo preces.
audite: fixus pendeat rupe aspera 1095
sanieque spargat aequor, et tabo fluat
prius, petito quam pedem figat vado
Troianus hospes. sin Iovis fatum volet
adnare terris prospere infandum caput
iactatus armis, finibus patriae suae 1100
extorris, etiam avulsus amplexu tuo,
Iule, quaerat exteram infaelix opem,
gentisque videat funus ac stragem suae.
nactusque pacem rursus e regno cadat,
vitaque iaceat truncus, algensque evomat, 1105
inhumatum arena cuncta quoque tumulum neget.
Elisa, Elisa fatur in tenuem prope
resoluta ventum, et spiritum ducens brevem.
  tum vos futuram stirpem et Aeneadum genus,
Tyria propago, cura iamdudum mea 1110
vexate, bellis desit odiisque exitus.
has consecrate funeri inferias precor
cinerique nostro, nullus aut populis amor
aut faedus esto. vindicem pariant mihi
haec ossa, cuius Dardanum extinguent faces 1115
ensesque gentem. fluctui fluctum imprecor
et tela telis obiici, et ripae obviam
pugnare ripam, denique aeternum petat

1083. pro *Stygios* vid. Comm. not. 1085. *aderitque Barce* Didoni tribuit B: corr. Binns 1089. *capientur* B 106. *negent* B

the cattle, place a fillet on her hair. You accompany her as escort. I shall now make offering to the god of the Styx.

BAR. Queen, Anna will heed your command, and Barce will be present. (*Exit Barce.*)

DI. Did I speak of Jupiter's rites? The rites I am performing can never be atoned for, when the earth, the sea, the sky hear of them, when the home of Dis hears, when all that exists is seized with loathing for my crime. Oh sun, borne on your flaming chariot, golden Titan, and you, accomplice in my undertaking, at once Jupiter's sister and wife, and Hecate, to whom men howl at crossroads, wild Eumenides, and you gods who are avengers of pious Elisa, hear me. Dying, I utter my final prayers.

Hear me. Let him hang from a sharp cliff, dripping blood into the ocean. Let our Trojan guest drip gore before setting foot on the shore he seeks. But if Jupiter's decree dictates that this unspeakable man float to the land, then let him, buffeted by fighting, an exile from his homeland, and, Iulus, torn from your embrace, seek foreign help. Let him see the death, the slaughter of his race and, having obtained peace, let him again be exiled from his kingdom. Let him lie, despoiled of life, shivering as he spews, let all the sands refuse him a tomb as he lies unburied. Elisa resolutely casts these words into the insubstantial wind, drawing on her breath that will soon cease.

And then, you progeny of Tyre, out of care for me you must harry his future stock, the race of Aeneas. Let there be no end to wars and hatred. I pray that you consecrate these sacrifices honoring the dead to my funeral, my ashes. Let there be no love or pact between our peoples. Let these bones find me an avenger whose torches and swords will exterminate the Dardanian race. I pray that wave will clash with wave, weapons with weapons, that shore will strike against shore. Let our descendants always attack theirs, I bid them

nepos nepotem, iubeoque aeternum petat.
 vos, vos priori tempore exuviae mihi 1120
dulces (iniquas quamdiu fatum vices
inhibuit) animam tristibus fessam malis
accipite meque liberam curis date.
vixi, et peregi quem dedit casus diem
iamque umbra terras subter evadet mea. 1125
 urbs alta per me condita et muris decor
praeclarus, ulta coniugem paenas tuli
de fratre. faelix heu nimis faelix forem
si constitissent littore in nostro rates
nunquam scelestae Phrygia quas rexit manus. 1130
an ergo iunulta moriar? at moriar tamen
sic. sic sub umbras ire pallentes iuvat.
hanc lustret oculis Dardanus flammam impiis,
omenque secum asportet indigenae necis.

scena iii

ANNA, BARCE, ANCILLAE SACRIFICANTES

BAR. eheu quod oculis perspicio factum meis? 1135
 regina moritur, impia incubuit sibi.

AN. moriturne?

BAR.   iacet exanguis.

AN.   o misera vices,
miseram sororem, misera divorum sacra.
ite, ite, famam spargite in vulgus, meet
ubique rumor. atria ingeminent sonum, 1140
vocemque mortis regiae, totam impleat
ululatus urbem, tecta lamentis fremant
planctuque caelum. o Dido, Sydonium decus,
germana Dido, respice sororem tuam.
an me petebas fraudibus? an istud rogus 1145
parabat? arae, cespites, taedae, faces?
deserta primum quid loquar, quidve ingemam?
carere poteras comite? non poteras idem

1132. *sic?* **B**

attack down through eternity.

Relics, sweet to me in former times (as long as my destiny forestalled misfortune), receive my soul, worn out by sad evils, grant me freedom from cares. I have lived, I have lived out my appointed span, and now my shade will journey beneath the earth.

I have founded a high city, the splendid glory of walls, I have avenged my husband and wreaked punishment on my brother. I would have been happy, alas, if those ships had never grounded on our shore, guided by Phrygian hands. So am I to die unavenged? But nevertheless thus I die. Thus I crave to join the wan shades. Let the Dardanian see this fire with his disloyal eyes, taking with him a sign of the death of a native woman. [*She stabs herself. Enter Anna, Barce, escorted by serving-women carrying materials for the sacrifice.*]

scena iii

ANNA, BARCE, MAIDS PARTICIPATING IN THE SACRIFICE

BAR. Ah, what deed do my eyes see? The queen is dying, she has wickedly done violence to herself.

AN. Is she dying?

BAR. She lies, drained of blood.

AN. Oh, miserable misfortune, miserable sister, miserable rites of the gods. Go, go spread the story among the people, let Rumor circulate everywhere. Let the hall resound with noise, with news of the royal death, let shrieking fill the entire city. Let our houses roar with laments, the heaven with our plaint. Oh Dido, glory of the Sidonians, my sister Dido! Consider your sister. Were you assailing me with deceit? Was this what the pyre was for? The altar, turf, torches, firebrands? Being abandoned, what should I say first, what should I bemoan? Could you lack a comrade? Could you not have shared your fate? How

     partire fatum? quam melius idem dolor
     eademque socias hora mactasset duas!   1150
     hisne ergo manibus ipsa funebrem pyram
     struxi, deosque precibus oravi meis
     ut sic abessem? te, soror, pessum dedi
     populumque, et urbem, meque et indigenas patres.
     date, date lymphas, vulnus intenta abluam,   1155
     atque ore si quis halitus superest legam

BAR. o spes inanes, omnis incassum labor
     locatur. ecce tollit ac ponit caput,
     cubitoque nixa decidit, in altum vibrat
     oculosque rursum claudit errantes. ubi   1160
     iam prisca virtus? prisca maiestas? honor
     antiquus urbis? exulat: reditus datur
     spes nulla. Dido dederat ac Dido abstulit.
     resolvar ecce gratia in planctus tua,
     lachrimisque nunquam deero. non reperit dolor   1165
     plus quod litaret, et frequens lacrimas dabit.

AN. o si miserta Iuno, quae thalami fuit
     author iugalis, posse iam sineret cita
     perire morte. pereat o superi cito.

scena iv

IRIS, ANNA

<*Caelitus dilapsa.*>

IR. Thaumante genita principis venio deae   1170
     ministra. fatum implere mandatur tuum,
     moramque mortis tollere urgentis prope.
     en hos capillos iussa Plutoni sacros
     dicabo, teque corpore exolvam tuo.

Exit.

AN. Elisa, nisi te forte necquicquam voco,   1175
     vale supremum, soror, in aeternum vale.
     compellat Anna mortuam. Dido, vale,

1150. *duas?* B 1151. *hiisne* **B** descriptio actionis ex descriptione Holingshedi supplevi

better the same grief, the same hour could have killed two companions! Did I therefore build your funeral pyre myself with these hands, offering up my prayers to the gods, thus to be apart from you? Sister, I worked great harm to you, our city, myself, our native forefathers. [*To the maids.*] Bring me water, I shall carefully wash her face, gathering with my lips whatever breath may linger.

BAR. Oh empty hopes, all our work is done in vain. See, she lifts her head, she drops it. She tries to raise herself on her elbow, but collapses, raises her wandering eyes, then closes them. Where is old-fashioned virtue? Our ancient majesty? The city's former honor? It is banished, and there is no hope for its return. Dido conferred it, Dido took it away. See how I am reduced to tears for your sake, I shall never cease my weeping. My grief finds no worthier object to spend itself on, it will often make me cry.

AN. Oh, if Juno, responsible for this marriage, had taken pity, she would have allowed her a speedy death. Oh gods, may she die quickly! [*Enter Iris.*]

scene iv

IRIS, ANNA

IR. [*Descending from heaven.*] Daughter of king Thaumas, I come as agent of the goddess. I am commanded to fulfil your destiny, to end the delay of your impending death. See how, bidden, I dedicate these hairs, consecrated to Pluto, and release you from your body. [*She cuts off a lock of Dido's hair. Dido dies and Iris exits.*]

AN. Elisa, unless I am calling on you in vain, farewell for the last time, sister, farewell for eternity. Anna is trying to rouse a dead woman. Farewell, Dido, never to return. Where

reditura nunquam. quo meas lachrimas feram?
aut quo querelas? taedet illarum deos,
et me pigebit ipsam, et assiduis parum est   1180
rigere lachrimis. aliud exequiae rogant
sororis. an vos o lares, miseri lares
viduata comite amplectar? an thalamos petam
relicta? caeli ac lucis aspectu fruar,
orbata? dira, invisa, devota omnia.   1185
cunctaris, Anna? propera, et inferias vove,
non has minores, anima pendatur tua.
elide fauces baltheo. en ferro prius
scrutata soror est viscera, et rupit fibras.
i, curre, sequere, munus authori suo   1190
gratetur. explet optimam hoc munus vicem.

CHORVS

quae vexant Tyriam fata propaginem?
quae clades agitat? quanta calamitas!
extinctus decor est urbis et invida
vitae tota fuit regia stirps suae.   1195
Annam Dido necat, perfuga Dardanus
Didonem, Tyriis utraque matribus
lugubrem subita morte tulit diem.
 o devota ratis quae dedit advenam
his oris Phrygium, saevior at ratis   1200
quae rursum pelago reddidit impium.
diris illa fides dignior omnibus
quae solvit thalamos perfida regios.
 Getulos metuit Punica gens prius,
illos esse malum tum rata maximum.   1205
nunc aerumna metum fortior expulit.
desperata salus nil penitus timet.
 sic fatum voluit, sic aliquis deus
iussit quisquis erat. stant adamantinis
consignata notis funera gentium.   1210
 quod nobis reliquum fecit adhuc dolor
defunctae dabimus. planctus erit frequens,
siccas nulla dies aspiciet genas.

1192. pro *vexant* vid. Comm. not.   1193. pro *calamitas* vid. Comm. not. (*calamitas?* B)   1195. pro *stirps* vid. Comm. not.

should I betake my tears, my laments? The gods tire of them, I myself grow ashamed, and it is a trifling thing to be numb with constant tears. My sister's funeral demands something more. Oh household gods, our poor household gods, shall I cleave to you, bereft of my companion? Or, left behind, should I seek a marriage? Shall I enjoy the sky, the sight of daylight, when left alone? Everything is horrible, loathsome, damnable. Do you hesitate, Anna? Hasten, and dedicate the sacrifices honoring the dead — not just the lesser ones. Let your life be payed out. Cut your throat with this sword. See, your sister has already plunged it into her guts and rent her entrails. Go, run, follow. Let this last service gratify the one who inspires it. This last dutiful act is for the best. [*Stabs herself and dies.*]

CHORUS

What Fates oppress the Tyrian race? What catastrophe pursues it? How great a calamity! Our city's glory is vanished, and the entire royal family has grown to hate its own life. Dido is the death of Anna, the Dardanian exile is the death of Dido. The both of them brought a sad day to the mothers of Tyre by their sudden deaths.

Oh, damnable ship which brought the Phrygian stranger to these shores, but even more savage the ship which returned the disloyal man to the sea. And yet more worthy of all dire things is that false faith which destroyed the royal marriage.

Before now the Punic nation feared the Getuli, then thinking them to be the greatest evil of all. Now a greater suffering has banished this fear. Hope for salvation, when abandoned, fears nothing greatly.

Thus destiny decided, thus some god, whoever he was, decreed. The destruction of nations stands graven in adamantine letters.

What our grief has left to us, we shall bestow upon our dead queen. Our lament will be constant, no day will see our cheeks unbathed by tears.

EPILOGVS

A p. 83

iam nacta tandem est exitum Dido suum,
utinam expetitum, quem tamen potuit tulit. 1215
et scriptam et actam tempus excuset breve.
   nunc quisque reputet quid sibi hinc referat boni.
Venus inimico credere antiquo vetat.
ut faveat hostis, cogitat semper dolos,
ut Iuno Teucris sit bona insidias struit. 1220
fidemque opemque regium est miseris dare.
hospitia claram magna nobilitant domum.
beneficio quicunque districtus manet,
capite minuitur, esse liber desinit.
sit gratus usque licet at "ingrate" audiet. 1225
Iunonia male expressa tempestas monet
habenda quae sit Prometheis posthac fides,
nec posse quenquam fulmen imitari Iovis.
decet obsequentes esse praemonitis deum,
omnisque nimia est, sit licet brevior, mora. 1230

p. 84

molles moveri faeminae lachrymis solent,
sed fortis aures obstruere debet suas.
promerita si maiora detineant bona
quacunque fuerint, neminem vinctum tenent.
externa raro connubia cedunt bene. 1235
vis magna amoris, faeminis gravior solet
corripere flamma, levior accendit viros.
sed vita paucas nostra Didones videt,
prudentiores faemanas factas reor,
amore nullam credo morituram gravi. 1240
   sed una longe, Elisa, te superat tamen.
regina virgo quot tulit casus pia!
quae regna statuit! quam dat externis fidem!
dignata nullo coniuge Sichaeo tamen,
animumque nullus flectat Aeneas suum. 1245
tamen, ecce, maior hospes Aenea hospite.
cui verba, Dido, rectius quadrent tua:
"quis iste nuper sedibus nostris novus
successit hospes? ore quem sese ferens!
quam fortis alto pectore armisque inclytus! 1250
genus esse divum credo, nec vana est fides."
   sed Elisa fato Tyria miserando occubat.
at nostra Elisa vivit, et vivat precor,

---

epilogum habet A   1226. *docet* pro *monet* B   1235. v. deest de A   1238. *tulit* pro *videt* B   1241. *Dido* pro *Elisa* B

EPILOGUE

Now *Dido* has had its conclusion. Would that it had been the one we would have chosen! But it took the ending it could. Let the speed with which it had to be prepared excuse its text and our performance.

Now let each spectator reckon up what good is to be derived from this play. Venus forbids us to trust an ancient foe, she is always inventing schemes to that an enemy will be favorable, setting snares so that Juno will be kind to the Trojans. It is royal to give trust and aid to the wretched, and hospitality ennobles a great house. But whoever remains dependent on charity is diminished in stature, ceasing to be a free man. Let him be ever so grateful, he will acquire the reputation of an ingrate. The storm, evilly raised by Juno, shows what faith is henceforth to be placed in Prometheuses, nor can anyone imitate Jupiter's lightning. We must heed the god's admonitions, and any delay in doing so, even a brief one, is too great. Pliable women are moved by tears, but the strong one must stop her ears. If the favors done you stand in the way of greater goods, no matter what they were, they oblige nobody. Foreign marriages rarely turn out well. Love's power is great. A greater fire affects women, a lighter one kindles men. But our times have produced few Didos, and I imagine our women have grown more prudent. I doubt any woman will die of a broken heart.

But, Dido, one woman surpasses you by far: our virgin queen. In her piety, how many reversals has she endured! What kingdoms has she founded! To what foreigners has she plighted her trust! But she has not condescended to marry any Sychaeus, and may no Aeneas sway her affections! But behold, here is a guest greater than Aeneas. To this man, Dido, your words would better apply: "What new guest has come to our home? How handsome his face! How brave with his deep chest, distinguished in battle! I believe he is descended from the gods, and this is no empty belief."

Tyrian Elisa came to a piteous end. But I pray our Eliza lives, will continue living, so that

talesque regnans hospites videat diu.
Sabae salutent undique, et magni duces.   1255
huic vos Elisae tollere applausum decet.

FINIS

as she reigns she will long see such guests. Queens of Sheba and great dukes hail her on all sides. You should give your applause for *this* Elisa.

Textual Commentary

Prologue 5ff. *Hesterna...scena* refers to the performance of Gager's comedy *Rivales* on the previous evening.

Prologue 7 Cf. Horace, *Ars Poetica* 81, *hunc socci cepere pedem grandesque cothurni*.

Prologue 10ff. These lines contain an unusually thoughtful *captatio benevolentiae*. Gager accepts the normal classicizing injunctions (issued, for example, by Horace in the *Ars Poetica*) about maintaining the proper distinctions between the various literary genres (a doctrine he was to return to, from a very different angle, in the *Prologus ad Criticum* written for *Ulysses Redux*), but adds an interesting twist. He is in effect saying "Tragedy is no less pleasant than comedy. Somebody would miss the point to add an admixture of sadness to a comedy, but there is a strong element of pleasure in tragedy. You can laugh until you cry, you can weep for joy. There is great pleasure in witnessing a tragedy, where you can have the fun of crying at the characters' misfortunes while safe in the knowledge that you yourself are quite free from danger. Therefore, dear spectator, you will have just as much entertainment now as you did last night." In his commentary Binns observed that line 10 echoes Horace, *A. P.* 343 *omne tulit punctum, qui miscuit utilie dulci*. The subsequent idea of the pleasurableness of tragedy is at least ultimately derived from the *Poetics* of Aristotle, who says at one point (p. 53^b14) "the poet should use representation to produce the pleasure [arising] from pity and terror" [tr. R. Janko].

Gager returned to both ideas in an oration delivered not long after the writing of *Dido*, *Eloquentiae Encomium* (printed here in Volume IV). In speaking of poets, he said *quorum ingenia sic sunt ad delitias nata, ut quanquam dulci aliquando utile misceant aspergantque, in dulci tamen semper magis elaborant*. And a bit further, speaking very significantly of the literary prototype of the present play, he asked rhetorically *quis est qui si quartum illum Aeneidos librum legerit, ut in nimis saepe laetitia fit, ita prae summa animi delectatione non abeat in lachrymas?*

Binns also pointed out the parallels to line 10 in Gager's notebook poetry: *nec levibus misce seria dicta iocis (Praecepta Isocratis* 45.2), *et tua lepidis seria mista iocis* (LXXVIII. 6), *et lepidis seria dicta iocis* (CXXIV.79).

Argumentum The first few lines establish the play's Carthaginian setting. Perhaps as the actor pronounces the word *tectis* in 22 he gestures towards the "house" used to represent Dido's palace. The entire play is set in this one location, save that Actus II is played as an interior scene within the palace: cf. the initial Commentary note on II.i. Other scenic features include: a.) in Actus I Venus and Cupid probably appear aloft, in the same "high place" from which Holinshed says Mercury and Iris made their descents later in the play; b.) one direction offstage leads to the cave-containing forest to and from which the hunting party progresses in Actus III and from which Cupid emerges at III.iii; c.) to the opposite direction undoubtedly lies the harbor of Carthage.

There evidently existed a tradition that *Dido* was the first Oxford play to employ movable scenery (cf. Thomas Seccombe and H. Spencer Scott, *In Praise of Oxford: An*

Anthology in Prose and Verse (London, 1912) II.500. Since the play contains no change of scene, this appears highly unlikely.

The Christ Church Disbursement Books for 1582-83 contain an entry "To Richard West, for felling of 4 timber trees at Chandence for the heaven and other new building on the stage, 3 other lesse, trees, squaring, dressing and cariage of 2 lodes. 6s 8d." The "heaven" in question was some sort of balcony or platform employed for the first of these special scenic features. (Some sort of crane-like machine would not require so much wood).

Argumentum 24 Dido's subjects are "double-tongued" because this is a mixed nation of Phoenician immigrants and Libyan natives. But there is also an allusion to the Carthaginians' notorious duplicity (the conceit is taken from Verg., *Aen.* I.661).

Actus I, scena i This scene is based in Verg., *Aen.* I.657 - 90.[1] The dramatic technique is un-Senecan, since each of the plays in the Senecan corpus begins with an extended introductory monologue.

Since the Actus of *Meleager* and *Ulysses Redux* are not divided into numbered scenae, this is as good a place as anywhere to remind the reader that in Gager's plays speaker lists, whether numbered as scenae or not, are not employed as scene divisions in the modern sense of the word; they do not mark any discontinuity of time or location, or any other kind of break in the action (for the sole arguable exception to this generalization, cf. the initial Commentary note on II.vi). Rather, according to the standard system employed by academic drama, derived from the manuscripts of Terence, each scena indicates a new grouping of speaking characters currently on the stage. Very often the use of such scenae functions as a way of marking entrances and exits.

I.52 Even if we replace a comma with a period at the end of the line, **B**'s text looks suspicious: *odium Minervae maius excepit malum.* This would mean "he encountered a hatred more evil than that of Minerva," but it would be odd to have *maius* modify another adjective. Since the errors would be equally easy from a paleographic standpoint, it is a matter of indifference whether we read *odio* or substitute *magis* for *maius*.

I.48 and 52 In some mythological accounts, Athena's anger over losing the Judgment of Paris was the cause of the Trojan War (and hence of the Trojans' woes).

I.65 B reads *mihi fas capessam iussa, tu iubeas modo* and it is modelled upon Verg., *Aen.* I.77 *mihi iussa capessere fas est.* As it stands, **B**'s line cannot be right. We must either punctuate after *fas* (with *est* to be supplied by the reader) or change *capessam* to *capessere*. The former expedient is less drastic. Another consideration that makes *capessere* seem slightly unlikely is that this change would create a line with an anapaest in all three even-numbered feet, but Gager's anonymous collaborator seems otherwise averse to lines containing more than two resolutions.

I.68f. Baumann-Wissemann observed the imitation of *Tr.* 199 - 201:

---

[1] Considerations of space forbid the quotation of Vergilian passages in these Commentary notes.

> *immoti iacent*
> *tranquilla pelagi, ventus abiecit minas*
> *placidumque fluctu murmurat leni mare.*

I.75 At *Aen.* I.321f. Venus pretends to be a huntress trying to find her sister.

I.83 Mercury was the son of Maia, daughter of Atlas.

I.92 The Trojans are sometimes called the Teucrians after a former king of Troy.

I.111f. Binns noted the parallel to *H. Oet.* 1366f.:

> *non ipse terris maior Oceanus meos*
> *extinguet vapores.*

Actus I, sc. ii The gods retire and the mortals enter. Dido's two counsellors Hanno and Maharbal are invented characters, and the present short scena is not based on the *Aeneid*.

Actus I, sc. iii Dido's advisors cease to speak when the Trojans enter. This and the following scenae closely follow Verg., *Aen.* I.520 - 630.

I.168 The time of the year when Orion is visible is stormy and makes for bad sailing weather.

I.185 Baumann-Wissemann translated *damit wir entweder nach dem Plan unseres Führers zusammen mit unseren Weggefährten*, unconcerned that *rege* is not in the genitive (nor can it be — it would create a spondaic fourth foot). Furthermore, the first two feet of B's line consist of a trochee and a spondee. Reading *recepto* solves all the problems: cf. *Aen.* I.553 *sociis et rege recepto*.

I.187 Sicania is an alternative name for Sicily.

Actus I, sc. iv In Vergil, Aeneas and Achates first appear wrapped in an invisibility-conferring cloud provided by Venus, and then suddenly step out of it to reveal themselves. Gager presumably abandoned this device because he and his technical advisor Peele could not figure out how to represent it on the stage. In the play, the two Trojans appear on one side of the stage where they can converse out of earshot of the other characters. Then, when they decide it is safe to approach Dido, they cross over to her.

I.239ff. Vergil (*Aen.* I.619ff.) tells the story more fully. The Greek Teucer, stepbrother of Ajax, when exiled from his native land, came to Sidon and was received by Dido's father Belus. He claimed kinship with the Trojans on the basis of his name, shared with a former king of Troy (cf. the Commentary note on I.i 92).

Actus I chorus The identity of the chorus is unstated, as often in Seneca: cf. D. F.

Sutton, *Seneca on the Stage* (Leiden, 1986) 35 - 7. There seems to have been a convention in the ancient theater that, when the chorus' identity is unspecified, we are to assume that it is composed of citizens of the town where the play is set. Or perhaps, since plays featuring a woman as the central character very often have female choruses, in such cases we are to assume a chorus of women of that town. If the same understanding is to be applied here, then the chorus is made of citizens, or women, of Carthage. Certainly this identification finds support in the extreme sympathy the Chorus displays towards Dido throughout the play.

Such ruminations about the power of Fate are commonplace in Seneca and Seneca-based tragedy, and numerous parallels could be adduced from other University tragedies. Baumann-Wissemann cited F. Kiefer, *Fortune and Elizabethan Tragedy* (San Marino, 1983).

The meter consists four hendecasyllables followed by an Adonic.

I 247ff. The Chorus' words seem to describe the action of a balance scale.

I 260ff. Binns compared Verg., *Aen.* II.354 *qui nil potest sperare, desperet nihil*, imitated at *Me.* 163 *qui nil potest sperare, desperet nihil*.

I 265f. *Sed intus io triumphat* refers to Aeneas' present condition. Cf. the staging of the following scena.

Actus II, scena i Dido is feasting the guests within her palace. The text supplies some clues that the first four scenae of this Actus are played as an interior scene: Dido's invitation to the Trojans to enter her house at I.iv 240 and the Chorus' reference to Aeneas "within" at I.265. Actus I was played before a "house" used to represent her palace. Now a doorcovering curtain has been pulled aside to reveal an interior scene. For the staging, compare the banquet scene of Thomas Legge's *Solymitana Clades*, Actio I.iv.i, with its very detailed stage direction.[1]

In Book I of the *Aeneid* Dido offers a feast to Aeneas and his men, during which Iopas, Dido's resident bard, performs and Aeneas recounts the fall of Troy and his wanderings. Gager does not dramatize this feast but rather a second one, having no Vergilian basis, that occurred on the following day, as is made clear by 293 *quae nocte genitor retulit hesterna altius*.

Boas (*op. cit.* 184) quotes an account record that shows that special wine was brought down from London for use in this scena and for a drinking-scene in *Rivales*. It is doubtful that any great concern would have been felt for the drinking pleasure of the actors. More likely, after the performance this wine and the marzipan confection used in the present scena were offered to the Pfalzgraf and other honored guests.

II.268 Binns observed that the sentiment is modelled on Verg., *Aen.* I.203 *forsan et haec olim meminisse iuvabit* and also on *H. F.* 656f.:

> *quae fuit durum pati,*
> *meminisse dulce est.*

---

[1] Printed as Vol. II of *Thomas Legge: The Complete Plays* (ed. D. F. Sutton, Bern - New York, 1993).

He also noted the parallel at poem XX.33f:

> *memora dulce est*
> *quod pati durum nihis ah fuisset.*

II.271 Baumann-Wissemann noted the echo of *Hipp.* 455, *curas Bacchus exoneret graves.*

II.279f. Cf. the Commentary note on *Meleager* 1858f.

II.296ff. This is of course the "marchpane patterne" mentioned by Holinshed: a large, multicolored confection dish in which a map of Troy was molded. A dish is round and so shield-like, and the conceit is a dramatic transformation of a stock epic device, the shield-descriptions such as one finds in Book XVIII of the *Iliad* and Book VI of the *Aeneid*. But in another sense the inspiration for this passage is Ovid, *Heroides* 31 - 6:

> *atque aliquis posita mostrat fera proelia mensa,*
> *pingit et exiguo Pergama tota mero:*
> *"hac ibat Simois, haec est Sigeia tellus,*
> *hic steterat Priami regia celsa senis.*
> *illic Aeacides, illic tendebat Ulixes.*
> *hic lacer admissos terruit Hector equos."*

II.298f. Tenedos, Cilla, and Chryse were local places sympathetic to Troy, taken by the Greeks before the capture of the city itself.

II.306 Anchises was of course Aeneas' aged father, whom his pious son tried to rescue from the sack of Troy by carrying him on his shoulders.

II.311 Sinon was the Greek who pretended to have been left behind by his departing comrades, and so persuaded the Trojans to admit the Trojan Horse within the walls.

II.317f. Baumann-Wissemann observed the imitation of *Tr.* 768 - 70:

> *cui demens ego*
> *laudes parentis bellicas, annos avi*
> *medios precabar.*

II.321ff. Vergil (*Aen.* I.740ff.) describes how, when the feasting was through, garlanded Iopas sang lore taught him by Atlas. As Boas (*op. cit.* 185) observed, he "chants the praises of the Trojan guest and of his royal hostess in words ingeniously designed to apply also to the Polish vistor and the English queen." This song is carefully designed: four stanzas are allocated to Aeneas, four to Dido, and two to the present happy occasion. The significant name Elisa is used repeatedly, and the final reference to the *ampla atria* refers equally to Dido's palace and to the dining hall of Christ Church.

The meter is Sapphic stanzas (three hendecasyllables and an Adonic).

Notes to pp. 280 - 86.

II.322 "Lycian" was an epithet of Apollo, based on his association with Lycia in Asia Minor.

II.341 Binns observed the echo of *Tr.* 1023, *est miser nemo nisi comparatus.*

II.368 To understand the following passage, it is necessary to realize that *fatum* is being used in a special way: prophetically revealed preconditions that had to be met before the Greeks could capture Troy.

II.371 One such precondition was that Priam's son Troilus had to die before reaching the age of twenty.

II.372 Helenus was the son of Priam and Hecuba, and a famous seer. When the Greeks found out that he knew secret oracles that protected Troy, Odysseus ("The Ithacan") kidnapped him. He then revealed his secrets.

II.373 Rhesus was a Thracian ally, coming to join the Trojans. An oracle had said that, once his horses pastured at Troy, the city would be invulnerable. Therefore Odysseus and Diomedes killed him and stole his horses before he could reach the city. Pyrrhus, also named Neoptolemus, was the son of Achilles. An oracle had foretold that his presence was necessary for a Greek victory.

II.378ff. Here the false Ascanius tells the story of the famous Palladium.

II.399ff. Now he tells the story of Philoctetes, son of Poeas. On the point of death, Hercules had bequeathed his bow and arrows to Philoctetes. Philoctetes had been bitten on the foot by a snake and, disgusted by the loathsome wound, the Greeks marooned him on island of Lemnos. Then, when they learned from Helenus that the presence at Troy of the bow and arrow, and also that of Philoctetes himself, was another precondition of victory, Odysseus was sent on a mission to retrieve him.

II.401ff. Baumann-Wissemann noted the imitation of *H. Oet.* 1648f.

> *"accipe haec," inquit, "sate*
> *Poeante, dona, et munus Alcidae cape."*

II.405f. They also noted the echo of *Oed.* 291f:

> *sacrate divis, proximum Phoebo caput,*
> *responsa solve; fare, quem poenae petant.*

II.419 (stage direction) Roberts-Baytop (*op. cit.* 38ff.) implausibly thought that *pompa larvalis* is meant to introduce the following invocation and sacrifice. Boas (*op. cit.* 185f.) suggested that these words indicate some sort of masque, an idea repeated by both Binns and Baumann-Wissemann. Although the Latin would also support the interpretation "procession of spectres," i.e., of the ghosts of the heroes killed at Troy, Boas'

Notes to pp. 286 - 90.

interpretation is mandatory in view of the stage direction at the beginning of Actus II of *Ulysses Redux, Proci primum larvati alicunde prodeunt, saltantque in scena, deinde exeunt in conclave*, which calls for a procession of Penelope's masked suitors.

Actus II, scenae iii and iv Since Gager's so-called scenae are really only speaker groups, and at least usually there is no discontinuity of time or place, whether we acknowledge this passage as two scenae with A, or as one with B, is immaterial. It is sufficient to observe that Aeneas seems to leave the stage at the end of scena ii, possibly in the company of the masquers; or at least, if he remains present, does not speak again before the end of scena iv. Ascanius remains, witnesses Dido's sacrifice, and then engages her in conversation. This formal libation follows *Aen*. I.723ff.

II.430 Binns noted the parallel at *Meleager* 249f.

> *dapibus ac ludis datum*
> *satis superque est.*

As noted in the Commentary note on those lines, they are indebted to *Thy*. 899f.

II.433 This line looks like a cue for some sort of musical interlude before the entrance of Dido's advisors. According to Boas (*op. cit.* 186 n.1) "The closing lines of the scene are intended to give an opportunity for clearing away the paraphernalia connected with the banquet, before the appearance of Maharbal and Hanno...Thus music diverted the attention of the audience while the stage was being cleared." Now the curtain closes, and the remainder of the Actus is performed outside the palace (cf. Hanno's reference to going indoors at 461). Although not mentioned in the text or stage directions, something may have been done to convey to the audience that a night passes between the banquet and scena v (for the problem of the Actus' internal time-scheme, cf. the initial Commentary note on II.vi).

Actus II, scena v In Vergil, Carthaginian reaction to Dido's romance is not an issue. Nor does Dido have somewhat paternalistic male advisors who feel entitled to form opinions about the wisdom or propriety of her actions, or to worry about their political, military, or diplomatic consequences (even if this stuff does little more than rehash what Anna says later, which reproduces what she says in Vergil, it has the effect of giving it extra emphasis). It is perhaps not extravagant, therefore, to think that this scena goes a fair distance towards recasting the situation in contemporary Elizabethan terms. Hanno and Maharbal are retrojections of, say, Burleigh and Walsingham.

II.443ff. Iarbas is one of the local princes slighted by Dido (*Aen*. IV.35f., 98ff.)

II.458f. Ariadne and Medea were two famous mythological heroines abandoned by false lovers.

Actus II, scena vi We now return to solid Vergilian ground. The interview between Dido and her sister Anna very closely follows *Aen*. IV.6 - 54.

Vergil's internal time-scheme is clearly marked and easily followed. On the first day,

Notes to pp. 290 - 98.

Aeneas lands at Carthage. That night, he and his companions are given a feast, and he delivers his long narrative. The next morning (*Aen.* IV.6f.) Dido has her first interview with Anna and alludes to the dream she had that night. On the night of the second day (IV.80ff.) Venus and Juno have their interview. On the third day (IV.129) occur the hunt, storm, and union of the lovers. We have already seen that Gager has altered this time-scheme. His banquet does not occur at the end of the first day, but at the end of the second (cf. the initial Commentary note on II.i) The reference to dreams (463), which is taken mechanically from Vergil, ought to mean that this scena transpires on the morning of his third day. Does, then, a night intervene between the end of scenae iv and the beginning of scena v, the only point in the Actus where an interval of time is possible? If so, it is not explicitly marked. Or is the Actus' internal time-scheme simply ill meditated? Certainly, in adapting Vergil's Dido story, Gager was forced to juggle requirements of dramatic convenience (and possibly some concern for observing the Unities) against the undeniable fact of Vergil's own scheme.

II.494ff. This *tour d' horizon* takes in the Getuli and the Numidians, native peoples of northwestern Africa, the inhabitants of the town of Barce, and the Syrte, a huge sandbank lying off the coast.

II.506ff. Dido's greedy brother Pygmalion had murdered her husband Sychaeus while he was standing at an altar offering sacrifice. She gained her revenge by assembling a following, leaving Tyre, and settling Carthage; as she was departing, she absconded with the royal treasury. Vergil tells the story at *Aen.* I.348ff.

Actus II chorus This chorus (including its magnificent simile of the deer) follows *Aen.* IV.65 - 78 and 86 - 91 very closely. The meter is anapestic dimeters.

III.551 Binns noted the parallel at poem CXXI.11f.:

> *abrupta pendent opera, et ingentes minae*
> *murorum, et alto machinae caelo pares.*

Actus III, scena i (initial stage direction) "...it is clear from Holinshed's account that, as in the case of Edwarde's *Palamnon and Arcyte* in 1566, full appeal was made to the sporting instincts of the audience. There was a 'goodlie sight of hunters with ful crie of a kennell of hounds.' It must have been an abrupt change from this cheerful spectacle to the Ghost of Sychaeus, who is introduced in Senecan fashion to foretell disaster to his fomer spouse if she marries one of the perfidious race of Troy. But his warnings are in vain, for the fateful tempest is at hand which joins the lovers in sudden and secret union." (Boas, *op. cit.* 186).

Actus III, scena i Ghost apparations are part of the traditional repertoire of scene-types in Senecan and Seneca-based tragedy (Seneca's *Agamemnon* and *Thyestes* both begin with such apparitions) and so are commonplace in Elizabethan drama. In a note on this passage Baumann-Wissemann cite G. Dahinten, *Die Geisterszene in der Tragödie vor Shakespeare, Zur Seneca-Nachfolge im englischen und lateinischen Drama des Elisabeth-*

anismus (Göttingen, 1958). Nevertheless, in the case of the present apparition, one is compelled to ask what this ghost is supposed to do. He makes no visible contribution to the supernatural machinery of the story, and seems even more superfluous than Megaera in the *Meleager*.

III.554f. Cf. the Commentary note on *Meleager* I.76ff.

III.561 Baumann-Wissemann observed the echo of *Tro.* 1168, *quo meas lacrimas feram?*

III.573 Here they noted the echo of *Thy.* 24, *furiis age.* Megaera is one of the three Furies.

III.i 575 Binns noted the echo of Seneca, *Thy.* 95, *stabo et arcebo scelus* (used also at *Panniculus* 53). In Seneca, the Ghost of Tantalus promises to remain and ward off the Fury's onslaught, then he passes into the palace, a fine visual metaphor. Evidently the Ghost of Sychaeus has a similar intention here, but his presence within Dido's palace has no more influence on the play's action than does the Ghost of Tantalus in *Thyestes*.

III.575 (second stage direction) "The single-word stage-direction 'Tempestas' [so it is given in **B**: D. F. S.] indicates that the storm was represented before the audience, and Holinshed adds the interesting details that 'it hailed small confects, rained rosewater, and snew an artificall kind of snow." Scarcely the most appropriate materials for the occasion, and out of harmony with the lamentations of the 'Nymphae plangentes' who bewail in doleful chorus 'hymenaeos, heu male iunctos'" (Boas, *op. cit.* 186f.).

One is compelled to admit that Holinshed seems to describe a remarkably cheerful storm, but it is likely that he gives an exaggerated impression. At first sight it might seem that his mention of "confits" implies sweetmeats being tossed out into the audience, in the manner of an Aristophanic comedy. But probably by "confits" he meant confetti employed to represent snowflakes.[1]

Actus III, scena ii It makes excellent dramatic sense to have the Nymphs sing this ironically inappropriate serenade to the couple who (as the Vergil-reading spectator knows) have taken refuge from the storm in a cave and are at this moment consummating their love. It serves to give a premonition of the sinister implications of what is ostensibly a happy occasion.

Gager got the idea for this song from Ovid, *Heroides* 94 - 6:

> *illa dies nocuit, qua nos declive sub antrum*
> *caerulis subitis conpulit imber aquis.*
> *audieram vocem. nymphas ululasse putavi —*
> *Eumenides fatis signa dedere meis!*

Each stanza consists of three anapestic dimeters followed by an anapaestic foot always re

---

[1] Unfortunately, there is no *Oxford English Dictionary* entry for the word "confetti," and this passage, and the definition it invites, are not noted in the *O. E. D.* article "comfit."

Notes to pp. 300 - 304.

solved so as an Adonic.

592ff. This brief monologue is generically similar to the even shorter one of Cupid at Marlowe's *The Tragedy of Dido Queen of Carthage* III.i:

> *Now, Cupid cause the Carthaginian Queene,*
> *To be inamourd of thy brother's lookes,*
> *Convey this golden arrowe in thy sleeve,*
> *Lest she imagine thou art Venus' sonne:*
> *And when she strokes thee softly on the head,*
> *Then shall I touch her breast and conquer her.*

III.592 Baumann-Wissemann observed the imitation of *Thy.* 279 and 889, *bene est, abunde est.*

III.597 There is a nearly untranslatable pun on *suavis* ("pleasant") and *suavium* ("kiss").

III.598 Again, there is a pun on the two meanings of *ludo,* "play" and "deceive."

III.603ff. These lines allude briefly to the interview between Venus and Juno at *Aen.* IV.90 - 128.

III.609 B has *maior* and A has *magnus*, and so, in accordance with the editorial policy adopted here, I duly print *magnus*. Nonetheless, the force of *etiam* would be more comprehensible if *maior* were selected. But then, what greater task could there be than what he has just accomplished?

III.610 (stage direction) In his poem *Iter Boreal* written later this same year (for which cf. the Commentary note on poem CXXXVIII.1f. in Volume III), Richard Eedes wrote of Matthew Harrison, landlord of the The Bear across the street from Christ Church, a fav-orite haunt of Christ Church men. Harrison kept a tame bear named Furze, and it would have created a hit with Gager's audience to have the hunters return with Furze in tow.

Actus III, scena iv Mercury's self portrait incorporates the description of his wand and its powers at Verg. *Aen.* IV. 242 - 46. But the winsomely self-satisfied tone is Gager's own contribution.

III.615 Baumann-Wissemann observed the imitation of *H. F.* 618, *utrumne visus vota decipiunt meos.*

III.618. Here they noted that *limen domus* comes from *Ag.* 7.

III.630 And that *ad infernam Styga* imitates *Thy.* 1007.

III.636 In Vergil "trusty Achates" (*fidus Achates*) is Aeneas' closest comrade.

Actus III, scena v Mercury's speech is based on that of Vergil, *Aen.* IV.259 - 76, incorporating additional material from IV.227 - 37.

III.653 Venus had rescued Aeneas after he was wounded by Diomedes, as recounted in Book V of the *Iliad*, and during the sack of Troy (cf. *Aen.* II.588 - 621).

Actus III, scena vi This scene is based on Vergil's brief description of Aeneas' profound shock at Mercury's message, his temporary vacillation and plans for departure, and his seeking for an auspicious moment to break the news to Dido (*Aen.* IV.279 - 95). But Gager transforms Aeneas' inner vacillation into a dialogue by introducing Achates as an interlocutor.

III.663 Euripus is the channel between Euboea and Boeotia.

III.676 Baumann-Wissemann observed that *credite experto mihi* echoes *Thy.* 81f.

III.683 Binns compared *Meleager* 430, *omnem hospitalis Iuppiter raptum vetat.*

III.724 Baumann-Wisseman note the echo of *Oed.* 14, *caelum deosque testor.*

Actus III chorus This description of Rumor closely follows Verg. *Aen.* IV.173 - 95. The meter is the same as that of the Nymphs' Song at III.ii.

III.734 Caeus and Enceladus were two of the Titans.

III.752 Binns points out that *luxus* is used mistakenly as a second declension noun.

Actus IV, scena i Cf. Vergil's description of the distraught Dido at *Aen.* IV.296 - 304.

IV.764 Baumann-Wissemann compared *H. F.* 1012 and *H. Oet.* 909, *quo misera pergis?*

Actus IV, scena ii This scene closely follows *Aen.* IV.305 - 87.

IV.772 Baumann-Wissemann noted the imitation of *Tr.* 464 - 7:

> *Strymonius altas Aquilo contorquent nives*
> *Libycusque harenas Auster ac Syrtes agit,*
> *nec manet in Austro. fit gravis nimbis Notus.*

IV.774 For Syrte, cf. the Commentary note on II.iv 494ff.

IV.783f. Baumann-Wissemann noted the echo of *Hipp.* 868 - 71:

Notes to pp. 316 - 18.

> *eheu, per tui sceptrum imperi,*
> *magnanime Theseu, perque natorum indolem*
> *tuosque reditus perque iam cineres meos,*
> *permitte mortem.*

IV.783 *Imperii* can be scanned as a trisyllable by taking the penultimate *i* as a semi-consonant, but this produces a spondaic sixth foot, not an iamb.

IV.785ff. Baumann-Wissemann noted the echo of *H. F.* 1269 - 71:

> *succurre, genitor, sive te pietas movet*
> *seu triste fatum sive violatum decus*
> *virtutus.*

IV.792 The "Nomads" are the Numidians (as at *Aen.* IV.320).

IV.795 Either the writer mistakenly scanned the first syllable of *seminanimis* short, or you can scan the fifth foot as a proceleusmatic with the final syllable shortened by *brevis brevians*. If this portion of the play was written by the anonymous collaborator, in view of his other metrical lapses, the former explanation is likelier. Certainly, *Dido* exhibits no other instance of *brevis brevians* or of proceleusmatic resolutions.

IV.798 Baumann-Wissemann noted the echo of *Tr.* 305, *solusne totiens spolia de nobis feres?*

IV.800ff. Baumann-Wissemann compared Ovid, *Heroides* VII.133 - 8:

> *forsitan et gravidam Dodon, scelerate, relinquas,*
> *parsque tui lateat corpore clausa meo.*
> *accedet fatis matris miserabilis infans,*
> *et nondum nati funeris auctor eris,*
> *cumque parente sua frater morietur Iuli,*
> *poenaque conexos auferet una duos.*

IV.803ff. Binns observed the imitation of *Tr.* 464 - 7:

> *hos vultus meus*
> *habebat Hector, talis incessu fuit*
> *habituque talis, sic tulit fortes manus,*
> *sic celsus umeris.*

IV.826ff. Baumann-Wissemann observed the echo of *Oct.* 115 - 7:

> *quam saepe tristis umbra germani meis*
> *offertur oculis, membra cum solvit quies*
> *et fessa fletu lumina oppressit sopor.*

IV.840ff. This speech follows Dido's similar one at Verg., *Aen.* 365ff. (also imitated at *Panniculus* 345f.

IV.841f. Procustes (or Procrustes) and Sinis were two wayfarer-molesting ogres defeated by Theseus in the course of his progress over the Isthmus of Corinth.
Baumann-Wissemann noted that this reference echoes *Hipp.* 1169f.:

> *membra — quis saevus Sinis*
> *aut quis Procrustes sparsit.*

IV.843 They also noted the echo of *Thy.* 1048f.:

> *quis inhospitalis Caucasi rupem asperam*
> *Heniochus habitans.*

IV.848 And of *Oct.* 692, *cur genae fletu madent?*

IV.851 *Pro...esse* is *prodesse* expressed by tmesis.

IV.855f. Baumann-Wissemann noted the echo of *Tr.* 753f., *vatem et insontes deos / praetendis?*

IV.869f. And of *Oct.* 267f., *meque perpetuo obruit / extincta luctu.*

Actus IV, scena iii This scena, included to provide a graphic display of Aeneas' determination to leave, has no basis in Vergil.
Initial speaker lists indicate the grouping of speakers for the ensuing scena. Although they are frequently employed as a device for indicating entrances and exits, they do not necessarily indicate that all such speakers are present from the beginning of the scena. Here, Aeneas' speech at 873ff. is probably a monologue, and Ilioneus enters only at 883.

IV.900 Baumann-Wissemann noted that this line is modelled on *Me.* 294, *etsi repugnat precibus infixus timor.*

IV.902. Baumann-Wissemann observed the echo of *Tr.* 56, *non tamen superis sat est.*

IV.912 Binns observed the echo of *H. Oet.* 886, *haut est nocens quicumque non sponte est nocens.*

Actus IV, scena iv This scena follows *Aen.* IV.408 - 36.

IV.919ff. Baumann-Wissemann noted the echo of *Hipp.* 438 - 43:

> *namque anxiam me cura sollicitat tui,*
> *quod te ipse poenis gravibus infestus domas.*
> *quem fata cogunt, ille cum venia est miser,*

> at si quis ultro se malis offert volens
> seque ipse torquet, perdere est dignus bona
> quis nescit uti.

IV.932 And of *Hipp.* 724, *secreta cum sit culpa, quis testis sciet?*

IV.937 And of *Hipp.* 1189, *o mors pudoris maximum laesi decus.*

IV.939 And of *H. Oet.* 10, *quid tamen nectis moras?*

IV.940 Binns noted the imitation of *Me.* 155, *levis est dolor qui capere consilium potest.*

IV.941f. Baumann-Wisseman compared *Tr.* 758f., *non vacat vanis diem / conterere verbis.* This line is also imitated at *Oedipus* 184 and *Meleager* 1041.

IV.944 They also compare Seneca, *Ag.* 744, *non ego antiquum decus.*

IV.946 They also observed the echo of *Ag.* 442, *ut aura plenos fortior tendit sinus.*

IV.948 Binns noted that this imitates *Ag.* 426, *omnis nimium longa properanti mora est.*

Act IV chorus The meter is the same as that of the Nymphs' Song at III.ii and the Actus III chorus.

IV.963ff. A previous instance of Trojan duplicity. "When Laomedon (the father of Priam) was building Troy, Poseidon and Apollo were doomed to serve Laomedon for wages. Apollo looked after the king's flocks on Mount Ida, whilst Poseidon helped to build the walls of Troy. When their work was completed, Laomedon refused them the promised reward": Binns' note *ad loc.*

IV.971 Another metrical slip: this line ends with an impossible cretic.

IV.988ff. The conceit of personified Virtue deserting the earth is suggested by the mythological idea of Astraea or Justice being the last of the immortals to abandon the world: cf. Vergil, *Eclogue* iv.6 and. Ps. - Seneca, *Octavia* 424ff.

Actus V, scena i Binns pointed out that this description is closely based on various passages of *Aeneid* IV, as follows: 985 - 1000 ≈ IV.529 - 47, 1000 - 1004 ≈ IV 494 - 7 and 507f., 1004 - 10 ≈ IV.478 - 80 and 483.
See the initial Commentary note to *Oedipus* V.

V.1007 The Massyli were an African people.

Actus v, scena ii In the *Aeneid* (IV.634ff.) Dido bids Barce to bring atonement-offerings so that she might "accomplish the rites of Stygian Jove, which I have duly prepared, to put an end to my cares and give over to the flames the pyre of that Dardanian man." This provides the pretext for an elaborate scene which, like Althaea's burning of the log in the *Meleager*, is modelled on the onstage magic ritual of Seneca's *Medea* (740 - 840).

Barce was Sychaeus' old nurse (*Aen.* IV.632f.). Vergil merely says that she is sent by Dido to fetch Anna. In the play this is turned into a Senecan *domina-nutrix* dialogue.

V.1022f. One cannot be quite sure about the purport of these lines. Evidently Dido is being assisted by some sort of priest or priestess. As suggested in the Introduction to this play, this looks like a musical cue.

V.1024 Colchis was Medea's native country (cf. the introductory note on this scena).

V.1025ff. Cf. Medea's similar invocation at *Me.* 740 - 7:

> comprecor vulgus silentum vosque ferales deos
> et Chaos caecum atque opacam Ditis umbrosi domum,
> Tartari ripis ligatos squalidae Mortis specus.
> supplicis, animae, remissis currite ad thalamos novos:
> rota resistat membra torquens, tangat Ixion humum,
> Tantalus securus undas hauriat Pirenidas.
> gravior uni poena sedeat coniugus socero mei:
> lubricus per saxa retro Sisyphum volvat lapis.
> vos quoque, urnis quas foratas inritus ludit labor,
> Danaides, coite: vestras hic dies quaerit manus.

V.1026f. Pluto, who abducted Proserpina.

V.1030 Hecate, daughter of the Titans Perseus and Asteria, was a divinity imported to Greece from Caria. She presided over witches and witchcraft. As Binns says in his note *ad loc.*, "she is often identified with Diana, Luna, and Proserpine, and is therefore portrayed with three heads."

V.1031f. Cf. the Commentary note on *Meleager* 506. Although the invocation of triform Hecate and triform Diana might seem redundant, these lines closely follow *Aen.* IV.510f.

V.1035f. Apollo slew the Python at Delphi.

V.1045ff. Like the Nurse in the *Meleager*, Barce takes a more active role in the procedings than the Nurse in Seneca's *Medea*; both try to dissuade their respective mistresses from continuing their ghastly rites.

V.1053 The remainder of scena ii is based on *Aen.* IV.590 - 662.

V.1083 The *st* in *Stygios* creates an illegal dactylic (or, at best, spondaic) second foot by positional lengthening.

V.1092 The Eumenides are the Furies.

V.1099 For *adnato* with the dative, the *Oxford Latin Dictionary* cites Silius Italicus X.610.

V.1132 Baumann-Wissemann compared Seneca, 584 *vidi inter umbras, ipse pallentes deos*.

Actus V, scena iii It is unusual to have a list of speakers at the begining of a scena note the present of non-speaking "extras."
Anna's long speech is closely based on *Aen*. IV.665 - 92.

Actus V, scena iv The appearance of Iris to claim Dido's life is based on *Aeneid* IV.693 - 705. The suicide of Anna, however, has no basis in Vergil.
I have added an extra stage direction because of Holinshed's description of "Mercurie and Iris descending from and to an high place." Whatever device was used to effect Mer-cury's previous entry and exit is employed again here.

V.1182ff. For a similar reproach "how can you die and leave me behind?" cf. *Oedipus* V.180.

Act V chorus The meter is lesser Asclepiads.

V.1192 Baumann-Wissemann observed that the first foot of the line is trochaic, a usage which *seit Horaz ungebräuchlich geworden war*.

V.1195 Another metrical slip: as at 1083, *st* should create positional lengthening.

V.1196 Baumann-Wissemann (p. 21) wrongly identified a metrical slip: *Auch in Vers 1196 verändert Gager die Quantitäten, indem er die 2. Silbe des Namens Dido fälchlich kurz mißt*. Final *o is commonly shortened in many 'silver age' poets, e.g. Juvenal, except in dative and ablative cases" (D. S. Raven, *Latin Metre: An Introduction* [London, 1965] 23).

V.1207 Cf. the Commentary note on I.260ff.

Epilogus 1214f. These line is susceptible to a double translation: "Now Dido has met her end. Would that her life had turned out the way one would want, but she chose the death she could," and "Now *Dido* s over. Would that it had ended as the spectator would have wished, but it took the only ending it could."

Epilogue 1220 For *insidias struit* cf. Catullus XXI.7, Ovid, *Metamorphoses* I.198, and Statius, *Thebais* II.501. Cf. also poem LXXXVI.6, *insidiasque struit*.

Epilogue 1227 The moral the spectator is supposed to draw here and the point of the allusion to Prometheus seem a trifle obscure. *Faute de mieux*, I suppose that the idea is that

Prometheus ("Foresight") stands for soothsaying and prophecy. At the time of the storm, and the resulting love affair of Dido and Aeneas, one would have predicted a happy union, but it did not turn out as foreseen. (Or is this a veiled criticism of fortune-tellers of the John Dee type?).

Epilogue 1230 Cf. the Commentary note on 948.

Epilogus 1243 This allusion to Elizabeth aiding foreigners seems too vague to be taken as a reference to any specific diplomatic or military initiative (it would be two more years before England openly entered into an anti-Spanish alliance with the Netherlands). The reference to the foundation of kingdoms could be taken as an allusion to English expansionism in Wales and Ireland. But since these efforts lay somewhat in the past, it is more likely that Gager alludes to Humphrey Gilbert's ill-starred American expedition of 1582, in the course of which Newfoundland had been claimed for England. In 1584 Gilbert's brother-in-law, Sir Walter Raleigh, would be issued a charter for American colonization, which led to the first Roanoke settlement in the following year.

Epilogue 1248 - 51 These lines = 464 - 6 of the play.

Epilogue 1255 Previous commentators have understood *Sabae* as "queens of Sheba," but the allusion also has classical implications: cf. Verg. *Aen.* I.416, Horace, *Ode* I.xxix. 3, Ovid., *Met.* X.480, Seneca, *H. Oet.* 376, etc.
Binns noted the phrase *te Saba salutat* in a poem addressed to the Queen (CXII.5).

APPENDIX: GAGER IN HIS POINTING: ON POINTING GAGER

As indicated in the General Introduction, after considerable thought I have adopted a policy of silently imposing modern punctuation on Gager's texts. As most editors leave punctuation more or less as they find it, under the impression that this is proper scholarly procedure, this decision perhaps requires justification, based on a consideration of Gager's pointing habits.

I. COLONS AND SEMICOLONS

Elizabethan punctuation practice does not square with contemporary theory. The definitive statement on the subject, familiar to every schoolboy, stood in William Lily's *A Short Introduction of Grammar Generally to be Used* (1549),[1] a standardized and expanded version of the 1529 Erasmus-Colet grammar prescribed for use in schools by Cardinal Wolsey:[2] *puncta ergo sive notae, quibus in scribendo utuntur eruditi, Latinis discuntur, Subdistinctio, Media distinctio, Plena ac perfecta distinctio. Graecis, Comma, Colon, Periodos.* ["And so the points or marks, which educated men employ in writing, are called in Latin the minor distinction, the middle distinction, and the full or perfect distinction; for the Greeks these were the comma, colon, and period."] This is a description of the original Roman tripartite system,[3] lifted from one of the Roman grammarians, and is at variance with the ostensibly quadripartite practice of English writers and printers for both Latin and vernacular texts: this definition excludes the semicolon, which they employed regularly.

So if we are to learn anything about pointing habits for the writing and printing of Latin poetry in Renaissance England, we must do so inductively. Gager's punctuation habits make an exceptionally interesting case study. For in *Dido* we have a rare situation of two holograph copies of the same literary text,[4] and it is instructive to observe the differences in pointing between them. Here we are interested in how the two manuscripts differ in their handling of colons and semicolons:

	A	**B**
2	*parit:*	*parit.*
17	*facit.*	*facit:*
22	*hospitem.*	*hospitem:*
29	*hospitem.*	*hospitem:*
31	*diem.*	*diem:*
33	*Lybia.*	*Lybia:*

---

[1] Reprinted with an Introduction by Vincent J. Flynn (New York, 1945).
[2] For a history of this textbook cf. T. W. Baldwin, *William Shakspear's Smalle Latine and Lesse Greeke* (Urbana, 1944) Vol. II, Appendix 2.
[3] Thomas N. Habinek, *The Colometry of Latin Prose* (Berkeley, 1985) Chapter 2.
[4] Two holographic copies of Robert Burton's *Philosophaster* allegedly exist.

279	*animum.*	*animum:*
280	*silet:*	*silet.*
334	*prisci:*	*prisci,*
336	*oras:*	*oras.*
341	*comparatus,*	*comparatus:*
365	*regna:*	*regna;*
374	*duo:*	*duo.*
383	*Ilus:*	*Ilus,*
391	*tibi:*	*tibi.*
401	*cape.*	*cape:*
419	*fuit.*	*fuit:*
425	*iucundam,*	*iucundam;*
426	*nostros.*	*nostros:*
459	*Medeae.*	*Medeae:*
469	*timor.*	*timor:*
483	*sepulchro.*	*sepulchro:*
489	*alit:*	*alit,*
519	*fraena,*	*fraena;*
526	*mentes:*	*mentes.*
529	*medullas,*	*medullas:*
540	*Elisa:*	*Elisa.*
542	*novam,*	*novam:*
570	*alienam,*	*alienam:*
595	*igne:*	*igne,*
605	*faedus:*	*faedus.*
617	*est,*	*est:*
749	*canens.*	*canens:*
1224	*disinit,* [sic]	*desinit:*
1242	*virgo.*	*virgo:*

Variations of punctuation involve:

1. Twenty alternations of colon with period: 2, 17, 22, 31, 33, 279, 280, 336, 374, 391, 401, 419, 426, 459, 469, 483, 526, 605, 749, 1242.

2.) Ten alternations of colon with comma: 334, 341, 383, 489, 529, 542, 570, 595, 617, 1224.

3.) One alternation of semicolon with period: 271.

4.) One alternation of colon with semicolon: 365.

5.) Two alternations of semicolon with comma: 425, 519.

In the course of editorial work, an initial assumption that Gager actually adhered to a disguised bipartite pointing system whereby he employed commas more or less as half stops and semicolons approximately as full stops, and that variations from this pattern could be regarded as individual lapses and corrected accordingly, proved increasingly difficult to sustain. The punctuation variants just listed go to show that Gager's use of the colon and semicolon was shifting and unstable. This is particularly true of colons, which alternate with both full and half stops; contrary to what one might predict, colons alternate with full stops twice as often as with half stops. The above list appears to attest a lesser degree of uncertainty about the semicolon, which in two or perhaps three cases is interchanged with half stops. Gager often employs the semicolon more or less as a heavy stop, using it to end sentences and even at the end of the occasional paragraph (e.g. at *Ulysses Redux* 2016). This contradictory evidence shows considerable vacillation and uncertainty about the value assigned this mark.

These observations scarcely encourage the belief that Gager followed a genuinely quadripartite punctuation system, with four marks used to designate four stops of progressively greater weight.[1] At most, he may have some idea of an intermediate stop corresponding to Lily's *media distinctio*. If so, this system is not applied systematically; even if it were, the ambiguity and confusion created by using four marks to implement a tripartite scheme would be obvious.

Gager employed the colon for other purposes as well. At times it is at least seemingly used more or less as we do today. Also, in poetic similes, a colon is regularly used to mark the comparison in similes (i.e, to separate the *qualis* clause from the *talis* clause). These are further instances of his willingness to employ the same sign for multiple purposes.

II. PERIODS AND COMMAS

Lily's prescription for distinguishing the comma from the period is simple and straightforward. It is therefore remarkable to observe how often commas and periods are alternated:

	A	B
380	*means.*	*means,*
381	*tenens.*	*tenens,*
101	*dapes,*	*dapes.*
444	*duces.*	*duces,*
567	*Paris,*	*Paris.*
606	*rotant,*	*rotant.*
618	*domus.*	*domus,*

---

[1] The system of punctuation employed in many modern editions of Latin poetry, such as Teubner texts, also features the regular use of comma, colon, semicolon, and period, evidently representing stops of ascending weight (though I have never seen a theoretical discussion of this convention). More likely it is a vestigal relict of Renaissance practice that is applied traditionally with little science.

624	*est.*	*est,*
631	*fugo.*	*fugo,*
1218	*vetat,*	*vetat.*

Again, these alternations are sufficiently frequent that it may be ill-advised to write them off as instances of copying carelessness; perhaps here too it would be more accurate to speak of a certain fluidity or instability of usage.

Usually commas are used to mark off syntactical units or sense-units within the sentence (although, as we have seen, colons, and even semicolons can also be used for this purpose). But two distinctly different comma functions are also employed. Lily's prescriptive statement about the comma is *subdistinctio seu Comma, est silentii nota, seu potius respirandi locus, utpote qua pronuntiationis terminus, sensu manente, ita suspenditur, ut quod sequitur, continuo succedere debeat.* ["The minor distinction or comma is a mark for a pause, or rather a place for a breath, so that there is a pause in the pronunciation with no break in the sense, which ought to flow unimpeded."] This use of the comma to indicate where the reader should make a pause is not necessarily the same thing at all. The most striking usage of this type is illustrated by the following lines from *Dido*:

45 *pariterque fratri, te pium praesta tuo.*

51 *aliam coactus quaerere, atque alibi domum.*

120 *meusque faelix casus, in casu fuit.*

125f.   *prima quae fecit deos pietas faventes, servat, id praesta modo.*

Here commas are introduced where there is no break in sense or syntax, as a device for marking the caesura of the line. On the other hand, the usage of commas to indicate pauses is employed no more systematically than any other form of punctuation. For example, commas (or parentheses) are infrequently introduced to mark off vocatives.

On rare occasions the use of commas to indicate pauses acquires a genuine literary interest when punctuation becomes, in effect, an indication to the actor on how to deliver his line. Most memorably, in *Meleager*, Oeneus reads aloud a letter in which Althaea confesses to the killing of Meleager (line 1679):

at relege: NATVM, ALTHAEA, MELEAGRVM, ABSTVLIT.

A comma is placed after each word in the letter to indicate the hesitant way in which Oeneus sounds out the words as he reads.

A third and completely different use of the comma is occasionally found in situations such as *Dido* 121f.:

nunc est videndum qui mihi constans status,

> *in urbe fiat,*

Here the comma at the end of 121 neither marks off a syntactical or sense unit, nor falls at a place where a reading pause could reasonably be inserted. In cases such as this, commas are irrationally inserted at the end of the line. This was perhaps done was done under the influence of early English blank verse in which a syntactical or sense unit is regularly concluded at the end of each line, so that most line-ends feature pointing.

It was Gager's regular habit to insert otiose commas between words linked by enclitics, where there is no syntactical break or, presumably, any pause. Thus he would have written *arma, virumque cano.*

III. QUESTION MARKS AND EXCLAMATION POINTS

The Elizabethan question mark performed essentially the same function as its modern equivalent. But a few special features deserve discussion.

In a modern question consisting of more than one part (*"Should I go to the store, or stay at home?"*) a question mark is only placed at the end of the entire sentence, with its internal parts demarcated by commas. Gager regularly placed a question mark after each part of the sentence. An example of this phenomenon is *Dido* 227f. as punctuated in **B**:

> *quae te tulerunt laeta mundo saecula?*
> *tantique talem qui dederunt principes?*

A modern writer would of course employ a comma at the end of 227.

In modern usage, the question mark is only applied to direct questions. Gager sometimes used it with indirect questions as well.

In both Gager's manuscript and printed works, there is frequent use of question marks for exclamation points.[1] Consider lines from the *Dido* such as these:

> 313   *o quam stupendi specimen ingenii datum?*
>
> 435f.   *ut vereor, Hanno, quem ferent ista exitum*
>   *hospitia?*
>
> 464 - 6   *quis iste nuper sedibus nostris novus*
>   *successit hospes? ore quem sese ferens?*
>   *quam fortis alto pectore, armisque inclytus?*

These are instances of a frequent tendency found throughout Gager's works to employ the question mark with sentences that are more or less clearly rhetorical exclamations; substitution of exclamation point for question mark also occurs, but far less frequently. This phenomenon suggests a certain fluidity or instability of usage regarding this sign, but there is

---

[1] This common Elizabethan confusion was doubtless encouraged by the fact that in many hands question marks are drawn as a line with only a slight oscillation from the vertical, which could easily be mistaken for exclamation points. But this observation does not apply to Gager, who drew his question marks as looping fish-hooks.

no reason for thinking that Gager regarded the question mark and the exclamation point as interchangable.

In the preceding paragraph I used the words "sentences that are more or less clearly rhetorical exclamations" advisedly, for Gager's ambiguity in the use of the question mark creates a number of situations where an editor or reader is uncertain whether he is looking at a rhetorical exclamation or a rhetorical question.

It is not uncommon for sentences that are more or less obviously questions to be given no special punctuation at all, or, conversely, for a question mark to be introduced needlessly. Again, this is illustrated by comparing variants between the two texts of *Dido* (oddly enough, the A copy is right in all four instances):

	A	**B**
309	*caedes.*	*caedes?*
366	*tuae?*	*tuae.*
553	*Elisam?*	*Elisam.*
635	*extulit?*	*extulit.*

IV. PERVASIVE CARELESSNESS

It is likely that the four instances just noticed are illustrations of the general principle that Gager was not a careful or a diligent pointer. This characteristic reveals itself in a negligence or indifference about the the point to be applied. Even worse, it is quite common to encounter situations in which some pointing is clearly obligatory at least desirable, but where none exists. Understandably, this phenomenon is commonest in A, written for private use. But none of his extended texts, handwritten or printed, is free of this fault. Its most troublesome form is failure to punctuate at the end of a sentence or major sense unit. *Dido* provides many examples, of which a few are:

> 64f.   *tuus est, videre quid velis fieri, labor*
>   *mihi fas capessam iussa tu iubeas modo.*

Some pointing (probably semicolon or period) must be placed at the end of 64, and it would be well to set off *capessam iussa* in 65.[1]

> 70f.   *quae prima vidit. vidit et Libyae solum*
>   *trabes ut aptet, sistit hic laceras rates,*

Heavy pointing is required after *solum*.

> 88 - 90   *proinde flammis cinge reginam novis,*
>   *dolisque falle fac sit Aeneae mei*
>   *amore capta,*

---

[1] If these two words should be retained in the text: but cf. the Commentary note *ad loc.*

Once again, a heavy stop must follow *falle*.

Examples like this, taken from any of Gager's works of substantial length, could be multiplied for a very long time indeed.

V. CONCLUSIONS

Such are Gager's most salient punctuation habits.[1] For present purposes there is no need to ask to what extent they are personal idiosyncracies, or to what extent they reflect the general practice of the age in the writing of Latin or vernacular texts. Such could only be discovered by compiling a number of such individual case studies and comparing them.[2] But for the prospective editor of Gager's works, the lessons of this study are highly instructive.

If an editor were convinced that Gager operated according to a reasonably systematic scheme of pointing, he could treat any deviations from that system as errors and fix them locally while retaining the system as a whole. Then, as long as the system was explained in the General Introduction, punctuation would not pose any difficulty. Such was my original expectation. The difficulty with such a procedure is that it is far from self-evident that Gager applied pointing according to any coherent system, or, if he did, precisely what that system might have been. It is particularly noteworthy that the values he placed on the colon and semicolon are shifting and elusive. The comma is used to designate at least three quite different things, and the question mark two. Even the period, which ought to be the least ambiguous mark of them all, is not quite exempt from this general aura of ambiguity. Nor are matters helped by Gager's carelessness about the whole matter of pointing. This causes great trouble for his editor. If one cannot be quite certain about the value he assigned to a given punctuation mark *in general*, then it becomes an exercise in futility to evaluate the alleged correctness or incorrectness of any particular example of that mark. Or at least there is perforce such a high degree of subjectivity involved in such judgments that the editor would be reduced to imposing his own pointing tastes on the texts under the guise of "correcting" the author.

One could dodge the problem by reproducing the punctuation as found, save for introducing the most obvious and necessary corrections and supplements. But such a policy would carry with it a heavy penalty in terms of reader comprehension. For, from an editor' viewpoint, in the last analysis it does not matter whether the punctuation that confronts him results from a pervasive multivalency of signs, the imperfect or negligent applicaton of a system, or the lack of any coherent system at all. In any event, the upshot is that the pointing found in Gager's texts often obscures his actual syntactic articulation, and so makes them unnecessarily difficult to read.

Scholarly accuracy is a fine thing. But so is coherence, and surely an editor should try to

---

[1] Generalizations about the punctuation of Gager's manuscript works apply equally to his printed ones. Evidently Barnes' typesetters faithfully reproduced what they saw in the manuscript copies from which they worked.

[2] One such is Albert Howard Carter, "The Punctuation of Shakespeare's *Sonnets* of 1609," in James G. McManaway, Giles E. Dawson and Edwin E. Willoughby (edd.) *Joseph Quincy Adams Memorial Studies* (Washington D. C., 1948), 409 - 28.

strike some sort of balance between these two imperatives. Anybody who has taught Latin on the secondary or undergraduate level must be keenly aware how a piece of maladroit punctuation can torpedo an inexperienced reader's understanding. If an editor feels his task is simply one of preparing a text for the benefit of professional students of Renaissance Latin, this issue would perhaps be unimportant. But if he thinks that his job is to produce something that can be read with ease and enjoyment by as many as possible, including those whose Latin is shaky or rusty, then punctuation becomes a matter of substantial concern. My suspicion is that, from the viewpoint of reader comprehension, retention of original punctuation is a far more critical issue than retention of original orthography. This is not a merely question of commercial self-interest: in introducing a writer who is not well or widely known, it is my conviction that one must serve as an advocate as well as an editor and make that writer comprehensible to a broad-based readership.

In the end, out of a conviction that such is the only really feasible choice, I have imposed modern punctuation on the text: that is to say, I have applied the modern English bipartite system in which period and comma are the only two general stops, with the rest of the marks being reserved for their specialized uses. Pointing is applied at the places, and only at the places, where modern usage requires. Normally I have done this silently. The alternative would involve disfiguring almost every page of text with a dense *apparatus criticus* conveying information of little interest to most readers. An *apparatus criticus* is of course still necessary, but in it I have held punctuation matters to the minimum possible. If, for example, a sentence standing as a question in the original text is repunctuated as a declarative sentence, the reader has a right to know it. But the reader need not be advised every time a period is substituted for a semicolon that seems to represent a heavy stop. The rare reader who feels that vital information is being withheld may console himself with the thought that much of Gager's work is readily available in modern photographic reproductions.

To further assist reader comprehension, all proper nouns (and only proper nouns) are capitalized, and quotation marks are introduced: Gager employed none save in *Pyramis*, where italics are used for the purpose.

For Product Safety Concerns and Information please contact our EU representative GPSR@taylorandfrancis.com
Taylor & Francis Verlag GmbH, Kaufingerstraße 24, 80331 München, Germany